Mastering
ORACLE®

Mastering ORACLE®
Featuring
ORACLE's SQL™ Standard

Daniel J. Cronin

HAYDEN BOOKS

A Division of Howard W. Sams & Company
4300 West 62nd Street
Indianapolis, Indiana 46268 USA

International Standard Book Number: *0-672-48419-6*
Library of Congress Catalog Card Number: *88-62905*

Acquisitions Editor: *Greg Michael*
Development Editor: *C. Herbert Feltner*
Manuscript Editor: *Amy Perry*
Illustrator: *Don Clemons*
Cover Artist: *Gregg Butler*
Technical Reviewer: *Howard Fosdick*
Compositor: *Weimer Typesetting Company, Inc.*

Printed in the United States of America

Overview

Contents

Foreword

Database management systems are our most important software products. They provide the tools with which programmers build applications, the environment in which software packages run, and the data management capability required by modern computer programs.

ORACLE is the premier database management system in the world today. ORACLE successfully integrates high-performance relational technology, the national standard SQL database language, and its own set of application development tools to provide an outstanding database environment. And—ORACLE runs under all major operating systems and in a broad variety of computers. That ORACLE leads the growth of the explosive database market can hardly be surprising.

Dan Cronin provides a simple, direct approach to learning ORACLE. He employs a case study approach and offers understandable examples that make learning ORACLE a pleasure rather than a chore. He covers everything you need to know in this one simple book.

The quickest and most modern way to develop applications is to learn ORACLE. *Mastering ORACLE, Featuring ORACLE's SQL Standard* is an investment in your professional future.

Howard Fosdick

Preface

When I was looking for the ideal application for ORACLE and its SQL system of managing relational databases, my search ended at the Movie House, a neighborhood video store I've haunted since its doors opened a few years ago. As a teaching vehicle the video application makes perfect sense. Home video rentals are a permanent fixture of everyday life, so the video business is *familiar* to most people. Also it presents many common business application problems such as inventory control, customer lists, rental transactions, and point-of-sale invoicing. Readers of this book needn't learn a specialized business simply to understand how to leverage the ORACLE application development to another environment.

Choosing the application was the easy part, however. The paramount challenge was to capture both the spirit and process of the ORACLE application development experience. For this I enlisted the help of friends, Joseph Lee and Mary Anne Lee of Venture Systems, Inc., who specialize in building value-added, turnkey systems based on the ORACLE technology.

Before this project began, we knew little more about the video business than the average home movie buff does. The application evolved in stages. Initially I spent hours at the Movie House, observing day-to-day operations, looking over shoulders, studying procedures, and interviewing personnel I would have interviewed if I had been going to actually install my system there. Joe and I then met several times over lunch at a tiny Greek restaurant down the hill from the Belmont headquarters of Oracle Corporation. I would impart my understanding of the business to Joe and then he would leave to sketch the business model and database schema. Over a series of meetings, Joe and I talked through the database design—sometimes heatedly—until we were satisfied that it depicted the real world. Efforts then turned to Mary Anne, who began prototyping the SQL*Forms application and defining the reports. After a few iterations, Mary Anne and I finalized the application, working independently to refine the user interface and to enhance application functionality. The net result of this collective effort was not only a viable application but a complete transcript of the development *process*—which I hope has been conveyed in this book.

Acknowledgments

I wish to express my gratitude to those generous souls who have contributed to this book in one significant form or another. My thanks to Amy Perry of Howard Sams for her diligent edits; to Howard Fosdick for his many helpful suggestions; to Alex Mollen of Oracle for his valuable lessons in CASE*Method theory; to Dennis Cochran and Eric Bond of Oracle for their astute technical reviews of the manuscript; and finally, to Larry Ellison, founder and CEO of Oracle, for his full support.

Trademarks

All terms mentioned in this book that are known to be trademarks or service marks are listed below. In addition, terms suspected of being trademarks or service marks have been appropriately capitalized. Howard W. Sams & Company cannot attest to the accuracy of this information. Use of a term in this book should not be regarded as affecting the validity of any trademark or service mark.

ORACLE and SQL*Plus are registered trademarks of ORACLE Corporation. SQL*Net, SQL*Forms, SQL*Menu, SQL*Loader, SQL*ReportWriter, CASE*Method, CASE*Dictionary, and CASE*Designer are trademarks of ORACLE Corporation.

UTS is a registered trademark of Amdahl Corporation.

Aegis-Domain/IX is a trademark of Apollo Computers, Inc.

UNIX and AT&T are registered trademarks of American Telephone and Telegraph.

PC-DOS is a trademark of CMC International.

COMPAQ DESKPRO 386 is a registered trademark of COMPAQ Computer Corporation.

CTIX is a trademark of Convergent Technologies.

The following are registered trademarks of Digital Equipment Corporation: DEC, ULTRIX, VAX, and VMS.

VOS is a trademark of Harris Corporation.

HP-UX is a trademark of Hewlett-Packard Corporation.

GCOS is a registered trademark of Honeywell-Bull.

The following are registered trademarks of International Business Machines Corporation: AT, IBM, and PS/2.

The following are trademarks of International Business Machines Corporation: AIX, DB2, DB2 Load Utility, MVS/SP, MVS/XA, and OS/2.

VME is a trademark of International Computer Limited.

MS-DOS and XENIX are registered trademarks of Microsoft Corporation.

PRIME is a registered trademark of Prime Computer, Inc.

OSx is a registered trademark of Pyramid.

DYNIX is a registered trademark of Sequent.

SINIX is a registered trademark of Siemens Capital Corporation.

SunOS 3.x is a trademark of Sun Microsystems, Inc.

Conventions Used in This Book

This book follows the SQL convention of using all caps for the names of tables. To avoid confusion as you walk through the creation of this application, here is a guide to the other conventions used.

Type of Term	Convention	Examples
SQL terms/operators	All caps	SELECT statement UPDATE clause WHERE clause AND operator
Key to press	Brackets	[Enter]
Table name	All caps	RENTALS table
Entity name	All caps	TRANSACTION entity
Attribute or column name		
—abbreviation	Italics	*prodno*
—in full	Initial cap and lowercase	Product Number
Other elements created in database*	All caps	YR_RENTALS view

* Includes attributes that also have become something else, such as a field or a view or a table.

Introduction to ORACLE and SQL

- Structured Query Language
- Beyond Fourth-Generation Languages: The Fourth-Generation Application Development Tools
- ORACLE's Fourth-Generation Development Environment
- Where We Are Going in This Book
- The ORACLE Products Cited in This Book
- Audience
- Assumptions
- Setting Up an ORACLE Account

1

Introduction to ORACLE and SQL

Computer technology has reached a level of accessibility unheard of in prior generations. Computer users at all levels—from data entry operators and non-DP professionals to systems analysts and application developers—are getting more sophisticated. They are demanding faster access to information and even greater productivity than ever before.

Within the corporate computing environment, roles continue to shift as they have for over three decades. During the 1970s, information processing was under the aegis of management information systems (MIS), a centralized organization, aloof, with a language all its own. As corporations evolved, the corporate structure fragmented into departments; into the late 1970s, the demands for immediate, accurate information grew proportionately. Departmental users became intolerant of an unresponsive MIS. In a word, MIS represented backlogs—delays in building new applications to keep up with growth and delays in modernizing existing applications to keep up with evolving needs.

The 1980s ushered in a new computing consciousness: do-it-yourself processing. Smaller, faster, and cheaper minicomputers allowed departments to become more self-sufficient in response to MIS backlogs. The trend toward decentralized computing crept into the corporate environment. Advances in personal computers soon brought mainframe horsepower to the desktop. Coupled with advanced networking solutions for sharing corporate data, PCs made self-reliance a permanent way of life.

Decentralized computing and the later acceptance of PCs accompanied another computing phenomenon: software productivity tools. Spreadsheets, word processors, database management systems and fourth-generation programming languages (4GLs) flourished. In 1979, Oracle Corporation introduced the ORACLE relational database management system (RDBMS). Following the blueprint developed by IBM's Dr. Ted Codd, the ORACLE system implemented the relational model—an innovative, user-oriented system of managing stored data by manipulating related data objects. Early on, Oracle Corporation made the decision to implement the Structured Query Language, or SQL (pronounced "Sequel"), as the sole database access language.

Structured Query Language

People often confuse SQL with relational databases, viewing them as a single entity. They are distinct technologies, although their developmental roots are intimately entwined. SQL is an access and manipulation language that interfaces to relational databases. (A few nonrelational databases have endorsed SQL but offer only partial implementations. Since they allow only a subset of standard SQL commands to be embedded in a proprietary programming language—often called a 4GL but more accurately a third-generation language—these partial implementations sacrifice much of SQL's power, ease of use, and query flexibility.)

When SQL first arrived, 4GLs were not a novelty, but they had failed to take root. The nonprocedurality of 4GLs was foreign, perhaps even uncomfortable, to traditional programmers. Programmers, used to laboring over complex constructs and managing each and every record, had difficulty with the concept of manipulating sets of records at a time and letting these apparently imprecise 4GLs navigate for them.

The rise of SQL began quietly but steadily gained momentum over the years. In May of 1986, the American National Standards Institute (ANSI) blessed SQL as the standard relational database language. Today, the popularity of SQL has developed into something of a frenzy.

Computer programming languages have changed radically from the early, faltering days of machine code programming, as Figure 1.1 shows. Each succeeding generation has boosted programmer productivity by quantum steps. In the 1950s, first generation languages were restricted to machine code—the binary world of absolutes, 1s and 0s. It was an achievement to build any application with machine code, let alone quickly, because the process was so tedious. Second and third-generations (assembly language and natural languages like COBOL) offered much improvement, but were succeeded by structured 3GLs like Pascal and FORTRAN 77. Structured 3GLs raised productivity by enforcing an organized, block-oriented approach to programming which minimized redundancy. Database management systems interfaced with fourth-generation languages like SQL became the next logical step in the evolution of productivity programming.

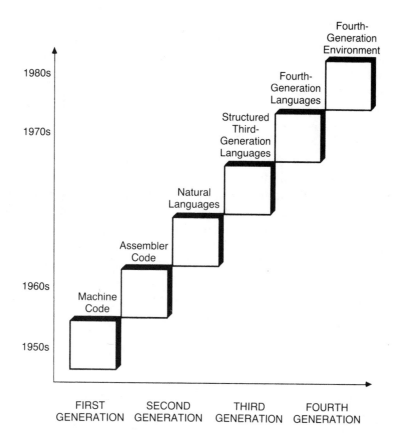

Figure 1.1   Generations of Programming Languages

SQL has made the corporate database accessible to a much wider audience than ever before. SQL is nonprocedural—you need only tell the
computer *what* data you want to view, not *how* the computer is to get at
that data. A non-DP person using SQL can be compared to a lay cook going
to restaurants in order to enjoy gourmet cooking. One may have the palate
of a gourmand but, unfortunately, lack all culinary talent. The benighted
gourmand experiments with dozens of recipes, following every instruction
faithfully, but invariably fails to recreate the flavors savored at four-star
restaurants. The amateur cook soon learns to leave the cooking up to experts. SQL enables a wide audience to have access to programming in the
same manner. SQL knows the recipes, and merely expects you, the application designer, to order what dishes are to be served. SQL then decides
the most efficient ways to serve them.

SQL is nondiscriminatory. SQL's nonprocedural approach is easily
understood by end-users, a community previously excluded from the information management business because traditional, esoteric program-

ming languages were the only access methods available. End-users can use SQL to maintain their own personal databases and execute simple interactive queries or reports without any previous programming experience. With SQL, systems design specialists, applications developers, and end-users can work together to better articulate the application requirements because they now speak a common language. SQL is the frame of reference.

Having one and the same SQL language accessible to end-users also gives professional developers a productivity tool with which to design database applications in record time. SQL lets designers spend the greater part of their time in the *design* and *prototyping* phases of the application development cycle, and devote far less time to actually writing code. Designers can then work out the user interface and functionality specifications in concert with users through iterative prototyping sessions. This prototyping process eliminates wasted coding effort, allowing the designer to reuse portions of the prototype as it evolves. The designer can then mold the prototype, step by step, like a piece of clay, into a completed, fully tested application.

Beyond Fourth-Generation Languages: The Fourth-Generation Application Development Tools

SQL and the relational database model have transformed the way application designers ply their craft. But SQL alone cannot satisfy the application development requirements. SQL was designed to be a database query language, not an application programming language. SQL lacks formatting, conditional procedures, and advanced data validation routines—functions which must be supplied by application tools layered on top of SQL. In reality, SQL provides the foundation for the next level of programmer productivity—the fourth-generation application development environment.

The touchstone of the fourth-generation environment (4GE) is a full complement of *integrated* fourth-generation application tools layered atop SQL. Extending the power of SQL, the 4GE tools are nonprocedural and provide the lion's share of functionality demanded by both single and multi-user business applications—without programming. The fourth-generation tools enable the application designer to move through the entire life cycle of an application—from defining the business model and building a prototype to implementing and maintaining the completed application—with a single set of integrated tools.

ORACLE's Fourth-Generation Development Environment

At the heart of ORACLE's 4GE toolset is SQL*Forms, the high-level screen painter and forms application generator. Via a menu-driven interface, the designer uses SQL*Forms to automatically generate the basic functionality, or *primitives*, for any application—the end-user interface, appropriate field attributes, validation rules to ensure accurate data entry, cursor navigation to control the application flow, and the screen manager to direct the flow of data traffic between the screen and the database.

SQL*Forms is extensible. For more robust applications, the default logic supplied by SQL*Forms can be augmented. SQL*Forms lets the designer embed SQL statements at various event points in the application to do unique validation checking, perform complex field computations, or retrieve related information from the database. While powerful, SQL statements are still not powerful enough for some sophisticated applications. Such specialized applications, ones requiring detailed statistical analysis, for example, may need the extra horsepower of procedural capability. SQL*Forms provides a macro language for reprogramming function keys, customizing the keyboard layout, calling other forms (to build on-line help systems, for example), performing if-then-else logic on field variables, and passing variable strings between forms within the application. SQL*Forms can also call 3GL programs via user exit points should the application warrant such specialized constructs. A future version of SQL*Forms will incorporate PL/SQL, ORACLE's procedural language superset of SQL, which will enable designers to perform extensive programmatic functions within triggers.

As Figure 1.2 shows, ORACLE's other fourth-generation tools supply the remainder of the application foundation requirements. These include

- ► SQL*ReportWriter, a nonprocedural report writer for controlling a range of report output formats

- ► SQL*Menu, a nonprocedural menuing system with a choice of menu styles for application integration

- ► CASE*Method, a proven, structured design methodology that provides application designers with practical techniques for analyzing users' requirements and then developing systems that fully satisfy those requirements

- ► CASE*Designer, a multi-user design dictionary to capture application information for system documentation. Information stored in the dictionary can also be used as source input for automatically generating the table design and the application code.

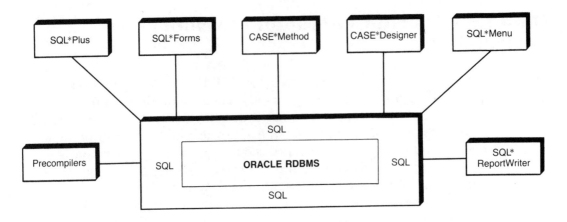

Figure 1.2   ORACLE's Fourth-Generation Environment Tools

Where We Are Going in This Book

Building a practical application that solves business problems is not something accomplished in one sitting. It is a dynamic process, and one that requires much thought and preparation in the early design phase, hands-on experimentation in the implementation phase, and trial-and-error testing in the fine-tuning phase.

This book puts you inside ORACLE's fourth-generation environment and teaches you how to use the ORACLE toolset to meet real business needs. The only way to do this is by hands-on experience. Therefore you will walk through the full development cycle of a real-world business application, taking occasional detours to learn some of the tips and tricks of using the ORACLE RDBMS. Once finished, you will have successfully built a multi-user video library management system for retail video stores. You will model the video rental application to solve the business problems of Video Quest, a fictitious video retail store. (Any resemblance to an actual business or to actual persons is purely accidental.) A video rental application is typical of the small business environment, but it can easily be expanded to manage the inventory of a vast tape library system within a distributed network or chain of stores.

The concepts and exercises demonstrated via this application are generic; they can be transferred to any other ORACLE application development experience. ORACLE is portable; the same application can be run unmodified on over 30 hardware platforms running under more than 16 operating systems. What you will learn in this book is completely portable to building business applications for the range of hardware environments, whether you are designing single-user PC systems for small businesses or large, multi-user systems with dozens of screens for minicomputers, or IBM mainframes in a corporate setting.

The ORACLE Products Cited in This Book

Every new release of an ORACLE tool must be ported from the base or *home* port (VMS for most products, and UNIX for newer, bit-mapped tools such as SQL*ReportWriter and future versions of SQL*Forms) to the various supported hardware environments. This need occasionally leads to a time delay between ports. For the most part, however, essential ORACLE application development tools become available on all strategic ports—VAX VMS, MS-DOS, UNIX, and System /370 mainframe environments—within a couple of months of one another.

Table 1.1 identifies the ORACLE products, including the 4GE application tools, covered in this book. Different versions of the products were used to build the sample video application on two hardware environments: Professional ORACLE for MS-DOS and ORACLE for VMS.

Audience

Anyone new to ORACLE may use this book as a thorough introduction to the ORACLE family of products. Application developers, such as independent consultants, value added resellers (VARs), or those on staff in MIS departments, who have outgrown their current databases and demand a more powerful RDBMS will profit from this book. Systems analysts, end-user specialists, project managers, and MIS professionals who are exploring 4GLs and relational database solutions may also want to scan this book.

Assumptions

Although no previous programming experience is required to build the application in this book, some exposure to a high-level language such as Pascal, FORTRAN or COBOL may help. You should at least be familiar with relational database concepts and terminology. You should also have read through the ORACLE documentation set, in particular the appropriate *ORACLE: Installation and User's Guide* for the computer you are working on, the *SQL*Plus User's Guide, SQL*Menu User's Guide*, and the complete set of SQL*Forms manuals.

Table 1.1   ORACLE Products Cited in This Book

Product	MS-DOS Version	VAX VMS Version	Purpose
ORACLE RDBMS	5.1A	5.1.17	The ORACLE relational "kernel" which manages the data storage environment and access to data. The ORACLE kernel maintains an active data dictionary and an extended application dictionary for SQL*Forms and SQL*ReportWriter objects.
ORACLE SQL	5.1A	5.1.22	ORACLE's SQL implementation, an access and data manipulation language for the ORACLE RDBMS.
SQL*Plus	2.0.14	2.1.13	ORACLE's SQL extensions designed for flexible formatting control of *ad hoc* queries or reports. SQL*Plus procedure files (SQL scripts) can be built for subsequent execution.
SQL*Menu	n/a	4.1.10	ORACLE's menuing facility for building dynamic, integrated application menus.
SQL*Forms	2.0.18	2.0.18	ORACLE's nonprocedural application builder and code-generator for forms-based applications. SQL*Forms interacts with ORACLE and DB2 databases via SQL; an application designer may extend functionality through the use of SQL statement and macro function triggers.
SQL*ReportWriter	n/a	1.0.11	ORACLE's nonprocedural reporting tool which provides advanced formatting control for SQL queries.
CASE*Method			ORACLE's business analysis and modelling system based on industry-standard entity-relationship modelling theories.
SQL*Loader	n/a	1.0	A bulk data loader utility.
EXPORT/IMPORT	5.1.17	5.1.22	Backup and recovery utilities for data and database structures (tables and views.)

Setting Up an ORACLE Account

ORACLE is shipped with the SYSTEM/MANAGER userid and password. The SYSTEM account has database administrator (DBA) privileges. DBA privileges are not to be taken lightly, since an ORACLE DBA has access to system tables that affect the core operations of the ORACLE database itself. After installing ORACLE, you should immediately change the default password MANAGER to ensure the security of your system.

Before you start to build the application for this book, you will want to set up a special ORACLE user account to store the Video Quest database. You do not want to clutter up the SYSTEM account, or any other account, with extraneous tables. You may also want to make a separate disk directory for the application files (the forms, report, and SQL command files) which you create by the end of this book.

For convenience, you might assign the new ORACLE account an obvious userid, such as VIDEO, with an equally memorable password of BOOK, perhaps. There is a short-cut way to create the new account which will be explained soon, but for now:

1. Log on to SQL*Plus using the SYSTEM userid:

   ```
   C> SQLPLUS SYSTEM/password
   ```

2. Use the GRANT command to create the new ORACLE user and authorize full database privileges:

```
SQL>GRANT CONNECT, RESOURCE, DBA to VIDEO identified by BOOK.
```

Automatic Log-On

When you log on to SQL*Plus or any other ORACLE tool, ORACLE security prompts you for a valid userid and password. While developing your sample application, you may want to shortcut this log-on procedure and run ORACLE tools directly from the operating system without having to log on and enter a password. ORACLE lets you set up an operating system (OPS$) user for automatic log-on.

To set up your new account as an OPS$ account, follow these instructions:

1. Log on to SQL*Plus using the SYSTEM userid:

   ```
   C> SQLPLUS SYSTEM/password
   ```

2. Use the GRANT command to create the new OPS$ user:

```
SQL>GRANT CONNECT, RESOURCE, DBA to OPS$VIDEO identified by BOOK.
```

3. Open the ORACLE CONFIG.ORA file and add the USERNAME command to it:

   ```
   USERNAME=VIDEO
   ```

When you now start an ORACLE tool, you may press [return] instead of entering a userid and password. ORACLE assigns the log-on privilege

OPS$VIDEO to anyone who presses [return] at log-on instead of entering a userid and password. Although this technique, known as *bypassing* log-on, circumvents the outer layer of defense, or moat, in ORACLE's security system, ORACLE provides many other commands to control user access and system security.

2

Inside the Video Rental Application

- The CASE*Method
- The Entity-Relationship Model
- The Database Design
- Forms for Fast Data Entry
- Planning the Reports
- Building a Menuing System
- Summary

2

Inside the Video Rental Application

Chapter 2 is an overview of the Video Quest video rental application which you will complete by the end of the book. This chapter highlights ORACLE's CASE*Method, an integrated collection of business analysis and modelling techniques, and steps you briskly through the application's foundation components—the database design, the user interface, the forms-based data entry screens, the reports, and the menuing system.

The CASE*Method

The application designer must perform an in-depth analysis of the business before writing a single line of code. The designer cannot presume to offer meaningful solutions without understanding the full scope of the business problems and functional requirements. The CASE*Method provides several modelling tools and techniques to assist the designer toward this end.

The CASE*Method embodies an integrated set of techniques. These include end-user interviews and feedback sessions, business and systems analysis, and modelling techniques to represent business functions, entity-relationships (related things or information which should be known about the business) and the flow of data through the business system.

The CASE*Method uses graphic models to express the business functions and data requirements. Visual modelling techniques facilitate communication between the designer and those who best understand the business, the management and the end-users.

The Entity-Relationship Model

The entity-relationship model defines *things* (or *entities*) which are important to the business and the *relationships* between these entities. An entity is anything of significance which the business application should know or hold information about. The entity-relationship model is a conceptual tool, not an implementation tool. By drawing graphic models of the business entities, the designer can easily visualize things of importance—not necessarily functions or actions—about the business. The graphic entity-relationship models also serve to document constraints about the business that may need to be implemented in the application. Entities typical of the video rental business include tapes, customers, titles, rental transactions, return transactions, and so forth.

A snapshot of Video Quest's complete entity-relationship model is shown in Figure 2.1.

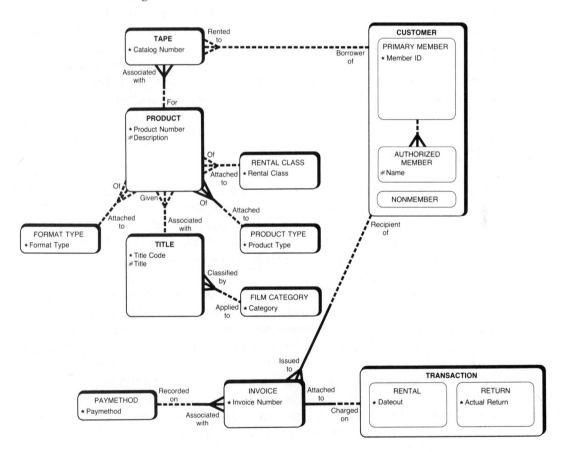

Figure 2.1   The Complete Video Quest Entity-Relationship Model

From this global picture, three major *entity groups*, or related collections of entity-relationships, can be identified. These related entities are your first clues to the identity of the *data elements*, or the individual pieces of related data, that will be stored in the database. Video Quest's three major entity groups are

▶ The TAPE-PRODUCT-TITLE trio

▶ The CUSTOMER entities

▶ The TRANSACTION entities

The elements of the Video Quest business—the rental, sale, and reservation of video tapes and accessory items—are represented by these three major entity groups at the highest level of organization. Film titles, rental and sale products (both video tapes and accessories), and multiple

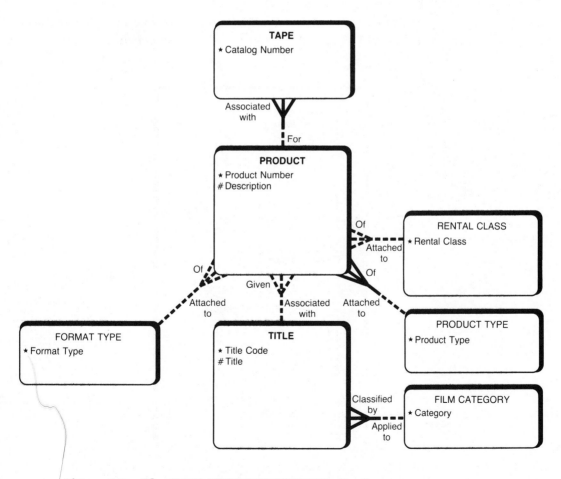

Figure 2.2   The TAPE-PRODUCT-TITLE Entity Group

copies of the same title (the video tapes themselves) are managed by the TAPE-PRODUCT-TITLE entities. The CUSTOMER entity manages the Video Quest's customer lists. The TRANSACTION entity manages activities concerned with the rental, sale, and reservation of video tapes, including tracking tapes through physical inventory and invoicing customers for each transaction.

Figures 2.2 through 2.4 represent blow-ups of the entity groups shown in Figure 2.1. Notice how either a solid or a broken line connects the entities; these lines symbolize the relationships the entities share with one another. Relationships often can be named or referred to with an English verb, such as "rented to." Chapter 3, on the CASE*Method, discusses how to develop this type of model in much greater depth.

The Database Design

Entity models hint at the kind of information the business application must know about, but they do not tell the designer precisely what infor-

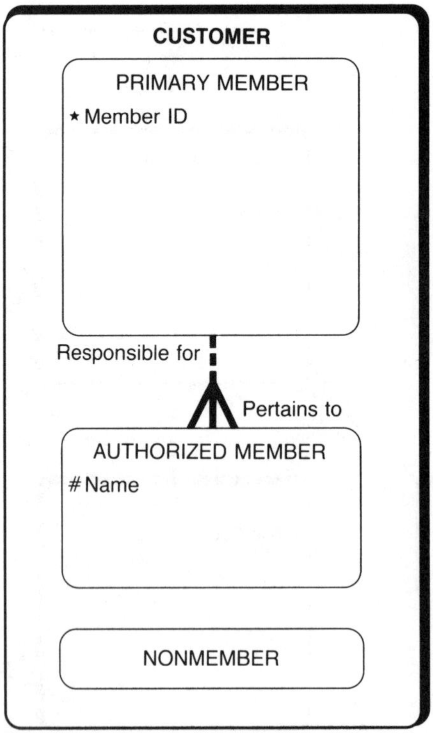

Figure 2.3   The CUSTOMER Entity Group

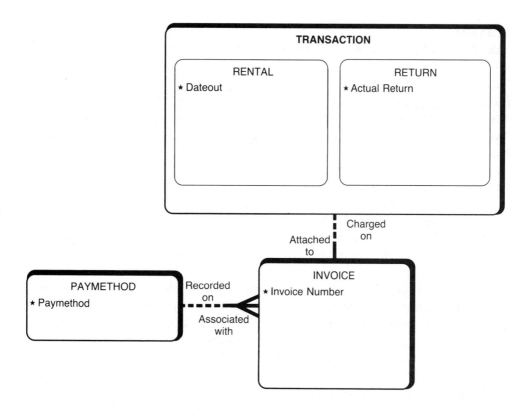

Figure 2.4   The TRANSACTION Entity Group

mation should be collected or how such information should be stored. For this you move on to creating the database design, or as it often is referred to in relational terms, the *schema*. The schema is the template or the structure of your database.

The hallmark of relational database systems is the storage of data in a two-dimensional tabular form as *rows* and *columns*, which make up *tables*. Tables are the logical framework for the collection of a related group of data and are the application's analog to the entities in the conceptual model in the diagrams. Columns organize your data logically. They refer to the categories of information that can be stored in the application and are analogous to the essential characteristics, or *attributes*, of each entity. Rows represent individual records, each a collection of values stored according to their associated columns. The following example table illustrates this basic principle—values relating to the PRODUCT entity have been collected into the PRODUCT Table and organized into columns and rows.

Product Number	Title Code	Format	Cost	Suggst Retail	Qty Rcv	Qty Oh	Qty Rent	Qty Sold
P100V	Soundmusic	Vhs	19.95	29.95	9	1	0	8
P450V	Crocdundee	Vhs	19.95	29.95	5	2	1	2
P460B	Critcondtn	Beta	59.95	69.95	6	5	0	1
P465B	Despsusan	Beta	49.95	59.95	5	3	2	0
P465V	Despsusan	Vhs	49.95	59.95	2	2	0	0
P470B	Ghostbuster	Beta	49.95	59.95	5	4	0	1
P470V	Ghostbuster	Vhs	49.95	59.95	5	3	2	0
P475V	Hitcher	Vhs	79.95	89.95	4	3	0	1
P480V	Shining	Vhs	69.95	79.95	3	2	1	0
P500V	Blank Tape	Vhs	2.99	4.99	30	20	0	10

Although a one-to-one correspondence doesn't exist between the entity models you develop and the schema you eventually design, they are usually close enough to be cousins. The Video Quest tables shown in the boxes in Figures 2.5 through 2.8 are based on the entities shown earlier in Figures 2.1 through 2.4. Study the tables to see just how closely they resemble the entity models. This should give you an idea of how closely the schema to be ultimately developed resembles the models it will be based on. (It is a SQL convention to use all uppercase letters for the names of tables. This book will use all uppercase letters both for the entity names and for the table names, since they are so closely related.)

After settling on the database tables, then create the column definitions for each one. Figures 2.5 through 2.8 show these underneath the Video Quest tables they come from. Most of the table columns are derived conveniently from the entity attributes—the essential characteristics—listed within each entity. Figures 2.5 and 2.6 show the TAPE-PRODUCT-TITLE database tables and the columns they generate. Figure 2.7 illustrates the CUSTOMER database table and its column definitions, and in Figure 2.8 we see the TRANSACTIONS tables along with their column definitions. (In the figures, "(F)" stands for *foreign key*, a concept explained in Chapter 4, Designing the Database.)

Forms for Fast Data Entry

An application not engineered for the ease and comfort of end-users is as conspicuous as spaghetti sauce on a yellow tie. Application designers have an obligation to end-users to provide a comfortable, consistent user interface for the data entry screens used to enter and retrieve data to and from the database.

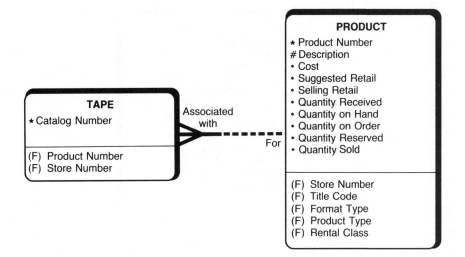

PRODUCT Table Data

PRODNO	DESCRIPTION	STORE	TITLECD	F	PRODTYPE	COST	SUGGRTL	QTYRCVD	QTYOH	QTYSOLD
P300B	Film	1	GONEWIND	B	RS	59.95	69.95	1		1
P300V	Film	1	GONEWIND	V	R			2	1	
P450V	Film	1	CKANE	V	RS	49.95	59.95	2	1	1
P470B	Film	1	GHOSTBUSTERS	B	RS	49.95	59.95	1	1	

TAPE Table Data

CATNUM	PRODNO	STORE
300	P300V	1
301	P300V	1
305	P300B	1
450	P450V	1
451	P450V	1
473	P450B	1

**Figure 2.5   TAPE and PRODUCT Tables with Corresponding
Column Definitions**

Oracle's nonprocedural SQL*Forms package relieves the application designer of much of the tedious programming effort required to build attractive data entry screens. The designer uses a screen painter to paint the form directly on the screen in WYSIWYG (What-you-see-is-what-you-get) fashion and then steps through a menu-driven interface to build and generate the form. The form's appearance can be customized with the SQL*Forms line drawing capability, its cut-and-paste functions for moving text, and its video highlighting for accenting effects, such as reverse video for fields and blinking fields to indicate error conditions.

TITLE Table Data

TILECD	TITLE	CAT	CENSOR	YEAR	STARRTG	RUNTIME	COLOR_BW
GONEWIND	Gone with the Wind	135	G	1939	*****	231 mins.	B/W
CKANE	Citizen Kane	135	PG-13	1941	*****	120 mins.	B/W
GHOSTBUSTER	Ghostbusters	120	PG	1984	*****	105 mins.	COLOR

TITLE SYNOPSIS Table Data

TITLECD	LINENO	DESCRIPTION
GHOSTBUSTER	1	When ghosts go on a rampage, only three men can save the world. It's
GHOSTBUSTER	2	GHOSTBUSTERS, starring Bill Murray, Dan Aykroyd and Harold Ramis as a maniacal
GHOSTBUSTER	3	band of parapsychologists specializing in psychic phenomena - and supernatural
GHOSTBUSTER	4	hilarity! Fired from university research jobs, Dr. Venkman (Murray),
GHOSTBUSTER	5	Stanz (Aykroyd) and Spengler (Ramis) set up shop as "Ghostbusters", ridding
GHOSTBUSTER	6	Manhattan ob bizarre apparitions.

Figure 2.6   TITLE and TITLE SYNOPSIS Tables with Corresponding Column Definitions

The Video Quest Master Forms

Video Quest's master forms facilitate data entry for the most commonly accessed database tables, the TITLE, PRODUCT, and CUSTOMER tables. These master forms, which are designed to resemble everyday business

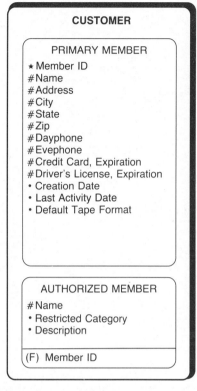

CUSTOMER

PRIMARY MEMBER
★ Member ID
Name
Address
City
State
Zip
Dayphone
Evephone
Credit Card, Expiration
Driver's License, Expiration
• Creation Date
• Last Activity Date
• Default Tape Format

AUTHORIZED MEMBER
Name
• Restricted Category
• Description

(F) Member ID

CUSTOMER Table Data

MEMBERID	NAME	AD1	CITY	STATE	ZIP	AREA	PRE	SUFX	CDLEXP
1	Jerry Barry	20 Davis Drive	Belmont	CA	94020	415	598	8125	01-JAN-89
2	Martha Kent	101 A Street	San Francisco	CA	94119	415	829	1928	01-JAN-89
3	Michelle Keaton	98 Sand Belois	Bolinas	CA	94777	707	445	2293	12-MAR-89
4	Jimmy Jimerino	1255 San Carlita	San Francisco	CA	94114	415	573	6992	28-JAN-91

CUSTNAME Table Data

MEMBERID	NAME	RESTRICT_CAT	DESCRIPTION
1	Carrie Barry	900	Adult
1	Chuck Barry	140	Musicals
2	Ken Kent	900	Adult
3	Dianne A. Keaton	899	Slasher
3	Buster A. Keaton	120	Comedy

Figure 2.7   CUSTOMER Tables with Corresponding Column Definitions

forms, are derived exclusively from the base database tables defined earlier. The TITLE form combines the base tables TITLE and SYNOPSIS; the PRODUCT form is based on the PRODUCT table; and the CUSTOMER form combines the CUSTOMER and CUSTNAME tables. Figures 2.9 through 2.12 present the master forms, complete with sample data.

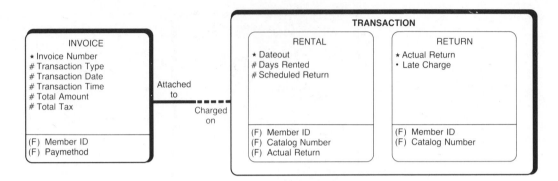

INVOICE Table Data

INVNO	MEMBERID	PAY	T	TRANDATE	TRANTIME	TOTAL	TAX
1	1	CA	R	15-MAR-88	11:07 am	3	.2
2	2	CA	R	28-MAR-88	12:14 am	3	.2
3	1	CA	R	09-APR-88	7:44 am	6	.39
4	1	CA	R	09-APR-88	7:45 am	6	.39

RENTALS Table Data

MEMBERID	CATNUM	DATEOUT	RENTDAYS	SCHDRTN	ACTRTN
1	100	15-MAR-88	1	16-MAR-88	16-MAR-88
2	300	28-MAR-88	1	28-MAR-88	29-MAR-88
1	200	09-APR-88	2	11-APR-88	
1	300	09-APR-88	2	11-APR-88	

RETURNS Table Data

MEMBERID	CATNUM	ACTRTN	LATECHARGE
1	100	16-MAR-88	
2	300	29-MAR-88	

Figure 2.8   TRANSACTION Tables with Corresponding Column Definitions

The *fields* in the TITLE form, shown in Figure 2.9, are derived from columns of the TITLE table, which is appropriately termed a *base table*. Any new values entered into the form fields are inserted directly into their corresponding table columns once the changes are committed. Any changes to existing fields are made on the form and will update their corresponding table columns.

The TITLE form offers a second screen (referred to as a *page* by SQL*Forms) for entering or querying a synopsis of the film title currently displayed on the first screen. Figure 2.10 illustrates this, called the TITLE SYNOPSIS form.

New products are inserted into the database via the PRODUCT form, shown in Figure 2.11. Product information, such as rental class, pricing changes or inventory positions, is updated through this form.

```
Video Quest TITLE Search

Title Code       Title
GHOSTBUSTER      Ghostbusters
Film Category
120  COMEDY

Released   Studio      Color/B&W   Running Time   Censor Rating   Star Rating
  1984   Columbia       Color       105              PG-13           *****

Directors
Ivan Reitman
Producers/Co-Producers
Ivan Reitman
Actors/Actresses
Bill Murray, Dan Aykroyd, Sigourney Weaver, Harold Ramis, Rick Moranis
Screenplay                            Academy or Foreign Film Awards
Dan Aykroyd, Harold Ramis

[Next Block] Synopsis    VIDEO QUEST RENTALS, Inc.    [Exit] Main Menu

      Char Mode: Replace  Page 1                     Count: 1
```

Figure 2.9 The TITLE Form

```
Synopsis for title: Ghostbusters

When ghosts go on a rampage, only three men can save the world.  It's
GHOSTBUSTERS, starring Bill Murray, Dan Aykroyd and Harold Ramis as a
maniacal band of parapsychologists specializing in psychic phenomena - and
supernatural hilarity!  Fired from university research jobs, Dr. Venkman
(Murray), Stanz (Aykroyd) and Spengler (Ramis) set up shop as "Ghostbusters",
ridding Manhattan of bizarre apparitions.

[Next Record] Scroll down   [Prev Record] Scroll up   [Prev Block] Title info
                      VIDEO QUEST RENTALS, Inc.

      Char Mode: Replace  Page 2                     Count: *0
```

Figure 2.10 The TITLE SYNOPSIS Form

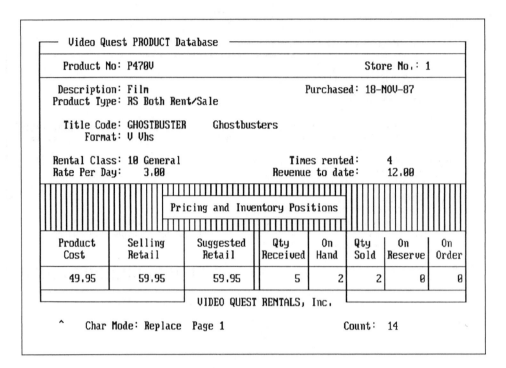

Figure 2.11   The PRODUCT Form

A Master-Detail Form

The Video Quest customer database is maintained via the CUSTOMER form, shown in Figure 2.12. The two database tables, CUSTOMER and CUSTNAME, are the foundation of this form. These two tables take on a new role at the forms application level. In forms terminology, the CUSTOMER and CUSTNAME tables represent a *master-detail* relationship.

A master-detail relationship expresses a one-to-many relationship through the forms-based medium; a master record, CUSTOMER, may or may not have one or more associated detail records, CUSTNAMES; but the detail record, CUSTNAME, must have one and only one master record, CUSTOMER. This concept is known as *referential integrity*, and these restrictions are enforced by the use of triggers in the SQL*Forms application. Chapter 7, Building Forms, will demonstrate how to build each form in elaborate detail, including how to use triggers.

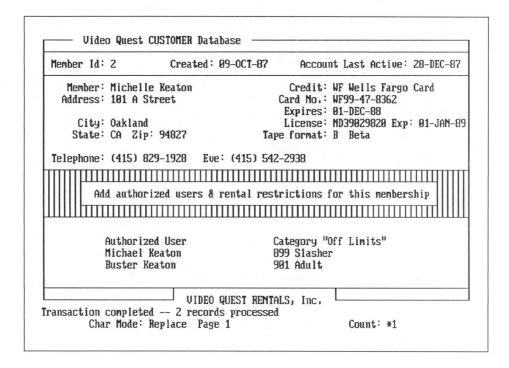

Figure 2.12   The CUSTOMER Form

Maintaining the Video Quest Codes

Store codes can be consolidated onto a single form, or separated into individual forms. On smaller machines, memory can be a precious resource. A single, multi-block form with many fields and form pages and SELECT statement triggers can consume a lot of memory. The ability for one form to automatically call another may allow you to design a seamless application while still conserving resources. This and other memory conservation tricks (discussed in Chapter 10) should be investigated *after* you've designed your application and have isolated resource problems; at the outset, concern yourself with ease of use. The Video Quest codes that must be maintained include

Catalog numbers	which feed the RENTALS and RETURNS tables
Film category codes	which feed the TITLE table
Rental class codes	which feed the PRODUCT table
Payment method codes	which feed the INVOICE table

Figures 2.13 through 2.15 illustrate each CODES screen.

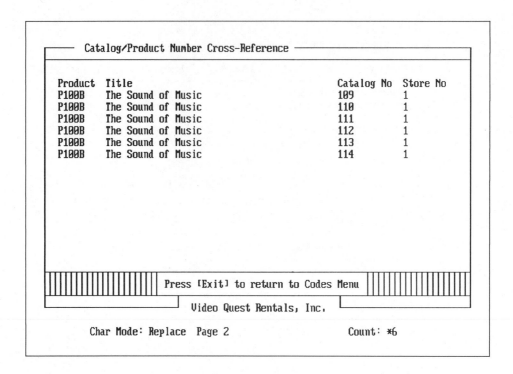

Figure 2.13   The CODES Form for Catalog Numbers

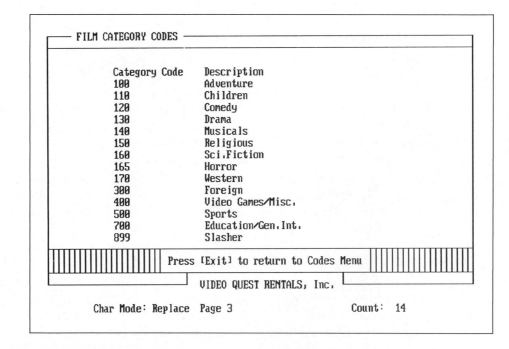

Figure 2.14   The CODES Form for Film Category Codes

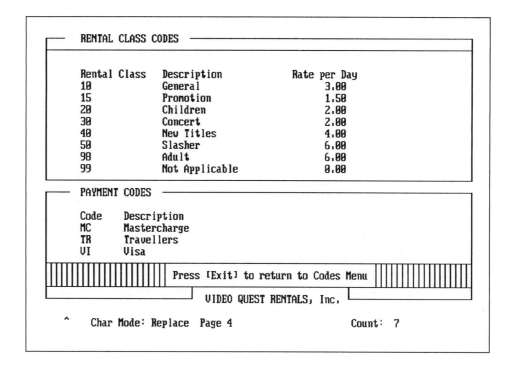

Figure 2.15   The CODES Form for Rental Class and Payment Codes

Managing the Rental and Return Transactions

The Video Quest application generates an invoice for rental transactions and a separate invoice for returns, if late charges are collected. Multiple tape rentals or returns can be combined on an invoice when rented or returned by a single customer. Maintaining separate data entry screens for each transaction enforces a logical separation between the two activities.

It would be perfectly logical to combine the two transactions, allowing a single invoice to contain both rentals and returns (and perhaps sales transactions). In this alternate scenario, the video application might have operators enter both rentals and returns on a single form. Applications often bow to stylistic preferences, either the preferences of the designer or those of the client. Neither method is right or wrong, although the approach we've opted to use is more suitable to our teaching purposes. Separating the transactions will help users new to ORACLE and SQL see the underlying table relationships more clearly.

The RENTALS and RETURNS forms are designed to emulate manual invoice forms—the kind typically perforated in multiple parts. Both forms closely resemble each other. In fact, rental and return invoices transactions are printed directly from the screen onto the same preprinted invoice paper stock. A consistent user interface goes a long way toward reducing training time, reducing operator errors, and accelerating data entry. For the same reasons, the screens of the master forms (TITLE, PRODUCT, and CUSTOMER) should convey a uniform look and feel. A good example of this is the RENTALS form illustrated in Figure 2.16.

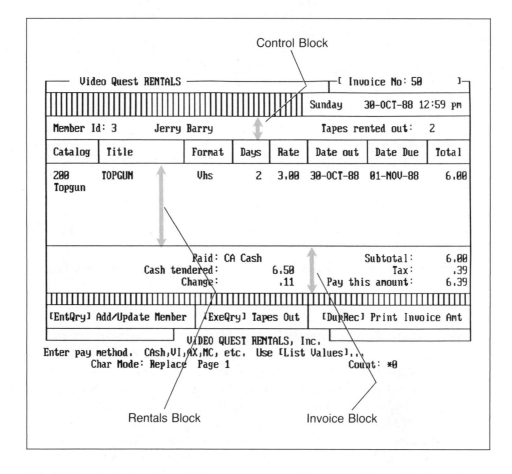

Figure 2.16   The RENTALS Form

The RENTALS form is divided into three sections, or *blocks*. The uppermost section of this form is called a control block because it does not refer to a database table. Control blocks are often used to display useful information not stored anywhere in the database, such as the current date and time as shown in the RENTALS form.

The middle and lower blocks of the RENTALS form are based on the RENTALS and INVOICE tables. Any changes made to these blocks are automatically updated in their corresponding RENTALS or INVOICE base tables.

The RETURNS form mirrors the RENTALS forms, as shown in Figure 2.17.

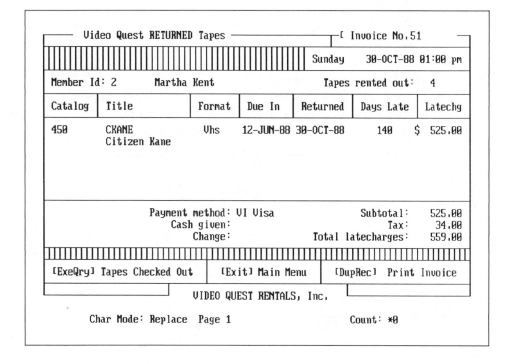

Figure 2.17   The RETURNS Form

Planning the Reports

Video Quest's continued success is dependent upon access to reliable, up-to-date information. With SQL, end-users can query the database interactively, experimenting with various SELECT commands to retrieve information from the database that answers specific questions. Since a SQL*Forms application uses SQL as the interface to the database, end-users can shape queries directly on a SQL*Forms screen with even greater ease.

Ad hoc queries satisfy a major portion of your immediate information needs, but not all. The fully automated business relies on various reports to provide a broad view of various activities and historical trends of the business. Management at Video Quest understands the need for comprehensive reporting, and has instituted store policies calling for the maintenance and generation of routine business reports. You will have a hand in building four types of these detailed reports for Video Quest, which are

- ▶ A Product Inventory Report
- ▶ A Tapes Overdue Report
- ▶ Daily Rentals Reports
- ▶ Year-to-Date Rental History Reports

Product Inventory Report

Let's glance at each of these. The Product Inventory Report provides current inventory positions for each product carried by the store. Figure 2.18 shows sample output of the inventory report output.

```
Fri Jun 10                                                                  page   1

                                   Video Quest Movie Rentals
                                  CURRENT INVENTORY POSITIONS


                                                 Qty   On  Qty   Qty    Actual
Product Format Description Title            Cost Recvd Hand Sold Rented Inventory <Variance>
------- ------ ----------- -------------------------------- ------- ------ ----- ----- ------- ---------- -----------
P100    Vhs    Film        The Sound of Music        $19.95     2         1     1       2
P200    Vhs    Film        Topgun                    $29.95     2               2       2
P300    Beta   Film        Gone with the Wind        $59.95     2         1     1       2
P300    Vhs    Film        Gone with the Wind        $59.95     2               2       2
P450    Vhs    Film        Citizen Kane              $49.95     2               2       2
P470    Beta   Film        Ghostbusters              $19.95     1    1                  1
P470    Vhs    Film        Ghostbusters              $19.95     2    1          1       2
P475    Vhs    Film        The Hitcher               $79.95     1    1                  1
P480    Vhs    Film        The Shining               $69.95     2         1             1         1
P500           Tape Case                              $2.99    30   20   10            30
                                                          ------ ----- ----- ------- ---------- -----------
                                                            46    23    13     9        45         1
```

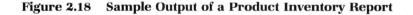

          Video Quest, Inc.
          Have A Good Day!

10 records selected.

This type of footer appears on every Video Quest report.

Figure 2.18   Sample Output of a Product Inventory Report

Tapes Overdue Report

Video Quest policy is to run a Tapes Overdue Report once a day, sometimes twice a day on busy days, and always twice daily on weekends. Figure 2.19 shows a sample of the output of the overdue report.

```
Fri Jun 10                                                                        page    1


                                     Video Quest Movie Rentals
                                       TAPES OVERDUE REPORT



                      Catalog            Scheduled      Days  Late     Member
Title                 Number    Format   Return Date    Late  Charge   Name                  Phone
-------------------   -------   ------   ------------   ----  -------  --------------------  -----------

Citizen Kane              451   Vhs        20 May , 88    22  $82.50   Jerry Barry           415-893-0050


Ghostbusters              470   Vhs        12 April , 88   60  $270.00  Daniel James Cronin  415-598-8125


Gone with the Wind        301   Vhs        14 April , 88   58  $217.50  Jerry Barry          415-893-0050

                          305   Beta       19 May , 88     23  $86.25   Daniel James Cronin  415-598-8125
```

Figure 2.19   Sample Output of a Tapes Overdue Report

Daily Rentals Reports

There are two types of Daily Rentals Reports, or Journals—a detailed report linking titles and customers and a summary report showing quantity and revenue totals by title. Figures 2.20 and 2.21 show sample outputs of both formats.

```
Fri Jun 10                                                                        page    1
                                     Video Quest Movie Rentals
                                      RENTALS JOURNAL - DETAILS


Rental                             Catalog   Film         Member
Date     Title              Format Number    Category     Name                  Phone
-------- -----------------  ------ -------   -----------  --------------------  -----------
10-JUN-88 Citizen Kane      Vhs       450    Classics     Martha Kent           453-392-4457

         Ghostbusters       Beta      473    Comedy       Jerry Barry           415-893-0050

         Gone with the Wind Vhs       300    Classics     Martha Kent           453-392-4457

         The Shining        Vhs       481    Horror       Martha Kent           453-392-4457
```

Figure 2.20   Sample Output of a Daily Rentals Report—Details

33

```
Fri Jun 10                                                              page    1
                                   Video Quest Movie Rentals
                                   RENTALS JOURNAL - SUMMARY


Rental                                             Total       Total
Date        Title                      Format    Tapes Out    Revenue
---------   ------------------------------  ------   ---------   --------
10-JUN-88   Citizen Kane               Vhs           1        $2.50

            Ghostbusters               Beta          1        $3.00

            Gone with the Wind         Vhs           1        $2.50

            The Shining                Vhs           1        $4.00

*********   ******************************            ---------   --------
sum                                                   4        $12.00
```

Figure 2.21   Sample Output of a Daily Rentals Report—Summary

Year-to-Date Rental History Reports

In the past, management had only the vaguest sense of rentals activity trends over a quarterly or yearly period. The Year-to-Date Rental History Reports, shown in Figures 2.22 and 2.23, change that.

The ORACLE tool currently offering the most *ad hoc* reporting mileage is SQL*Plus, a compilation of proprietary, nonprocedural SQL extensions designed for flexible formatting and report control. The Video Quest reports you will build were chosen to give you the widest possible exposure to these SQL*Plus commands.

You will also get a preview of ORACLE's newest report writer, SQL*ReportWriter, a powerful reporting tool which sports a familiar spreadsheet-style interface and offers tremendous nonprocedural formatting control. SQL*ReportWriter is new technology which, at the time of this writing, is available only on a few VAX and UNIX platforms. SQL*ReportWriter will be available to Professional ORACLE users in late 1988.

```
Fri Jun 10                                                                      page    1
                                 Video Quest Movie Rentals
                                 SUMMARY RENTAL ACTIVITY
                                 Ranked By Film Category

     Film                                                                              Yearly
YR   Category      Title                  F    Jan Feb Mar Apr May Jun Jul Aug Sep Oct Nov Dec  Total
--   ------------  ---------------------  ---- --- --- --- --- --- --- --- --- --- --- --- --- ------
88   Adventure     Topgun                 Vhs              1   1                                    2

     ************  *********************        --- --- --- --- --- --- --- --- --- --- --- --- ------
     sum                                                   1   1                                    2

     Classics      Gone with the Wind     Vhs          1   2   1   1                                5

                   Citizen Kane           Vhs                  2   1                                3

                   Gone with the Wind     Beta                 1                                    1

     ************  *********************        --- --- --- --- --- --- --- --- --- --- --- --- ------
     sum                                              1   2   4   2                                9

     Comedy        Ghostbusters           Beta                     1                                1
                                          Vhs              1                                        1

     ************  *********************        --- --- --- --- --- --- --- --- --- --- --- --- ------
     sum                                                   1       1                                2

     Horror        The Shining            Vhs              1       1                                2

     ************  *********************        --- --- --- --- --- --- --- --- --- --- --- --- ------
     sum                                                   1       1                                2

     Musicals      The Sound of Music     Vhs          1       1                                    2

     ************  *********************        --- --- --- --- --- --- --- --- --- --- --- --- ------
     sum                                              1       1                                    2

**                                             --- --- --- --- --- --- --- --- --- --- --- --- ------
sum                                                2   5   6   4                                  17




                                 Have a Good Day!
                                 Rentytd.SQL

8 records selected.
```

Figure 2.22   Sample Output of a Year-to-Date Rental History Report, Ranked by Film Category

```
Fri Jun 10                                                                        page    1

                                        Video Quest Movie Rentals
                                      RENTAL ACTIVITY FOR CURRENT YEAR
                                           Ranked By Quantity


                                                                                 Yearly
YR Title                    F    Jan Feb Mar Apr May Jun Jul Aug Sep Oct Nov Dec  Total
-- ------------------------- ---- ---- ---- ---- ---- ---- ---- ---- ---- ---- ---- ---- ---- -------
88 Gone with the Wind       Vhs           1    2    1    1                             5

   Citizen Kane             Vhs                     2    1                             3

   The Shining              Vhs                1         1                             2

   The Sound of Music       Vhs           1         1                                  2

   Topgun                   Vhs                1    1                                  2

   Ghostbusters             Beta                         1                             1
                            Vhs                1                                       1

   Gone with the Wind       Beta                    1                                  1

** **********************************  ---- ---- ---- ---- ---- ---- ---- ---- ---- ---- ---- ---- -------
sum                                      2    5    6    4                             17
```

Figure 2.23   Sample Output of a Year-to-Date Rental History Report, Ranked by Quantity

Building a Menuing System

A menuing system binds the application components together to provide full application integration. End-users should be able to navigate through various menu levels and menu options with ease, but they should only have access to those forms or functions which they are authorized to use. The more sophisticated menuing system controls user access dynamically based on log-on ID and password and may also allow for parameter entry and parameter passing to the applications they invoke.

Store Clerk's Application View
The application menus and submenus shown in Figures 2.24 through 2.26 are available to Video Quest store clerks: Store Clerk's Main Menu, Store Clerk's Master Tables Submenu, and Store Clerk's Transactions Submenu.

Management's Application View
In contrast to the store clerk, Video Quest management personnel (both Assistant Managers and store owners) have much wider access to information in the Video Quest application. The Main Menu presented to management is shown in Figure 2.27.

In addition to the options available to store clerks, management can access the Code Maintenance and Business Reports submenus shown in Figures 2.28 and 2.29.

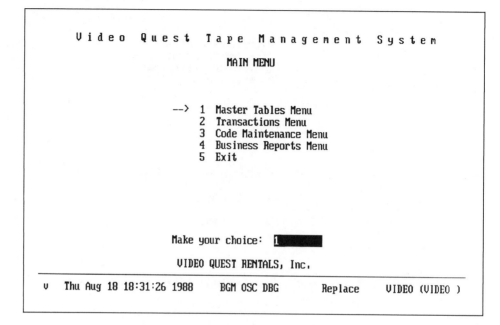

Figure 2.24   Store Clerk's Main Menu

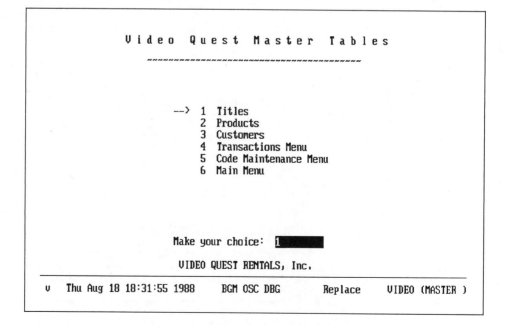

Figure 2.25   Store Clerk's Master Tables Submenu

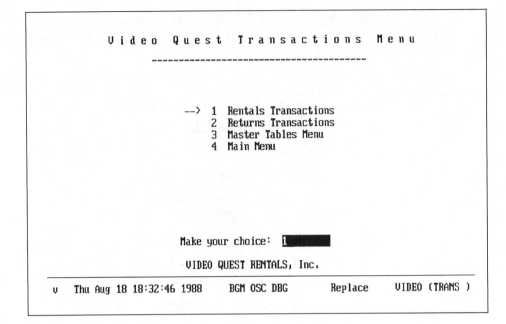

Figure 2.26   Store Clerk's Transactions Submenu

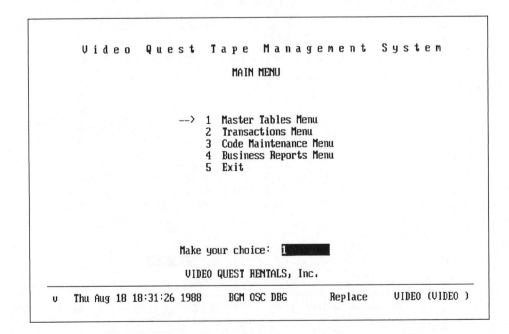

Figure 2.27   Management's Main Menu

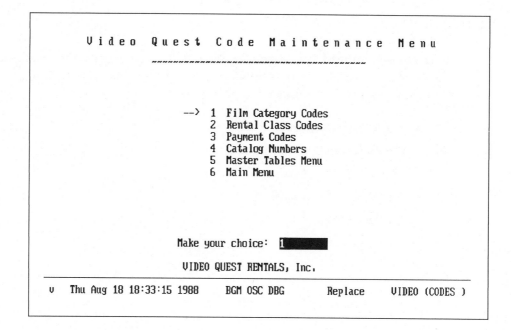

Figure 2.28   Management's Code Maintenance Submenu

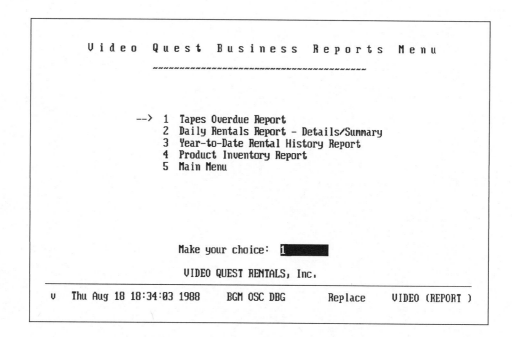

Figure 2.29   Management's Business Reports Submenu

Summary

This chapter toured you through the Video Quest application serving as the tutorial example for this book. It gave you an overview of the application foundations, including

- ► The CASE*Method
- ► Database design techniques
- ► The Video Quest forms
- ► The Video Quest reports
- ► The menuing system

3

Building the Business Model

3

Building the Business Model

Chapter 3 introduces you to ORACLE's fourth-generation application development environment. It focuses on the business problems of our fictitious video retail store. You will become familiar with the policies of Video Quest in order to design a comprehensive application which solves its problems. By doing so, you will learn the principles of the SQL development philosophy formalized in the CASE*Method, Oracle's business analysis and modelling system.

Objectives of a Development Method

Traditional 3GL development environments are trapped in their own histories, often entrenched in outdated development theories and techniques. Communication between the designer and the client—the end-user—is stilted. The development methods used are more often reactive than proactive. During the life cycle of any application, end-user requirements always change; this is an *a priori* truth. Rather than design a flexible application from the very start, one that allows ease of expansion and modification, the traditional answer is to throw more people at the problem. This is an inelegant and costly solution.

A sound development method is anything but reactive. It is a complete, self-documenting method immediately understood by end-users and DP professionals alike. The development method becomes the framework for controlling all phases of the application life cycle, yet it must also be flexible and responsive to changes, such as new demands by end-users or new trends in technology.

The CASE*Method

The CASE*Method, originally developed in the United Kingdom, successfully addresses the problems of the traditional 3GL development environments. The CASE*Method leverages the strengths of SQL, offering a top-down development method that puts end-users and business management in touch with the development process. CASE*Method gives application designers the necessary skills to quickly identify the application requirements within the business and technical constraints and to document them as a basis for the actual implementation of the application.

The CASE*Method embodies an integrated set of techniques. These include end-user interviews and feedback sessions, business and systems analysis, and modelling techniques to represent business functions, entity-relationships (related things or information which should be known about the business), and the flow of data through the business system. CASE*Method breaks down the development life cycle into six distinct phases and weighs them according to the average amount of time devoted to each:

Strategy	5%
Analysis	15%
Design	40%
Build	25%
Transition	10%
Production	5%

Through each phase, CASE*Method controls the movements and actions of application designers to refine their design and prototyping skills and to make the most productive use of their time.

The CASE*Method stresses the use of models to express the business functions and data requirements. The CASE*Method modelling techniques facilitate communication between the designer on one hand and the management and the end-users on the other hand. These are the people who best understand the business—in other words, they are the experts. As the application gradually evolves, the system must of course be documented in writing. Diagrammatic models do not replace documentation, but augment it. Visual models are simply tools to help the business experts clearly visualize their business requirements. As a rule, experts will disagree on the particulars of the business, sometimes vehemently. Visual models bring about a much quicker resolution.

At each phase of the development life cycle, models are used to move both designer and experts to the next development phase, as Figure 3.2 shows.

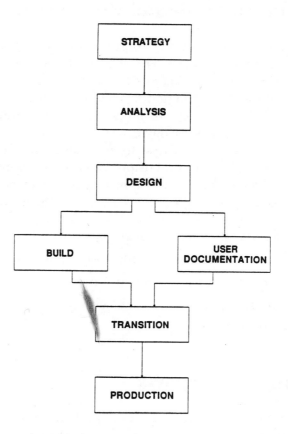

Figure 3.1 **Stages of the Development Life Cycle** *Courtesy of Oracle Corporation*

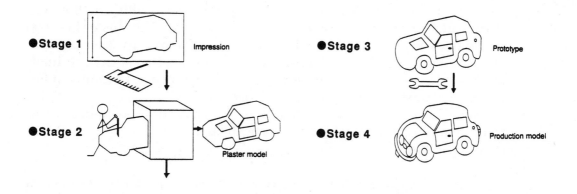

Figure 3.2 **Models for All Phases of the Development Life Cycle** *Courtesy of Oracle Corporation*

Defining the Video Rental Business Model

Video Quest has been in operation for over two years and has grown into a successful small business. The store is so successful, in fact, that its manual operations are cracking at the seams. The current volume of business has made it impossible to handle everyday tasks manually—tracking tapes in circulation, invoicing customers, managing the tape inventory, and maintaining the customer database.

It is time for Video Quest to automate. You, the ORACLE consultant, have been hired to build a custom video rental application to solve Video Quest's problems. Your first task in fulfilling your charter is to analyze the Video Quest business. Applying the CASE*Method, you will

- ▶ Interview the business experts
- ▶ Define the functional model of the business
- ▶ Define the entity-relationship model
- ▶ Conduct a feedback session with the original team of experts
- ▶ Build the data flow model

Interviewing the Experts

The information gathering phase is perhaps the most critical of all. After interviewing the business experts, you should know enough about the organization to make a first pass at drawing up the blueprint of the business. Interviewing clients may be second nature to you, but even so, there are some special ground rules for the CASE*Method interview process. As in any interview session, it is essential to establish rapport with the interviewees and make the best use of the time they spend with you. But even more critical is asking the right questions. Each player has his or her own perceptions about what is important in the business. To get a sharper focus on the global business environment, you must elicit precise information from each interviewee. Sifting through extraneous, tangential information is a waste of your and your client's time.

Your opening questions should be broad and thought-provoking. Some questions that CASE*Method consultants typically open with include the following:

"Would you please tell me, in your own words, about the essence of your business?"

"What is your organization's structure and what do each of your people do?"

"Where do you think the business will go in the future?"

"What key things do you need to know to do your job, and why?"

"What (else) do you do and what information does this demand?"

If the interview session is dragging on too long, gently prompt the subject to move on to crucial information with a leading question like:

"Could you explain in a little more detail your most pressing problems?"

It wouldn't hurt to acquire some background information about the business before conducting your interviews, if only to properly guide the interviewee when he or she strays from the path. Be prepared to ask some specific questions about the business or particular operations of the business. Time permitting, you might ask the same questions of each expert to observe the range of responses and to get a better feel for what things or functions are significant. For example, you might prepare a list of the following topics or questions before your first interview at Video Quest:

1. Membership policies

   Fees

   Deposits required?

   Can members share a single membership card or is the policy one card per member?

   Can only members rent tapes?

2. Rental and return policies

   Limit on number of tapes rented at one time?

   Rental rates—based on classes of films? Also, any discount days or promotions?

   Rates and accrual of late charges, including ability of clerk to optionally waive late charges?

   Special penalty fees—rewind charges, lost tapes?

   Does the store provide a night drop service?

3. Invoicing and payment policies

   Rentals payable in advance or upon return?

   Cash only or credit card ok?

Can the rental of a tape and the purchase of a tape or accessory be posted to a single invoice, or must separate invoices be generated?

Are late charges invoiced?

4. Reservations

Advance reservations or same day only?

Tape held for a limited time?

Reservation privilege revoked at any time (for the offenders who consistently fail to pick up reservations)?

The interview session should never come to an abrupt end. You don't want to rush the interviewee because you risk alienating a valuable resource, one that you will probably want to visit with again. Leave yourself plenty of time to cover the appropriate ground; then gradually bring the session to a close with a round of brief closing questions. Such closing questions might be as general as

"Let's go through your organization again quickly, and see whether we've missed anything."

"Who else would you recommend that I talk to, and why?"

"Are there any other problems which you have to deal with?"

"Is there anything else you would like to tell me about?"

Take careful notes during each interview. Inaccurate or incomplete notes are an insult to the interviewee and will obviously not help to increase your understanding of the business, particularly when you must review the mass of material at the end of the interview process. At a minimum, your notes should contain significant elements in the business, details of the organization, business procedures, emphatic statements and revealing quotations made by interviewees, summaries, types of things or entities used by the business, references to people and documents, and your impressions of the organization.

Defining the Functional Model

After the final interview session, you will begin constructing the business model for Video Quest. You will start with the most fundamental component, a model illustrating the business functions of the video rental business and any functions peculiar to Video Quest's approach to this business.

The goal of a functional model is to define in the simplest terms what the business actually does. The functional model will drive a more detailed analysis and also serve to cross check the accuracy of your subsequent entity-relationship analysis. Since it is a template of all of the business functions, this simple model will eventually help you select implementation areas for the final application.

The functional model is hierarchical. You begin with a single strategic business statement—a sweeping description of the entire business—and break this down, typically into seven or eight major functions. You then break each of these major functions down into more detailed descriptions to cover the scope of the business. The process of building this model is, appropriately, termed *functional decomposition.* Video Quest's mission in life can be summed up as follows:

> "To service customers with the rental, sale and reservation of video tapes and accessories from a large inventory of merchandise located across a chain of video retail stores."

From this statement, one can cull at least five of Video Quest's major functions: tape rentals, tape sales, tape reservations, inventory control, and customer maintenance. The remaining business functions, taken from your copious interview notes, will flesh out the list. CASE*Method expresses this upper level of the functional hierarchy (known as the Top Function Split) as shown in Figure 3.3.

Every function noted in your model, including the top line, should begin with a verb. In the real world, nearly every business function translates into an action; your functional model should mirror reality.

Functional decomposition becomes more challenging the further down the hierarchy you go. Functions often overlap, and they often occur conditionally, only when triggered by another event or function. Another problem is that application designers, having spent so much time interviewing clients, are apt to confuse functions with people or jobs.

One trick many CASE*Method consultants use when doing functional decomposition is to write down every function that comes to mind randomly on a separate 3″ by 5″ index card. Once they've built up a hefty stack of cards, they lay the cards out on the table and then arrange them in a logical hierarchical order. The freedom resulting from the randomness of the first step of this process eliminates having to make premature decisions about the grouping or sequence of certain functions.

```
┌─────────────────────────────────────────────────────────────┐
│ Service customers with the rental, sale, and reservation of   │
│ video tapes and accessories from a large inventory of          │
│ merchandise located among a chain of video retail stores.      │
└─────────────────────────────────────────────────────────────┘
        1
   ┌─────────────────────────────────────────────────────────┐
   │ Manage rentals and returns of tapes and accessories       │
   └─────────────────────────────────────────────────────────┘
        2
   ┌─────────────────────────────────────────────────────────┐
   │ Sell cassettes, accessories, and equipment                │
   └─────────────────────────────────────────────────────────┘
        3
   ┌─────────────────────────────────────────────────────────┐
   │ Reserve tapes and equipment for customers                 │
   └─────────────────────────────────────────────────────────┘
        4
   ┌─────────────────────────────────────────────────────────┐
   │ Manage information about the customer base                 │
   └─────────────────────────────────────────────────────────┘
        5
   ┌─────────────────────────────────────────────────────────┐
   │ Purchase tapes and equipment                              │
   └─────────────────────────────────────────────────────────┘
        6
   ┌─────────────────────────────────────────────────────────┐
   │ Maintain store inventory                                  │
   └─────────────────────────────────────────────────────────┘
        7
   ┌─────────────────────────────────────────────────────────┐
   │ Administer store prices and accounting procedures         │
   └─────────────────────────────────────────────────────────┘
        8
   ┌─────────────────────────────────────────────────────────┐
   │ Analyze rental and sales trends                           │
   └─────────────────────────────────────────────────────────┘
```

Figure 3.3   Video Quest—Top Function Split

The core of Video Quest's business is the rental of video tapes. Since rentals are inextricably tied to customers, maintenance of the customer database is equally important. Sample hierarchies of these primary functions appear in Figures 3.4 and 3.5. Observe that this modelling technique is consistent in its numbering convention; functions are numbered in a strict hierarchical fashion.

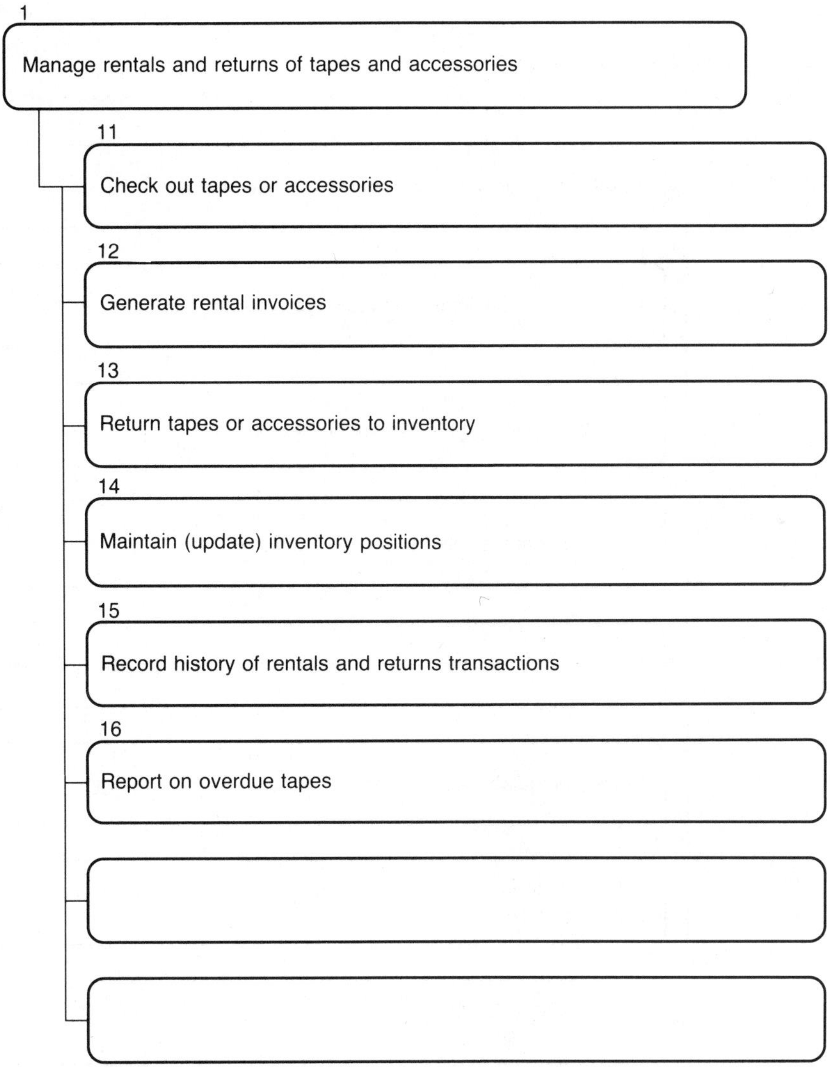

1

Manage rentals and returns of tapes and accessories

    11

    Check out tapes or accessories

    12

    Generate rental invoices

    13

    Return tapes or accessories to inventory

    14

    Maintain (update) inventory positions

    15

    Record history of rentals and returns transactions

    16

    Report on overdue tapes

Figure 3.4   Functional Hierarchy—Rentals and Returns

Defining the Entity-Relationship Model

If the functional model is one half of the equation, the entity-relationship model is the other half. An entity model assists the designer in defining and understanding the *things of significance about which information needs to be known or held* and also the *relationships* between these things. In contrast to business functions, which translate into actions, the business entity is conceptual. It is a noun or any named thing. Some examples of

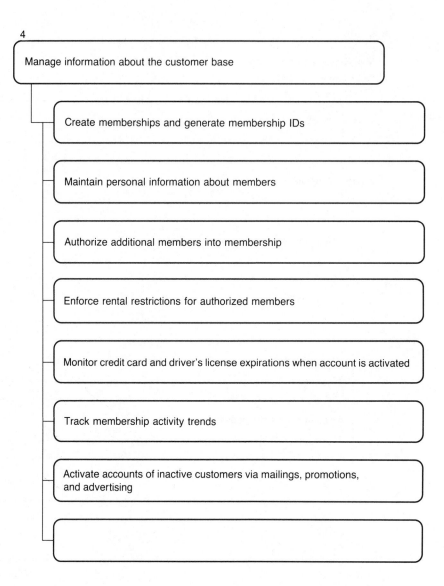

Figure 3.5   Functional Hierarchy—Managing Customer Information

entities in the business community are a person, a project, a division, a corporation, an employee, a client, or a supplier. In the video retail business, an entity may be a tape, a customer, a title, a product, a store, a rental transaction, or an invoice. (Although it may seem awkward, one normally speaks of an entity in the singular, not the plural, unless specifically referring to two or more discrete entities.)

An entity-relationship is a carefully chosen CASE*Method term that defines the connection or relationship between two entities. In CASE*Method jargon, a *relationship* is *any significant way in which two* *things of the same or different type may be associated.* A relationship must always have a name. Some examples of relationships are

Entity 1	Relationship	Entity 2
Project	for	Client
Person	responsible for	Project
Person	employed by	Corporation
Corporation	employer of	Person
Division	part of	Corporation

The Video Quest Entity-Relationship Model

The technique for crafting an entity model is based on the same hierarchical premise as the functional model: find the lowest common denominator and gradually add layers of complexity to it. With entity models, you define the simplest core relationships and build up from there, layer by layer. What are the two core entities of the video rental business? Tapes and customers. There is a unique relationship between these two entities, which would be expressed as in Figure 3.6.

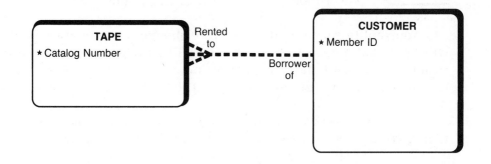

Figure 3.6   Entity-Relationship—TAPE and CUSTOMER

The TAPE-CUSTOMER relationship can be described narratively as follows:

A tape [may be] rented to [only one] customer.

and:

A customer [may be] the borrower of [one or more] tapes.

What this means is that a single, unique tape may be rented to only one customer at a time. A customer, however, may borrow more than one tape at any one time. In relational database terms, this entity-relationship represents the classic one-to-many relationship. (Roughly 90% of all entity-relationships in real-world applications fall into this category.)

In the diagram, note the single line attached to the customer box and the three splayed lines, called *crow's feet*, attached to the tape box. These are CASE*Method notation conventions that express the relationships between entities. A single line always means that one and only one entity exists, and the crow's feet indicate that one or more exist.

Another entity-model convention is the connecting line between entities, which can be either dotted or solid. Notice that a dotted line connects both the TAPE and the CUSTOMER entities. A dotted line signifies that the relationship is not mandatory, that is, it *may* be true. A tape may be rented to a customer, but no law says it must. Similarly, a customer may rent the tape, but nothing is stopping the customer from renting another tape instead. Quite often, you will see a solid line attached to one or another entity. This indicates the opposite condition, a mandatory connection, that is, it *must* be true.

To recap these four basic symbols:

———————	one and only one	---------- may be
<————	one or more	——————— must be

Your entity model will get more elaborate as you progress. Entities will be added, and your descriptions will gain precision as the entity-relationships start to take shape. For now, you want to identify each entity with at least one attribute—some aspect that clearly distinguishes or qualifies the entity.

Entity attributes are of three types: primary key, required, and optional. These attributes are expressed with the following symbols:

- ★ Primary key attribute
- # Required attribute
- • Optional attribute

The primary key attribute of an entity is not the same as the primary key of a relational database. These are similar concepts, but don't confuse them. The primary key of an entity is something that uniquely identifies the entity, whereas a database key refers to a column in a database table that uniquely identifies each row in the table. An entity model is just a conceptual tool; you are not bound to it. The entity model is not necessarily what you will implement in the final database design. Of course, you may ultimately choose to implement the primary key attributes as database keys, but it is far too premature at this stage to make such implementation decisions.

The attributes defined for both the TAPE and CUSTOMER entities are primary keys. Since each tape is unique, the TAPE attribute refers to a unique catalog number; likewise, a unique Member ID identifies each customer.

Adding the TITLE Entity

Our research into the video business tells us that a few titles, particularly new titles or classics such as *Gone with the Wind*, are much in demand. The responsible video store will stock several copies of a popular title to meet this demand. This ancient principle of supply and demand introduces a new entity into the landscape—the film TITLE. The TITLE entity shares a special relationship with the TAPE entity, a relationship implied by the context in which it was introduced. While there may be several copies—that is, several unique tapes—of a given title, each tape must be identified by one and only one title. Figure 3.7 shows the original model of the TAPE-CUSTOMER entity relationship expanded to include the new TITLE entity:

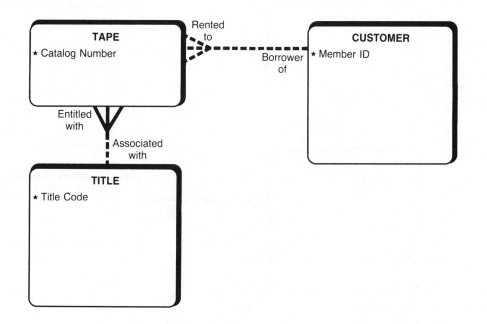

Figure 3.7   Adding the TITLE Entity

The TITLE-TAPE relationship can be described narratively as follows:

A title [may be] associated with [one or more] tapes.

and:

A tape [must be] entitled with [one and only] one title.

Rental tapes are typically classified into film genres—drama, comedy, children's, horror, sci-fi, western, classics, and so forth. These classifications satisfy the industry's preoccupation with organization, but, more importantly, they become a guideline for studios and distributors to better manage the distribution of their offerings. Most video stores use these film categories for convenience; the store's tape library is normally organized by genre, and the blank boxes laid out for customer perusal are organized this way. To present a consistent image, the store's customized catalog would also follow suit.

The FILM CATEGORY entity must be added to the model to further describe the TITLE entity. It would look like the model in Figure 3.8:

A film category [may be] applied to [one or more] titles.

A title [must be] classified by [one and only one] film category.

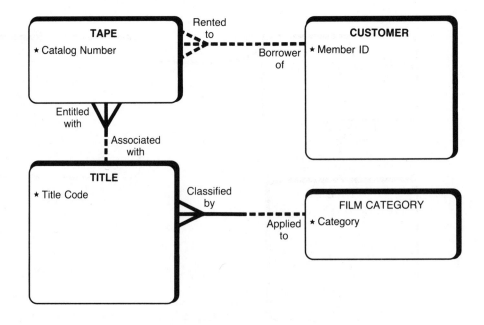

Figure 3.8   Adding the FILM CATEGORY Entity

Correcting the Video Quest Model

Unfortunately, Video Quest's current entity model is flawed. A profitable chunk of the business is not reflected. This is the rental or sale of nontape items—video recorders or accessories such as blank tapes, VCR head cleaners, tape cabinets, and so forth. Such accessories have nothing in common with the TITLE entity and certainly have no bearing on the rental or sale of video tapes. An additional entity must be created to hold these nontape items. To preserve the integrity of the model, however, the entity should also bear some relationship to both TITLE and TAPE. We'll call this all-encompassing entity PRODUCT and express it as shown in Figure 3.9.

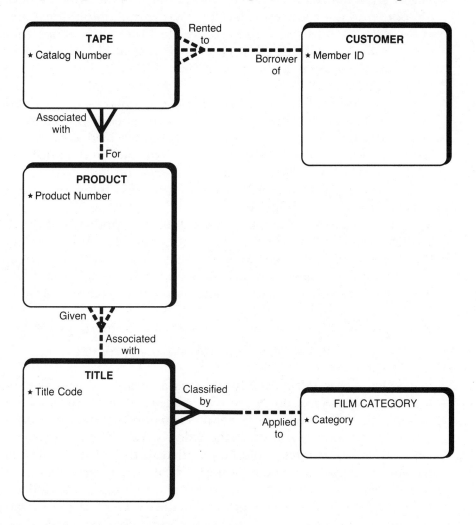

Figure 3.9   Adding the PRODUCT Entity

A product [may be] given [one and only one] title.

A title [may be] associated with [one or more] products.

and:

A product [may be] for [one or more] tapes.

A tape [must be] associated with [one and only one] product.

Since PRODUCT is an umbrella entity that may include rental tapes and accessory merchandise, the relationship between TITLE and PRODUCT is not required. There may or may not be a title associated with a product, so the connection is expressed with a dotted line. The flip side of the PRODUCT-TITLE relationship is the TAPE entity. When the product refers to a video tape, it must carry a title. Multiple copies of a title are thus expressed through the intermediary PRODUCT entity as noted in the above entity model.

We also discovered that products (both video tapes and nontape accessories) can either be rented or sold. Some special products—overstock copies of *Ghostbusters*, for instance—may be classified as both a rental and purchase product, leaving the store owner the flexibility to decide at a later date which individual tapes would be rented or sold. (Without having to reclassify the product type, the owner can also sell a previously rented tape at a used discount price.)

These options prompt the creation of another entity, PRODUCT TYPE, which ties the products down in further detail. The primary key of PRODUCT TYPE would be called Product Type as well and would probably contain the values of rental, sale, and both rental/sale. Video Quest's expanded entity model might be expressed as in Figure 3.10.

A product type [may be] attached to [one or more] products.

A product [must be] of [one and only one] product type.

Video stores often classify films as a means of affixing rental rates. Rental classifications, not to be confused with film categories, commonly include such headings as General, Promotion, Children, Concert, New Titles, Slasher, and so forth. If the video store's inventory were relatively small, then rental rates could be handled in the PRODUCT entity, but for a larger database, this would be impractical. Rental rates change; it's much more efficient to change a rate once (for an entire class of films) and let the system apply the rate change automatically to several titles, rather than wasting an operator's time making the same change over and over again to each title. (In addition, not all products are rentable; for example, blank tapes, so a product does not have to have a rental class.)

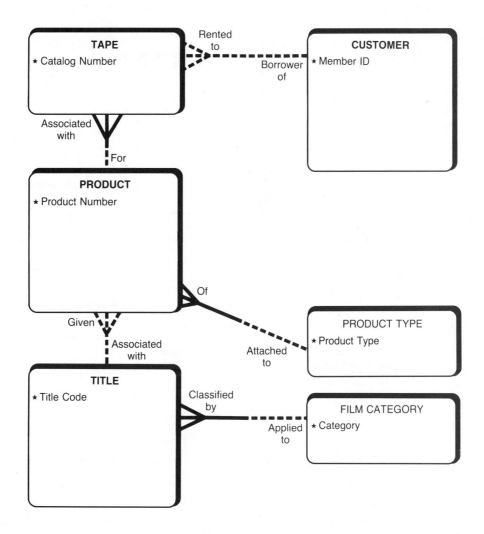

Figure 3.10   Adding the PRODUCT TYPE Entity

The new entity, RENTAL CLASS, must therefore be added to the model. As Figure 3.11 shows,

A rental class [may be] attached to [one or more] products.

A product [may be] of [one and only one] rental class.

There is one more small detail about the PRODUCT entity which mustn't be ignored. If the product is a rental tape, how will the system distinguish between different tape formats? A video tape can be in either Beta, VHS, or CD format (and there probably will be others in the future, at the rate technology is racing). Tape formats complicate things, but our system can accommodate new information because the entity model is not

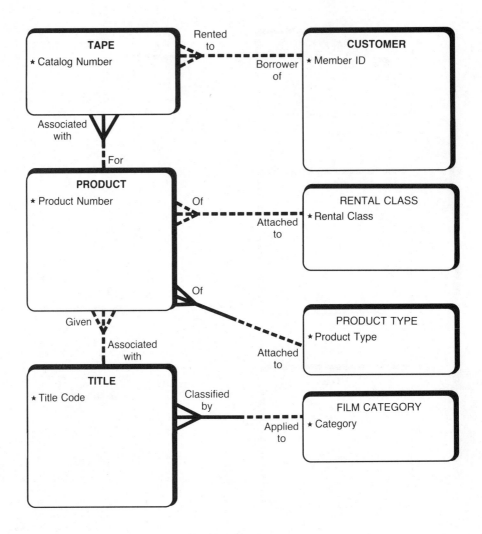

Figure 3.11   Adding the RENTAL CLASS Entity

cast in stone. One of the chief reasons for defining the business model beforehand is to work these relationships out well before the system is implemented, before it's too late.

Similar to PRODUCT TYPE, a new FORMAT TYPE entity must be added to further describe any product which specifically refers to a video tape. It doesn't matter whether this tape is rented or sold outright. Either way, the tape must have a distinct format. Since Beta VCRs are on the wane in the video industry, stores are rapidly phasing out tapes in Beta format. Nearly 20% of Video Quest's current film inventory is in Beta format; in other words, with 20 copies of *Topgun* in stock, four would be in Beta and 16 copies would be in VHS format. This is the kind of detailed inventory information that must be monitored closely in the video retail business.

Adding FORMAT TYPE, the complete entity model would now be expressed as in Figure 3.12.

A format type [may be] attached to [one or more] products.

A product [may be] of [one and only one] format type.

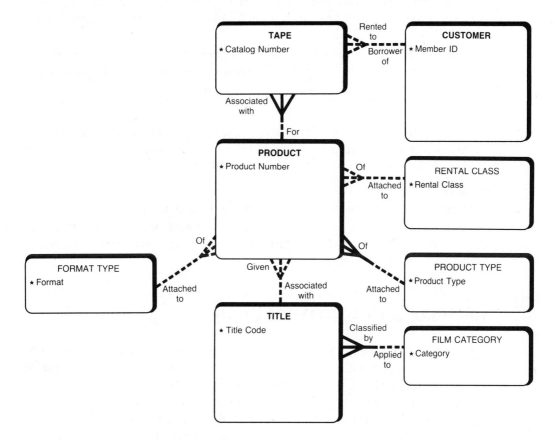

Figure 3.12   Adding the FORMAT TYPE Entity

Since a FORMAT TYPE refers only to video tape products, and not to nontape accessories, then the attribute Format Type listed under the PRODUCT box is optional. However, the Format Type attribute uniquely identifies each item of its host entity, FORMAT TYPE, so it becomes the primary key attribute for this entity. (This book will use initial caps and lowercase for attributes when speaking of them as attributes, and all caps when they are in their capacity as entities or as tables.)

Let's briefly summarize the relationships between PRODUCTs, TAPEs, and TITLEs. Three scenarios are possible:

Scenario 1

A PRODUCT may be a video tape which is either rented, sold or available for rental/sale (identified by R, S, or RS in the PRODUCT TYPE entity).

This PRODUCT carries a TITLE and a FORMAT TYPE (currently either VHS, Beta, or CD).

If the PRODUCT is rentable, it carries a specific RENTAL CLASS to determine the rental rate (children's, rock videos, exercise tapes, new titles, and so forth.)

There may be several copies of this video tape, each uniquely identified by the primary key attribute, "catalog number," held by the TAPE entity.

Scenario 2

A PRODUCT may be a tape without any associated TITLE, such as a blank tape. Such a product would have a particular FORMAT TYPE, and would probably be for sale only (an S PRODUCT TYPE).

Scenario 3

A PRODUCT may also be a nontape item such as a VCR drive cleaner or a tape cabinet. Such accessories may be either rented or sold, thus they are identified by a PRODUCT TYPE. This type of product would have neither a TITLE nor a FORMAT TYPE.

Expanding the CUSTOMER Entity

A video store can handle customer memberships many different ways. The central issue is who will be responsible for the membership card. Should every customer wishing to rent tapes have his or her own personal card? If business is prosperous, this approach could generate a mass of cards to maintain. Should a membership, therefore, be assigned to a group or family with only one person responsible for it, one who can grant the privilege of using the card to others?

Video Quest has found it more efficient—and economical—to assign group memberships, which means that the CUSTOMER entity will have to be refined. The CUSTOMER entity would be split into two subtypes, PRIMARY MEMBER and AUTHORIZED MEMBER, and might be expressed as in Figure 3.13.

A primary member [may be] responsible for [one or more] authorized members

An authorized member [must] pertain to [one and only one] primary member

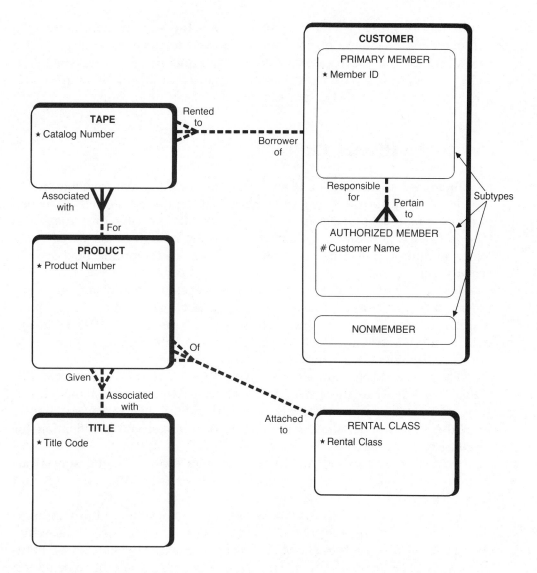

Figure 3.13   Expanding the CUSTOMER Entity

Entity subtypes are akin to the larger entity, analogous to cousins. The PRIMARY MEMBER at Video Quest is wholly responsible for the membership account. He or she can sponsor anyone onto the account, but must pay the price for lost or delinquent video tapes. The AUTHORIZED MEMBER owes allegiance to one and only one PRIMARY MEMBER; this secondary member cannot legally rent tapes on any other membership card.

One need not be a member of Video Quest to walk in and purchase a tape or accessories. Memberships are relevant only to rental privileges, so a third entity must be created which covers the sale of merchandise to nonmembers. (Members obviously are allowed to purchase merchandise as well.) Thus the above CUSTOMER entity model includes the third sub-type, NONMEMBER. The NONMEMBER has no direct relationship to the other member types and is more or less an island unto itself.

Creating a History Entity

Most business applications collect some form of historical information. In the video retail business, access to historical data is imperative. A record of every rental, sale, and return transaction must be kept to manage the tape inventory, generate invoices, balance daily receipt totals, satisfy customer enquiries, perform auditing functions, and monitor business or growth trends.

For simplicity, the Video Quest model singles out one global entity for the storage of historical information: TRANSACTION. Since Video Quest maintains more than one kind of transaction, this TRANSACTION entity will be subdivided into RENTAL and RETURN subtypes and, optionally, the SALE, RESERVATION, and STOCK RECEIPT subtypes.

These last three transactions (SALE, RESERVATION, and STOCK RE-CEIPT) are added to the diagram to illustrate a more robust model, but they will not be implemented in our application. They vary so slightly from the base transactions that there is no educational justification for discussing them here.

Observe how the TRANSACTION entity is drawn, paying special attention to the multiple relationships shared with the original TAPE and CUSTOMER entities, shown in Figure 3.14.

Clearly, TAPEs and CUSTOMERs are the focal points of both transactions. The TAPE is the subject of RENTAL and RETURN transactions, while the CUSTOMER is the initiator of both transactions. Between them, a complete, closed system is formed. The most significant piece of information held by the RENTAL entity (besides the catalog number of the tape and the member ID of the customer responsible) is the date the rental transaction was created. Similarly, the date the tape was actually returned is the primary attribute of the RETURN transaction.

The Distributed Environment

Our current entity model has concentrated on the operations of an isolated Video Quest store. The fictional Video Quest enterprise commands a chain of video retail stores spanning northern California. Currently, each

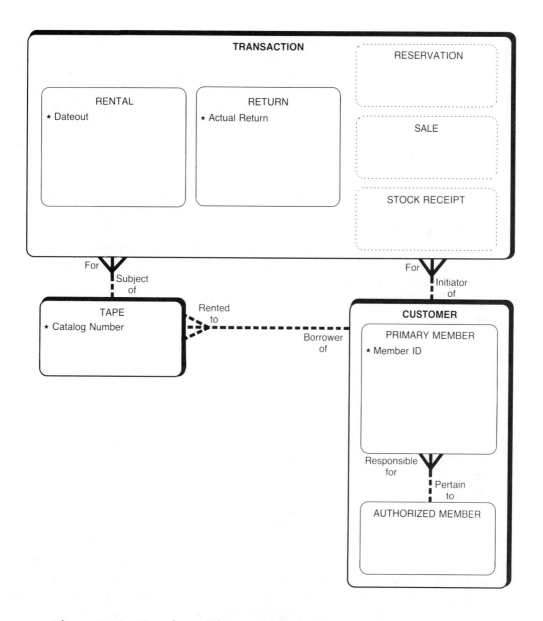

Figure 3.14   Creating a History Entity—TRANSACTION

store is autonomous, carrying its own tape inventory, managing an exclusive customer base (a customer must apply for separate membership cards to belong to two Video Quest stores), and purchasing tapes or accessories for only that store.

During the interview process, management emphasized a long-term goal for Video Quest: to link stores in a distributed computer network environment. One scenario would let each store continue to maintain its own inventory (an arrangement called *a limited site autonomy*) but have corporate headquarters assume the purchasing, accounting and, possibly, the customer service responsibilities for all stores. A large, central database at headquarters would tie into individual store databases within a global network. To make intelligent purchasing decisions, headquarters would require access to inventory status and historical information stored on the local databases and would need to be able to query information remotely.

Video Quest chose ORACLE as a system in part for its networking and distributed database support. With ORACLE facilities, application designers are free from the drudgery of writing the protocols and network control software to run applications in a networking environment. However, the designer must factor into the application design some flexibility to support distributed capabilities. To do this, when modelling the distributed relationships, simply add an entity labelled STORE that shares a unique relationship to each TAPE and TRANSACTION.

As shown in Figure 3.15, the STORE entity shares a one-to-many relationship with the TRANSACTION entity, and also a one-to-many relationship with the TAPE entity. A STORE may be the initiator of one or more TRANSACTIONs, but a TRANSACTION must occur at one and only one store. Now a STORE will certainly own more than one tape, but a single tape can only be located at one store. A store number uniquely identifies each value in the STORE entity.

Generating Customer Invoices

Video Quest clerks are instructed to generate a customer invoice for each rental or sale transaction. An invoice might also be generated for returns, if late charges have accrued. Customers appreciate the personal touch of receiving a receipt, and a receipt is also necessary for maintaining a history of these transactions by number. Without a unique invoice number, performing transaction audits any time in the future—such as inquiring into sales or purchase trends by customer, or balancing daily receipt totals—would be nearly impossible to do.

The blow-up of the TRANSACTION model in Figure 3.16 illustrates the new INVOICE entity.

A transaction [may be] charged on [one and only one] invoice.

An invoice [must be] attached to [one and only one] transaction.

Customer invoicing can be handled a variety of ways; the rationale for choosing one approach over another depends on the business the appli-

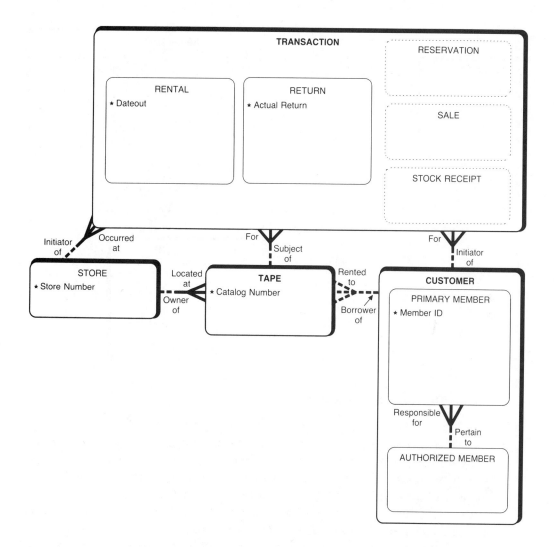

Figure 3.15   The Distributed Environment—The STORE Entity

cation is designed for, but is also a matter of style. Is it most efficient to combine all transactions for a customer onto a single invoice? Or is it simpler to invoice each transaction separately, using one invoice for all rental transactions and another for sales transactions? Considering that the video business garners most of its profits from tape rentals, it seems that rental transactions should be handled separately from sales. Most of a clerk's time will be spent checking out tapes and updating the rentals side of the database. (As you'll soon see, the forms-based application clearly separates the rental, sales, and return transactions by implementing a separate screen for each.)

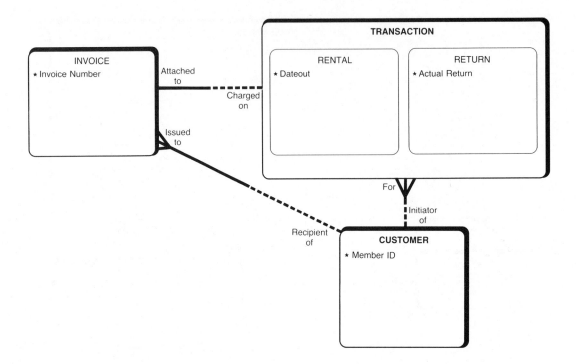

Figure 3.16   The INVOICE Entity

An invoice would rarely (we hope!) be issued for a return transaction; this would happen only if late charges were applied, as we saw earlier. So, the entity model illustrates the possibility, but not the probability, of a transaction generating an invoice. A customer may be the bearer of more than one invoice; however, a single invoice can only be issued to one customer. Invoices are tied exclusively to a customer.

Payment methods are normally restricted by the retail store. No retail business accepts every bank card issued nationally, but all will accept a subset, such as VISA, Master Charge, American Express, and the like. Such payment information must be recorded on every invoice and is necessary to balance the cash register at the end of the day. Bank deposits require separate totals for cash (or check) and charges.

The relationship between the INVOICE and PAYMETHOD entities is illustrated in Figure 3.17.

A payment method [may be] recorded on [one or more] invoices.

An invoice [must be] associated with [one and only one] payment method.

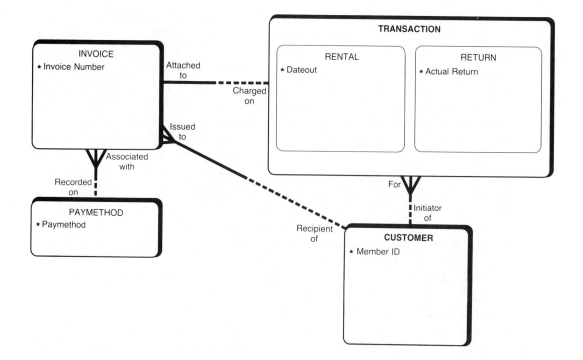

Figure 3.17   The INVOICE-PAYMETHOD Relationship

Building the Data Flow Model

Now that Video Quest's functional model and entity-relationships are committed to paper, you are prepared to move on to the final analytical phase—building the data flow model. The data flow model binds the business functions and entities, providing a graphic representation of their interrelatedness. While two-dimensional, the data flow model is active, capturing the input and output flow of data through the entire business system. The data flow model ultimately serves as a platform for the application foundations—the database design, menus, screens and reports. It integrates everything you've learned about the business and the problems the application is designed to solve.

The Feedback Session

It is suicide to jump into this advanced stage of analysis until you fully understand the entire business model. If you do so prematurely, you risk getting tied up in conceptual knots, and you will probably wind up with a system that is logically and functionally incomplete or inept. This is why ORACLE consultants typically gather the original team of experts, the interviewees, for a powwow before tackling the data flow model. This meeting, called a feedback session, gives the designer an opportunity to present what he or she has learned about the business, using the functional model, entity-relationship diagrams, or any other documents that might be appropriate. If anything is wrong, missing, overstated, or underemphasized— errors which have probably occurred in direct proportion to the number of experts who have been interviewed—the experts have an opportunity to tell you at this point. The goal of a feedback session is to refine the business model, raise everyone's level of understanding about the business, and encourage resolution, or buy-in, from both management and end-users as to the strategy of the business application. This refining process naturally *must* take place well before the designer can think of constructing the data flow model.

The data flow model starts with a major business function; it then charts the entities that either hold data used by the function or capture data results as output from an action. One of the checks and balances of the data flow modelling technique is to ensure the completeness of your data models (the entity-relationships). If you can determine that the *output*

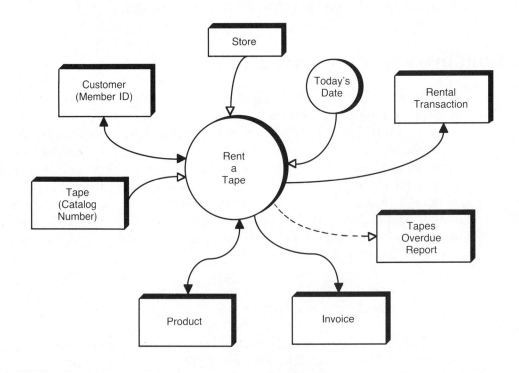

Figure 3.18   Data Flow Model for Renting a Tape

information can be derived from all of the *input* information, you can be confident of a fairly complete system.

The example in Figure 3.18 describes a data flow model built around the fundamental Video Quest function, renting a tape.

Input information flows from the left of the nucleus function to generate output information on the right. The boxed items refer to data elements that are held, called data stores. Arrows pointing to the nucleus function convey input information and the arrows pointing outward convey output information. Double arrow connections, as shown with the customer and product elements, convey a two-way communication of input and output.

As we've learned, the key input information for any rental is the tape (by catalog number), the customer (by member ID) and the store in which the transaction occurred (the store is significant only for distributed network environments). In most transactions, a common data element required as input is the current date and time.

The customer and product data elements provide two-way communication. A customer serves as input, but also stores output information in that the application will update an activity field for each membership to track activity trends.

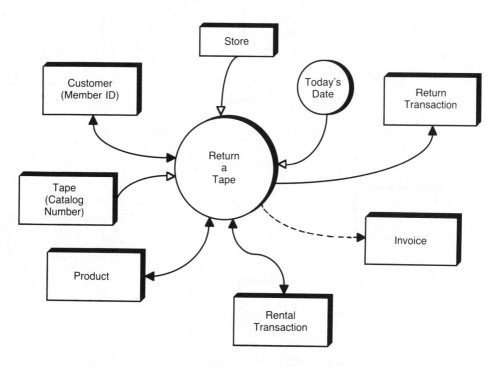

Figure 3.19   Data Flow Model for Returning a Tape

A product becomes input to the rental transaction because it relates a TITLE to an individual TAPE, as shown in Figure 3.2, which illustrates the entity model defining the TITLE-PRODUCT-TAPE relationship. The only way to get title information for any one tape is via the product number. On the other hand, the product data element serves as output information as well. Since inventory status information will eventually be held in the PRODUCT entity, every rental transaction must update the inventory position for every product (i.e., must decrement the current inventory by one for each tape that goes out the door).

The rental function would generate a rental transaction and an invoice as output information; it might also generate a tapes overdue report for this member (or for all members).

The model in Figure 3.19 captures the data flow of the counterpart to renting tapes—returning them. Observe how closely the returns data flow reflects the flow of its counterpart. The only significant difference is that the return transaction must tie directly back to the rental transaction, a two-way communication both to verify that the tape being returned was correctly recorded as outstanding and to update the actual return date to close the rental transaction record properly.

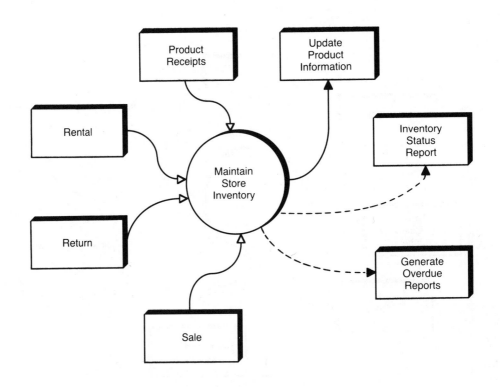

Figure 3.20 Data Flow Model for Maintaining the Store Inventory

The last data flow model, shown in Figure 3.20, represents the central function of maintaining the inventory of Video Quest's large tape library. All four major transactions—initial product shipments (stock receipts), rentals, returns, and sales—have a direct impact on current inventory positions on an ongoing basis. Since historical inventory information is recorded in the PRODUCT entity, any changes due to transactions are held as output in this data store. Inventory status reports and tapes overdue reports can be issued optionally.

Summary

Business analysis is the first critical step of any sound application development method. The application designer must analyze the business and its problems before expecting to offer a meaningful solution. The CASE*Method provides several modelling tools to assist the designer toward this end. This chapter explained the CASE*Method and covered

- ► Interview techniques
- ► Functional modelling
- ► Entity-relationship modelling
- ► The feedback session
- ► Data flow modelling

4

Designing the Database

Designing the Database

Chapter 4 explores the Video Quest database. Before you can create the database design, you must first finalize the entity-relationship model to determine what data elements are to be stored in the database. Only then can you move on to creating the schema—the *template* or the structure that holds the tables and columns of your database.

This chapter describes how to make the transition from your entity models to the database design—the tables, columns, and rows. You will work with the SQL data definition commands used to create and modify database tables and learn a few other commands useful for managing data in the database.

You will find a complete listing of the table definitions for the Video Quest database at the end of this chapter, as well as sample data that will be used through the course of this book.

Inside the Video Quest Database

The CASE*Method offers an easy migration path from one phase to another of the application life cycle. The business models you built in the last chapter, particularly the entity-relationship model, will be referred to time and again, tested, expanded, and refined during the next phase of the application life cycle, the database design phase.

Before SQL-based relational database systems became popular, the database designer's role was a highly specialized one, demanding an intimate understanding of operating systems and low-level system services. Primitive, convoluted data definition languages were required to define the underlying database structures, and equally primitive job control languages had to be run to create the database. Skill in these languages was usually out of the reach of most application designers within MIS; application designers were dependent upon a centralized database administrator (DBA) to define and manage the databases which their applications would access.

The simplicity of SQL as a database access language demystifies the process of creating databases, while the ORACLE relational database management system makes the business of accessing and managing stored information painless. The ORACLE RDBMS automates these tasks, leaving application designers free to concentrate on what they do best—providing business solutions and meeting end-user requirements.

Identifying the Entity Attributes

If you were to combine the entity relationships you've defined thus far into one composite model, it would look like the model in Figure 4.1.

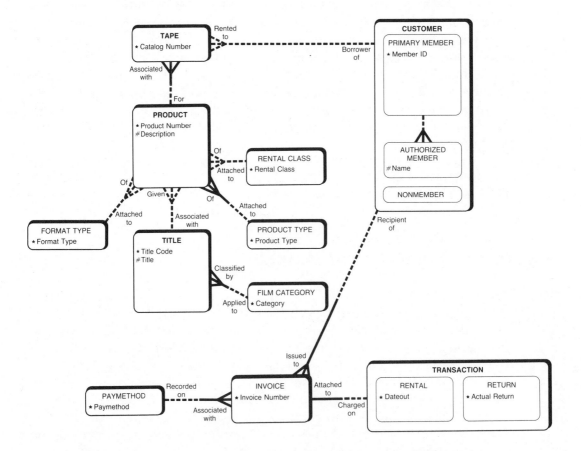

Figure 4.1   The Complete Video Quest Entity-Relationship Model

This global picture enables you to quickly identify clusters of closely related entities. These related entities give you your first clues as to the method of identifying the *data elements*, the individual pieces of related data, that will be stored in the database tables. Entity models hint at the kind of information the business application must know about, but they do not tell the designer how such information should be stored in the database.

The schema ultimately defines *how* the data will be stored in the database. At present, however, you haven't yet nailed down *what* data elements are to be collected in the Video Quest application. To define these elements, you must finalize the entity-model relationships. Each and every attribute associated with an entity must be defined, in minute detail. In many cases, this definition can be altered later using the ALTER TABLE command.

An attribute signifies an overt characteristic of an entity. Although an attribute need not be *unique*, the same attribute cannot refer to more than one entity at a time. The more precisely you define the attributes of these entities the closer you will be to determining what data will be stored. Our earlier discussion of entity attributes (primary key, required, and optional) was rather brief. It is appropriate now to explore these attributes in more detail.

Attributes of the TAPE-PRODUCT-TITLE Trio

The TAPE-PRODUCT-TITLE trio, by now well known to you, is the nucleus of Video Quest's entity model. The attributes for each of these entities appear in Figure 4.2, as well as the attributes for the satellite entities, PRODUCT TYPE, FORMAT TYPE, STORE, FILM CATEGORY, and RENTAL CLASS.

These attributes are derived, of course, from what we've learned about the business. Let's consider them each in turn.

Attributes of the TAPE Entity

The significant thing about a tape is its Catalog Number, so this primary key is the sole attribute of the TAPE entity. There will be hundreds, perhaps even thousands, of tapes in the Video Quest tape library and each must be tracked individually by this unique catalog number.

Attributes of the PRODUCT Entity

This entity is more complex because it encompasses many different product types and many different activities. A product is uniquely identified by a Product Number; thus, this is a product's primary key attribute.

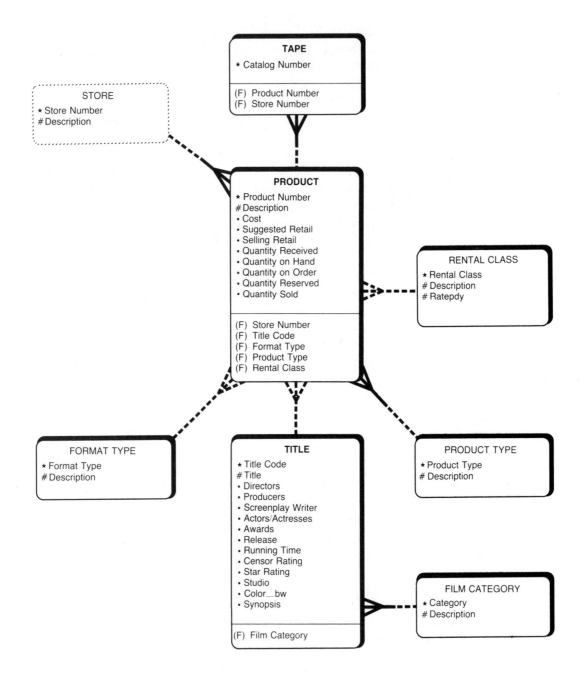

Figure 4.2   Attributes of the TAPE-PRODUCT-TITLE Trio

A description of the product would be more than helpful; in fact, a brief Description is required for users to quickly identify the product. Product codes are cryptic, at best.

Since Video Quest is a relatively small business, maintaining the video tape inventory is a straightforward process. Tracking up-to-date inventory positions is done at the PRODUCT entity level; much larger systems would probably manage inventory information in a separate, self-contained entity to avoid reading information into memory unnecessarily for typical queries. Video Quest is concerned with tracking only essential information, so we have the attributes Quantity Received, Quantity On Hand, Quantity Sold, Quantity Ordered, and Quantity Reserved. These inventory facts are optional for our application, as the optional attributes symbol indicates.

Product pricing information should be stored in a place chosen intuitively, namely with the products, for quick look-up. This information, such as the Cost of the product, Suggested Retail Price, and Selling Retail Price, should be stored as optional attributes of the PRODUCT entity. You can be sure that the attribute references the appropriate entity if it is dependent on the key, the whole key, and nothing but the key.

In a high-volume retail business, pricing information would be managed in a separate table. The volume of retail merchandise would presumably be high and the pricing information would change often because of discounts, seasonal price fluctuations, and price variances between suppliers. Video Quest's bread and butter is the rental of tapes, not the sale of tapes or accessories, so at this point it is still convenient to manage sales pricing information with the PRODUCT entity. Rental rates, as discovered in the previous chapter, are managed by the separate entity RENTAL CLASS.

Attributes of the TITLE Entity

The Title Code is the unique identifier of a title—and thus is its primary key attribute. A description of the film—the Title Description—must also be stored, so this attribute is required.

The system designer has an opportunity to be creative in choosing the TITLE entity's attributes. One of the keen advantages of the relational model is to allow users the flexibility to manipulate their data in a myriad of ways. Users have the utmost freedom in querying the database, being able to look at different logical *views* of their data without worrying about how the data is physically stored in the database.

Designers can take advantage of ORACLE's query capability by collecting not only useful but also interesting information, the kind that casual users might enjoy perusing. There are numerous examples of title trivia that might appeal to moviegoers and fanatics alike. Such optional title information would be included in the attributes Directors, Producers, Actors and actresses, Screenplay writers, and Film Awards. Also useful would be the year of the film's Release, the length or Running Time of the film, the Censorship Rating (PG-13, R, X), a critical Star Rating of the film

(Video Quest uses Siskel and Ebert's ratings), the Studio that produced the film, the color or black-and-white format of the film, and perhaps a brief Synopsis of the film. We saw earlier that the Synopsis attribute will have a table too.

Attributes of the PRODUCT TYPE Entity

This satellite entity simply holds the primary key attribute, Product Type, and a required Description. Since there are only three possible values for the product type, R for rental, S for sale, and R/S for both rental and sale, it's unlikely that you will store this data in a separate table. It is impractical to use up storage space and waste system overhead to maintain a database table for such a small number of static values. These values will eventually be stored with the products themselves when you implement the database design.

Attributes of the FORMAT TYPE Entity

This entity holds the primary key attribute, Format Type, and a required description. This entity is similar to the PRODUCT TYPE entity in that it currently holds but three values—in this case VHS, Beta, or Compact Disc. (The Video Quest store currently carries only VHS and Beta tapes, but management has expressed interest in expanding the inventory to include CDs.)

The format data ultimately will be stored with products; only those products that carry a format, however, will contain a Format Type value. (Remember, some products are nontape accessories for which the Format Type attribute does not apply.)

Attributes of the STORE Entity

This entity holds the primary key attribute, Store Number, and a required attribute for Store Location to distinguish each within a distributed chain of Video Quest retail stores.

Attributes of the FILM CATEGORY Entity

This entity holds the primary key attribute, Film Category Code (called Category), to uniquely identify each film classification. A Description is required.

Attributes of the RENTAL CLASS Entity

This satellite entity holds the primary key attribute, Rental Class, to uniquely identify each rental class. The rental class determines the rental rate for a title. A rental rate, Rate Per Day, and a Description of the rental class both are required attributes.

Understanding Relational Fields

The schema—the database structure—can descend directly from the entity-relationship model. The key to ensuring a smooth transition between the two is the appropriate use of the primary key attribute. When moving from the entity model to defining a database table, the primary key attribute takes on new meaning. The primary key often becomes a *relational field*, a key field that joins or links two or more related entities.

As the attribute diagram for the TAPE-PRODUCT-TITLE trio in Figure 4.2 shows, the PRODUCT and TITLE entities are bound together in a one-to-many relationship. The actual link is the Title Code, the primary key attribute for TITLE entity. To enforce this logical link, you must also store the Title Code with the PRODUCT entity. The Title Code then becomes a relational field—not an attribute of the latter entity. The rules of entity modelling discourage the duplication of attributes across entities in general, but redundancy of a primary key attribute is a heinous crime. The Title Code is not a true characteristic of the PRODUCT entity; it is merely a field that seals the logical connection between PRODUCT and TITLE.

Because Title Code is a primary key of TITLE, it becomes a *foreign key* of the associated PRODUCT entity. Understanding the relationship between primary keys and foreign keys is fundamental to understanding the relational model. Primary and foreign keys form the logical substructure binding relational database tables. This results in a powerful advantage over most nonrelational database management systems: related information can be stored in separate physical locations to reduce data redundancy and conserve storage (a process known as *normalization*), but it can be joined together logically when retrieved from the database.

Figure 4.3 illustrates the rest of the primary and foreign key relationships surrounding the TAPE-PRODUCT-TITLE trio.

Defining the CUSTOMER Attributes

Video Quest is a service-oriented business. Promoting solid customer relations and providing special customer services are tenets that management needs to follow to attain success. The application designer must make the ease of managing the customer database a priority and plan to implement some advanced customer features in the application. Collecting important customer information is the first step toward accomplishing these goals.

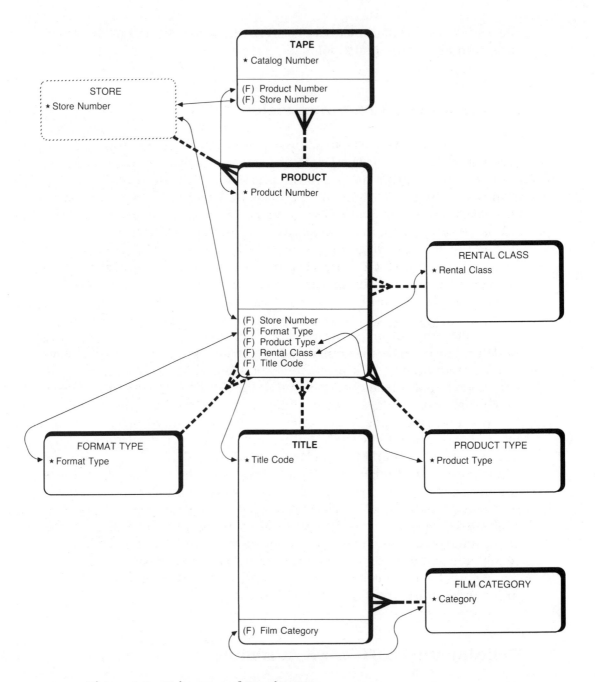

Figure 4.3 Primary and Foreign Keys

Figure 4.4 illustrates the CUSTOMER attributes held for both the PRIMARY MEMBER and AUTHORIZED MEMBER subtypes.

```
┌────────────────────────────────────┐
│            CUSTOMER                │
│  ┌──────────────────────────────┐  │
│  │       PRIMARY MEMBER         │  │
│  │  ★ Member ID                 │  │
│  │  # Name                      │  │
│  │  # Address                   │  │
│  │  # City                      │  │
│  │  # State                     │  │
│  │  # Zip                       │  │
│  │  # Dayphone                  │  │
│  │  # Evephone                  │  │
│  │  # Credit Card, Expiration   │  │
│  │  # Driver's License, Expiration │
│  │  • Creation Date             │  │
│  │  • Last Activity Date        │  │
│  │  • Default Tape Format       │  │
│  │                              │  │
│  └──────────────────────────────┘  │
│  ┌──────────────────────────────┐  │
│  │      AUTHORIZED MEMBER       │  │
│  │  # Name                      │  │
│  │  • Restricted Category       │  │
│  │  • Description               │  │
│  │  ────────────────────────────  │
│  │  (F)  Member ID              │  │
│  └──────────────────────────────┘  │
│  ┌──────────────────────────────┐  │
│  │          NONMEMBER           │  │
│  └──────────────────────────────┘  │
└────────────────────────────────────┘
```

Figure 4.4   Attributes of the CUSTOMER Entity

Let's turn our attention to these attributes to understand the reasons for choosing them.

Attributes of the PRIMARY MEMBER Subtype

Every membership granted to the primary member must be identified by a unique identification number; thus the primary key attribute, Member ID. A Video Quest membership card would be issued to the primary, or responsible, member the day the account is opened.

To keep memberships current—and to keep members accountable for their rental transactions—several vital statistics must be filed away about the primary member. The system must maintain these attributes: Name, Address, City, State, Zip Code. Both Day Phone and Evening Phone numbers are required because Video Quest is open late into the evening every night. Two pieces of identification are required to open a membership; thus the attributes of Credit Card and Driver's License. Both cards must be current, and to ensure this, the PRIMARY MEMBER entity should hold the attribute of Expiration Date for each.

The date the account is opened, Creation Date, is useful, but not critical, information. Just as useful would be a real-time record of the date the account had its Last Activity. Such historical information would let the store owner compare customer activity trends via *ad hoc* queries or generate a report of customer activity over a designated period of time. To lend a personal touch for customers, the system might optionally have an attribute for storing the Default Tape Format for each customer. When the customer rented a tape, the staff could use this information to validate that they had pulled the correct tape format.

Attributes of the AUTHORIZED MEMBER Subtype

Since an authorized member can only be hosted onto the system by a primary member, the system will issue only one membership number and card. Here is a classic example of the primary key-foreign key relationship. The primary key attribute, Member ID, is passed on to the authorized member—not as an attribute, remember, but as a relational field. The Member ID becomes a foreign key of the AUTHORIZED MEMBER subtype.

The customer name is the only bit of information required to be held with the AUTHORIZED MEMBER. As we saw earlier, this entity corresponds to a table named CUSTNAME.

Video Quest management personnel posed an intriguing challenge to the application designer. Authorized members are often teen-aged family members, most of whom are not allowed by their parents to watch the gory horror or slasher films which are currently the teen video rage. (Their parents restrict them from viewing adult films as well, but it is a company policy of Video Quest not to rent or sell such material.) Legally, the video store owner is not responsible for monitoring viewing restrictions; this is a parental prerogative. The problem is this: how can the system police viewing restrictions without involving the store owner?

The solution is to incorporate a clever validation routine into the application. It will be up to the primary member to inform Video Quest of any viewing restrictions for those authorized to use the membership card. Whenever an authorized member rents a tape, the system will automatically verify that the film doesn't belong to a film class he or she is restricted from viewing. If the tape is restricted, the store clerk will be alerted immediately and the transaction cancelled.

The simplest way of storing this restriction information is to add an optional attribute, Restricted Category, to the AUTHORIZED MEMBER subtype. A Description of this category might also be added to enhance the user interface.

Defining the TRANSACTION Attributes

The RENTAL and RETURN transactions are the basis of the Video Quest operations. The information captured by these transactions affects every major function of the business; inaccuracies can cause damaging side-effects such as incorrect purchasing decisions, distorted cash flow projections, and inflated inventory balances.

Handling on-line transaction processing in a busy environment can be a challenge for the application designer. It is nearly impossible, however, to build demanding on-line applications without the right tools. The video application has to be properly designed and tuned to process the high volume of transactions as fast as possible. Performance is of major concern; users haven't the luxury—nor customers the patience!—to wait around for the computer system to process a lot of data. The transactions must be small, and the amount of information collected brief and to the point, in order to process many transactions in rapid-fire sequence.

Figure 4.5 illustrates the attributes for the RENTAL and RETURN transaction subtypes and the attributes for the associated INVOICE Entity.

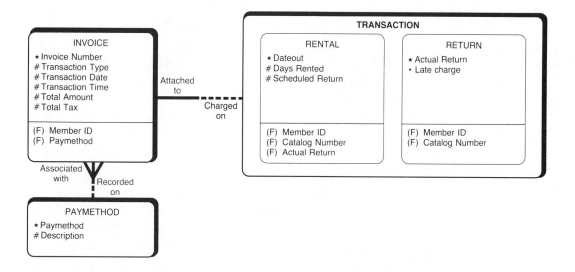

Figure 4.5   Attributes of the TRANSACTION Entity

Let's briefly step through the attributes of these TRANSACTION sub-types.

Attributes of the RENTAL Entity

The RENTAL entity does not have a primary key. The table itself is nothing more than a real-time collection of historical information derived from other sources.

The most critical information for each rental transaction comes from the CUSTOMER and TAPE entities, that is the Member ID and the Catalog Number. Both pieces of information are primary key attributes of their respective entities, and both will be stored as foreign keys in every RENTAL transaction.

The date the tape was rented out (called *dateout*), the number of Days Rented, and the Scheduled Return Date are the three chief attributes of the RENTAL transaction. The *dateout* becomes the primary *database* key attribute. Combined with the Member ID, Catalog Number, and Actual Return keys (the latter will be added later), these three required attributes store a snapshot of every rental transaction and let you track any given tape through the entire system.

Attributes of the RETURN Entity

The RETURN transaction mirrors the RENTAL transaction. For every rental transaction, there must be a complementary return transaction at some point in time; otherwise, a rented tape would be lost from the system.

Primary keys are not required in the RETURN transaction entity, because the critical rentals information is derived from the CUSTOMER and TAPE entities. The primary key attributes, Member ID and Catalog Number, respectively, become foreign keys of the RETURN transactions.

The significant attribute held by the RETURN entity is the Actual Return date. This attribute ultimately updates the rentals transaction to close the logical loop.

A Late Charge, if collected, would be stored with the RETURN transaction.

Attributes of the INVOICE Entity

A unique invoice number is generated for every rental and every return transaction. (Sales transactions, if implemented, would also have a unique invoice number.) The Invoice Number is thus the primary key attribute.

Since every invoice is tied to a customer, the Member ID becomes a foreign key of the INVOICE entity. Every invoice must also store a Payment Method, such as Cash, Visa, MasterCharge; *paymethod*, the primary key of the PAYMETHOD entity, becomes a foreign key here.

The required attributes of INVOICE are the Transaction Type (R for rental, S for sale, and L for late charge), Transaction Date, Transaction Time, Total Amount and Total Tax. Combined with the *memberid* and *paymethod* keys, these attributes provide enough historical information about invoices to perform customer billing; to trace rentals, sales or late returns by invoice number; and to generate daily receipt totals or receipts activity reports for a given period of time.

The Database Design

Whether you realize it or not, your high-level database design is nearly complete. Your efforts in building the entity models and pinning down the entity attributes have paid off; erecting the schema is a mechanical task from this point. Although there isn't a one-to-one correspondence between your detailed entity models and the schema, the resemblance is close. Some practical storage management and tuning issues account for minor differences.

Video Quest's major entity groups—CUSTOMER, TRANSACTION, and TAPE-PRODUCT-TITLE—might translate into the tables shown in Table 4.1.

Table 4.1   Video Quest Database Design

Entity Group	Entity	Table
TAPE-PRODUCT-TITLE	TAPE	TAPE
	PRODUCT	PRODUCT
	TITLE	TITLE
	FILM CATEGORY	CATEGORY
	RENTAL CLASS	RENTAL CLASS
CUSTOMER	PRIMARY MEMBER	CUSTOMER
	AUTHORIZED MEMBER	CUSTNAME
TRANSACTION	RENTAL	RENTALS
	RETURN	RETURNS
	INVOICE	INVOICE
	PAYMETHOD	PAYMETHOD

After settling on the database tables, you would then create the column definitions for each one. Database tables are made up of columns in the same manner that entities are made up of attributes. Columns, or categories of information, organize the stored data. For the most part, these columns are simply logical extensions of the entity attributes you've already defined. We'll point out a few exceptions to this rule as they crop up in the video retail application.

Tables 4.2 through 4.6 show the Video Quest database tables dissected to show their column definitions.

Table 4.2   TAPE and PRODUCT Table Design

Table Column	Derived From Entity Attribute	Entity	Key
TAPE Table			
catnum	Catalog Number	TAPE	\<Pr\>
prodno	Product Number	PRODUCT	\<F\>
storeno	Store Number	STORE	\<F\>
PRODUCT Table			
prodno	Product Number	PRODUCT	\<Pr\>
description	Product Description	PRODUCT	
storeno	Store Number	STORE	\<F\>
titlecd	Title Code	TITLE	\<F\>
format	Format Type	FORMAT TYPE	\<F\>
prodtype	Product Type	PRODUCT TYPE	\<F\>
rentclass	Rental Class	RENTAL CLASS	\<F\>
cost	Cost	PRODUCT	
suggrtl	Suggested Retail Price	PRODUCT	
sellrtl	Selling Retail Price	PRODUCT	
qtyrecvd	Quantity Received	PRODUCT	
qtyoh	Quantity On Hand	PRODUCT	
qtysold	Quantity Sold	PRODUCT	
qtyord	Quantity On Order	PRODUCT	
qtyrsv	Quantity Reserved	PRODUCT	

Table 4.3   TITLE and SYNOPSIS Table Design

Table Column	Derived From Entity Attribute	Entity	Key
TITLE Table			
titlecd	Title Code	TITLE	\<Pr\>
category	Film Category	FILM CATEGORY	\<F\>
title	Title Description	TITLE	
directors	Directors	TITLE	
producers	Producers	TITLE	
screenplay	Screenplay Writer	TITLE	
actors	Actors/actresses	TITLE	
awards	Film Awards	TITLE	
release	Year Film Released	TITLE	
runtime	Running Time (length)	TITLE	
censorrtg	Censorship Rating	TITLE	
starrtg	Critic's Star Rating	TITLE	
studio	Studio Producer	TITLE	
color_bw	Color or B/W format	TITLE	
SYNOPSIS Table (tied to TITLE table)			
titlecd	Title Code	TITLE	\<F\>
description	Synopsis (1 line of)	TITLE	
lineno	Line Number	TITLE	

It may seem odd that the title synopsis, an attribute of the TITLE entity, is now stored in its own database table. A synopsis can be quite lengthy; it often is at least a paragraph or more of data. The database should manage such text data separately rather than cluttering up an already sizable table like TITLE. (As a rule, relational database tables are best managed when lean, or normalized. This rule has some implications for performance which are discussed in Chapter 10, Advanced Concepts and Features.)

Table 4.4   FILM CATEGORY and RENTAL CLASS
Table Design

Table Column	Derived From Entity Attribute	Entity	Key
FILM CATEGORY Table			
category	Category Code	FILM CATEGORY	<Pr>
description	Category Description	FILM CATEGORY	
RENTAL CLASS Table			
rentclass	Rental Class Code	RENTAL CLASS	<Pr>
description	Class Description	RENTAL CLASS	
ratepdy	Rate Per Day	RENTAL CLASS	

Table 4.5   CUSTOMER Table Design

Table Column	Derived From Entity Attribute	Entity	Key
CUSTOMER Table			
memberid	Member ID	PRIMARY MEMBER	<Pr>
name	Name	PRIMARY MEMBER	
ad1	Address	PRIMARY MEMBER	
ad2	Address	PRIMARY MEMBER	
city	City	PRIMARY MEMBER	
state	State	PRIMARY MEMBER	
zip	Zip	PRIMARY MEMBER	
day_area	Day Phone	PRIMARY MEMBER	
day_prefix	Day Phone	PRIMARY MEMBER	
day_suffix	Day Phone	PRIMARY MEMBER	
eve_area	Eve Phone	PRIMARY MEMBER	
eve_prefix	Eve Phone	PRIMARY MEMBER	
eve_suffix	Eve Phone	PRIMARY MEMBER	
creditcard	Credit Card	PRIMARY MEMBER	
cardexp	Expiration Date	PRIMARY MEMBER	
cdlno	Driver's License	PRIMARY MEMBER	
cdlexp	Expiration Date	PRIMARY MEMBER	
date_created	Date Membership Created	PRIMARY MEMBER	
last_act	Last Activity Date	PRIMARY MEMBER	
format	Default Tape Format	PRIMARY MEMBER	

Table 4.5   (*continued*)

Table Column	Derived From Entity Attribute	Entity	Key
CUSTNAME Table			
memberid	Member ID	PRIMARY MEMBER	<F>
name	Authorized Member Name	AUTHORIZED MEMBER	
restrict_cat	Restricted Tape	AUTHORIZED MEMBER	

An additional address column has been added to the CUSTOMER table to allow for longer addresses. Also note that phone numbers have been broken down into component parts—area code, prefix, and suffix. Storing numbers in this manner promotes data consistency.

Table 4.6   TRANSACTION Table Design

Table Column	Derived From Entity Attribute	Entity	Key
RENTALS Table			
memberid	Member ID	CUSTOMER	<F>
catnum	Catalog Number	TAPE	<F>
actrtn	Date Tape Returned	RETURN	<F>
dateout	Date Tape Rented	RENTAL	
rentdays	Number of Days Rented	RENTAL	
schdrtn	Date Tape Due Back	RENTAL	
RETURNS Table			
memberid	Member ID	CUSTOMER	<F>
catnum	Catalog Number	TAPE	<F>
actrtn	Date Tape Returned	RETURN	
latecharge	Late Charges Accrued	RETURN	
INVOICE Table			
invno	Invoice Number	INVOICE	<Pr>
memberid	Member ID	CUSTOMER	<F>
paymethod	Paymethod	PAYMETHOD	<F>
trantype	Transaction Type	INVOICE	
trandate	Transaction Date	INVOICE	
trantime	Transaction Time	INVOICE	
total	Total Invoice Amount	INVOICE	
tax	Total Tax Amount	INVOICE	
PAYMETHOD Table			
paymethod	Paymethod	PAYMETHOD	<Pr>
description	Payment Description	PAYMETHOD	

Creating the Tables

Creating a database table is a simple procedure with ORACLE. You use the CREATE TABLE command to specify

- ▶ the name of the table
- ▶ the name of each column
- ▶ the format of each column, which includes

> the type of data stored (the *datatype*)
>
> the column width
>
> whether or not the column must have a value in it.

Creating the TAPE Table

Since you've completed the design of the TAPE table, *creating* it is merely a formality. To refresh your memory, review Table 4.2, which illustrates the table columns derived from the TAPE entity attributes. As you walk through the creation of this application, at times you may forget the exact form of a word you need to type in when referencing a part of the database previously created. The table in Appendix E can be used as a quick reference guide to the Video Quest schema—and of course can be added to—as you progress through the application.

Table 4.2 indicates the columns you need to create, but ORACLE also needs to know the *datatype* and the width of each column, and whether or not each column can hold *null values*.

To create the TAPE table, you would enter the following CREATE TABLE command through SQL*Plus:

```
CREATE TABLE tape
     (catnum    number     not null,
      prodno    char(25)   not null,
      storeno   number     not null)
```

The three columns of the TAPE table are enclosed in parentheses and are described as follows:

Catnum

The Catalog Number column represents the primary key of this table; *catnum* will contain number values, and may not contain null values.

A primary key can never take a null value. By definition, the primary key column uniquely identifies a row, so a value must exist. The null value option does not, however, enforce uniqueness. To do this, you must create a *unique index* on the column; the use of indexes is discussed in some detail in Chapter 10, Advanced Concepts and Features.

You do not need to specify the width of the number column; ORACLE assumes 44 column positions, unless specified otherwise. When you specify a column width, ORACLE automatically checks to see whether data entered into the column contains only that specified number of values; if a user enters more or fewer values, ORACLE rejects the entry and displays an error message.

Prodno

The Product Number column represents a foreign key of the PRODUCT table; *prodno* will contain character values (both alpha and numeric characters) up to 25 characters wide and cannot contain null values.

A foreign key may take a null value, but it need not. This depends on the database design. The *prodno* column does not allow nulls because each catalog number must have one and only one product number, as determined earlier in the entity model.

Video Quest's product numbers are currently no longer than five characters wide, but it is advisable to plan ahead. We've increased the column width to 25 characters comfortably, allowing the database to expand with the growth of the business. Five years down the road, the store may carry hundreds of thousands of product numbers, and the prodno column may need to hold a much larger number.

Storeno

The Store Number column represents a foreign key of the STORE entity; *storeno* will contain number values, and cannot contain null values.

A Word About Null Values

The concept of null values is a slippery one. Database systems often confuse nulls with blanks or zeroes, but these are not synonymous at the physical storage level. A null is the *absence of value* and should be reflected as such in the database, that is, nothing should be stored.

Database systems that do not provide null value support cannot distinguish between nulls, blanks, and zeroes. A column not containing a value is often represented by a blank (a space character) or a zero. A major problem with the use of zeroes to represent nulls is that the results of mathematical operations on this field can be skewed. A zero is not the absence of value; a zero *is* a legitimate number.

Creating the PRODUCT Table

The PRODUCT column definitions evolve conveniently from their corresponding entity attributes. Review Table 4.2 to refresh your memory. With the column names already assigned, you now use the CREATE TABLE command to define the tables and fill in the column format information.

To create the PRODUCT table, enter

```
CREATE TABLE product
        (prodno        char(25)              not null,
        storeno        number                not null,
        description    char(30),
        titlecd        char(12),
        format         char(1),
        prodtype       char(2),
        rentclass      number,
        cost           number(10,2),
        suggrtl        number(10,2),
        sellrtl        number(10,2),
        qtyrecvd       number,
        qtyoh          number,
        qtysold        number,
        qtyord         number,
        qtyrsv         number)
```

A couple of these column definitions deserve comment—the *format* and *cost* columns:

Format
The format column refers to the tape format, which can be either VHS, Beta, or CD. You might question why the column has been defined as only one character wide. To conserve disk space, only the value V, B, or C will be stored.

Cost
The cost column refers to a money value which may store decimal numbers (cents values). An ORACLE numeric datatype stores decimal numbers with up to 42 significant digits. The cost column definition—number(10,2)—is interpreted as being ten digits long, with two of these ten digits following the decimal point (for example, 50.75).

The same decimal number format applies to the other money columns in the PRODUCT table, *suggrtl* and *sellrtl*.

Creating the TITLE and SYNOPSIS Tables

There are few surprises in the creation of the TITLE and SYNOPSIS tables; the table definitions take their cues from the TITLE entity. Here are the CREATE TABLE commands for both tables.

To create the TITLE Table, enter

```
CREATE TABLE title
      (titlecd    char(15)    not null,
      title       char(78),
      category    char(3),
      directors   char(78),
      producers   char(78),
      screenplay  char(78),
      actors      char(78),
      awards      char(78),
      release     char(4),
      runtime     char(10),
      censorrtg   char(7),
      starrtg     char(5),
      studio      char(15),
      color_bw    char(6))
```

To create the SYNOPSIS Table, enter

```
CREATE TABLE title
      (titlecd     char(15)   not null,
      lineno       number     not null,
      description  char(78))
```

The technique used to store text in the SYNOPSIS table may puzzle you at first. Each row of the SYNOPSIS table holds a single line of text, stored in the *description* column. A unique line number is associated with row to ensure that when subsequently retrieved, the text displays in the correct order.

ORACLE manages the physical storage environment automatically, shuffling database storage blocks where appropriate. One should never assume that the order in which the data was entered will be the order in which it is retrieved. There is no guarantee of this, nor is it necessary. With

SQL, you have logical control over your data. SQL gives you the flexibility to retrieve the data in almost any order you please.

The Video Quest application will allow synopsis text to be entered interactively on the SYNOPSIS screen. With SQL*Forms, you will design SQL-based application logic to automatically generate the line number for each line of text committed to the database. Since most terminal screens are 80 characters wide, the *description* column in the SYNOPSIS table is clipped to a 78-character width.

ORACLE supports a LONG datatype which allows up to 65,535 characters to be stored in a single column. Unfortunately, SQL*Forms does not support LONG fields. Applications designed with SQL*Forms are restricted to working with textual data in CHAR fields, each being limited to 240 characters.

Creating the CODES Tables

Two final tables must be created to complete the schema of the TAPE-PRODUCT-TITLE entity group—the FILM CATEGORY and RENTAL CLASS tables. These tables contain application codes. Film categories identify classes of films, such as western or sci-fi films. The rental class determines the rental rate for a title, such as a New Title or a Children's film. The CREATE TABLE commands for both tables appear below.

To create the FILM CATEGORY table, enter

```
CREATE TABLE category
     (category     number      not null,
     description   char(20))
```

To create the RENTAL CLASS table, you enter

```
CREATE TABLE rentclass
     (rentclass    number      not null,
     ratepdy       number,
     description   char(20))
```

Working with the Tables

You have now created the master tables of the TAPE-PRODUCT-TITLE entity trio. These tables are empty—mere shells ready for you to pour rows of data into them. In the following exercises, you will learn a few basic SQL commands used to insert, retrieve and manipulate data in the database tables you've created. These commands and their functions are

INSERT	adds a new row to a table
DESCRIBE table	displays the columns in order defined
DELETE	deletes a row or rows
SELECT	retrieves and displays data
DROP table	drops existing table, erasing all data
RENAME table	renames an existing table

If you are sitting before your terminal and logged on to ORACLE SQL*Plus, you might experiment with these commands as you read along. This assumes, of course, that you have created the TAPE, PRODUCT, TITLE, and SYNOPSIS tables described in the previous section.

Inserting Rows into a Table

To insert rows into a table, you use the INSERT command. The INSERT command contains a value for each column in the table. Values are entered, separated by commas, in the same order as the columns were defined when the table was first created.

If you've forgotten the column order of the TAPE table, issue the DESCRIBE table command like this:

```
DESCRIBE tape
```

and SQL*Plus will display the columns and format information in the original order.

To add a new tape to the TAPE table, you enter:

```
INSERT INTO tape VALUES (100, 'P100V', 1)
```

Columns inserted → catnum prodno storeno

Notice that the value for *prodno* is enclosed in apostrophes. The INSERT command expects constant CHAR and DATE values to be enclosed in apostrophes.

The SQL SELECT Command

To verify that the new row was actually inserted, you can issue a simple SELECT statement to *query* the table:

```
SELECT *
  FROM tape
```

The SELECT * command retrieves *all* rows and columns currently stored in the TAPE table specified in the FROM clause:

```
CATNUM   PRODNO   STORENO
------   ------   -------
   100   P100V          1
```

Practice using the INSERT command by loading the sample Video Quest data below into the TAPE table.

```
CATNUM   PRODNO   STORENO
------   ------   -------
   100   P100V          1
   101   P100V          1
   200   P200V          1
   201   P200V          1
   300   P300V          1
   301   P300V          1
   305   P300B          1
   450   P450V          1
   451   P450V          1
   470   P470V          1
   471   P470V          1
   473   P470B          1
   475   P475V          1
   480   P480V          1
   481   P480V          1
```

SQL*Plus supports a line editor which eliminates having to retype the SQL statement each time (Chapter 6, Advanced SQL Capabilities, covers this in more detail).

Deleting Rows From a Table

If you have been working through these exercises, then you've just inserted a duplicate row into the TAPE table—the first row identified by Catalog Number 100. To verify this, enter

```
SELECT *
  FROM tape
```

To delete the duplicate rows, you will use the DELETE command. A WHERE clause is added to point to the specific row or rows you wish to delete. In this example, you are deleting the redundant rows where the Catalog Number for each is 100. Observe:

```
DELETE FROM tape
  WHERE catnum = 100
```

If you omit the WHERE clause, *every* row in the TAPE table will be deleted. Enter

```
SELECT *
  FROM tape
```

to verify that the duplicate rows have been deleted successfully. You may now re-insert the same row, so that only a single record with Catalog Number 100 appears in the TAPE table.

Inserting Rows with Null Values

When inserting a row that contains null values, you must explicitly type the word NULL for each. A common oversight is simply to leave the null column blank in the INSERT statement; SQL*Plus requires a value to be entered for every referenced column.

To insert a row into the PRODUCT table, enter

```
INSERT INTO product values ('P100V', 1, 'Film',
'SOUNDMUSIC', 'V', 'RS', 10, 19.95, 29.95, 29.95, null,
null, null, null, null)
```

This may seem like a lot of superfluous typing, and it is. For times when you are inserting a row containing several null fields, there is a shortcut you can use. Instead of typing NULL for each blank column, you can list only the columns and values you wish to enter.

For example, suppose you have a rental-only product. Sales pricing information wouldn't apply for this type of product. The inventory columns would be null because no history information has been collected. For this example, you could use a shortcut which instructs the INSERT command to automatically insert nulls:

```
INSERT INTO tape (prodno, storeno, description,
            titlecd, format, prodtype, rentclass)
VALUES      ('P300V', 1, 'Film', 'GONEWIND', 'V',
            'R', 25)
```

You should now query the PRODUCT table to see the results of the two previous INSERT commands. Enter

```
SELECT *
  FROM product
```

and SQL*Plus displays:

Product	Store	Description	Title Code	F	Type	Rental Class	Cost	Sugg Retail	Sell Retail	Qty Recvd	Qty Oh	Qty Sold	Qty Ord	Qty Rsrv
P100V	1	Film	SOUNDMUSIC	V	RS	10	19.95	29.95	29.95					
P300V	1	Film	GONEWIND	V	R	25	59.95							

The Sample Product Data

You might practice inserting longer, more complex rows of data to get more comfortable with the INSERT command. Start by entering the following sample data into the PRODUCT table:

Product	Store	Description	Title Code	F	Type	Rental Class	Cost	Sugg Retail	Sell Retail	Qty Recvd	Qty Oh	Qty Sold	Qty Ord	Qty Rsrv
P100V	1	Film	SOUNDMUSIC	V	RS	10	19.95	29.95	29.95	2	1	1		
P200V	1	Film	TOPGUN	V	RS	10	29.95	39.95	9.95	2	1			
P300B	1	Film	GONEWIND	B	RS	25	59.95	69.95	69.95	1		1		
P300V	1	Film	GONEWIND	V	R	25	59.95			2				
P450V	1	Film	CKANE	V	RS	25	49.95	49.95	59.95	2	1	1		
P470B	1	Film	GHOSTBUSTER	B	RS	10	19.95	29.95	29.95	1	1			
P470V	1	Film	GHOSTBUSTER	V	RS	10	19.95	29.95	29.95	2	1			
P475V	1	Film	HITCHER	V	RS	50	79.95	89.95	89.95	1	1			
P480V	1	Film	SHINING	V	RS	45	69.95	79.95	79.95	2		1		
P500	1	Tape Case	n/a	V	S	99	2.99	4.99	4.99	30	20	10		

Inserting volumes of data into a table one row at a time can be a laborious chore, especially with longer rows containing many null values. There are easier ways. One is to use forms built with the SQL*Forms application generator. You will learn how to build the Video Quest forms in Chapter 7. Most of your sample data can then be entered directly through the forms. Another technique is to use the SQL*Loader bulk data loader facility, which is briefly descibed in Chapter 10, Advanced Concepts and Features. For this and the next two chapters, you will need sample data to practice a few preliminary exercises. Entering small amounts of data via SQL commands is relatively painless.

Updating Rows in a Table

You can change data that exists in a table with the UPDATE command. Similar to the DELETE command, an UPDATE can take a WHERE clause to point to a specific row or rows to be changed. In the following update example, change the description of product P500 to read 'Tape Case' and not 'Blank Tape' as it is currently.

```
UPDATE product
   SET description = 'Tape Case'
 WHERE prodno = 'P500'
```

If you omit the WHERE clause, the description of *every* product in the table will be changed to 'Tape Case.'

Modifying Table Definitions

A table may need to be modified after it has already been created. You may want to add a new column or change the length of an existing column. You will use the ALTER TABLE command with either the ADD or MODIFY parameters to perform these operations.

Adding a New Column

After reviewing the PRODUCT table design, it occurs to you that you might want to know when a given product was last purchased from a supplier. You decide to add the column *purchase_date* to this table.

To add the new column to the PRODUCT table, enter:

```
ALTER TABLE product
ADD (purchase_date date)
```

The datatype of the *purchase_date* column is an ORACLE date datatype. Dates are represented in the standard ORACLE format like this:

```
25-DEC-88
```

The ORACLE date format is written in the format mask 'DD-MON-YY'. Valid dates range from January 1, 4712 BC to December 31, 4712 AD. Several different date formats may be displayed by a simple technique of date format conversion (discussed in Chapter 6 in the section *Working with Date Values*).

To verify that the column has actually been added, enter the DE-SCRIBE product command to display all the column definitions for the PRODUCT table in the order in which you defined them:

```
DESCRIBE product
```

The screen should display:

```
NAME               Null?        Type
-----------        --------     -----------
PRODNO             NOT NULL     CHAR(25)
STORENO            NOT NULL     NUMBER
DESCRIPTION                     CHAR(30)
TITLECD                         CHAR(15)
FORMAT                          CHAR(1)
PRODTYPE                        CHAR(2)
RENTCLASS                       NUMBER
COST                            NUMBER(10,2)
SUGGRTL                         NUMBER(10,2)
SELLRTL                         NUMBER(10,2)
QTYRECVD                        NUMBER
QTYOH                           NUMBER
QTYSOLD                         NUMBER
QTYORD                          NUMBER
QTYRSV                          NUMBER
PURCHASE_DATE                   DATE
```

Modifying an Existing Column

To modify an existing column, you use the ALTER TABLE command with the MODIFY parameter. There are other ways to redefine tables which will be explored later in the book.

Suppose you have an unusually long film title, and cannot create a *titlecd* with less than 13 characters. You need to increase the length of the *titlecd* column from 12 to 15 characters in the PRODUCT table (*and* the TITLE and SYNOPSIS tables). To do this, you would enter:

```
ALTER TABLE product
MODIFY (titlecd char(15))
```

While you can *add* a column at any time—whether the column is empty or not—you are restricted with the MODIFY parameter. You can always *lengthen* a column, but you cannot reduce the width of a column if it contains data. SQL*Plus protects you from inadvertently truncating your data by reducing the column width.

Try to reduce the *titlecd* column width back to 12 characters. SQL*Plus won't let you; it displays the error message:

```
ORA-1441: Column to be modified must be empty to decrease
          column length
```

Only in rare cases would you need to reduce the width of a column that contains data. It can be done, but it requires a few extra steps. You must create a new table that copies all the column definitions and data from the old table except for the column in question. Then you add the modified column to the new table and update each row to add the data for that column. With larger databases, this procedure can be more trouble than it is worth. When you are designing SQL queries or reports, the physical column definition is immaterial, for you can always change the column width any time, due to the dynamic nature of ORACLE-SQL.

Creating a New Table From an Existing Table

Suppose you wanted to drop a column from a table. SQL*Plus does not provide a drop column function to complement the ADD functions. To do this, you must create a new table based on an existing table, discard the old table, and then rename the new one. The new table will contain every column from the old table, except the one column you wanted to drop.

To create a new table based on an existing table, you will use the CREATE TABLE AS (SELECT . . .) command. The SELECT statement is used in a *subquery* of the CREATE TABLE AS command. The SELECT subquery effectively copies the existing column definitions and data of the columns you specify into the new table. For example, if you wanted to drop the *purchase_date* column you added to the PRODUCT table a moment ago, you would enter:

```
CREATE TABLE product1
AS
SELECT  prodno, storeno, description,
        titlecd, format, prodtype, rentclass,
        cost, suggrtl, sellrtl, qtyrecvd,
        qtyoh, qtysold, qtyord, qtyrsv
  FROM  product
```

You create the new table PRODUCT1 and extract the definitions and data from each column listed in the SELECT subquery. Notice that the column definitions and data will be copied in exactly the same order as they appear in the SELECT subquery. (In the following chapter, you will be working with SELECT subqueries in more detail.)

Dropping a Table

After creating the new table PRODUCT1, you will want to discard the older table from the database. Before you do, however, issue the command

```
SELECT COUNT(*)
  FROM product1
```

to verify that the data got moved first. To drop a table, including all the data in it, you use the DROP TABLE command like so:

```
DROP TABLE product
```

SQL*Plus has discarded the PRODUCT table and column definitions from the data dictionary and erased all of its contents.

Renaming a Table

We're now left with a single table containing Video Quest products. However, this table is called PRODUCT1, a rather nondescript name. You should rename the table back to its original name, using the RENAME command.

To rename the PRODUCT1 table to PRODUCT, enter

```
RENAME PRODUCT1 to PRODUCT
```

A Complete Listing of the Video Quest Tables

The following documents the CREATE TABLE statements for the entire Video Quest database. Before moving on to the next chapter, you should create each of these tables.

The TRANSACTION entity includes one table you've not seen—the CNTL table. This table holds control and store policy information by store number, such as sales tax rate, the maximum number of tapes a member can rent at a time, late charge percentages, and so forth. Be sure to create this table too.

What follows now is a listing of the CREATE TABLE statements grouped by the three major entity groups.

TAPE-PRODUCT-TITLE Tables

PRODUCT Table

```
CREATE TABLE product
        (prodno       char(25)        not null,
        storeno       number          not null)
        description   char(30),
        titlecd       char(15),
        format        char(1),
        prodtype      char(2),
        rentclass     number,
        cost          number(10,2),
        suggrtl       number(10,2),
        sellrtl       number(10,2),
        qtyrecvd      number,
        qtyoh         number,
        qtysold       number,
        qtyord        number,
        qtyrsv        number)
```

TAPE Table

```
CREATE TABLE tape
        (catnum   number    not null,
        prodno    char(25)  not null,
        storeno   number    not null)
```

TITLE Table

```
CREATE TABLE title
        (titlecd     char(15)   not null,
        title        char(78),
        category     char(3),
        directors    char(78),
        producers    char(78),
        screenplay   char(78),
        actors       char(78),
        awards       char(78),
        release      char(4),
        runtime      char(10),
        censorrtg    char(7),
        starrtg      char(5),
        studio       char(15),
        color_bw     char(6))
```

SYNOPSIS Table

```
CREATE TABLE synopsis
      (titlecd     char(15)    not null,
      lineno       number      not null,
      description char(78))
```

FILM CATEGORY Table

```
CREATE TABLE category
      (category    number      not null,
      description char(20))
```

RENTAL CLASS Table

```
CREATE TABLE rentclass
      (rentclass   number      not null,
      ratepdy      number,
      description char(20))
```

CUSTOMER Tables

CUSTOMER Table

```
CREATE TABLE customer
      (memberid    number       not null,
      name         char(30),
      ad1          char(30),
      ad2          char(30),
      city         char(30),
      state        char(2),
      zip          char(10),
      day_area     char(3),
      day_prefix   char(3),
      day_suffix   char(4),
      eve_area     char(3),
      eve_prefix   char(3),
      eve_suffix   char(4),
      creditcard   char(2),
      credcdno     char(20),
      cardexp      date,
      cdlno        char(10),
      cdlexp       date,
```

```
        date_created date,
        last_act     date,
        format       char(2))
```

CUSTNAME Table

```
CREATE TABLE custname
        (memberid    number       not null,
        name         char(30),
        restrict_cat number)
```

TRANSACTION Tables

RENTALS Table

```
CREATE TABLE rentals
        (memberid   number            not null,
        catnum      number            not null,
        invno       number            not null,
        dateout     date,
        rentdays    number,
        schdrtn     date,
        actrtn      date,
        ratepdy     number(10,2))
```

RETURNS Table

```
CREATE TABLE returns
        (memberid    number    not null,
        catnum       number    not null,
        actrtn       date,
        latecharge   number)
```

INVOICE Table

```
CREATE TABLE invoice
        (invno      number    not null,
        memberid    number    not null,
        paymethod   char(2),
        trantype    char(1)   not null,
        trandate    date      not null,
        trantime    char(8)   not null,
        total       number,
        tax         number)
```

PAYMETHOD Table

```
CREATE TABLE paymethod
     (paymethod   char(2),
      description char(20))
```

CONTROL Table

```
CREATE TABLE cntl
     (storeno        number,
      last_invoice   number,
      last_memberid  number,
      slstaxpct      number,
      latechgpct     number,
      maxrent        number)
```

Video Quest Sample Data

The sample data below will carry you through the exercises appearing in Chapters 5 and 6. Additional sample data will be entered later via forms screens.

You will create SQL command files to insert the sample data into the respective database tables. Use your host line editor to create these command files (Professional ORACLE users can get by with EDLIN, the PC-DOS line editor, while VAX VMS users can make do with EDIT) or any programming text editor you wish. Be sure to enter the data *exactly* as it appears in the listings below, being careful to enclose CHAR and DATE fields in apostrophes and to separate each value with a comma. (A common error to avoid is placing an apostrophe *outside* a comma separating a value: what is correct in the formal rules of punctuation is a violation of SQL syntax.)

TAPEDATA Command File

The following SQL script creates the TAPEDATA command file to insert records into the TAPE table. Enter the insert statements into an edit file named TAPEDATA.SQL. To load the database directly from the file, log on to SQL*Plus and then enter

```
START tapedata
```

Enter

```
rem * Tapedata.sql
rem * SQL script — Inserts TAPE table data
```

```
insert into tape values (100, 'P100V', 1);
insert into tape values (101, 'P100V', 1);
insert into tape values (200, 'P200V', 1);
insert into tape values (201, 'P200V', 1);
insert into tape values (300, 'P300V', 1);
insert into tape values (301, 'P300V', 1);
insert into tape values (305, 'P300B', 1);
insert into tape values (450, 'P450V', 1);
insert into tape values (451, 'P450V', 1);
insert into tape values (470, 'P470V', 1);
insert into tape values (471, 'P470V', 1);
insert into tape values (473, 'P470B', 1);
insert into tape values (475, 'P475V', 1);
insert into tape values (480, 'P480V', 1);
insert into tape values (481, 'P480V', 1);

rem * end TAPE table inserts
```

PRODUCT Data Command File

```
rem * Proddata.sql
rem * SQL script - Inserts PRODUCT table data

insert into product values ('P100V', 1, 'Film', 'SOUNDMUSIC',
'V', 'RS', 10, 19.95, 29.95, 29.95, 2, 1, 1, null, null);

insert into product values ('P200V', 1, 'Film', 'TOPGUN',
'V', 'RS', 10, 29.95, 39.95, 39.95, 2, 2, null, null, null);

insert into product values ('P300B', 1, 'Film', 'GONEWIND',
'B', 'RS', 25, 59.95, 69.95, 69.95, 1, null, 1, null, null);

insert into product values ('P300V', 1, 'Film', 'GONEWIND',
'V', 'R', 25, null, null, null, 2, null, null, null);

insert into product values ('P450V', 1, 'Film', 'CKANE','V',
'RS', 25, 49.95, 59.95, 59.95, 2, 1, 1, null, null);

insert into product values ('P470B', 1, 'Film',
'GHOSTBUSTER', 'B', 'RS', 10, 19.95, 29.95, 29.95, 1, 1,
null, null, null);

insert into product values ('P470V', 1, 'Film','GHOSTBUSTER',
'V', 'RS', 10, 19.95, 29.95, 29.95, 2, 1, null, null, null);
```

```
insert into product values ('P475V', 1, 'Film', 'HITCHER',
'V', 'RS', 50, 79.95, 89.95, 89.95, 1, 1, null, null, null);

insert into product values ('P480V', 1, 'Film', 'SHINING',
'V', 'RS',45, 69.95, 79.95, 79.95, 2, null, 1, null, null);

insert into product values ('P500', 1, 'Tape Case', 'na',
'V', 'S', 99, 2.99, 4.99, 4.99, 30, 20, 10, null, null);

rem * end PRODUCT table inserts
```

TITLE Data Command File

```
rem * Titledat.sql
rem * SQL script - Inserts TITLE table data

insert into title values ('SOUNDMUSIC', 'The Sound of Music',
140, 'Robert Wise', 'Saul Chaplin', 'Ernest Lehman',
'Julie Andrews, Christopher Plummer', '1965 Academy Award
(Best Picture)', '1965', 172, 'G', '*****', 'Paramount',
'Color');

insert into title values ('TOPGUN', 'Topgun', 100, 'Tony
Scott', 'Don Simpson, Jerry Bruckheimer', 'Jim Cash, Jack
Epps, Jr.', 'Tom Cruise, Kelly McGillis', null, '1987', 109,
'PG', '***', Paramount, 'Color');

insert into title values ('GONEWIND', 'Gone with the Wind',
135, 'Victor Fleming', 'David O. Selznick', 'Margaret
Mitchell', 'Clark Gable, Vivien Leigh, Leslie Howard',
'Academy Award (Best Picture, Actress, Supporting Actress)',
'1939', 231, 'G', '*****', 'MGM', 'B/W');

insert into title values ('CKANE', 'Citizen Kane', 135,
'Orson Welles','Orson Welles', 'Orson Welles', 'Orson Welles,
Joseph Cotten, Agnes Moorehead', null, '1941', 120, 'PG-13',
'*****', '20th Fox', 'B/W');

insert into title values ('GHOSTBUSTER', 'Ghostbusters', 120,
'Ivan Reitman','Ivan Reitman', 'Dan Aykroyd, Harold Ramis',
'Bill Murray, Dan Aykroyd, Sigourney Weaver, Harold Ramis,
Rick Moranis', null, '1984', 105, 'PG-13', '*****',
'Columbia', 'Color');
```

```
insert into title values ('SHINING', 'The Shining', 165,
'Stanley Kubrick', 'Stanley Kubrick', 'Stanley Kubrick, Diane
Johnson', 'Jack Nicholson, Shelley Duvall', null, '1980',
144, 'R', '****', 'Warner Brothers', 'Color');

insert into title values ('HITCHER', 'The Hitcher', 899,
'Robert Harmon', 'Kip Ohman, David Bombyk', 'Eric Red',
'Rutger Hauer, C. Thomas Howell', null, '1986', 93, 'R','**',
'Thorn EMI', 'Color');

rem * end TITLE table inserts
```

CATEGORY Data Command File

```
rem * Catdata.sql
rem * SQL script – Inserts CATEGORY table data

insert into category values (100, 'ADVENTURE');
insert into category values (120, 'COMEDY');
insert into category values (135, 'CLASSICS');
insert into category values (140, 'MUSICALS');
insert into category values (165, 'HORROR');

insert into category values (899, 'SLASHER');

rem * end CATEGORY table inserts
```

RENTCLASS Data Command File

```
rem * Rentclass.sql
rem * SQL script – Inserts RENTCLASS table data

insert into rentclass values (10, 3, 'General');
insert into rentclass values (25, 2.5, 'Classics');
insert into rentclass values (45, 4, 'Horror');
insert into rentclass values (50, 6, 'Slasher');
insert into rentclass values (90, 0 'Not applicable');

rem * end RENTCLASS table inserts
```

PAYMETHOD Data Command File

```
rem * Paymethod.sql
rem * SQL script – Inserts PAYMETHOD table data
```

```
insert into paymethod values ('CA', 'Cash');
insert into paymethod values ('MC', 'Mastercharge');
insert into paymethod values ('VI', 'Visa');
insert into paymethod values ('VT', 'Versateller');
```

```
rem * end PAYMETHOD table inserts
```

RENTALS Data Command File

```
rem * Rentdata.sql
rem * SQL script - Inserts RENTALS table data
```

```
insert into rentals values (1, 100, 1, '15-MAR-88', 1,
'16-MAR-88', '16-MAR-88', 3);
```

```
insert into rentals values (2, 200, 2, '28-MAR-88', 1,
'29-MAR-88','29-MAR-88', 3);
```

```
insert into rentals values (1, 200, 3, '09-APR-88', 2,
'11-APR-88', null, 3);
```

```
insert into rentals values (1, 300, 4, '09-APR-88', 2,
'11-APR-88', null, 2.5);
```

```
insert into rentals values (1, 470, 5, '10-APR-88', 2,
'12-APR-88', null, 3);
```

```
insert into rentals values (1, 480, 6, '10-APR-88', 1,
'11-APR-88', null, 4);
```

```
insert into rentals values (2, 301, 7, '12-APR-88', 2,
'14-APR-88', null, 2.5);
```

```
rem * end RENTAL table inserts
```

Summary

This chapter explored the inner workings of the Video Quest database. You finalized the entity-relationships models introduced in the previous chapter and learned the mechanics of designing, creating, and loading an ORACLE database. This chapter covered

- ▶ Defining entity attributes
- ▶ Principles of database design
- ▶ Creating and modifying ORACLE tables

    The CREATE TABLE command

    The ALTER TABLE command

    The DROP TABLE command

    The RENAME TABLE command

- ▶ Working with tables

    The INSERT command

    The SELECT command

    The DELETE command

5

Querying the Database

5

Querying the Database

SQL's ease of use is both a blessing and a curse to application designers. SQL's characteristic set-at-a-time processing is foreign to traditional programmers. SQL processes entire groups or sets of records at a time, in contrast to procedural languages which perform repetitive processing on single records. Confronted with SQL, traditional programmers have to rethink and revise their approach to solving real-world application problems. Once they overcome the culture shock, however, most programmers embrace the SQL solution expressly for its ease of use.

Though powerful, SQL does not offer as much flexibility or programming control as procedural languages offer. SQL is not a full programming language; SQL is a database access and manipulation language. However, procedural flexibility comes at a price. Programmers are forced to weigh the added control of procedural languages against drastically reduced productivity—often a difficult choice to make. SQL makes possible a new generation of application tools: the fourth generation development environment. With SQL as the platform, the 4GE application tools satisfy the majority of your programming needs.

This chapter exposes you to the many facets of SQL and ORACLE's extensions to ANSI-standard SQL, SQL*Plus. Via a series of exercises, you learn how to sculpt queries in a variety of ways, retrieving information in as much or as little detail as you need. Chapter 5 unravels the SQL SELECT command. The SELECT command is your passport to retrieving information from the database.

The SELECT Command

The SELECT command is disarmingly simple to use. End-users and DP professionals immediately grasp the concept, and can quickly put the

SELECT command to work extracting data from tables with little or no prior training. However, the same SELECT command in its manifold permutations is used by professional programmers to build elaborate queries spanning pages of code. Building complex queries presupposes a mastery of the SQL language.

The SELECT exercises in this chapter steadily increase in difficulty, so you should plan to work through them at your own pace. Those of you familiar with SQL may want to skim through this chapter and concentrate on Chapter 6, *Advanced SQL Capabilities*. All exercises use the sample data listed at the close of the previous chapter. If you haven't yet loaded this sample data, you should do so now.

Retrieving Film Title Information

Enter the generic SELECT * command against the TITLE table:

```
SELECT *
  FROM title
```

and observe the results displayed on screen. Not a very interesting display, is it? The TITLE table, a master database table as distinguished from the leaner transaction tables, holds a fair amount of information. Many of the Title columns are wide—78 characters wide. To extract film title information in more meaningful ways, you must refine your queries, specifying only a few columns at a time.

Specifying Columns in a Table

Suppose you want to see the title of every film stored in the TITLE database. You would specify the *title* column after the SELECT command to do this.

Exercise 5.1
To display titles from the TITLE table, enter

```
SELECT title
  FROM title
```

The query returns all titles found in the table:

```
TITLE
------------------------------------------------------------
Ghostbusters
The Hitcher
The Sound of Music
Topgun
Gone with the Wind
Citizen Kane
The Shining
```

Suppose you also want to know which actors and actresses starred in each film. You would display the title, followed by the Actors column.

Exercise 5.2
To retrieve Titles and Actors from the TITLE table, enter

```
SELECT title, actors
  FROM title
```

and the query returns

```
TITLE
------------------------------------------------------------
ACTORS
------------------------------------------------------------
Ghostbusters
Bill Murray,Dan Aykroyd,Sigourney Weaver,Harold Ramis,Rick Moranis

The Hitcher
Rutger Hauer,C. Thomas Howell,Jeffrey DeMann

The Sound of Music
Julie Andrews,Christopher Plummer,Richard Haydn,Eleanor Parker

Topgun
Tom Cruise, Kelly McGillis

Gone with the Wind
Clark Gable, Vivian Leigh, Leslie Howard

Citizen Kane
Orson Welles, Joseph Cotten, Agnes Moorhead
```

continued

```
The Shining
Jack Nicholson, Shelley Duvall
```

Response time permitting, the results of your query will display rapidly on the screen. Enter the SET PAUSE ON command at the SQL> prompt to cause SQL*Plus to pause the display after each screenful. (At installation, ORACLE sets the default pagesize to 25 lines, or an entire screenful. Unless you've changed the page size with the SET PAGESIZE *nn* command, SET PAUSE ON should properly halt the display after each screenful.)

Now expand the query to include the directors, the year the film was released, and the star rating for each title.

Exercise 5.3

To display the Title, Actors, Directors, Release Date, and Star Rating from the TITLE table, enter

```
SELECT title, actors, directors, release, starrtg
   FROM title
```

The query returns

```
TITLE
------------------------------------------------------------------
ACTORS
------------------------------------------------------------------
DIRECTORS
------------------------------------------------------------------
RELE STARR
---- -----
Ghostbusters
Bill Murray,Dan Aykroyd,Sigourney Weaver,Harold Ramis,Rick Moranis
Ivan Reitman
1984 *****

The Hitcher
Rutger Hauer,C. Thomas Howell,Jeffrey DeMann
Robert Harmon
1986 **

The Sound of Music
Julie Andrews,Christopher Plummer,Richard Haydn,Eleanor Parker
Robert Wise
1965 *****
```

```
Topgun
Tom Cruise, Kelly McGillis
Tony Scott
1987 ***

Gone with the Wind
Clark Gable, Vivian Leigh, Leslie Howard
Victor Fleming
1939 *****

Citizen Kane
Orson Welles, Joseph Cotten, Agnes Moorhead
Orson Welles
1941 *****

The Shining
Jack Nicholson, Shelley Duvall
Stanley Kubrick
1980 ****
```

You can easily change the order in which the columns display by specifying the columns in the order you wish to see them.

Changing the Column Display

SQL*Plus displays column names as defined when the table was created, and truncates them according to column width. When issuing a query, you can change the name of a column on the fly by adding a new name, often called an *alias* name, after the column name.

Exercise 5.4
Change the names of the *release* and *starrtg* columns, and the order in which the columns appear by entering

```
SELECT title, release year, starrtg stars, actors, directors
  FROM title
```

Changing the Column Format

While you can change the name of a column in a query, the new name lives only for the life of that query. An alternative approach is to use the COLUMN format command, a SQL*Plus command far more flexible and enduring. The COLUMN format command lets you alter the format of the column and heading—including the column name, its width, its justification position, and whether to wrap or truncate text—and the new format endures for the duration of your SQL*Plus session. A changed column displays the new format any time the column is referred to by *any query* until it is redefined or until you exit SQL*Plus.

The COLUMN format command is issued at the SQL> prompt, and would look similar to the following example:

```
SQL> COLUMN title FORMAT a25 HEADING 'Film Title'
```

The FORMAT parameter controls the column width. Different format models are available for character, number, and date fields. (These format elements are described in detail in Chapter 1 of the *SQL*PLus Reference Guide.*) As in the above example, the width of a character field is defined with an a, followed by the new width of the column; the width of a number field is defined by the digit 9 repeated once for each digit of the new width.

The HEADING parameter controls the displayed column name. If the new heading contains blanks or punctuation, it must be enclosed in single quotes.

You can reset a column to its default format—the format originally defined when the table was created—by using the DEFAULT parameter like this:

```
SQL> COLUMN title DEF[ault]
```

To view the column format for a given column, simply enter the COLUMN command followed by the column name, like so:

```
SQL> COLUMN title
```

Exercise 5.5

To change the formats of the Title, Release, Star Rating, Directors, and Actors columns, enter

```
COLUMN title      FORMAT a25      HEADING 'Film Title'
COLUMN release    FORMAT a8       HEADING 'Released'
COLUMN starrtg    FORMAT a15      HEADING "Critic's Choice"
COLUMN directors  HEADING 'Director'
COLUMN actors     HEADING 'Starring'
```

Now enter the query:

```
SELECT title, release, starrtg, directors, actors
  FROM title
```

and observe the results:

Film Title	Released	Critic's Choice

Directed By

Starring

Ghostbusters   1984   *****
Ivan Reitman
Bill Murray, Dan Aykroyd, Sigourney Weaver, Harold Ramis, Rick Moranis

The Hitcher   1986   **
Robert Harmon
Rutger Hauer,C. Thomas Howell,Jeffrey DeMann

The Sound of Music   1965   *****
Robert Wise
Julie Andrews, Christopher Plummer,Richard Haydn,Eleanor Parker

Topgun   1987   ***
Tony Scott
Tom Cruise, Kelly McGillis

Gone with the Wind   1939   *****
Victor Fleming
Clark Gable, Vivian Leigh, Leslie Howard

Citizen Kane   1941   *****
Orson Welles
Orson Welles, Joseph Cotten, Agnes Moorhead

The Shining   1980   ****
Stanley Kubrick
Jack Nicholson, Shelley Duvall

To display the column format settings defined for your current log-on session, enter

```
SQL> COLUMN
```

and you should see the following:

```
column    title ON
heading   'Film Title'
format    a25

column    release ON
heading   'Released'
format    a8

column    starrtg ON
heading   'Critic's Choice'
format    a15

column    actors ON
heading   'Starring'

column    directors ON
heading   'Directed By'
```

Sorting Rows: The ORDER BY Clause

You can control the order in which the rows of a query are displayed with the ORDER BY clause. Typically the last statement of a query, the ORDER BY clause is followed by a column name indicating the column by which the rows will be ordered. The ORDER BY clause normally puts rows in *ascending* order (smaller values first); thus character fields are ordered alphabetically. For example, if you added "ORDER BY title" to the previous query, SQL*Plus would display the results in alphabetical order by title. To reverse this order, you can specify the DESC parameter and the query would return the rows in *descending* order.

Rows can be ordered on multiple columns by specifying each column after the ORDER BY clause; SQL*Plus then orders the rows in succession. Rows are ordered first by the first column specified and then within that column; multiple rows are ordered by the second column specified; and so forth.

Exercise 5.6

To order the previous query in alphabetical (ascending) order by Title, enter

```
SELECT    title, release, starrtg, directors, actors
  FROM    title
 ORDER    BY title
```

To order the same query in ascending order by release date, enter

```
SELECT    title, release, starrtg, directors, actors
  FROM    title
 ORDER    BY release
```

The query will display the older titles first and the more recent titles last. To reverse the order and display the rows in descending release date, enter

```
SELECT    title, release, starrtg, directors, actors
  FROM    title
 ORDER    BY release DESC
```

The ORDER BY column does not have to be displayed when specified. For example, you can order rows by descending release date without displaying the date as well. Observe:

```
SELECT    title, starrtg, directors, actors
  FROM    title
 ORDER    BY release DESC
```

Editing SQL Commands

SQL*Plus temporarily stores the SQL command you enter in a buffer. The command remains in the buffer until you enter a new SQL command or explicitly clear the buffer. With the aid of several SQL edit commands, you can examine, modify, or rerun the current SQL command without re-entering it.

The SQL edit commands are line-oriented, allowing you to manipulate—change, append, delete and add—only a single SQL command line at a time. They are handy when constructing a query that is constantly being modified and re-executed. However, when working with longer queries or highly formatted reports composed of multiple queries, you must graduate to a text editor.

The SQL edit commands are listed for you in Table 5.1.

Table 5.1   SQL Edit Commands

Command	Abbreviation	Purpose
APPEND	A text	add text at the end of a line
CHANGE	C/old/new	change *old* text to *new* in a line
CHANGE	c/text/	delete text from a line
CLEAR BUFFER	CL BUFF	delete everything in buffer
DEL		delete current line
INPUT	I	add an indefinite number of lines
INPUT	I text	add a line of text
LIST	L	list all lines in SQL buffer
LIST n	L n	list one line
LIST m n	L m n	list range of lines (m to n)
RUN	R	rerun the current SQL command
/		run the current SQL command

Retrieving Specific Rows: The WHERE Clause

The ease and power of SQL become evident when you construct your first queries that retrieve specific rows of data from a table. The WHERE clause is like a pointer leading you through row after row of a table. The *predicate*, or search criteria of the WHERE clause, is your destination point, the exact rows of data you need. A SELECT command with a WHERE clause retrieves *only* the row or rows that meet the specified search criteria.

Exercise 5.7
To retrieve the Title, Release and Censorship Rating of all films made by 20th Century Fox studios, enter

```
SELECT title, release, censorrtg
  FROM title
 WHERE studio = '20 Century Fox'
```

This query results in

```
Film Title                                       Release  Censorr
-----------------------------------------------  -------  -------
The Sound of Music                               1965     G
Citizen Kane                                     1941     PG-13
```

This query compares the Studio column to a character value, '20 Century Fox'. Translated, the SELECT statement with the WHERE clause actually reads

Grab all the rows from the TITLE table that contain the value '20 Century Fox' in the Studio column.

Number and date values can also be included in the WHERE clause. Date and character values must be enclosed in single quotes, however. For example, you may want to search the TITLE table to extract all films that are two hours long, no more and no less.

Exercise 5.8

To retrieve the Title, Release and Censorship Rating of all films whose running time is 120 minutes, enter

```
SELECT title, release, censorrtg
  FROM title
 WHERE runtime = 120
```

The query returns

```
Film Title                                  Release  Censorr
-----------------------------------------   -------  -------
Citizen Kane                                 1941     PG-13
```

A reminder: use the SQL edit commands to minimize retyping when you test and modify queries on-line. The query just entered merely altered the WHERE clause of the previous query. You could have saved time by refreshing the current SQL buffer, and modifying the single command line. For instance, here is what you could have entered and what each command would have done:

1. `SQL> L` would have listed the previous query
2. `SQL> DEL` would have deleted the current line
3. `SQL> INPUT` where runtime = 120
4. `SQL> /` would have re-executed the query

Logical Operators in the WHERE Clause

The WHERE conditions in the two query examples you've just entered compare an *equal* condition by using the = or *equal to* logical operator. When the WHERE condition, or *expression*, is satisfied and a row or rows returned, then the expression is considered *true*. On the flip side, if no rows are returned, then the expression is *false*. Since the answer can only be either true or false, the expression in a WHERE clause is often termed a *logical expression*.

Several other operators can be used to compare columns against values (or columns against other columns) with logical expressions. The operators you can use to create different expressions are listed for you in Table 5.2.

Table 5.2   Logical Operators

Operator	Meaning
=	equal to
!=, ^ = or < >	not equal to
>	greater than
> =	greater than or equal to
<	less than
< =	less than or equal to
*BETWEEN . . . AND . . .	between two values
*IN (list . . .)	any values in the specified list . . .
*LIKE	match a character pattern
*IS NULL	where the value is null (no value)

*The last four operators can be made negative by using the NOT operator: NOT BETWEEN, NOT IN, NOT LIKE, IS NOT NULL.

Experiment with these operators by working through the following exercises.

Exercise 5.9

To retrieve the Title, Release Date, Censorship Rating, and length (*runtime*) of all films whose running time is 120 minutes *or* longer, enter

```
SELECT title, release, censorrtg, runtime
  FROM title
 WHERE runtime > = 120
```

The query returns:

Film Title	Release	Censorr	Runtime
The Sound of Music	1965	G	172
Gone with the Wind	1939	G	231
Citizen Kane	1941	PG-13	120
The Shining	1980	R	144

Before moving on to the next exercise, reformat the *censorrtg* and *runtime* columns so that they are consistent in appearance with the other columns. Enter the following SQL*Plus commands:

```
SQL> COLUMN censorrtg format a6 heading 'Censor'
SQL> COLUMN runtime heading 'Running Time'
```

Exercise 5.10
To retrieve the Title, Release Date, Censorship Rating, and length of all films whose running time is *less than* 120 minutes, and to order them by *runtime*, enter

```
SELECT    title, release, censorrtg, runtime
  FROM    title
 WHERE    runtime < 120
 ORDER    BY runtime
```

The query returns:

```
Film Title                       Release  Censor  Running Time
------------------------------   -------  ------  ------------
The Hitcher                      1986     R                 93
The Ghostbusters                 1984     PG               105
Topgun                           1987     PG               109
```

Now recast the query to retrieve all rows whose value in the runtime column is *not equal to* 120 minutes. Using SQL edit commands, enter

1. SQL> L3   (To list the line, making it the current line)
2. SQL> C/</!=/   (To replace the less than operator with the not equal to operator)

and rerun the query:

```
SELECT    title, release, censorrtg, runtime
  FROM    title
 WHERE    runtime != 120
 ORDER    BY runtime
```

Every title but 'Citizen Kane' should display:

```
Film Title                     Release  Censor  Running Time
------------------------       -------  ------  ------------
The Hitcher                    1986     R                 93
The Ghostbusters               1984     PG               105
Topgun                         1987     PG               109
The Shining                    1980     R                144
The Sound of Music             1965     G                172
Gone with the Wind             1939     G                231
```

We obviously haven't gathered enough data to draw any definite conclusions; however, our query indicates a growing trend—modern films seem to be getting shorter all the time!

Exercise 5.11
To retrieve all films released *between* 1980 and 1986, and to order them in descending order by release date, enter

```
SELECT    title, release, censorrtg, runtime
  FROM    title
 WHERE    release BETWEEN '1980' AND '1987'
 ORDER    BY release DESC
```

The screen displays

```
Film Title                     Release  Censor  Running Time
------------------------       -------  ------  ------------
Topgun                         1987     PG               109
The Hitcher                    1986     R                 93
The Ghostbusters               1984     PG               105
The Shining                    1980     R                144
```

Notice that both the high and low ends of the range specified for the BETWEEN operator are included in the results. The same holds true for number values. (Comparing date values is slightly more involved; an entire section is devoted to this topic in the following chapter.) For example, rewrite the query to compare a range of *runtime* values, such as

```
SELECT    title, release, censorrtg, runtime
  FROM    title
 WHERE    runtime BETWEEN 120 AND 231
 ORDER    BY release DESC
```

and the query displays

```
Film Title                         Release   Censor   Running Time
------------------------------     -------   ------   ------------
Gone with the Wind                 1939      G                 231
Citizen Kane                       1941      PG-13             120
The Sound of Music                 1965      G                 172
The Shining                        1980      R                 144
```

Sometimes you will want to search for a particular value but are uncertain of its full spelling, or whether it is the only value stored in the column. SQL*Plus offers the LIKE operator to let you search character values against a pattern mask.

Suppose you want to find the films in which Clark Gable starred, or all films directed or co-directed by Stanley Kubrick. You would use the LIKE operator to satisfy these queries.

Exercise 5.12
To find all films starring Clark Gable, enter

```
SELECT title, release, censorrtg, runtime, actors, directors
  FROM title
 WHERE actors LIKE '%Clark Gable%'
```

The query displays

```
Film Title                         Release   Censor   Running Time
------------------------------     -------   ------   ------------
Starring
------------------------------------------------------------------
Directors
------------------------------------------------------------------
Gone with the Wind                 1939      G                 231
Clark Gable, Vivian Leigh, Leslie Howard
Victor Fleming
```

The percent sign framing the value 'Clark Gable' tells SQL*Plus to find any records that include those characters *anywhere* in the actors column. If you had entered a single percent sign after the name (like *'Clark Gable%'*), SQL*Plus would have returned only the rows in which Clark Gable appeared as the *first* entry in the Actors column. Conversely, a percent sign preceding the name, like *'%Clark Gable'*, would have returned all the rows listing Clark Gable as an actor, but not if his name was the first value in the column. (The only exception to this would be if Clark Gable was the *only* value listed in the Actors column; in that case the LIKE operator written with the percent sign preceding the name would still pick the row up.)

Try this principle yourself. Erase the second percent sign in our original query and then rerun it. No records should be selected, since the logical expression written this way is false.

To find any films directed by Stanley Kubrick, enter

```
SELECT title, release, censorrtg, runtime, actors, directors
  FROM title
 WHERE directors LIKE '%Stanley Kubrick%'
```

and the query returns:

```
Film Title                         Release  Censor  Running Time
--------------------------------   -------  ------  ------------
Starring
-----------------------------------------------------------------
Directors
-----------------------------------------------------------------
The Shining                        1980     R                144
Jack Nicholson, Shelley Duvall
Stanley Kubrick
```

Building Compound Expressions

You can combine logical expressions within a single WHERE clause to either broaden or restrict the radius of your search. When you mix logical expressions, the effect is to build a *compound expression*. The components of a compound expression are connected by either the AND or the OR boolean operators, or both. Compound expressions let you build powerful, complex queries to perform precise table searches.

The AND Operator

Suppose you want to find all films that were released between the years of 1980 and 1987, but only those rated PG. You would use the AND operator to create this query.

Exercise 5.13

To retrieve all PG rated films released *between* 1980 and 1987, and to order them in descending order by release date, enter

```
SELECT    title, release, censorrtg, runtime
  FROM    title
 WHERE    release BETWEEN '1980' AND '1987'
   AND    censorrtg = 'PG'
 ORDER    BY release DESC
```

The screen displays

Film Title	Release	Censor	Running Time
Topgun	1987	PG	109
Ghostbusters	1984	PG	105

From a previous query, we learned that there are two other films released between these years, but they are both rated R. The AND operator lets you restrict the query to only those films rated PG.

The AND operator states that both logical expressions must be true for the entire compound expression to be true. Watch what happens when you add another ANDed expression to the query, one that further restricts the search to only those films running longer than 120 minutes:

```
SELECT    title, release, censorrtg, starrtg, studio
  FROM    title
 WHERE    release BETWEEN '1980' AND '1987'
   AND    censorrtg = 'PG'
   AND    runtime > 120
 ORDER    BY release DESC
```

The query returns

```
no records selected
```

No records were selected because the last ANDed expression was false, invalidating the entire WHERE clause. Experiment with the AND operator by working through some additional exercises.

Exercise 5.14

To retrieve all films released by MGM studios that also have received a five-star rating by Siskell and Ebert, enter

```
SELECT title, release, censorrtg, starrtg, studio
  FROM title
 WHERE studio = 'MGM'
   AND starrtg = '*****'
```

The query displays

```
Film Title                 Release  Censor  Critic's Choice
------------------------   -------  ------  ----------------
Studio
-----------------------------------------------------------
Gone with the Wind         1939     G               *****
MGM
```

Exercise 5.15
To retrieve all films released by 20th Century Fox that have received a five star rating AND were directed by Orson Welles, enter

```
SELECT title, release, censorrtg, starrtg
  FROM title
 WHERE studio = '20 Century Fox'
   AND starrtg = '*****'
   AND directors = 'Orson Welles'
```

Reformat the studio column for a uniform appearance, and the query displays

```
Film Title                 Release  Censor  Critic's Choice
------------------------   -------  ------  ----------------
Studio
-----------------------------------------------------------
Citizen Kane               1941     PG-13           *****
20 Century Fox
```

Exercise 5.16
To select all films that have received an academy award, are rated five stars, and whose censorship rating is not equal to R, enter the following, also remembering to reformat the Awards column:

```
SELECT title, release, censorrtg, starrtg, awards, studio
  FROM title
 WHERE starrtg = '*****'
   AND awards is not null
   AND censorrtg != 'R'
```

The screen displays

```
Film Title                      Release  Censor  Critic's Choice
-----------------------------   -------  ------  ---------------
Academy Awards
---------------------------------------------------------------
Studio
---------------------------------------------------------------
The Sound of Music              1965     G              *****
1965 Academy Awards (Best Picture)
20 Century Fox

Gone with the Wind              1939     G              *****
Academy Awards (Best Picture, Actress, Supporting Actress)
MGM
```

One of the unwritten laws of building queries, particularly those containing compound expressions or subqueries, is to be mindful of performance issues. ORACLE processes all the AND expressions in the order in which they are written, and it utilizes whatever index paths are available to the query optimizer to improve performance. It pays to design your query in such a way as to force each successive AND expression to restrict the radius of search as much as possible, selecting the fewest number of rows. Each successive AND expression should extract fewer and fewer rows until the query is satisfied and the desired rows selected. This will help improve search performance, unless of course no index paths exist; in this case, ORACLE would have to scan all rows in the database sequentially. Chapter 10 covers performance issues in much greater depth.

For example, suppose you request all Clark Gable films that have won Academy Awards. The query is simple enough, but with a large table, the order in which the AND expressions are written could yield dramatically different performance results.

The OR Operator

The OR operator broadens the radius of your search criteria. The compound expression in a query using the OR operator is true—that is, it will successfully return a row or rows—if any *one* of the logical expressions in the WHERE clause is true. (There is no syntactical restriction on the number of expressions you can connect with the OR operator.)

If you can pose the query as a choice between two mutually exclusive values, this tells you that you can use the OR operator. For example, suppose you are in the mood to see only two types of films on an evening—either an Academy award winner, OR a comedy in which Bill Murray is starring.

Exercise 5.17

To retrieve the films that either have received an academy award or star Bill Murray, enter

```
SELECT title, release, censorrtg, starrtg, actors, awards
  FROM title
 WHERE awards is not null
    OR actors like '%Bill Murray%'
```

The query displays

```
Film Title                        Release  Censor  Critic's Choice
------------------------------    -------  ------  ---------------
Starring
--------------------------------------------------------------------
Academy Awards
--------------------------------------------------------------------
Ghostbusters                      1965     G       *****
Bill Murray, Dan Aykroyd, Sigourney Weaver, Harold Ramis, Rick Moranis

The Sound of Music               1965     G       *****
Julie Andrews, Christopher Plummer, Richard Haydn, Eleanor Parker
1965 Academy Awards (Best Picture)

Gone with the Wind               1939     G       *****
Clark Gable, Vivian Leigh, Leslie Howard
Academy Awards (Best Picture, Actress, Supporting Actress)
```

When searching a column for a *list* of values, you can cut corners by using the IN logical operator; the IN operator is similar to the OR operator in that it returns rows based on a choice of criteria; if any of the listed criteria is true, the entire OR expression is true. The IN operator works in place of the equal operator (=) only, however, and is restricted to searching a list of values within a given column. Unlike the OR operator, IN cannot be used to connect WHERE expressions in a compound expression.

Exercise 5.18

To retrieve the films that star Bill Murray, were directed by Tony Scott, or have a critical star rating of *either* four OR five stars, enter

```
SELECT    title, release, censorrtg, starrtg, actors, directors
   FROM    title
  WHERE    actors like '%Bill Murray%'
     OR    directors like '%Tony Scott%'
     OR    starrtg IN ('*****', '****')
ORDER BY starrtg DESC
```

This results in

```
Film Title                      Release   Censor   Critic's Choice
------------------------------  -------   ------   ---------------
Starring
-----------------------------------------------------------------
Directors
-----------------------------------------------------------------
Ghostbusters                     1965       G        *****
Bill Murray, Dan Aykroyd,Sigourney Weaver,Harold Ramis,Rick Moranis
Ivan Reitman


The Sound of Music               1965       G        *****
Julie Andrews, Christopher Plummer, Richard Haydn, Eleanor Parker
Robert Wise


Citizen Kane                     1941      PG-13     *****
Orson Welles, Joseph Cotten, Agnes Moorhead
Orson Welles


Gone with the Wind               1939       G        *****
Clark Gable, Vivian Leigh, Leslie Howard
Victor Fleming


The Shining                      1980       R        ****
Jack Nicholson, Shelley Duvall
Stanley Kubrick


Topgun                           1987      PG        ***
Tom Cruise, Kelly McGillis
Tony Scott
```

Operator Precedence

When AND and OR operators are combined in a compound expression,
ORACLE performs the AND expressions first. ANDed WHERE clauses are

said to have *higher precedence* than ORed clauses. This is important to bear in mind when constructing queries that contain mixed operators. Unless you properly block the AND and OR expressions, you are bound to wind up with unexpected query results. (It is possible to modify operator precedence rules by using parentheses as you will see in examples occurring in later sections of this book.)

Suppose you want to find all black and white films directed by either Victor Fleming, Orson Welles or Stanley Kubrick, OR any other films which bear a five-star rating. To do this, you build a compound WHERE clause with both AND and OR expressions, being careful that they accurately portray the desired search condition.

Exercise 5.19
To retrieve the black and white films directed by Victor Fleming, Orson Welles or Stanley Kubrick, OR those with a five-star rating, enter

```
SELECT description, release, censorrtg, starrtg, directors
  FROM title
 WHERE directors in ('Victor Fleming', 'Orson Welles',
       'Stanley Kubrick')
   AND color_bw = 'BW'
    OR starrtg = '*****'
```

The screen displays

Film Title	Release	Censor	Critic's Choice
Directors			
Ghostbuster Ivan Reitman	1965	G	*****
The Sound of Music Robert Wise	1965	G	*****
Gone with the Wind Victor Fleming	1939	G	*****
Citizen Kane Orson Welles	1941	PG-13	*****

Given the way the query is designed, ORACLE groups the compound expression into two discrete units, evaluating each separately. ORACLE first processes the expressions

```
[where directors in 'Victor Fleming', 'Orson Welles',
'Stanley Kubrick') AND color_bw = 'BW']
```

and then processes the second expression:

```
[OR starrtg = '*****']
```

Notice that the above query did not select any films directed by Stanley Kubrick, because the one Kubrick film in our sample data, *The Shining*, is in color, not black and white.

To impress upon you the importance of constructing your queries cautiously, let's alter this query a bit. Suppose you want to retrieve all black and white films directed by either Victor Fleming, Orson Welles, or Stanley Kubrick which have a five star rating. This is not the same query as before. Observe:

```
SELECT description, release, censorrtg, starrtg, directors
   FROM title
  WHERE directors IN ('Victor Fleming', 'Orson Welles',
        'Stanley Kubrick')
    AND (color_bw = 'BW' OR starrtg = '*****')
```

This results in

Film Title	Release	Censor	Critic's Choice
Directors			
Gone with the Wind Victor Fleming	1939	G	*****
Citizen Kane Orson Welles	1941	PG-13	*****

As written, this query restricts the search to only those black and white, five-star films directed by any of these three master directors. ORACLE interprets the WHERE clause in this fashion because AND expressions have higher precedence.

By enclosing the combined OR expressions in parentheses, you are telling ORACLE to apply both OR conditions to the AND expression. *Both* conditions must be true for the entire WHERE clause to be true. Thus, ORACLE interprets the entire WHERE clause as containing both of these two expressions:

```
WHERE directors IN ('Victor Fleming', 'Orson Welles',
      'Stanley Kubrick')
  AND (color_bw = 'BW')
```

and:

```
WHERE directors IN ('Victor Fleming', 'Orson Welles',
      'Stanley Kubrick')
  AND (starrtg = '*****')
```

Working with Groups of Rows

The queries you've constructed thus far have returned a value for each row selected; this is referred to as returning *individual* or *detail results*. SQL also provides functions that let you evaluate summary information about *groups* of rows. These GROUP functions retrieve a single value for the entire query, not for each selected row. Table 5.3 shows the most frequently used GROUP functions.

Table 5.3 GROUP Functions

Function	Example	Result
NUMBER values only:		
AVG	AVG(runtime)	Computes the average running time of all titles.
SUM	SUM(qtysold)	Computes the total quantity of products sold in the PRODUCT table.
NUMBER, CHARACTER, and DATE values:		
COUNT	COUNT(title)	Returns the total number of titles.
MAX	MAX(cost)	Selects the highest Cost value of all products in the PRODUCT table.
MIN	MIN(cost)	Selects the lowest Cost value of all products in the PRODUCT table.

The following exercises explain these GROUP functions further.

Exercise 5.20
To find out the total number of film titles in the TITLE table, you would use the COUNT function. Null values, if present, are not counted. Enter

```
SELECT COUNT(title)
  FROM title
```

and you get

```
COUNT(TITLE)
------------
           7
```

You can make this display more attractive by assigning an alias column name when entering the query, such as

```
SELECT COUNT(title) "Total Titles"
  FROM title
```

and you get

```
Total Titles
------------
           7
```

If you wanted a count of the number of records stored in the entire table, you would use a special form of the COUNT function, the COUNT(*) function. Enter

```
SELECT COUNT(*)
  FROM title
```

Exercise 5.21

To display the value of the most expensive product in the PRODUCTS table, use the MAX function. Enter

```
SELECT MAX(cost)
  FROM product
```

and get

```
MAX(COST)
---------
    79.95
```

And to display the value of the cheapest product, use the MIN function. Enter

```
SELECT MIN(cost)
  FROM product
```

and get

```
MIN(COST)
---------
     2.99
```

GROUP functions are often used when performing arithmetic on fields. The results of any field computations would be temporarily stored in a *virtual field*—one that is created extemporaneously just to display computed or comparative data. (Arithmetic can be performed on any numeric fields in SQL; this ability is not limited to GROUP functions.)

For example, you can create a virtual field that computes the *difference* between the cheapest and the most expensive Video Quest products, and displays the results on screen.

Exercise 5.22
To display both the least and most expensive products in the PRODUCT table, and the difference in price between them, enter

```
SELECT MAX(cost), MIN(cost), MAX(COST) - MIN(COST) "Price
       Difference"
  FROM product
```

and get

```
MAX(COST)  MIN(COST  Price Difference
---------  --------  ----------------
    79.95      2.99             76.96
```

Exercise 5.23
To calculate the AVERAGE running time of all film titles in the TITLE table, use the AVG function. Enter

```
SELECT AVG(runtime) "Average Length"
  FROM title
```

and get

```
Average Length
--------------
    139.142857
```

If a query doesn't require this much numeric precision, you can round the query to a specific decimal point explicitly with the ROUND function. A film's length is measured in minutes, so you would probably want the query result rounded to the nearest whole number to avoid confusion. Observe:

```
SELECT ROUND(avg(runtime), 0) "Average Length"
  FROM title
```

produces

```
Average Length
--------------
           139
```

The ROUND function rounds decimal numbers to the nearest hundredths, or second decimal position, unless you specify otherwise, as we did in the above example.

Summarizing Several Groups in a Query: The GROUP BY Clause

With the COUNT function, you determined the number of film titles stored in the TITLE table. Suppose you wanted this total broken down into a count of the titles in *each* of the four censorship groups—G, PG, PG-13, R. Now, you could do this by writing a separate COUNT(title) query for each censorship group, such as

```
SELECT COUNT(title)
  FROM title
 WHERE censorrtg = 'G'
```

However, SQL provides a far more efficient technique in the GROUP BY clause. The GROUP BY clause divides the table into the groups of rows found in the column you specify after the clause. In the above query, for example, your aim is to display a separate count of the titles in each censorship group. To do this, you must design the query to break the table up into groups by *censorrtg*, that is, you have the query GROUP BY *censorrtg*. It would help identify these groups if you were to display the *censorrtg* column in the query as well.

Exercise 5.24

To list the censorship rating categories, and to COUNT the total number of titles in each of these groups, enter:

```
SELECT    censorrtg, count(title) "Number of Titles"
  FROM    title
 GROUP    BY censorrtg
```

The screen then displays

```
Censor  Number of Titles
------  ----------------
G                      2
PG                     2
PG-13                  1
R                      2
```

A Caveat for Using Group Functions

Group functions and individual functions simply do not mix. The single most important rule for using a group function is

> *Don't attempt to summarize groups and select individual results in the same query.*

Until new users get accustomed to working with group functions, they frequently bump into this problem. For instance, you cannot perform the following query:

```
SELECT title, AVG(runtime)
  FROM title
```

If you do, ORACLE displays

```
ERROR at line 1: ORA-0937: not a single group set function
```

The reason is that it is impossible for the results of both selections to be displayed at the same time. The title column returns a value for every row (and we know there are seven titles in the table), and AVG(runtime), being a group function, can select only *one* value, that is one row for the entire query. It would be quite a feat for SQL to break treaty with logic and display seven rows against one column and one row against another, at one and the same time.

There are two exceptions to this rule: in cases when group functions are used in the GROUP BY clause, as discussed in the preceding section, and in *subqueries*.

If the SELECT command contains a subquery (a separate, distinct query used in the clause of another query, a SQL or a SQL*Plus command), then you may use group functions in the subquery while individual results can be selected in the main query, or vice versa. An example of a subquery which uses a group function appears below, though the detailed discussion of subqueries is saved for the following chapter, Advanced SQL Capabilities.

Exercise 5.25

To retrieve the title, running time, and critical rating of the longest film in the database, enter

```
SELECT title, starrtg, runtime
  FROM title
 WHERE runtime =
       (SELECT  max(runtime)
          FROM  title)
```

The screen returns

Film Title	Critic's Choice	Running Time
Gone with the Wind	*****	231

Building a SQL Command File

When working with longer queries or designing highly formatted reports, you will want to work with a text editor and build SQL command files. However, while constructing a query on-line, you can save it to a text file at any time. (This query might be the basis for a complex report at some later point.) You save the contents of the current SQL buffer to disk with the SAVE command, which can be recalled or run directly from the command file.

ORACLE appends the suffix .SQL to the saved file unless you specify a different suffix. Be careful when naming your command files, which are also known as *SQL script* files. On the PC, ORACLE overwrites any file by the same name without warning; on the VAX, however, new versions of the file are created.

The operative commands for working with script files within SQL*Plus are as shown in Table 5.4.

Table 5.4   Command File Commands

Command	Purpose
SAVE file	Saves current SQL buffer to the named files.
GET file	Retrieves named file to the current SQL buffer
START file	Retrieves the named file and runs it automatically
HOST dir *.sql	Lists the SQL script files stored in the current operating system directory (PC, VAX)

Suppose you want to peruse all the five-star films that star Jack Nicholson or were directed by Orson Welles. Toying with the query, you first enter

```
SELECT title, release, censorrtg, starrtg, actors, directors
  FROM title
 WHERE actors like '%Jack Nicholson%'
    OR directors = 'Orson Welles'
   AND starrtg '*****'
```

and you save the query to a file named "5STARS," like so:

```
SQL> SAVE 5STARS
```

While the command is still in the buffer, you run it, and you get

```
Film Title                      Release  Censor  Critic's Choice
------------------------------  -------  ------  ---------------
Starring
-----------------------------------------------------------------
Directors
-----------------------------------------------------------------
Citizen Kane                    1941     PG-13   *****
Orson Welles, Joseph Cotten, Agnes Moorhead
Orson Welles

The Shining                     1980     R       ****
Jack Nicholson, Shelley Duvall
Stanley Kubrick
```

Of course, these aren't the results you wanted. (The Jack Nicholson film is rated only four stars!) You then rewrite the query to better articulate the search:

```
SELECT title, release, censorrtg, starrtg, actors, directors
  FROM title
 WHERE (actors like '%Jack Nicholson%' OR directors =
        'Orson Welles')
   AND starrtg = '*****'
```

(Don't let the position of the AND expression at the end fool you; no matter where they are placed within the WHERE clause, ANDed expressions have higher precedence.)

The results become

```
Film Title                    Release  Censor  Critic's Choice
---------------------------   -------  ------  ---------------
Starring
-----------------------------------------------------------
Directors
-----------------------------------------------------------
Citizen Kane                  1941     PG-13   *****
Orson Welles, Joseph Cotten, Agnes Moorhead
Orson Welles
```

Satisfied, you save the updated query to the "5STARS" file; if desired, you can also go into your text editor and edit the file. Perhaps you want to add remarks, some column format commands used repeatedly, a CLEAR BUFFER command to clear the current SQL buffer before loading the new query, and the SPOOL file command, which writes the results of the query out to the named file. If so, the "5STARS" file might include

```
rem *    Script to execute 5 Star Films by Orson Welles
rem *    or starring Jack Nicholson.

COLUMN title      FORMAT a45     HEADING 'Film Title'
COLUMN release    FORMAT a8      HEADING 'Released'
COLUMN starrtg    FORMAT a15     HEADING "Critic's Choice"
COLUMN censorrtg  FORMAT a6      HEADING 'Censor'
COLUMN directors                 HEADING 'Director'
COLUMN actors                    HEADING 'Starring'
COLUMN awards                    HEADING 'Academy Awards'
COLUMN runtime                   HEADING 'Running Time'
```

continued

```
CLEAR BUFFER
SPOOL 5STARS.lis

SELECT title, release, censorrtg, starrtg, actors, directors
  FROM title
 WHERE (actors like '%Jack Nicholson%' OR directors =
        'Orson Welles')
   AND starrtg = '*****'

SPOOL OFF
rem * end
```

To retrieve this file and edit it on-line, enter

```
SQL> GET 5STARS
```

You may also run the query directly from the file by entering

```
SQL> START 5STARS
```

Using Parameters in the Command File

By using parameters, you can execute a query that searches for different criteria *each time* the query is run. Quite often, you will build a query and want to reuse it, modifying the search criteria only slightly. Normally, you would have to rewrite the query and save it to a new command file.

A much easier way is to enter one or more parameters after the START command, and you get the same results as if the parameters had been written into the command itself. This is a neat trick; the technique is to embed a substitution variable in the WHERE clause of the command, instead of the specific search criteria.

Take a simple query, one that retrieves all the films in which Tom Cruise stars:

```
SELECT title, release censorrtg, starrtg, actors, directors
  FROM title
 WHERE actors like '%Tom Cruise%'
```

Save this query to a file named "STARRING." Now suppose you also want to review the films in which *other* actors or actresses have starred, such as Jack Nicholson or Vivian Leigh. Instead of writing separate queries for each new actor or actress, simply substitute the value "Tom Cruise" with an ampersand (&) followed by one numeral for each parameter. Enter

```
SELECT title, release censorrtg, starrtg, actors, directors
  FROM title
 WHERE actors like '%1%'
```

When you START the command, you can then specify the name of any actor or actress you want, and the query will execute as though that name had been written in the command originally. You might enter

```
SQL> START starring 'Vivian Leigh'
old 3: where actors like '%1%'
new 3: where actors like '%Vivian Leigh%'
```

ORACLE displays the line number of the original command and the variable that will be substituted, and then it returns these results:

```
Film Title                Release  Censor  Critic's Choice
----------------------    -------  ------  ---------------
Starring
------------------------------------------------------------
Directors
------------------------------------------------------------
Gone with the Wind        1939     G       *****
Clark Gable, Vivian Leigh, Leslie Howard
Victor Fleming
```

If you want to suppress the display of the "old" and "new" lines, you can enter the environment command SET VERIFY OFF.

Summary

This chapter introduced you to the power of SQL and ORACLE's SQL extensions, SQL*Plus. You learned a few basic SQL commands, and also some fundamental formatting techniques. This chapter covered

▶ Specifying columns in a table

▶ Formatting columns

▶ The ORDER BY clause to control the order of displayed rows

▶ The WHERE clause to retrieve specific rows

▶ The AND and OR operators of the WHERE clause

▶ The GROUP BY clause for working with groups of rows

▶ SQL Edit commands

▶ Building a SQL command file

6

Advanced SQL Capabilities

6

Advanced SQL Capabilities

Chapter 6 takes you to the next level of mastering SQL—working with advanced SQL functions. This chapter builds on what you've learned so far. It highlights the concepts and techniques of constructing complex SELECT statements and demonstrates some additional SQL functions which allow you to design more elaborate queries. These advanced SQL capabilities include

- ▶ Character, arithmetic and date expressions
- ▶ Subqueries
- ▶ Multiple subqueries
- ▶ Relational joins
    - Multi-way joins
    - Outer joins
- ▶ Views

Working with Character Expressions

Character values, such as products, titles, customers, addresses, and other text, are normally displayed in the same form as they were entered into the database. If you entered a title code in uppercase, for example, it will be displayed in uppercase—unless you enlist one of the many SQL*Plus *character expressions* or *functions* that can transform the way character values appear when displayed.

153

SQL*Plus lets you combine character columns and constants (the CHAR values themselves) into *character expressions*. A character expression can be manipulated and selected as though it were a single column.

A discussion of some useful character expressions follows.

Field Concatenation

One prevalent use of character expressions is to string two or more columns together and display them as a single column. This is called *field concatenation*.

To concatenate fields, you use the concatenate operator (¦¦) in a query like this:

```
SELECT category¦¦description
  FROM category
```

The result would be

```
CATEGORY¦¦DESCRIPTION
--------------------
100ADVENTURE
120COMEDY
135CLASSICS
140MUSICALS
165HORROR
899SLASHER
```

Squished together, the values are unintelligible. When concatenating fields, SQL*Plus removes any *trailing blanks* (the blank spaces after the last character and to the end of the field) in the first column you specify. To fix the appearance of the display, you might separate the values with literal blanks enclosed in single quotes and perhaps add an alias column name like this:

```
SELECT category¦¦' '¦¦description "Film Category"
  FROM category
```

to return

```
Film Category
-----------------------------------
100 ADVENTURE
120 COMEDY
135 CLASSICS
140 MUSICALS
165 HORROR
899 SLASHER
```

LOWER Function

Perhaps you don't care for the overshadowing appearance of the upper-case description values. Change this with the LOWER function:

```
SELECT category¦¦' '¦¦ LOWER(description) "Film Category"
  FROM category
```

and you would get

```
Film Category
---------------------------------------
100 adventure
120 comedy
135 classics
140 musicals
165 horror
899 slasher
```

INITCAP Function

This still doesn't look right to you. It would probably improve the appearance to capitalize the first character of description and make the other characters lowercase. You would use the INITCAP function instead:

```
SELECT category¦¦' '¦¦ INITCAP(description) "Film Category"
  FROM category
```

which displays

```
Film Category
---------------------------------------
100 Adventure
120 Comedy
135 Classics
140 Musicals
165 Horror
899 Slasher
```

LENGTH Function

Having worked with the COLUMN command, you have learned how to adjust column widths of individual columns. Some additional character functions provide even greater flexibility in adjusting column widths and positioning columns in reports.

To verify the *length* of the character values stored in a column, you can use the LENGTH function:

```
SELECT category, LENGTH(description)
  FROM category
```

This returns

```
CATEGORY   LENGTH(DESCRIPTION)
--------   -------------------
     100                     9
     120                     6
     135                     8
     140                     8
     165                     6
     899                     7
```

The LENGTH function can also figure as a condition in the WHERE clause of a query. Suppose you are having difficulty fitting columns within a limited space on a report. You have eight characters to work with and want to know whether any description values are more than eight characters long. You enter

```
SELECT category, LENGTH(description)
  FROM category
 WHERE LENGTH(description) > 8;
```

to learn, unfortunately:

```
CATEGORY   LENGTH(DESCRIPTION)
--------   -------------------
     100                     9
```

RPAD and LPAD Functions

The RPAD (right pad) and LPAD (left pad) functions justify character values to either the right or left of the string; leading or trailing blanks are padded with any character you choose for the length of the field specified in the command.

The following RPAD example right justifies the Title column and fills in blanks with periods to make the lines easier to read. This is a standard convention in Tables of Contents, for example.

```
   SELECT prodno, RPAD(title, 45, '.') "Titles", cost
     FROM product, title
    WHERE product.titlecd = title.titlecd
ORDER BY prodno
```

gets you

```
Product  Titles                                        Cost
-------  --------------------------------------------- -----
P100V    The Sound of Music ......................... 19.95
P200V    Topgun ..................................... 29.95
P300B    Gone with the Wind ......................... 59.95
P300V    Gone with the Wind ......................... 59.95
P450V    Citizen Kane ............................... 49.95
P470B    Ghostbusters ............................... 19.95
P470V    Ghostbusters ............................... 19.95
P475V    The Hitcher ................................ 79.95
P480V    The Shining ................................ 69.95
```

The only difference between the RPAD and the LPAD function is that in the LPAD function fill characters are added to the left of the specified character string. LPAD is particularly useful for right justifying columns on a report.

Suppose you are working with CUSTOMER addresses which are to be printed out on invoices, labels, or reports. You want to restrict address information to 35 character fields and present a uniform appearance; however, the variable length of the CITY, STATE, and ZIP code fields seems to complicate matters. (The CITY column is 20 characters wide, the STATE column is fixed at 2 characters, and the ZIP column is 10 characters wide to accommodate both 5- and 10-digit zip codes. This yields a total of 32 possible characters.) Solving this problem is tricky, but it can be done by a combination of concatenating the CITY, STATE, and ZIP fields and left justifying ZIP fields and padding the values with blanks. Here are the results you're looking for:

```
Address
------------------------------
San Francisco, CA       94109
Belmont, CA             94020
Berkeley, CA         94707-4444
```

Concatenating the CITY and STATE fields is a straightforward process. Separate them with a comma followed by a space, like this:

```
SELECT city||', '||state
```

Figuring out how to concatenate *and* left justify the ZIP field is the tricky part. The CITY fields vary in length, so you cannot specify a constant field length when padding the ZIP field. For example, given the above values, if you were to specify the width of the ZIP field as 15 characters like this

```
SELECT city||', '||state||LPAD(zip, 15, ' ')
```

and attempt to squeeze each line within 35 characters, the ZIP values would not fit:

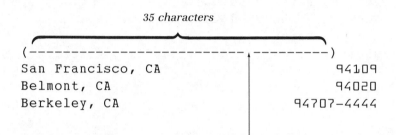

35 characters

```
(---------------------------,----------)
San Francisco, CA                  94109
Belmont, CA                        94020
Berkeley, CA                  94707-4444
```

end of concatenated CITY, STATE column

One way to nail down the width of the ZIP field is by specifying the length of the variable CITY field as the column width—instead of a constant value—and then doing some arithmetic. Observe:

```
SELECT city||', '||state||LPAD(ZIP, (35-4-(LENGTH(CITY))), ' ')
    "Address"
```

The width expression in the LPAD function translates to

"Take the 35-character width of your address, subtract 4 characters (the combined length of the comma, space, and constant STATE field), then subtract the variable length of the CITY field (which SQL*Plus learns from the LENGTH function.)"

SUBSTR and DECODE Functions

SUBSTR and DECODE are popular character functions often used in concert with one another. The SUBSTR function lets you extract part of a character string (hence its name, *sub-string*) and display only that part, while DECODE works in complementary fashion, letting you expand the display of a character value into longer, more intuitive text. DECODE enables you to substitute expressions as well as constants, opening the door to powerful IF-THEN-ELSE validation processing on column values.

Perhaps you have built some intelligence into the Video Quest product codes. All film-related products have a letter designator at the end of the code to signify the format of the film (V for VHS, B for Beta, C for Compact Disc). The SUBSTR function could be used to extract this piece of information and display the product code in two parts, like so:

```
SELECT SUBSTR(prodno, 1, 4), SUBSTR(prodno, 5, 1)
  FROM product
  ORDER BY prodno
```

with the result:

```
SUBS S
---- -
P100 V
P200 V
P300 B
P300 V
P450 V
P470 B
P470 V
P475 V
P480 V
P500
```

The format of the SUBSTR function is as follows:

```
                   CHAR string
                     |
                 ⌒⌒⌒⌒
SELECT SUBSTR(prodno, 1, 4) . . .
                     | |
              start position   extract this many characters
```

Having extracted the format code with SUBSTR, you can now utilize the DECODE function to expand the code into more meaningful text. DECODE takes each substring value that is returned and translates it into the text string specified in the command. Observe:

```
SELECT SUBSTR(prodno, 1, 4),
       DECODE(SUBSTR(prodno, 5, 1), 'V', 'Vhs', 'B', 'Beta','C',
              'Compact Disc', null, 'Non-Film', 'Not Applicable')
  FROM product
```

This yields

```
SUBS DECO
---- ----
P100 Vhs
P200 Vhs
P300 Beta
P300 Vhs
P450 Vhs
P470 Beta
P470 Vhs
P475 Vhs
P480 Vhs
P500 Non-Film
```

The DECODE function requires three variables—the character string column, a value, and the text to be substituted for this value. The DECODE function in the example

```
DECODE(SUBSTR(prodno, 5, 1), 'V', 'Vhs', 'B', 'Beta','C',
          'Compact Disc', null, 'Non-Film', 'Not Applicable')
```

translates to

"For every value 'V', display 'VHS';

For every value 'B', display 'Beta';

For every value 'C', display 'Compact Disc';

For every null value, display 'Non-Film';

If no match, display the default 'Not Applicable'."

DECODE is a powerful function. By expanding text, DECODE enables the application to store values in abbreviated, coded format to conserve costly disk storage space. Further, by allowing expressions as well as constants, DECODE can be used to perform powerful IF-THEN-ELSE logic on values.

Table 6.1 summarizes the character functions we've discussed and others less frequently used.

Table 6.1   SQL*Plus Character Functions

Function	Purpose
DECODE	Translates a string to another string. Translates constants as well as expressions to perform IF-THEN-ELSE validation processing.
INITCAP	Capitalizes only the first character of a string.
INSTR	Finds the position of a substring in a string.
LENGTH	Returns the length of a string.
LOWER	Converts a string to lowercase.
RPAD/LPAD	Pads blanks with any chosen character to the right or left of a string.
RTRIM/LTRIM	Erases blanks to the right of left of a string.
SOUNDEX	Finds values whose consonants sound similar to a string.
SUBSTR	Extracts a substring from a string.
UPPER	Converts a string to uppercase.

Working with Arithmetic Expressions

Similar to character expressions, number columns and values can be combined in *arithmetic expressions*. You can perform calculations in an arithmetic expression and display the result as if it were an actual column. Arithmetic expressions can also be used as selection criteria in the WHERE clause of a query, or to perform calculations with group functions. Arithmetic operations support the standard arithmetic operators:

+	Add
−	Subtract
*	Multiply
/	Divide

For example, suppose you want to calculate the rental fee for a film that is being rented for two days. You would use an arithmetic expression to multiply the *rentdays* by the rate per day of the film, and display this in Rental Fee, a virtual column. Observe:

```
SELECT catnum, rentdays, (rentdays * 3.00) "Rental Fee"
  FROM rentals
 WHERE catnum = 300
```

This yields

```
Catalog Rentdays Rental Fee
------- -------- ----------
    300        2       6.00
```

Suppose you want to retrieve all the tapes which brought a rental fee of $3.00 or less per transaction. (For simplicity, let's assume that the daily rental rate for each tape is $3.00.) To perform this calculation, you would enter

```
SELECT memberid, catnum, dateout, schdrtn, actrtn
  FROM rentals
 WHERE (rentdays * 3.00) <= 3.00
```

and get

Member Id	Catalog	Date Rented	Scheduled Return	Actual Return
1	100	15-MAR-88	11-APR-88	16-MAR-88
2	200	28-MAR-88	29-MAR-88	29-MAR-88
2	480	10-APR-88	11-APR-88	

Now you want to select the average rental fee taken in for all rental transactions. This calculation employs the AVG group function:

```
SELECT AVG(rentdays * 3.00)
  FROM rentals
```

and results in

```
AVG(RENTDAYS*3.00)
------------------
4.71428571
```

Arithmetic Functions

By default, SQL*Plus displays numbers with up to ten digits of numeric precision. For most applications, money fields require only two decimal positions. The ROUND function rounds numbers and expressions *up* to the specified decimal position, while the complementary TRUNC function truncates numbers and expressions to the specified position.

To display the average rental fee of all transactions, rounded to the nearest cent, for example, enter:

```
SELECT ROUND(AVG(rentdays * 3.00), 2)
  FROM rentals
```

to get

```
ROUND(AVG(RENTDAYS*3.00),2)
---------------------------
                       4.71
```

The NVL Function

When working with arithmetic expressions, you must take into account whether a column contains null values. A null is not a number—it is the absence of value—and it does not abide by the rules of arithmetic. *Anything added to or subtracted from a null value is a null value*. If you plan to do arithmetic on a column containing nulls, then you must convert the nulls to numeric values or else the calculations will be skewed. SQL*Plus provides the NVL function to do this. The NVL function can also be used to display the meaning of a null in a column, as in our earlier DECODE example, where a null value translated to the string 'Not Applicable', for example, NVL(*col*, 'Not Applicable').

Suppose you are generating rental receipt totals at the end of the day to balance the cash register. Working with the INVOICE table, you calculate the total amount taken in for all rental transactions (*total*), and perform a separate calculation for the total tax received (*tax*). A third calculation combines the two in the same query to generate a grand total. The NVL function is used just in case null values exist in either the *total* or *tax* column. You enter

```
SELECT nvl(sum(total), 0) "Total",
       nvl(sum(tax), 0) "Tax",
       (nvl(sum(total), 0) + nvl(sum(tax), 0)) "Grand Total"
  FROM invoice
 WHERE trantype = 'R'
```

which might yield

```
Total   Tax  Grand Total
-----   ----  -----------
   24  1.61        25.61
```

Table 6.2 summarizes the SQL*Plus arithmetic functions you can use in expressions.

Table 6.2 SQL*Plus Number Functions

Function	Purpose
ABS(*number*)	Returns the absolute value of a positive or a negative number.
CEIL(*number*)	Returns the smallest integer greater than or equal to *number*.
GREATEST(*value1, value2 . . .*)	Returns the MAX value in a list of number values.
LEAST(*value1, value2 . . .*)	Returns the MIN value in a list of number values.
MOD(*number1, number2*)	Returns the remainder of *number1* when divided by *number2*.
NVL(*expression, expression*)	Converts null values in an *expression* with a character or numeric *expression*.
POWER(*number1, number2*)	Raises *number1* to the power of *number2*.
ROUND(*number*[, *decimal places*])	Rounds *number* up to *decimal places*; default is 2.
SIGN(*number*)	Gives −1 if *number* <0; 0 if *number* = 0; 1 if *number* > 0.
SQRT(*number*)	Gives the square root of *number*.
TRUNC(*number*[, *decimal places*])	Truncates *number* to *decimal places*; default is 0.

Working with Dates

Columns defined with the DATE data type store both a date and a time for each value. By default, the time in a DATE field is 12:00 am (midnight) if no time is entered. ORACLE dates are stored on disk in a special format—the number of days since 4712 BC and the number of seconds since midnight last night. High noon on April Fool's Day, 1987, would be internally stored as 2447252/43200, for example; almost two and a half million days have elapsed since the 4712 BC origin date. (There are 86,400 seconds in a day, so high noon represents 43,200 seconds.)

Date Format Conversions

When date values are retrieved by a query, ORACLE displays the values in the default format 'DD-MON-YY', or '25-DEC-88'. You can change this default format by converting the date value into a character string in a new *format mask*, or pattern. SQL*Plus has countless format masks giving you a lot of flexibility in how you display dates.

For example, perhaps you want to display the scheduled return date of all outstanding rental tapes in a different format to make it stand out. You would enter

```
SELECT memberid, catnum, dateout, rentdays, TO_CHAR(schdrtn,
       'FMDay FMMonth DD, YYYY') "Scheduled Return"
  FROM rental
 WHERE actrtn is null
```

to retrieve

Member Id	Catalog	Date Rented	Days	Scheduled Return
1	200	09-APR-88	2	Monday April 11, 1988
1	300	09-APR-88	2	Monday April 11, 1988
1	470	10-APR-88	2	Tuesday April 12, 1988
2	480	10-APR-88	1	Monday April 11, 1988
3	301	12-APR-88	2	Thursday April 14, 1988

Note that both the DAY and MONTH format elements have been pre-fixed with 'FM' for *fill-mode*. Fill-mode suppresses any blank padding, leaving a variable-length date output format for a uniform, attractive format display.

The conversion of the *schdrtn* date column to a character string in the above format translates to

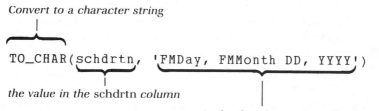

Convert to a character string

TO_CHAR(schdrtn, 'FMDay, FMMonth DD, YYYY')

the value in the schdrtn *column*

in the date format 'Monday, April 11, 1988'

When you want to store a date whose format has been changed, you must convert the date back to its ORACLE default format. While you use the TO_CHAR function to convert a date to a character string, the converse operation requires the TO_DATE function.

To convert the string back to a date format acceptable to ORACLE for internal storage, enter

Convert to ORACLE date format

TO_DATE(TO_CHAR(schdrtn, 'FMDay, FMMonth DD, YYYY'))

the character string in the schdrtn *column*

currently in 'Monday, April 11, 1988' format

Converting Constants

If you want to convert a constant string to a date, you must first convert it to a date and then to a character string in the specified format. The two-step conversion is required because the value must be a date value to change its format mask—which is why it is necessary to convert the value to a character string in the first place.

Consider the constant character string '01-APR-88'. To convert this string to a date format in the following mask, you enter

```
SELECT TO_CHAR(TO_DATE('01-APR-88'), 'FMMonth DDth,
      YYYY')
  FROM dual
```

and get

```
TO_CHAR(TO_DATE('01-APR-88'), 'FMMonth DDTH, YYYY')
--------------------------------------------------
April 01ST, 1988
```

Although the string '01-APR-88' appears to be in the ORACLE default date format, it is merely a character string to SQL*Plus because you haven't retrieved it from a DATE column. In the above example, the string has been converted *outside* the tables created in your database application. An ORACLE-supplied table, DUAL, has been used to perform the conversion.

DUAL is a one-column, one-row *dummy* table containing the value 'X.' DUAL is a device to let you test SQL SELECT statements or data manipulation operations without having to modify legitimate production tables. Because DUAL is the smallest conceivable table, you get better performance using it to test values than using one of your production tables. DUAL serves to satisfy SQL syntax, which demands that you must SELECT FROM a table, or the statement will fail with a syntax error. When selecting from DUAL, the SQL statement you are testing is *true* if a single row is returned; conversely, the statement is *false* if the row is not returned.

You will become adept at using both the TO_CHAR and TO_DATE functions after practicing with the date format conversion exercises in the following chapter.

Date Format Masks

The *SQL*Plus Reference Guide* charts the numerous date format masks allowed by SQL*Plus. Here is just a sampling of possibilities for a single date, April 1, 1988:

Date Format Mask	Displays
'Day, Month DD, YY'	Friday, April 1, 88
'FMMonth DDth, YYYY'	April 01st, 1988
'DD, FMMonth YYYY'	01, April 1988
'Dy MON DD YY'	Fri APR 1 88
'MM/DD/YY'	04/01/88
'MM.DD.YY'	04.01.88
'FMMonth DD, YYYY am HH24'	April 1, 1988 am
'DY-MON-DD-YY HH:MM:SS'	FRI APR-01-88 12:00:00

Date Arithmetic

Dates can be manipulated in arithmetic expressions just as numbers can. In fact, dates *are* numbers to ORACLE because they are internally stored as numbers. The date arithmetic operations you may use are

date + number	Adds a number of days to a date, producing a later date.
date − number	Subtracts a number of days from a date, producing an earlier date.
date − date	Subtracts one date from another, producing the number of days that has elapsed between them.

Let's say you want to calculate when a rental tape is due. On April 1st, this rental tape was checked out for two days. A simple date calculation:

```
SELECT catnum, dateout, (dateout + 2) "Scheduled Return"
  FROM rentals
 WHERE catnum = 100
```

yields the Scheduled Return Date:

```
          Date
Catalog   Rented    Scheduled Return
-------   --------- ----------------
    100   01-APR-88 03-APR-88
```

This is precisely the method used to determine the scheduled return date for every rental transaction in Video Quest's SQL*Forms application; the calculated date is ultimately committed to the *schdrtn* column in the RENTALS table.

Take this example a step further. Suppose you want to calculate the number of days each outstanding rental tape is late in being returned. To get this answer, you must calculate the number of days that have elapsed between the scheduled return date and the current date. You would request

```
SELECT memberid, catnum, dateout, schdrtn,
       (sysdate - schdrtn) "Days Late"
  FROM rentals
 WHERE actrtn is null
```

to get this result:

```
                       Date       Scheduled
Member Id   Catalog    Rented     Return      Days Late
---------   -------    ------     ------      ---------
        1       200    09-APR-88  11-APR-88   22.818669
        1       300    09-APR-88  11-APR-88   22.818669
        1       470    10-APR-88  12-APR-88   21.818669
        2       470    10-APR-88  11-APR-88   22.818669
        3       301    12-APR-88  14-APR-88   19.818669
```

Notice that the date expression uses a virtual or *pseudo-column*, *sysdate*, to perform the arithmetic. *Sysdate* represents the current date and time, derived from the system clock on your host computer. *Sysdate* acts like any other date value in arithmetic expressions and is invaluable for calculating past or future dates and lapses of time between dates.

Calculations with *sysdate* invariably return a fractional number. Like any other date column, *sysdate* stores both a date and time. In this application, however, we've elected to specify only the date value for *schdrtn*, not the exact time. (If you do not specify a time when inserting a date value, ORACLE assigns a default time of 12:00 midnight.) When the current date and time of *sysdate* are subtracted from the *schdrtn* date, then a fractional number results.

You can use either the ROUND or the TRUNC function to ensure that the result of this rounded to a whole number. Both ROUND and TRUNC set the time of each date value to 12:00 AM (noon). By making the time of day the same for each value, you cancel out the effect the difference in time has on the calculation. The nature of your application should dictate which function to use; ROUND rounds up to the nearest whole number, while TRUNC truncates to the nearest whole number.

Applying TRUNC to the above query like this:

```
SELECT memberid, catnum, dateout, schdrtn,
       TRUNC(sysdate - schdrtn) "Days Late"
  FROM rentals
 WHERE actrtn is null
```

produces

Member Id	Catalog	Date Rented	Scheduled Return	Days Late
1	200	09-APR-88	11-APR-88	24
1	300	09-APR-88	11-APR-88	24
1	470	10-APR-88	12-APR-88	23
2	480	10-APR-88	11-APR-88	24
3	301	12-APR-88	14-APR-88	21

We've used the TRUNC function to give a customer the benefit of the date. If a tape is returned before the store opens (as through a bulk drop window), the day after it is due, then TRUNC turns back the clock to midnight. Thus, grudgingly we treat returning the tape a half day late as acceptable.

Now that you know the number of days each tape is late, you can easily calculate the accrued late charges. You multiply the daily rental rate by the number of days each tape is late:

```
SELECT memberid, catnum, dateout, schdrtn,
       TRUNC(sysdate - schdrtn) "Days Late"
       (TRUNC(sysdate - schdrtn)) * ratepdy "Latecharge"
  FROM rentals
 WHERE actrtn is null
```

to produce

Member Id	Catalog	Date Rented	Scheduled Return	Days Late	Latecharge
1	200	09-APR-88	11-APR-88	24	72
1	300	09-APR-88	11-APR-88	24	60
1	470	10-APR-88	12-APR-88	23	69
2	480	10-APR-88	11-APR-88	24	96
3	301	12-APR-88	14-APR-88	21	52.5

Date Functions

SQL*Plus offers many functions to empower date arithmetic expressions. In the previous examples, you used numbers to add or subtract calendar days to and from dates. With the ADD_MONTHS function, you can manipulate calendar months in arithmetic expressions as well. For example, you can pinpoint the exact date six months from April 1st, 1988 by entering

```
SELECT ADD_MONTHS('01-APR-88', +6)
  FROM dual
```

which returns

```
ADD_MONTH
---------
01-OCT-88
```

To find the date six months ago, you can replace the +6 parameter with −6, which returns

```
ADD_MONTH
---------
01-OCT-87
```

Instead of using a constant, you can plug in the pseudo-column *sysdate*. To find the exact date 15 months from today (assume today's date is '15-APR-88'), enter

```
SELECT ADD_MONTHS(sysdate, +15)
  FROM dual
```

to display

```
ADD_MONTH
---------
15-JUL-89
```

Suppose you want to know the date of the last day of the current month. The LAST_DAY function applied to *sysdate* like this:

```
SELECT LAST_DAY(sysdate)
  FROM dual
```

returns

```
LAST_DAY
---------
30-APR-88
```

If you want the date of a specific day of the week, you use the NEXT_DAY function with *sysdate*. To determine the date of the following Monday (given that today's date is '15-APR-88', a Friday), you would enter

```
SELECT NEXT_DAY(sysdate, 'Mon')
  FROM dual
```

to display

```
NEXT_DAY
---------
18-APR-88
```

By combining date functions, you can build powerful search criteria. Suppose you want to analyze Video Quest's rental activity over a designated period of time. First display the tapes that been rented out over the last month (again, *sysdate* is '15-APR-88').

```
SELECT *
  FROM rentals
WHERE DATEOUT BETWEEN ADD_MONTHS(sysdate, +1) AND sysdate
```

The result is

Member ID	Catalog	Date Rented	Days	Scheduled Return	Actual Return	Rate
1	100	15-MAR-88	1	16-MAR-88	16-MAR-88	3
2	200	28-MAR-88	1	29-MAR-88	29-MAR-88	3
1	200	09-APR-88	2	11-APR-88		3
1	300	09-APR-88	2	11-APR-88		2.5
1	301	12-APR-88	2	14-APR-88		2.5
1	470	10-APR-88	2	12-APR-88		3
1	480	10-APR-88	1	11-APR-88		4

Now refine this query to display the tapes rented out *this month alone* (i.e., since the first of the month). You would do this by combining the LAST_DAY and ADD_MONTHS functions. Enter

```
SELECT *
  FROM rentals
 WHERE DATEOUT BETWEEN LAST_DAY(ADD_MONTHS(sysdate, -1)) + 1
   AND sysdate
```

This yields

Member ID	Catalog	Date Rented	Days	Scheduled Return	Actual Return	Rate
1	200	09-APR-88	2	11-APR-88		3
1	300	09-APR-88	2	11-APR-88		2.5
1	301	12-APR-88	2	14-APR-88		2.5
1	470	10-APR-88	2	12-APR-88		3
1	480	10-APR-88	1	11-APR-88		4

Since today's date is 15-APR-88, the WHERE clause breaks down as follows:

```
ADD_MONTHS(sysdate, -1)
```

yields

```
15-MAR-88
```

or "exactly one month ago today."

```
LAST_DAY(ADD_MONTHS(sysdate, -1)
```

yields

```
31-MAR-88
```

or "the last day of last month."

```
LAST_DAY(ADD_MONTHS(sysdate, -1) +1
```

yields

```
01-APR-88
```

or "add one day to the last day of last month."

Table 6.3 summarizes the SQL*Plus date functions you can use in arithmetic expressions.

Table 6.3   SQL*Plus Date Functions

Function	Purpose
ADD_MONTHS(*date*, +/− *number*	Adds or subtracts *number* of months to or from *date*.
GREATEST(*date1, date2*)	Returns latest date from a list.
LEAST(*date1, date2*)	Returns earliest date from a list.
LAST_DAY(*column*)	Displays the last day of the month containing *column*.
MONTHS_BETWEEN(*column1, column2*)	Displays the number of months between *column1* and *column2*.
NEXT_DAY(*column1, day*)	Returns the date of the first *day* after date in *column1*.
ROUND(*column* [*expression*])	Rounds *column* or *expression* to the nearest whole number.
TO_CHAR(*column, format mask*)	Converts date value in *column* to character string in *format mask*.
TO_DATE(*chardate, format mask*	Converts character string containing a date to a date value in *format mask*.

Building Subqueries

Subqueries let you build complex queries out of simple ones. A subquery—also termed a *nested SELECT*—is a complete and distinct query that is used in the WHERE or SET clause of a SQL command (a SELECT, INSERT, UPDATE, DELETE, or CREATE command). A complex query supporting a subquery is often more efficient to use than executing several individual queries. Depending on the nature of the search, a subquery can provide much greater precision, as well.

The key to knowing when to use a subquery is when your search condition itself depends on finding specific values stored in a table. In its simplest form, a subquery is used to locate the rows that contain these values; the values are then compared against the WHERE clause expression in the *main query* to find any matching rows.

For example, the query, "What products are as expensive as the *Ghostbusters*?" cannot be answered unless you first know the cost *value* of the *Ghostbusters* product. If the query is phrased in terms of an attribute (like *Ghostbusters* in this example) as opposed to a specific value (the *cost* of *Ghostbusters*), then this is a clue that you must enlist a subquery to find the answer.

Remember to be specific when expressing your query as a question. The question should be phrased explicitly in terms of actual attributes or table columns. This will make it easier to restate a question in the often confusing form of a subquery. The question, "What products are as expensive as the *Ghostbusters*?" should be rephrased as "Which products *cost* the same as the *Ghostbusters* product?" "Are any films longer than *Gone with the Wind?*" might become "What titles have a *runtime* longer than the title *Gone with the Wind?*"

Let's turn to the PRODUCT table to explore the notion of subqueries. Suppose you are interested in finding out which products cost the same as the products with the title code of SOUNDMUSIC. (Notice that we are using all uppercase letters for our title codes.) You need to determine a couple of things to get this answer. First, you must find out how much the SOUNDMUSIC products cost; second, you must find out whether any other products cost the same amount.

You could take the long route and execute separate queries to ultimately get the right answer. To find out how much the SOUNDMUSIC products cost, you would enter

```
SELECT cost
  FROM product
 WHERE titlecd = 'SOUNDMUSIC'
```

and get

```
   COST
-------
  19.95
```

With the cost in hand, you then use it to compare against the costs of all other products to see if any match. Enter

```
SELECT prodno, titlecd
  FROM product
 WHERE cost = 19.95
```

to yield

```
PRODNO  TITLECD
------  ------------
P470B   GHOSTBUSTERS
P470V   GHOSTBUSTERS
P100V   SOUNDMUSIC
```

Now a subquery added to a main query would do the same trick—and more efficiently. Combining the two simple queries, you can design a broader query to look like this:

```
SELECT prodno, titlecd
  FROM product
 WHERE cost =
       (SELECT cost
          FROM product
         WHERE titlecd = 'SOUNDMUSIC')
```

You then get

```
PRODNO  TITLECD
------  -----------
P470B   GHOSTBUSTERS
P470V   GHOSTBUSTERS
P100V   SOUNDMUSIC
```

The second query, or *inner query*, retrieves the information your main query depends on to satisfy its search criteria, namely, the cost of the product entitled SOUNDMUSIC. The main query, also called the *outer query*, ultimately displays the query results, while the inner query merely functions to pass the critical information up to the main query.

Subqueries Returning More Than One Row

The previous example illustrates the simplest kind of subquery—one that returns a value from a single row. (There is but one product with the title code, SOUNDMUSIC.) Quite often you won't be able to predict how many rows the subquery will return, or you may deliberately construct a subquery that returns values from more than one row. When a subquery returns multiple rows, the syntax of the query must be altered to accommodate this condition.

For example, suppose you wanted to find out the products that cost the same as those with the GHOSTBUSTERS title code, instead of the SOUNDMUSIC title code. The query would be exactly the same, except that you substitute GHOSTBUSTERS for SOUNDMUSIC in the WHERE clause of the subquery. Observe:

```
SELECT prodno, titlecd
  FROM product
 WHERE cost
       (SELECT cost
          FROM product
         WHERE titlecd = 'GHOSTBUSTERS')
```

The screen returns

```
ERROR: ORA-1427: single-row subquery returns more than
one row no records selected
```

The ORACLE error announces that this subquery, designed to return only one value, would actually return more than one value. (There are two GHOSTBUSTERS products, one Vhs and one Beta, and the products cost the same amount.) While this query is perfectly logical, you must modify the comparison operator in the WHERE clause of the main query (COST =) to allow for a multiple row comparison. When a subquery returns more than one value, you must use either the ANY or the ALL operators between the comparison operators (=, !=, >, >=, <, <=) and the subquery.

The ANY and ALL operators specify how multiple rows are to be used in the main query. The ANY operator is analogous to the OR operator that compares logical expressions; if *any* one of the multiple rows in a subquery is true, then the entire subquery is true. Conversely, the ALL operator is analogous to the AND operator; the entire subquery is true only if each and every row returned by the subquery is true.

In the above example, you must determine the cost of any product with the GHOSTBUSTERS title code to complete the query. Since you know that the cost of every GHOSTBUSTERS product is the same, you can safely use the ANY operator: the cost value for any one of the GHOSTBUSTERS products will suffice. Adding the ANY operator, you would now write the query as

```
SELECT prodno, titlecd
  FROM product
 WHERE cost = ANY
       (SELECT cost
          FROM product
         WHERE titlecd = 'GHOSTBUSTERS')
```

You may use abbreviations for the ANY and ALL operators. The IN operator may be substituted for = ANY, and NOT IN for != ALL. Users find the IN operator intuitively easier to use.

The following exercises utilize data from the PRODUCT and the TITLE tables. From here on out, the exercises will shift between various sample tables to better acquaint you with the contents of the Video Quest database.

You may want to reformat the PRODUCT columns before diving into these exercises. One strong suggestion is to create a format file, called

COLFORM.SQL, which contains the following column format definitions. You can continually add definitions as you experiment with new tables, and you can then reload the format definitions directly from the file without having to retype them.

```
COLUMN storeno      FORMAT 99999    HEADING 'Store'
COLUMN prodno       FORMAT a6       HEADING 'Product'
COLUMN prodtype     FORMAT a4       HEADING 'Type'
COLUMN description  FORMAT a12      HEADING 'Description'
COLUMN titlecd                      HEADING 'Title Code'
COLUMN cost         FORMAT 999.99   HEADING 'Cost'
COLUMN rentclass    FORMAT 999999   HEADING 'Rental!Class'
COLUMN qtyrecvd     FORMAT 99999    HEADING 'Qty!Recvd'
COLUMN qtyoh        FORMAT 999      HEADING 'Qty!Oh'
COLUMN qtysold      FORMAT 9999     HEADING 'Qty!Sold'
```

Suppose you want to review the product numbers and title codes of all products in the same rental class as product P470V, the GHOSTBUSTERS. A moderately simple subquery that returns multiple rows would achieve this. Your query must do two things: ascertain the rental class of the GHOSTBUSTERS (which happens to be rental class 10, General), then select the products that also fall under this rental class.

Exercise 6.1

To select the product numbers and title codes of the products assigned the same rental class as product P470V, GHOSTBUSTERS, enter

```
SELECT prodno, titlecd
  FROM product
 WHERE rentclass in
       (SELECT rentclass
          FROM product
         WHERE prodno = 'P470V')
```

You will get

```
Product  Title Code
-------  ------------
P470B    GHOSTBUSTERS
P470V    GHOSTBUSTERS
P100V    SOUNDMUSIC
P200V    TOPGUN
```

Subqueries Returning More Than One Column

Of the products in the same rental class as GHOSTBUSTERS, perhaps you only want to see those that cost the same as the GHOSTBUSTERS. This new condition narrows your search even further. The subquery must now select on two columns—the Rental Class *and* the Cost columns. For the query to be true, the subquery must return values for both of these columns.

Exercise 6.2
To list the product numbers and title codes of the products with the same rental class *and* cost as product P470V, the GHOSTBUSTERS, enter

```
SELECT prodno, titlecd
  FROM product
 WHERE (rentclass, cost) in
       (SELECT rentclass, class
          FROM product
         WHERE titlecd = 'GHOSTBUSTERS')
```

The query returns

```
Product   Title Code
-------   ------------
P470B     GHOSTBUSTERS
P470V     GHOSTBUSTERS
P100V     SOUNDMUSIC
```

Notice that both columns are enclosed in parentheses in the WHERE clause of the main query. When the subquery is to return more than one column, you must enclose the specified columns in parentheses *on this side* of the comparison operator. Observe also that the subquery is using the title code, GHOSTBUSTERS, as the search criteria instead of the product number, 'P470V'.

Using Multiple Subqueries

Perhaps you want to expand on this query. In addition to finding the products that share the rental class and cost of GHOSTBUSTERS, you also want to find the products that cost the same as the *most expensive product* in the table. This last fact is your clue to how to design the query. A group function must be used in the subquery to ascertain the cost of the most expensive product.

Exercise 6.3

To list the products, title codes, and costs of all products that share the rental class and cost of the GHOSTBUSTERS, *or* those that cost the same as the most expensive product, enter

```
SELECT prodno, titlecd, cost
  FROM product
 WHERE (rentclass, cost) in
       (SELECT rentclass, cost
          FROM product
         WHERE prodno = 'P470V')
   OR cost =
      (SELECT max(cost)
         FROM product)
```

You will get

Product	Title Code	Cost
P470B	GHOSTBUSTERS	19.95
P470V	GHOSTBUSTERS	19.95
P100V	SOUNDMUSIC	19.95
P475V	HITCHER	79.95

This complex query features multiple subqueries connected by the OR operator. Any number of combinations of subqueries and ordinary conditions connected by the AND and OR operators can be defined in the WHERE clause of a query.

The additional subquery uses the MAX group function. Since a group function returns a single value, a subquery is a perfect vehicle for combining a group function with a main query that returns individual results. (Recall our caveat against mixing a group function with a query that returns a value for each row.) In this query, the MAX function identifies the cost of the most expensive product and passes that value to the main query to satisfy the ORed condition.

Do not overuse multiple subqueries. Longer, more complex queries containing multiple combinations of subqueries and compound search conditions can become labrynthian—difficult to build and debug, and even harder to optimize. One can assume that the denser the query, the more processing the system must perform. By clarifying what information you want to retrieve and experimenting with various queries, you may discover a more direct path to your data, one that doesn't depend on a query weighted with multiple subqueries and numerous, often redundant, conditions. On the other hand, a complex query may very well be the most efficient means of extracting the data you need.

Try a couple of multiple subquery examples on your own.

Exercise 6.4

Find the product numbers and title codes of all products that cost less than product P480V, SHINING, and more than product P100V, SOUND-MUSIC. Enter

```
SELECT prodno, titlecd
  FROM product
 WHERE cost <
       (SELECT cost
          FROM product
         WHERE prodno = 'P480V')
   AND cost >
       (SELECT cost
          FROM product
         WHERE prodno = 'P100V')
```

to return

```
Product   Title Code
-------   ----------
P200V     TOPGUN
P300B     GONEWIND
P450V     CKANE
```

Exercise 6.5

Find the product numbers and title codes of all products that cost less than product P475V, HITCHER, and cost more than *any* of the products available in Beta format. Enter

```
SELECT prodno, titlecd
  FROM product
 WHERE cost <
       (SELECT cost
          FROM product
         WHERE prodno = 'P475V')
   AND cost > ANY
       (SELECT cost
          FROM product
         WHERE format = 'B')
```

This query returns

```
Product   Title Code
-------   ----------
P200V     TOPGUN
P300B     GONEWIND
P300B     GONEWIND
P450V     CKANE
P480V     SHINING
```

Referencing Different Tables in the Main and Inner Queries

Perhaps you want to see the titles of all video tape products that are available in Beta format. You must first find the title codes of all the Beta products, and then select the titles associated with these title codes. Two separate tables are referenced in this complex query: the main query references the TITLE table while the inner query references the PRODUCT table.

Exercise 6.6
To retrieve the titles of all video tape products available in Beta format, enter

```
SELECT title
  FROM title
 WHERE titlecd in
       (SELECT titlecd
          FROM product
         WHERE format = 'B')
```

This results in

```
Film Title
-----------------
Ghostbusters
Gone with the Wind
```

The title code is the primary key of the TITLE table, which also is the relational column for the PRODUCT table. Relational columns are used to retrieve values from separate tables for use in subqueries and to *join* rows from separate tables. (*Joining* is a wholly different topic which will be discussed shortly.)

Nested Subqueries

Let's recast the preceding query in a different light. Still focusing on Beta products, suppose you want to see the titles of all video tape products that cost more than the *average* cost of the Beta products. This query involves a *nested subquery*, or a subquery within a subquery. The innermost subquery will use the AVG group function to find the average cost of all Beta tape products.

Exercise 6.7
To list the titles of all video tape products which cost more than the average cost of those in Beta format, enter

```
SELECT title
  FROM title
 WHERE titlecd in
       (SELECT titlecd
          FROM product
         WHERE cost >
               (SELECT AVG(cost)
                  FROM product
                 WHERE format = 'B'))
```

to retrieve

```
Film Title
------------------
Citizen Kane
Gone with the Wind
The Hitcher
The Shining
```

If you were to dissect this complex query into its component subqueries, you would see the connections as follows:

```
     Innermost ─────────────────────→  Inner ──────────────────────→  Main
       Query                           Query                          Query
```

```
SELECT AVG(COST)          SELECT titlecd              SELECT title
  FROM product              FROM product                FROM title
 WHERE format = 'B'        WHERE cost > 39.95          WHERE . . .
```

yields   *yields*   *yields*

```
AVG(COST)                 Title Code                  Film Title
─────────                 ──────────────────          ──────────────────
    39.95                 HITCHER                     Citizen Kane
                          GONEWIND                    Gone with the Wind
                          GONEWIND                    The Hitcher
                          CKANE                       The Shining
                          SHINING
```

You will shift gears now and work with the TAPE table while experimenting with a few more complex subquery examples. You may want to add the following Catalog Number column to your COLFORM.SQL format file. *Catnum* is the primary key of the TAPE table and should be reformatted as

```
COLUMN catnum HEADING 'Catalog'
```

Suppose you want to peruse catalog and product numbers of rental-only tape products. To do this, you build a complex query that references both the TAPE and PRODUCT tables. The main query selects rows from the TAPE table, while the inner query selects rental-only products from the PRODUCT table. The relational column linking the two tables is *prodno*.

Exercise 6.8

To select catalog numbers and product numbers of all rental-only tapes, enter

```
SELECT catnum, prodno
  FROM tape
 WHERE prodno in
         (SELECT prodno
            FROM product
           WHERE prodtype = 'R')
```

You will get

```
Catalog  Product
--------- -------
      300  P300V
      301  P300V
```

Now refine the above query to retrieve the catalog and product numbers of the tapes that are *not* rental-only and whose cost is between $20 and $60.

Exercise 6.9
To select catalog and product numbers of the tapes that are not rental only and cost between $20 and $60, enter

```
SELECT catnum, prodno
  FROM tape
 WHERE prodno in
       (SELECT prodno
          FROM product
         WHERE prodtype != 'R'
           AND cost between 20 and 60)
```

The result is

```
Catalog  Product
--------- -------
      200  P200V
      201  P200V
      305  P300B
      450  P450V
      451  P450V
```

This next exercise adds even more muscle to the previous query. The challenge is to find the catalog numbers of the rental/sale products which have not sold a single copy and whose suggested retail price is greater than the minimum suggested retail price of all beta tapes. Your query will combine subqueries and ordinary conditions with the MIN group function nestled in a nested subquery.

Exercise 6.10
Find the catalog and product numbers of the rental/sale product types which have never been sold, and whose suggested retail price (the *suggrtl* column) is greater than the minimum suggested retail price of the beta products. Entering

```
SELECT catnum, prodno
  FROM tape
 WHERE prodno in
```

```
(SELECT prodno
   FROM product
  WHERE prodtype = 'RS'
    AND qtysold is null
    AND suggrtl >
        (SELECT min(suggrtl)
           FROM product
          WHERE format > 'B'))
```

results in

```
Catalog  Product
-------- -------
    200  P200V
    201  P200V
```

Relational Joins

One of the most powerful features of SQL is the ability to join tables—to retrieve information from several tables at once in a single SELECT statement. This capability is at the very heart of the relational model. The relational join gives SQL its characteristic logical data independence. Users needn't be concerned *where* the tables physically reside. To harvest information scattered across several tables, a user simply specifies the desired columns, the names of the tables where they reside, and how the tables are to be related.

Suppose you want to analyze historical information about Video Quest RENTAL transactions. First review the structure and contents of the RENTALS table with the generic statement

```
SELECT *
  FROM rentals
```

This returns

MEMBERID	CATNUM	INVNO	DATEOUT	RENTDAYS	SCHDRTN	ACTRTN	RATEPDY
1	100	1	15-MAR-88	1	16-MAR-88	16-MAR-88	3
2	200	2	28-MAR-88	1	29-MAR-88	29-MAR-88	3
1	200	3	09-APR-88	2	11-APR-88		3
1	300	4	09-APR-88	2	11-APR-88		2.5
1	470	5	10-APR-88	2	12-APR-88		3
2	480	6	10-APR-88	1	11-APR-88		4
3	301	7	12-APR-88	2	14-APR-88		2.5

7 records selected.

Before you proceed, you may want to reformat the columns of this new RENTALS table. Save the following definitions to your COLFORM.SQL format file:

```
COLUMN memberid     HEADING 'Member Id'
COLUMN invno        HEADING 'Invoice'      FORMAT 999
COLUMN dateout      HEADING 'Date!Rented'
COLUMN rentdays     HEADING 'Days'         FORMAT 999
COLUMN schdrtn      HEADING 'Scheduled!Return'
COLUMN actrtn       HEADING 'Actual!Return'
COLUMN ratepdy      HEADING 'Rate'         FORMAT 9999
```

The RENTALS table tracks rental tapes by catalog number. You realize immediately that you need more information to evaluate this data. For starters, you must know the Product Numbers (and perhaps the Store Numbers) associated with these tapes. Product numbers are the key to tapping a wealth of product information and related title information.

To locate product numbers for each tape, you must look to the TAPE table. Review the contents of the TAPE table by entering

```
SELECT *
  FROM tape
 ORDER by catnum
```

This query gets you

```
    Store   Catalog   Product
  --------   -------   -------
         1       100   P100V
         1       101   P100V
         1       200   P200V
         1       201   P200V
         1       300   P300V
         1       301   P300V
         1       305   P300B
         1       450   P450V
         1       451   P450V
         1       470   P470V
         1       471   P470V
         1       473   P470B
         1       475   P475V
         1       480   P480V
         1       481   P480V
15 records selected.
```

Now you want to execute a single SELECT statement that combines the tables and produces a joint listing. By joining the tables, you can fill in the product information absent from the RENTALS table. How would you do this? Your first guess might be to issue SELECT * from both tables, as in

```
SELECT *
  FROM rentals, tape
```

But that would be wrong. Try it and see what happens:

Store	Catalog	Product	Member Id	Catalog	Date Rented	Days	Scheduled Return	Actual Return	Rate	Invno
1	100	P100V	1	100	15-MAR-88	1	16-MAR-88	16-MAR-88	3	1
1	101	P100V	1	100	15-MAR-88	1	16-MAR-88	16-MAR-88	3	1
1	200	P200V	1	100	15-MAR-88	1	16-MAR-88	16-MAR-88	3	1
1	201	P200V	1	100	15-MAR-88	1	16-MAR-88	16-MAR-88	3	1
1	300	P300V	1	100	15-MAR-88	1	16-MAR-88	16-MAR-88	3	1
1	301	P300V	1	100	15-MAR-88	1	16-MAR-88	16-MAR-88	3	1
1	305	P300B	1	100	15-MAR-88	1	16-MAR-88	16-MAR-88	3	1
1	450	P450V	1	100	15-MAR-88	1	16-MAR-88	16-MAR-88	3	1
1	451	P470V	1	100	15-MAR-88	1	16-MAR-88	16-MAR-88	3	1
1	470	P470V	1	100	15-MAR-88	1	16-MAR-88	16-MAR-88	3	1
1	471	P470V	1	100	15-MAR-88	1	16-MAR-88	16-MAR-88	3	1
1	473	P470V	1	100	15-MAR-88	1	16-MAR-88	16-MAR-88	3	1
1	475	P470V	1	100	15-MAR-88	1	16-MAR-88	16-MAR-88	3	1
1	480	P470V	1	100	15-MAR-88	1	16-MAR-88	16-MAR-88	3	1
1	481	P470V	1	100	15-MAR-88	1	16-MAR-88	16-MAR-88	3	1
1	100	P100V	1	200	28-MAR-88	1	29-MAR-88	29-MAR-88	3	2
1	101	P100V	1	200	28-MAR-88	1	29-MAR-88	29-MAR-88	3	2
1	200	P200V	1	200	28-MAR-88	1	29-MAR-88	29-MAR-88	3	2
1	201	P200V	1	200	28-MAR-88	1	29-MAR-88	29-MAR-88	3	2
.						.	.	.		
.						.	.			
1	481	P480V	1	100	12-APR-88	2	14-APR-88		4	7

```
105 records selected.
```

Both tables are indeed joined, but the information is anything but useful. SQL has merely taken each row of the RENTALS table, and tacked on to the front of it *each row* of the TAPE table; the combined result thus displays all possible combinations of rows. Since the RENTALS table contains 7 records and the TAPE table contains 15 records, the errant join displays the total possible combination, 105 records. (7 records times 15 = 105 records.) This exhaustive compilation of information is referred to as the *Cartesian product* of the two tables, a far cry from a relational join.

Note that the Catalog Number column appears twice in this display. *Catnum* is the column that both tables have in common; it is the *join column*. When relating these two tables, you are only interested in displaying the rows where the catalog number in the TAPE table *is the same as* the catalog number in the RENTALS table. Any other displayed rows, as in the Cartesian example above, are meaningless for your present question. Your goal is to display the product and store numbers associated with each catalog number, so you only want to retrieve the rows where the catalog numbers in each table match.

To correctly join the rows from the RENTALS and TAPE tables, enter

```
SELECT *
  FROM rentals, tape
 WHERE rentals.catnum = tape.catnum
```

SQL does not employ a JOIN command to do a join; as shown in this example, one merely specifies the join column common to both tables in the WHERE clause of the query. This type of relational join is known as an *equi-join*, or the joining of two or more tables where the comparison operator in the WHERE predicate specifies an equality condition.

SQL adheres to a strict syntax convention for columns that appear in more than one table, however. Any time you list a column that exists in more than one referenced table, you must precede the column name with a table name followed by a period (table name.column name). Also bear in mind that it is not necessary to include columns in the SELECT list in order to join or ORDER BY them.

The result of this two-table join is

Store	Catalog	Product	Member Id	Catalog	Date Rented	Days	Scheduled Return	Actual Return	Rate	Invno
1	100	P100V	1	100	15-MAR-88	1	16-MAR-88	16-MAR-88	3	1
1	200	P200V	2	200	28-MAR-88	1	29-MAR-88	29-MAR-88	3	2
1	200	P200V	1	200	09-APR-88	2	11-APR-88		3	3
1	300	P300V	1	300	09-APR-88	2	11-APR-88		2.5	4
1	301	P300V	3	301	12-APR-88	2	14-APR-88		2.5	5
1	470	P470V	1	470	10-APR-88	2	12-APR-88		3	6
1	480	P480V	2	480	10-APR-88	1	11-APR-88		4	7

Again the Catalog column appears twice. You can prevent this by specifying the columns you want in the order they should appear. For example, you might enter

```
    SELECT memberid, tape.catnum, prodno, dateout, rentdays,
           schdrtn, actrtn
      FROM tape, rentals
     WHERE tape.catnum = rentals.catnum
  ORDER BY tape.catnum
```

and the results would be

Member Id	Catalog	Product	Date Rented	Days	Scheduled Return	Actual Return
1	100	P100V	15-MAR-88	1	16-MAR-88	16-MAR-88
2	200	P200V	28-MAR-88	1	29-MAR-88	29-MAR-88
1	200	P200V	09-APR-88	2	11-APR-88	
1	300	P300V	09-APR-88	2	11-APR-88	
3	301	P300V	12-APR-88	2	14-MAR-88	
1	470	P470V	10-APR-88	2	12-APR-88	
2	480	P480V	10-APR-88	1	11-APR-88	

Observe that the *catnum* column is qualified by a table name (tape.catnum) in the selection list and the ORDER BY clause. If you fail to precede every reference to *catnum* with a table name, ORACLE will return the error message:

```
ORA-0918: column ambiguously defined
```

As a matter of fact, you could have qualified the catnum column with the RENTALS table name (*rentals.catnum*) and the results would have been the same. SQL syntax requires the name of at least one of the tables in which this column appears.

Multi-Way Joins

Suppose you also want to display the Title Code for each tape. Title codes immediately identify the tapes that have been rented. While catalog and product numbers are critical pieces of information, they are not very meaningful to users by themselves.

Title codes are stored by product number in a third table—the PROD-UCT table. (The title code is a primary key of the TITLE table, and a foreign key of the PRODUCT table, as you recall.) Since you now know the product numbers for each tape, the product number is your clue for finding the associated title code.

To retrieve the title codes for each tape, your query must be expanded to perform a three-table join. Here is the query you would request:

```
    SELECT memberid, invno, tape.catnum, product.prodno,
           titlecd, rentdays, schdrtn, actrtn
      FROM rentals, tape, product
     WHERE rentals.catnum = tape.catnum
       AND tape.prodno = product.prodno
  ORDER BY tape.catnum
```

The result is the following (the *dateout* and *ratepdy* columns have been omitted to confine the results to an 80-character display):

```
                                                   Scheduled Actual
Member Id Invoice Catalog Product Title Code  Days Return    Return
--------- ------- ------- ------- ------------ ---- --------- ---------
        1       1     100 P100V   SOUNDMUSIC      1 16-MAR-88 16-MAR-88
        2       2     200 P200V   TOPGUN          1 29-MAR-88 29-MAR-88
        1       3     200 P200V   TOPGUN          2 11-APR-88
        1       4     300 P300V   GONEWIND        2 11-APR-88
        3       5     301 P300V   GONEWIND        2 14-MAR-88
        1       6     470 P470V   GHOSTBUSTERS    2 12-APR-88
        2       7     480 P480V   SHINING         1 11-APR-88
```

This three-table join combines columns extracted from the TAPE, RENTAL, and the PRODUCT tables. The TAPE and RENTAL tables are joined together by their common values in the *catnum* column, and the TAPE and PRODUCT tables are joined together by common values in the *prodno* column. Figure 6.1 illustrates this.

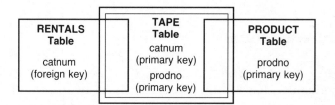

Figure 6.1   Three-Table Join

The Outer Join

When rows of one join table do not match any rows in another join table, they are usually not displayed. Sometimes, however, you will want to display these nonmatching rows.

Suppose you want to review the inventory positions of all Video Quest products. For readability, you want to include the titles of all film-related products in your query, which necessitates linking the TITLES and PRODUCTS tables on the Title Code column. Herein lies the problem. Products include both film and nonfilm items; films have title codes, whereas nonfilm products, such as blank cassettes, do not. A straight join of the TITLE and PRODUCT tables will retrieve only the products with matching title codes and will not display products without title codes. To get around this problem, you must use the *outer join* operator. An outer join lets you view the nonmatching rows as well.

Review the products currently stored in the PRODUCT table by requesting

```
SELECT prodno, description, titlecd
  FROM product
 ORDER BY prodno
```

You will get

Product	Title Codes	Description
P100V	SOUNDMUSIC	Film
P200V	TOPGUN	Film
P300B	GONEWIND	Film
P300V	GONEWIND	Film
P450V	CKANE	Film
P470B	GHOSTBUSTERS	Film
P470V	GHOSTBUSTERS	Film
P475V	HITCHER	Film
P480V	SHINING	Film
P500		BASF Blank Tape

You can see that product P500 is a nonfilm product, and has a null value in the title code slot. Ignore this fact for the moment and build your query to perform an ordinary join of the two tables. To join PRODUCTS and TITLES, you would enter

```
SELECT prodno, product.description, title, cost, qtyrecvd,
      qtyoh, qtysold
  FROM product, title
 WHERE product.titlecd = title.titlecd
 ORDER BY prodno
```

The results of the join are

Product	Description	Film Titles	Cost	Qty Recvd	Qty Oh	Qty Sold
P100V	Film	The Sound of Music	19.95	2	1	1
P200V	Film	Topgun	29.95	2	1	
P300B	Film	Gone with the Wind	59.95	1		1
P300V	Film	Gone with the Wind	59.95	2		
P450V	Film	Citizen Kane	49.95	2	1	1
P470B	Film	Ghostbusters	19.95	1	1	
P470V	Film	Ghostbusters	19.95	2	1	
P475V	Film	The Hitcher	79.95	1	1	
P480V	Film	The Shining	69.95	2		1

Now you modify the query to perform an outer join. The outer join operator is simply a plus sign, (+) added to the name of the matching column in the table where the missing rows are to be found.

If you request an outer join like this:

```
SELECT prodno, product.description, title, cost, qtyrecvd,
       qtyoh, qtysold
  FROM product, title
 WHERE product.titlecd = title.titlecd (+)
 ORDER BY prodno
```

the complete list follows:

Product	Description	Film Titles	Cost	Qty Recvd	Qty Oh	Qty Sold
P100V	Film	The Sound of Music	19.95	2	1	1
P200V	Film	Topgun	29.95	2	1	
P300B	Film	Gone with the Wind	59.95	1		1
P300V	Film	Gone with the Wind	59.95	2		
P450V	Film	Citizen Kane	49.95	2	1	1
P470B	Film	Ghostbusters	19.95	1	1	
P470V	Film	Ghostbusters	19.95	2	1	
P475V	Film	The Hitcher	79.95	1	1	
P480V	Film	The Shining	69.95	2		
P500	BASF Blank Tape		2.99	30	20	10

The outer join operator tells SQL to add null rows to the join result where there is a row in one table that does not match the other. You must be sure to place the outer join operator *after* the column name of the table that contains the missing rows, or the outer join will not work properly. For example, if you placed the operator like so:

```
WHERE product.titlecd (+) = title.titlecd
```

you will get the original incomplete result because there are no un-matched rows in the PRODUCT table. The TITLE table is the offender, for there is no title code in TITLE to match the null title code value for product P500.

Join Exercises

Practice working with relational joins on your own now by doing the following exercises. Any combination of ordinary conditions, compound expressions connected by AND and OR operators, or subqueries can be used in concert with joins to lend precision to your search. Such conditions may reference any column in *any* of the joined tables.

Exercise 6.11
Select the product numbers and titles of all products in VHS format; order the results by product number. (Hint: This is a two-table join of the PRODUCT and TITLE tables.) Enter

```
SELECT prodno, title
  FROM product, title
 WHERE product.titlecd = title.titlecd
 ORDER BY prodno
```

to get

```
Product Film Titles
------- ------------------
P100V   The Sound of Music
P200V   Topgun
P300B   Gone with the Wind
P300V   Gone with the Wind
P450V   Citizen Kane
P470B   Ghostbusters
P470V   Ghostbusters
P475V   The Hitcher
P480V   The Shining

9 records selected.
```

Once you've targeted the tables that must be joined, identify the join column. The join column contains the values common to both tables, and it is typically the primary key column of one table and a foreign key of the other table(s).

When writing join queries, get into the habit of referencing the join columns in the same order as the tables are listed. For example, the product table is listed before the title table in the example above; thus, the *product.titlecd* reference comes before the *title.titlecd* reference in the WHERE clause. This small tip will assist you in keeping your column and table references straight.

Exercise 6.12

Select the product number, title, runtime, and cost of all film products in VHS format that cost less than $50 and that have a running time of longer than *The Hitcher*; order the results by product number. Enter

```
SELECT prodno, title, runtime, cost
  FROM product, title
 WHERE product.titlecd = title.titlecd
   AND format = 'V'
   AND cost < 50
   AND runtime >
       (SELECT runtime
          FROM title
         WHERE title = 'The Hitcher')
```

to retrieve

Product	Film Titles	Running Time	Cost
P100V	The Sound of Music	172	19.95
P200V	Topgun	109	29.95
P450V	Citizen Kane	120	49.95
P470V	Ghostbusters	105	19.95

4 records selected.

Exercise 6.13

Select the product number, title, film category code and category description of the products that are *not* rental-only products; order the results by product number. Enter

```
SELECT prodno, title, category.category "Code"
       category.description "Category"
  FROM product, title, category
 WHERE product.titlecd title.titlecd
   AND title.category = category.category
   AND product.prodtype != 'R'
 ORDER BY prodno
```

and you get

```
Product  Film Titles         Code  Category
-------  ------------------  ----  --------
P100V    The Sound of Music  140   Musicals
P200V    Topgun              100   Adventure
P300B    Gone with the Wind  135   Classics
P450V    Citizen Kane        135   Classics
P470B    Ghostbusters        120   Comedy
P470V    Ghostbusters        120   Comedy
P475V    The Hitcher         165   Horror
P480V    The Shining         165   Horror
```

8 records selected.

Exercise 6.14

Select the Member ID, catalog number, product number, title, number of days rented, and scheduled return date of all outstanding rental tapes; order the results by scheduled return date. (Hint: This involves a four-table join.) Enter

```
SELECT memberid, tape.catnum, product.prodno, title,
       rentdays, schdrtn
  FROM rentals, tape, product, title
 WHERE rentals.catnum = tape.catnum
   AND tape.prodno = product.prodno
   AND product.titlecd = title.titlecd
   AND actrtn is null
 ORDER BY schdrtn
```

This returns the following (the actual return date, *actrtn*, is omitted because this query lists the tapes not yet returned):

Member Id	Catalog	Product	Title Code	Days	Scheduled Return
1	200	P200V	Topgun	2	11-APR-88
1	300	P300V	Gone with the Wind	2	11-APR-88
2	480	P480V	The Shining	1	11-APR-88
1	470	P470V	Ghostbusters	2	12-APR-88
3	301	P300V	Gone with the Wind	2	14-MAR-88

Exercise 6.15

Select the Member ID, catalog number, product number, title, film category, and scheduled return of the Adventure or Horror films still rented out; order the results by scheduled return date. (Hint: This is a five-table join.) Enter

```
SELECT memberid, tape.catnum, product.prodno, title,
       category.description "Category", schdrtn
  FROM rentals, tape, product, title, category
 WHERE rentals.catnum = tape.catnum
   AND tape.prodno = product.prodno
   AND product.titlecd = title.titlecd
   AND title.category = category.category
   AND actrtn is null
   AND category.description in ('Adventure', 'Horror')
 ORDER BY schdrtn
```

This returns the following (the *rentdays*, *ratepdy*, and *invno* columns are omitted to confine the display to an 80-column width):

Member Id	Catalog	Product	Film Titles	Category	Scheduled Return
1	200	P200V	Topgun	Adventure	11-APR-88
2	480	P480V	The Shining	Horror	11-APR-88

Creating Views

The complex five-table join you just entered requires a lot of manual typing to reproduce. It would be tedious to have to rekey the entire query every time you needed the information in this format. There are two alternatives to rekeying. You could save the query to a command file and start it up in either a form or a report procedure. Another method is to create a virtual table, known as a *view*, from the columns listed in the query.

A view is a window on the database. Through a view, information can be queried or modified in a single table or several tables at once. Views are often created for security reasons. With a view you can restrict user access to a subset of columns in a table, thus protecting sensitive information by controlling data access at the object level. (ORACLE security facilities are further discussed in Chapter 10, Advanced Concepts and Features.)

Views are also defined to simplify complex queries. Like a multi-paned window, a view can access information from the landscape of tables in the database. Here is how you would set up a view of a five-table join query:

```
CREATE VIEW rentals_out
(memberid, catnum, prodno, title, category, schdrtn)  ---¦
AS                                                        ¦
SELECT memberid, tape.catnum, product.prodno, title,  ---¦
       category.description, schdrtn
  FROM rentals, tape, product, title, category
 WHERE rentals.catnum = tape.catnum
   AND tape.prodno = product.prodno
   AND product.titlecd = title.titlecd
   AND title.category = category.category
   AND actrtn is null
```

You create a view just as you would create a table from another table (with the CREATE TABLE AS command). The column definitions and values for the RENTALS_OUT view are taken from the columns specified in the SELECT statement.

The chief difference between a view and a table is that a view exists only temporarily. It is an artifice; no physical table exists for RENTALS_OUT because the data remains in the *base* tables (TAPE, RENTALS, PRODUCT, TITLE, and CATEGORY.) However, you can select information from RENTALS_OUT just as though it were an actual table. You can now enter the simple query:

```
SELECT *
  FROM rentals_out
```

and you get

Member Id	Catalog	Product	Film Titles	Category	Scheduled Return
1	200	P200V	Topgun	Adventure	11-APR-88
1	300	P300V	Gone with the Wind	Classics	11-APR-88
1	301	P301V	Gone with the Wind	Classics	14-APR-88
1	470	P470V	Ghostbusters	Comedy	12-APR-88
1	480	P480V	The Shining	Horror	12-APR-88

without having to enter the complex join query again. You may have observed that the RENTALS_OUT view was not designed to search for all outstanding Adventure or Horror films, as originally requested in the five-table join. The view takes care of the hard part—replicating the five-table join. Generally, you do not want to hard code such detailed search criteria into a view. Leave the view open, for you have the flexibility to add explicit search conditions whenever you select against the view. For example, you can now request

```
SELECT *
  FROM rentals_out
 WHERE category.description in ('Adventure', 'Horror')
```

and get the results of the original five-table join:

Member Id	Catalog	Product	Film Titles	Category	Scheduled Return
1	200	P200V	Topgun	Adventure	11-APR-88
1	480	P480V	The Shining	Horror	12-APR-88

Using Group Functions in Views

One common application of views is using them to select the results of individual sets and group functions in a single query. This is not the same as using a group function in a subquery; with subqueries, you are still limited to selecting individual results in the main query. A view, on the other hand, gives you the flexibility of joining tables to combine the results of single and group functions in the same query.

For example, you wrote an outer join query earlier to report on current product inventory positions. Suppose you wanted a more detailed look at these inventory positions. Here are the results of the original query:

Product	Description	Film Titles	Cost	Qty Recvd	Qty Oh	Qty Sold
P100V	Film	The Sound of Music	19.95	2	1	1
P200V	Film	Topgun	29.95	2	1	
P300B	Film	Gone with the Wind	59.95	1		1
P300V	Film	Gone with the Wind	59.95	2		
P450V	Film	Citizen Kane	49.95	2	1	1
P470B	Film	Ghostbusters	19.95	1	1	
P470V	Film	Ghostbusters	19.95	2	1	
P475V	Film	The Hitcher	79.95	1	1	
P480V	Film	The Shining	69.95	2		
P500	BASF Blank Tape		2.99	30	20	10

Though useful, the information is incomplete. You want to expand this query to include the current outstanding rentals for each product as well. You will add another column to the display: *qty_rented*. Because rentals are tracked by catalog number and because there is a many-to-one relationship between catalog numbers and products, this involves slightly more than a simple query. The following steps are necessary to get this information:

1. Create the view, PRODUCTS_RENTED, to join the TAPES, RENTALS, and PRODUCTS tables, and list the product numbers of all outstanding rental tapes.

2. Create a second view, QTY_RENTED, to count the total number of catalog numbers rented out for every product. (This group function view is based on PRODUCTS_RENTED.)

3. Create a third view to extract product inventory positions from the PRODUCT table and add to it the outstanding rental positions from QTY_RENTED.

Creating the PRODUCTS_RENTED View

PRODUCTS_RENTED is a straightforward join view that combines values from the TAPE and RENTALS tables. It serves chiefly to retrieve the product numbers of the rental tapes currently out. This view can be the basis for several procedures; a global inventory report is but one application. To create PRODUCTS_RENTED, enter

```
CREATE VIEW products_rented
(memberid, catnum, prodno, dateout, schdrtn)
AS
SELECT memberid, tape.catnum, product.prodno, dateout,
       schdrtn
  FROM rentals, tape, product
 WHERE rentals.catnum = tape.catnum
   AND actrtn is null
```

You can then select all records from PRODUCTS_RENTED by entering

```
SELECT *
  FROM products_rented
 ORDER BY schdrtn
```

and getting

Member Id	Catalog	Product	Date Rented	Scheduled Return
1	200	P200V	09-APR-88	11-APR-88
1	300	P300V	09-APR-88	11-APR-88
2	480	P480V	10-APR-88	11-APR-88
1	470	P470V	10-APR-88	12-APR-88
3	301	P300V	12-APR-88	14-MAR-88

As you can see, a view column accepts column format definitions as if it were any other table column.

Creating the QTY_RENTED View

The QTY_RENTED view calculates the total outstanding rentals for each product. QTY_RENTED counts the catalog numbers and groups them by product. This view is meaningless unless PRODUCTS_RENTED is created first; QTY_RENTED draws its information exclusively from the PRODUCTS_RENTED view. To create QTY_RENTED, enter

```
CREATE VIEW qty_rented
(prodno, qty_rented)
AS
SELECT prodno, count(catnum)
  FROM products_rented
 GROUP BY prodno
```

If you were to select all records from QTY_RENTED, the results would be

```
Product   QTY_RENTED
-------   ----------
P200V              1
P300V              2
P470V              1
P480V              1
```

Creating the INVENTORY View

With access to the totals, by product, of all outstanding rentals, you can now complete your product inventory report. Simply create a view based on a join of the PRODUCT and TITLE tables and fold in the rental quantity information from the QTY_RENTED view. Review the syntax of the outer join example created earlier in this chapter:

```
SELECT prodno, product.description, title, cost, qtyrecvd,
       qtyoh, qtysold
  FROM product, title
 WHERE product.titlecd = title.titlecd (+)
 ORDER BY prodno
```

This outer join lays the foundation for the third view, INVENTORY, which now provides a more complete snapshot of the product inventory information. Observe:

```
CREATE VIEW inventory
(prodno, description, title, cost, qtyrecvd, qtyoh, qtysold,
rented)
AS
SELECT prodno, product.description, title, cost, qtyrecvd,
       qtyoh, qtysold, qty_rented
  FROM product, title, qty_rented
 WHERE product.titlecd = title.titlecd (+)
   AND product.prodno = qty_rented.prodno (+)
```

By selecting all records from INVENTORY, you now see

Product	Description	Film Titles	Cost	Qty Recvd	Qty Oh	Qty Sold	Qty Rented
P100V	Film	The Sound of Music	19.95	2	1	1	
P200V	Film	Topgun	29.95	2	1		1
P300B	Film	Gone with the Wind	59.95	1		1	
P300V	Film	Gone with the Wind	59.95	2			2
P450V	Film	Citizen Kane	49.95	2	1	1	
P470B	Film	Ghostbusters	19.95	1	1		
P470V	Film	Ghostbusters	19.95	2	1		1
P475V	Film	The Hitcher	79.95	1	1		
P480V	Film	The Shining	69.95	2		1	1
P500	BASF Blank Tape		2.99	30	20	10	

Views are not restricted to queries but are best used for this purpose. Whenever data is modified in any of the base tables, the changes are of course *seen* through the associated views. It is possible to modify data in the underlying tables directly through a view, but there are restrictions on this ability. You cannot insert, update, or delete rows from a join view, for example; you can do these only if the view is created from a single base table. Other restrictions apply which we won't explore now, but the important point is that modifying data through views is not always the wisest policy. Data manipulation should be carefully controlled in the application design. If countless views are used to modify underlying tables, then it makes it that much harder to troubleshoot problems that may occur, such as rows being updated incorrectly or not being updated at all.

Summary

Building on what you had learned in the previous chapter, Chapter 6 challenged you with more advanced SQL concepts and techniques. It taught you how to work with character, number, and date values in expressions, how to construct complex SELECT statements with subqueries and relational joins, and how to create views. This chapter covered

- ▶ Character expressions
- ▶ Arithmetic expressions
- ▶ Working with dates
- ▶ Building subqueries
- ▶ Relational joins
- ▶ Creating views

7

Building Forms

7

Building Forms

Chapter 7 presents advanced techniques for building custom forms with ORACLE's application development tool and code generator, SQL*Forms. This chapter demonstrates the process of creating forms, defining low-level field validation, and enhancing the appearance of your forms with the SQL*Forms screen painter. You will concentrate, however, on customizing forms by adding complex application logic with SQL*Forms *triggers*.

This chapter assumes that you have perused the SQL*Forms documentation set, and are sufficiently grounded in the mechanics of SQL*Forms. If you haven't explored the documentation, it would be wise to do so now. At the very least, you should have worked through the exercises in the *SQL*Forms Designer's Tutorial V2.1*.

Forms: The Fourth-Generation Application Interface

Application users rarely interact with database tables directly. Forms are the traditional medium of exchange. Forms provide the user interface for most fourth-generation applications. When a form is displayed, it presents fields that generally correspond to database columns, and text such as form titles, field names, and function key legends. Via forms, users can quickly insert, update, or delete records in corresponding database tables. Users can also query records directly on screen, using the screen fields to enter search criteria. This fill-in-the-blanks technique of querying records is known as *query-by-example*.

Forms make querying records easier, but also serve to preserve the integrity of the database. Field and record validation protect the database by ensuring that only the correct values are entered—and in the correct format. More sophisticated forms provide several other functions to control data entry:

- ▶ a list of values to indicate a range of values for certain fields
- ▶ automatic display of related data (*table look-ups*)
- ▶ automatic generation of control or sequence numbers
- ▶ automatic computation of field values
- ▶ referential integrity to maintain consistency across database tables
- ▶ cursor navigation to control user movement through the application
- ▶ triggers to prevent inserts or updates to certain fields and to disable certain function keys
- ▶ default values

Forms Terminology

Forms have a language all their own. Terms that have special meaning when referring to the database can mean something else entirely at the forms application level. For example, what is called a column in the database is called a *field* in forms terminology; what is called a row in the database is called a *record* in forms. Some forms terms are exclusive to the forms environment. Here is a glossary of terms you should be familiar with at the outset:

Page	The part of the form currently displayed on a full screen at one time. A form can span many pages.
Block	The section of a form that contains a group of related fields. The fields hold data and text that normally reference a single table.
Base Table	The table on which a block is based.
Record	Data from one row of a database table.
Field	A designated area on the screen that can display a value. The value normally corresponds to a value from a column in the database table.
Single-record Block	A block that can display only one record.
Multi-record Block	A block that can display more than one record.

Figure 7.1 illustrates these terms. It shows the two-block CUSTOMER form which you will build later in the chapter.

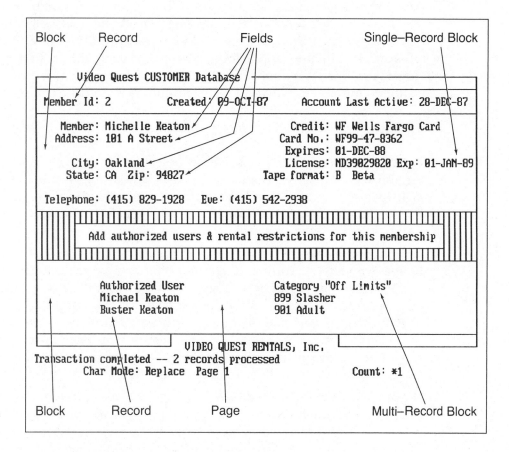

Figure 7.1   Forms Terminology

The SQL*Forms Design Program

SQL*Forms contains two parts—the SQL*Forms (Design) used to design and create forms and SQL*Forms (Runform) to execute forms built with the Design program. These are separate programs. In every ORACLE environment except the PC (Version 5.1A and earlier), you can execute a form with Runform from within the SQL*Forms (Design). The reason for this is that memory restrictions and the single-user architecture of MS-DOS prevent running multiple processes at once. SQL*Forms spawns a subprocess to execute Runform within the Design component. The ability to run a form from the Design program cuts down debugging time because you needn't log out of the program to generate and execute the form, then log back when you are finished. You will learn a couple of tricks to regain much of this time in PC environments, however.

SQL*Forms lets you design a form on the screen and modify it interactively until you are satisfied with it. The SQL*Forms (Design) offers a steady migration path from the initial design and prototype of a form to the full-scale production application. You can begin with a simple default form and then gradually add functionality as you work out the application requirements with end-users. No code is wasted, no code thrown away.

There are essentially three levels of form design:

1. *Creating the blocks and fields*. The simplest form is merely a window on the base tables without any special validation or functionality. SQL*Forms generates this kind of form automatically with the DEFAULT BLOCK option. You can also paint the fields on screen individually.

2. *Defining the blocks and fields*. Once the form is laid out, you can enhance it by adding rudimentary validation or functions to assist operator entry. The application logic at this level fulfills the minimal requirements, or *primitives*, of the application. The nonprocedurality of SQL*Forms is demonstrated by the way you define this default logic. By selecting items from pull-down menus, you can specify field ranges for validation, default values, update restrictions, upper or lowercase entry, or simple help messages on fields.

3. *Defining triggers*. At this advanced level, you take the foundation of the form and mould it into a robust application. You provide complex validation and enhanced operator control by writing *triggers*. These are parcels of logic constructed of SQL statements, macro statements, or SQL*Forms commands which are executed at certain event points in the form or when certain function keys are pressed.

The Video Quest Forms

Perhaps the best indoctrination to the Video Quest forms is to observe how they serve the business. By following an individual video tape through its entire life cycle, you will see where each form comes into play. Let's track one such tape—a copy of *Ghostbusters*.

The TITLE Form
Long before a video tape reaches the tape library, it must be assigned a title and a product code. The TITLE form is the first stop on its journey.

```
┌── Video Quest TITLE Search ─────────────────────────────────────┐
│ Title Code      Title                                           │
│ GHOSTBUSTER     Ghostbusters                                    │
│ Film Category                                                   │
│ 120  COMEDY                                                     │
│                                                                 │
│ Released    Studio      Color/B&W   Running Time  Censor Rating   Star Rating │
│  1984       Columbia    Color       105           PG-13           *****       │
│                                                                 │
│ Directors                                                       │
│ Ivan Reitman                                                    │
│ Producers/Co-Producers                                          │
│ Ivan Reitman                                                    │
│ Actors/Actresses                                                │
│ Bill Murray, Dan Aykroyd, Sigourney Weaver, Harold Ramis, Rick Moranis │
│ Screenplay                           Academy or Foreign Film Awards │
│ Dan Aykroyd, Harold Ramis                                       │
│                                                                 │
│ ▮▮▮▮▮▮▮▮▮▮▮▮▮▮▮▮▮▮  ▮▮▮▮▮▮▮▮▮▮▮▮▮▮▮▮▮▮▮▮▮▮  ▮▮▮▮▮▮▮▮▮▮▮▮▮▮▮ │
│   [Next Block] Synopsis  ║  VIDEO QUEST RENTALS, Inc.  ║  [Exit] Main Menu │
└─────────────────────────────────────────────────────────────────┘
         Char Mode: Replace   Page 1              Count:  1
```

Figure 7.2   The TITLE Form

An operator keys in the critical TITLE information—the title code, title, and film category—and can then enter other optional information. TITLE information could be made available to Video Quest customers as well as to store personnel. In a local area network configuration, one or two terminals tied to the Video Quest database could be placed strategically on the shop floor. Customers would be invited to query the TITLE database to answer movie trivia questions like "What Jack Nicholson films were made between 1981 and 1986?" and to verify film availability themselves. This self-help service would relieve clerks of having to answer the same question repeatedly and of having to look up answers to obscure questions.

If the store has access to the information, an operator can page to the SYNOPSIS screen and enter synopsis text for *Ghostbusters*. By pressing the [Page Down] key, an operator accesses the SYNOPSIS screen. The application automatically copies the film title from the TITLE block to the top line of the SYNOPSIS screen to properly coordinate the blocks and enhance the visual interface.

The PRODUCT Form

As you know, Video Quest rents and sells other products besides films. If Video Quest dealt exclusively with films, there wouldn't be any need to

```
Synopsis for title: Ghostbusters
|||||||||||||||||||||||||||||||||||||||||||||||||||||||||||||||||||
When ghosts go on a rampage, only three men can save the world.  It's
GHOSTBUSTERS, starring Bill Murray, Dan Aykroyd and Harold Ramis as a
maniacal band of parapsychologists specializing in psychic phenomena - and
supernatural hilarity!  Fired from university research jobs, Dr. Venkman
(Murray), Stanz (Aykroyd) and Spengler (Ramis) set up shop as "Ghostbusters",
ridding Manhattan of bizarre apparitions.




                                                         
|||||||||||||||||||||||||||||||||||||||||||||||||||||||||||||||||||
[Next Record] Scroll down | [Prev Record] Scroll up | [Prev Block] Title info

                        VIDEO QUEST RENTALS, Inc.

      Char Mode: Replace  Page 2                Count: *0
```

Figure 7.3   The TITLE SYNOPSIS Form

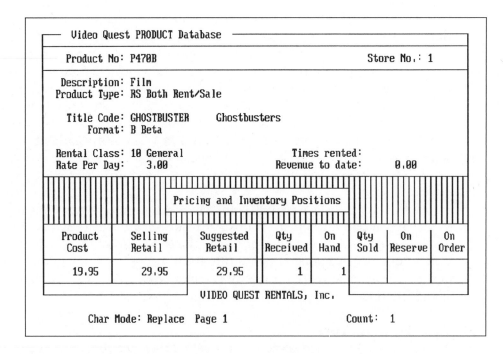

Figure 7.4   The PRODUCT Form

maintain product codes. Such is not the case. Product codes and related product information are entered for each title on the PRODUCT form. Of course, nonfilm products such as blank video tapes start their journey through the system from this form.

Since *Ghostbusters* is a film product, the operator must enter a *titlecd* and a *rentclass*. If the operator enters an invalid title code, or one not set up in the TITLE table, the system rejects the entry immediately.

Inventory status information is displayed on the PRODUCT form, but the fields themselves are not enterable. It is the duty of the Video Quest application to automatically update inventory positions. For example, when a product is rented, the RENTALS form automatically updates the On Hand position by decrementing the value in the *qtyoh* column in the PRODUCT table. You will define a trigger in the RENTALS form to do this.

Video Quest carries the *Ghostbusters* title in both VHS and Beta Format. Separate product codes are assigned for each format, P470V and P470B, respectively; the PRODUCT table thus maintains a separate row for each product.

The CATALOG Form

The operator has assigned *Ghostbusters* a title code and two product codes against this title—one for VHS format and another for Beta format. However, the store undoubtedly owns multiple copies of each tape format. The operator must now enter a unique catalog number for each copy, that is, each physical video tape, which the store owns. A tape is not legitimized until it is given a catalog number. The operator invokes the CATALOG form to assign and manage the catalog numbers.

The CATALOG form is built almost exclusively from the base TAPE table. It is created as a default form by SQL*Forms and is embellished with the screen painter. A TITLE field is added to better identify the catalog numbers and associated product numbers. You will create this form and the other default-generated code maintenance forms, RENTAL_CLASS, CATEGORY, and PAYMENT, on your own.

The CUSTOMER Form

The CUSTOMER form manages the vital statistics for Video Quest customers. Both primary and authorized member information is inserted and updated via this two-block form.

The CUSTOMER form represents the classic master-detail design, or parent-child relationship as it also is called. A single primary member can support several authorized members, each of whom "borrows" the host's Membership ID when renting out a tape. This underlying entity relationship is formalized as a master-detail relationship in the form.

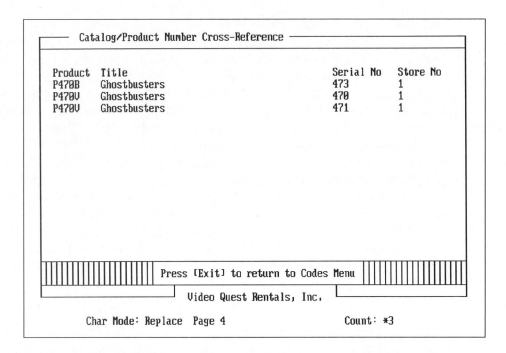

Figure 7.5   The CATALOG Form

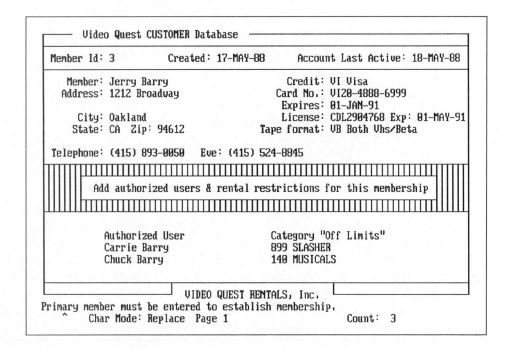

Figure 7.6   The CUSTOMER Form

The RENTALS Transaction Form

Video tapes are rented out and invoiced from the RENTALS form. This is a three-block form based on the RENTALS transaction table, the INVOICE table, and a header, or *control block*.

The three RENTALS blocks are linked together by the primary key field, *memberid*, which an operator enters into the control block. When entered, the *memberid* is verified by a look-up to the CUSTOMER table; if the value is valid, the appropriate customer name is displayed.

Although the RENTALS form appears simple enough, complex validation is being performed behind the scenes. A dragnet of field-, block-, and form-level triggers are written to automate processing and preserve the integrity of the database.

The RETURNS Transaction Form

The RETURNS form completes the RENTALS loop. When a customer returns a tape, it is checked in via this form, and an invoice is generated if any late charges are collected.

The RETURNS form has the same three-block structure as the RENTALS form. The key difference is that the middle block inserts records into the RETURNS transaction table instead of into the RENTALS table. The trigger logic performed in the background is much the same as well. You will create this form and design the triggers on your own.

Building the TITLE Form

The TITLE form is relatively simple. It is a two-block form composed of the TITLE and SYNOPSIS blocks. The TITLE form is an ideal candidate for using the SQL*Forms DEFAULT BLOCK option. Each block fills up an entire form page, or screen. Forms that squeeze multiple blocks onto a single page, such as the RENTALS form, are difficult to generate with DEFAULT BLOCK unless the base tables are small. DEFAULT BLOCK tends to spread fields thinly across the screen. When using it to place more than one block on a page, the fields rarely fit. With such forms, it is often more efficient to paint the fields on screen one at a time.

Creating the TITLE Block

The following exercises, illustrated in Figures 7.9 through 7.12, walk you through the creation of the TITLE block with the DEFAULT BLOCK option. We will not elaborate on the details of the Designer menu options. The SQL*Forms documentation covers this material in ample detail.

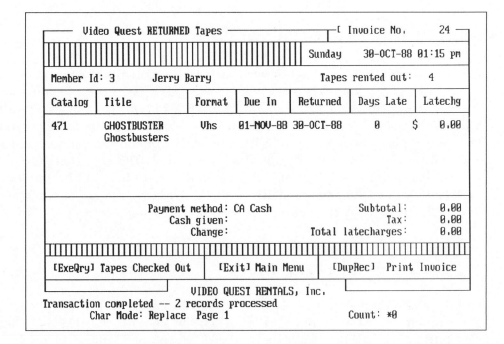

Figure 7.7   The RENTALS Form

```
 ┌── Video Quest RETURNED Tapes ──────────────┐[ Invoice No.    24 ──┐
 │▐▌▐▌▐▌▐▌▐▌▐▌▐▌▐▌▐▌▐▌▐▌▐▌▐▌▐▌▐▌▐▌▐▌▐▌│ Sunday   30-OCT-88 01:15 pm │
 │ Member Id: 3      Jerry Barry         Tapes rented out:  4         │
 │ Catalog │ Title       │ Format │ Due In  │ Returned │ Days Late │ Latechg │
 │ 471       GHOSTBUSTER   Vhs      01-NOV-88 30-OCT-88      0      $  0.00   │
 │           Ghostbusters                                                     │
 │                                                                            │
 │             Payment method: CA Cash          Subtotal:        0.00         │
 │                 Cash given:                       Tax:        0.00         │
 │                     Change:             Total latecharges:    0.00         │
 │▐▌▐▌▐▌▐▌▐▌▐▌▐▌▐▌▐▌▐▌▐▌▐▌▐▌▐▌▐▌▐▌▐▌▐▌▐▌▐▌▐▌▐▌▐▌▐▌▐▌│
 │ [ExeQry] Tapes Checked Out │ [Exit] Main Menu │ [DupRec]  Print Invoice │
 │                    VIDEO QUEST RENTALS, Inc. ──┘                           │
 Transaction completed -- 2 records processed
              Char Mode: Replace   Page 1                 Count: *0
```

Figure 7.8   The RETURNS Form

1. Enter the name *title* on the CHOOSE FORM window and select CREATE. This displays the CHOOSE BLOCK window.

2. Enter the block name, TITLE, for the first block of the form.

3. Select DEFAULT to display the DEFAULT BLOCK window.

4. Choose the COLUMNS item to select the columns from the list you wish to include in the default block. Choose ALL. If you know ahead of time that you want to include every column, you can simply press [Accept] after entering this window.

5. Return to the DEFAULT BLOCK window. The TITLE block is a single record block. The Rows Displayed value controls whether you are defining a single- or multi-record block. Leave the value at *1*.

6. Return to the CHOOSE BLOCK window. Select MODIFY to enter the screen painter.

You are now in the SQL*Forms screen painter. You can rearrange the fields on the screen to create any visual interface desired. With the SQL*Forms line-drawing capability—the DRAW BOX/LINE function—you can further enhance the form's appearance by drawing boxes around groups of fields, drawing accent lines, and so forth. Text can be entered directly on the screen to relabel fields, for example, or to add header and/ or footer titles and function key legends.

The text identifying the TITLE fields, known as field *labels*, can be erased with the [Delete] key on your keyboard, and relabelled. They also can be moved with the fields themselves using the CUT and PASTE functions.

It will take a few moments, but you can transform the DEFAULT TI-TLE form to resemble the enhanced TITLE form appearing in Figure 7.13.

Using the CUT and PASTE functions, first rearrange the fields to mirror the enhanced form, then change the field labels. You can cut and paste a single field at a time or several fields at once. If you make a mistake cutting or placing a field, press [Undo] to correct it.

Some of the base fields must be resized to fit within the boundaries of your screen. Resize these fields with the [Resize Field] function key as follows:

```
Field Name   New Field Length
----------   -------------------------------
TITLE        60 characters
SCREENPLAY   37 characters / 78 Query Length
AWARDS       38 characters / 78 Query Length
```

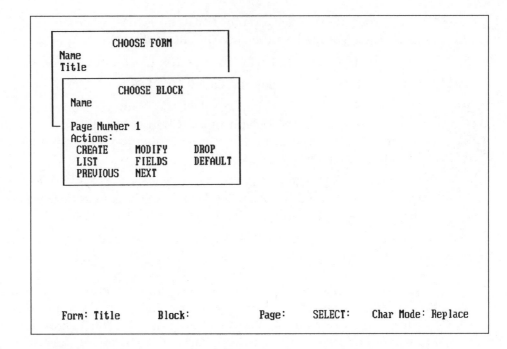

Figure 7.9   The CHOOSE FORM and CHOOSE BLOCK Windows

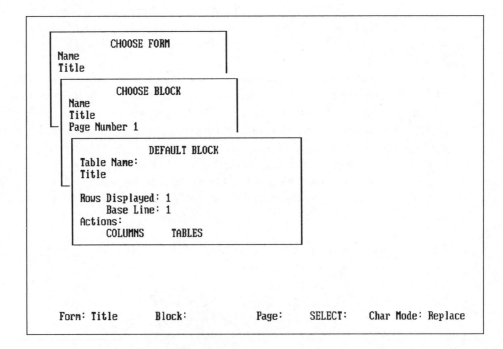

Figure 7.10   The DEFAULT BLOCK Option Window

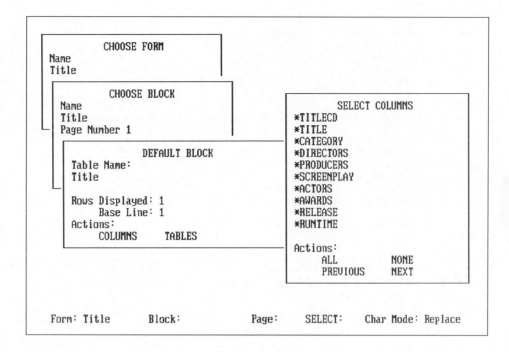

Figure 7.11   The SELECT COLUMNS Window

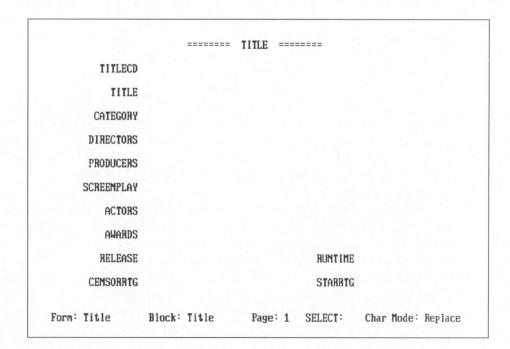

Figure 7.12   The DEFAULT TITLE Form

```
┌─────────────────────────────────────────────────────────────────┐
│  ┌─ Video Quest TITLE Search ────────────────────────────────┐   │
│  │ Title Code      Title                                      │   │
│  │ Film Category                                              │   │
│  │                                                            │   │
│  │ Released   Studio     Color/B&W   Running Time  Censor Rating   Star Rating │
│  │                                                            │   │
│  │ Directors                                                  │   │
│  │                                                            │   │
│  │ Producers/Co-Producers                                     │   │
│  │                                                            │   │
│  │ Actors/Actresses                                           │   │
│  │                                                            │   │
│  │ Screenplay                        Awards                   │   │
│  │                                                            │   │
│  │                                                            │   │
│  │ ▓▓▓▓▓▓▓▓▓▓▓▓▓▓▓▓▓▓▓ ▓▓ ▓▓▓▓▓▓▓▓▓▓▓▓▓▓▓▓▓▓▓ ▓▓ ▓▓▓▓▓▓▓▓▓▓▓▓ │   │
│  │ [PgDn] Title Synopsis ║║ VIDEO QUEST RENTALS, Inc. ║║ [Exit] Main Menu │   │
│  └────────────────────────────────────────────────────────────┘   │
│                                                                   │
│  Form: title        Block: title        Page: 1    SELECT:    Char Mode: Replace │
└─────────────────────────────────────────────────────────────────┘
```

Figure 7.13   The Enhanced TITLE Form

After the fields are arranged, draw the boxes around the screen and function key legends. The decorative vertical lines at the bottom of the screen (above the *Video Quest Rentals, Inc.* footer title) were drawn using a shortcut. If you draw one line and then cut it with the CUT function, you can paste it repeatedly. The CUT function stores the last object cut, which can be pasted as many times as you like.

By now you've certainly noticed that a couple of fields are missing. One must be created from scratch; we will get to this in a moment. The other field, RUNTIME, has already been created, but it was placed on the second page of the form. The DEFAULT BLOCK could not fit all the TITLE fields on the first page, so this field spilled over to the next one.

To get to Page 2 of the form, simply enter 2 for the Page Number on the CHOOSE BLOCK window, then enter the screen painter. Move the RUN-TIME field to its proper location back on Page 1. You can move fields freely within a form and between forms. Be sure to erase the title text at the top of the screen before finally leaving this page. Be careful, though. The PASTE buffer only remembers the last object cut; if you've cut the RUN-TIME field in anticipation of moving, but then cut the title text before actually pasting the RUNTIME field anywhere, you will have overwritten the PASTE buffer and have lost the RUNTIME field.

Adding A Table Look-Up Field

The CATEGORY field at the top of the page displays the category code assigned for every title. A code by itself is not very meaningful to users. You will add another field beside it to display a description of the code, derived from the CATEGORY table, whenever an operator enters a new code or a title is queried. This field is known as a *look-up field*. The ability to display data on the screen with a look-up field lets you conserve valuable disk space; you needn't store a category description in the TITLE table along with the code. You will design a trigger shortly to display this related data.

With the CREATE FIELD function, add a field named CATDESC on the same line as the CATEGORY code. CATDESC should be sized as follows:

Field Name	Field Length	Field Type
CATDESC	20 characters	CHAR

Displaying Data to Enhance the Interface

You will add a second field to the TITLE block to enhance the human interface of the form. When an operator moves to the SYNOPSIS block to insert a synopsis for a new title, the XTDESC field automatically displays the title of the film at the top of the page. XTDESC is a nondatabase field. It is the last field of the TITLE block, and it is the only field for this block to appear on the second page of the form.

At the top of Page 2, add the XTDESC field as shown in Figure 7.14. The XTDESC field should be sized and labelled as follows:

Field Name	Field Length	Field Type
XTDESC	56 characters	CHAR

Defining the Form Fields

The DEFAULT BLOCK option accepts the underlying column definitions when creating the default fields. In a forms environment, these inherited characteristics double as basic field validation. For example, the *titlecd* column, originally defined with a CHAR data type, immediately becomes a CHAR field in a form. An operator cannot enter a number value into this field.

Default fields inherit other characteristics, known as *field attributes*, from the corresponding columns. Let's look at the attributes for the TITLECD field.

```
┌─────────────────────────────────────────────────────────────────────┐
│                                                                       │
│    Synopsis for title: ▓▓▓▓▓▓▓▓▓▓▓▓▓▓▓▓▓▓▓▓▓▓▓▓▓▓▓▓▓▓▓▓              │
│                                                                       │
│                                                                       │
│                                                                       │
│                                                                       │
│                                                                       │
│                                                                       │
│                                                                       │
│                                                                       │
│                                                                       │
│                                                                       │
│                                                                       │
│                                                                       │
│                                                                       │
│                                                                       │
│                                                                       │
│    Form: title      Block: synopsis   Page: 3  SELECT:   Char Mode: Replace │
│                                                                       │
└─────────────────────────────────────────────────────────────────────┘
```

Figure 7.14   The XTDESC Field Placement

1. Choose MODIFY from the CHOOSE BLOCK window and specify Page 1 to enter the screen painter.
2. On the TITLECD field (now labelled 'Title Code'), press [Define Field] to display the DEFINE FIELD Window, illustrated in Figure 7.15.

   The DEFINE FIELD window is a thoroughfare to several other windows which let you:

   redefine field attributes

   adjust the display format of the data type

   add field validation

   include help messages for operators

   add field comments to aid designers maintaining the application at a later date

   define SQL*Forms triggers for advanced validation.

   You can modify field attributes in the SPECIFY ATTRIBUTES window by doing the following:

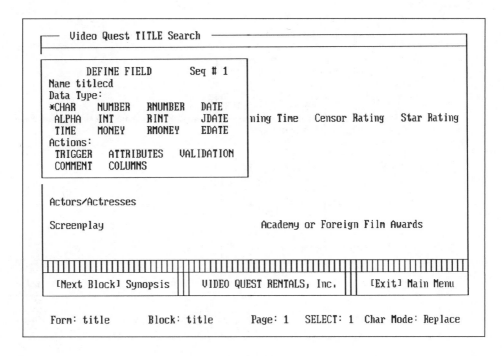

Figure 7.15   The DEFINE FIELD Window

3. From the DEFINE FIELD window, choose ATTRIBUTES to display the SPECIFY ATTRIBUTES Window.

As shown in Figure 7.16, a default field like TITLECD has these characteristics: it is a database field (derived exclusively from the base table); it is a displayed field (as opposed to a field which can be hidden from view); operator input is allowed (some fields only display data and cannot be entered); the field is queryable (only base table fields can be queried); values can be updated through this field (if this item was not selected, you could insert a new value, but not change it through the form afterward); and the field is mandatory.

Take the opportunity now to add a new field attribute for TITLECD—the Uppercase attribute. A Video Quest data entry convention is to enter any codes in uppercase letters, including title codes, product codes, film category codes, and so forth.

4. Select the Uppercase attribute. This automatically converts entered data to uppercase letters.

5. Return to the DEFINE FIELD window. Choose VALIDATION to display the SPECIFY VALIDATION window (Figure 7.17).

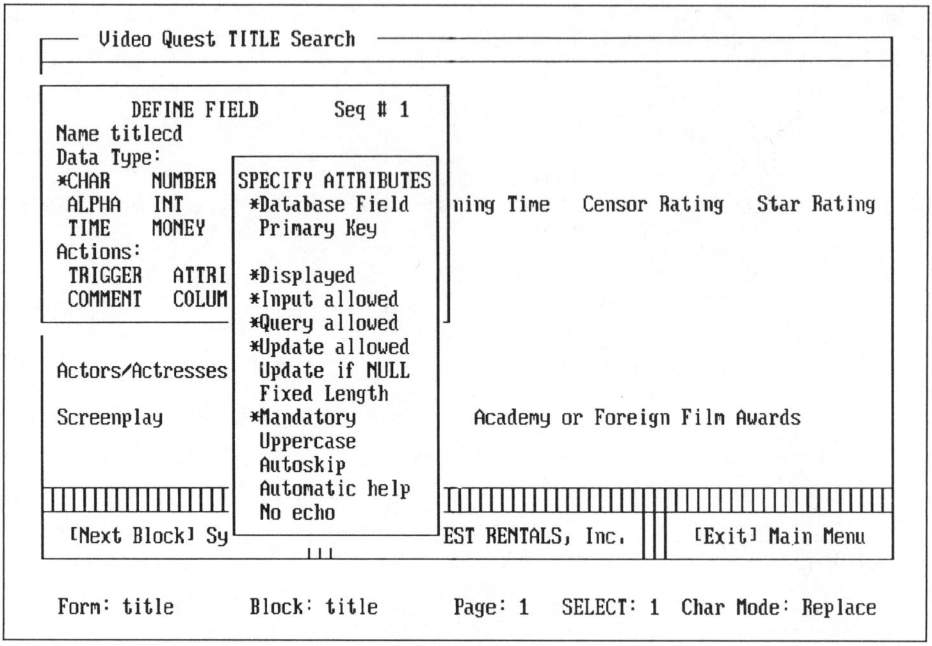

```
┌─────────────────────────────────────────────────────────────┐
│  ┌─ Video Quest TITLE Search ──────────────                   │
│  │                                                            │
│  ┌──────────────────────────────────────┐                    │
│  │    DEFINE FIELD      Seq # 1          │                    │
│  │ Name titlecd                          │                    │
│  │ Data Type:                            │                    │
│  │ *CHAR   NUMBER  SPECIFY ATTRIBUTES│ning Time  Censor Rating  Star Rating│
│  │ ALPHA   INT    *Database Field    │                         │
│  │ TIME    MONEY   Primary Key       │                         │
│  │ Actions:                          │                         │
│  │ TRIGGER  ATTRI *Displayed         │                         │
│  │ COMMENT  COLUM *Input allowed     │                         │
│  │                *Query allowed     │                         │
│  │                *Update allowed    │                         │
│  │ Actors/Actresses Update if NULL   │                         │
│  │                 Fixed Length      │                         │
│  │ Screenplay     *Mandatory      Academy or Foreign Film Awards│
│  │                 Uppercase         │                         │
│  │                 Autoskip          │                         │
│  │                 Automatic help    │                         │
│  │                 No echo           │                         │
│  │  [Next Block] Sy           EST RENTALS, Inc.   [Exit] Main Menu│
│  │                                                            │
│  │  Form: title     Block: title    Page: 1   SELECT: 1  Char Mode: Replace│
└─────────────────────────────────────────────────────────────┘
```

Figure 7.16   The SPECIFY ATTRIBUTES Window

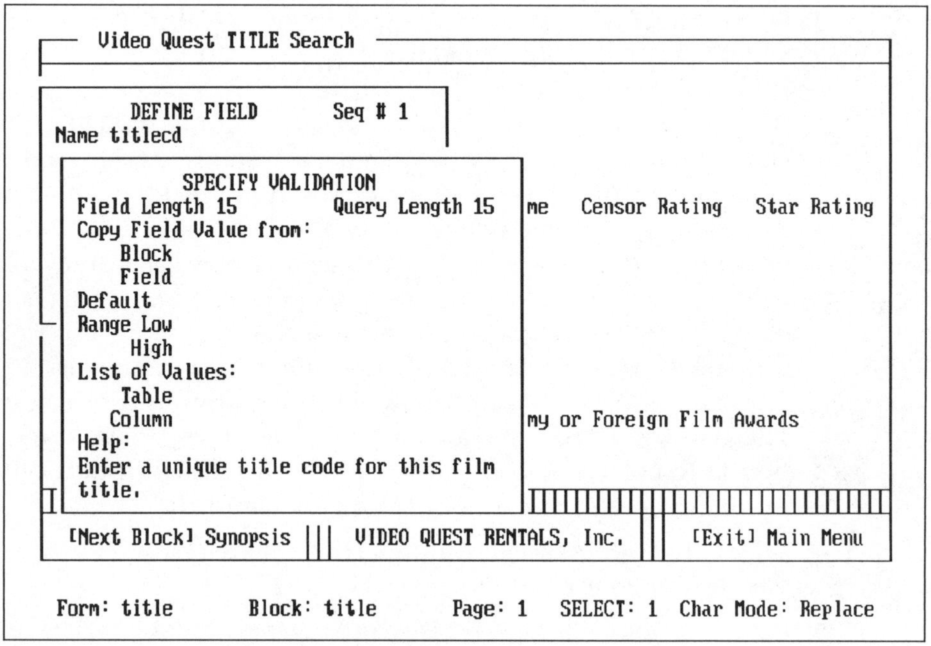

```
┌─────────────────────────────────────────────────────────────┐
│  ┌─ Video Quest TITLE Search ──────────────                   │
│  ┌──────────────────────────────────────┐                    │
│  │    DEFINE FIELD      Seq # 1          │                    │
│  │ Name titlecd                          │                    │
│  │      SPECIFY VALIDATION               │                    │
│  │ Field Length 15     Query Length 15  me  Censor Rating  Star Rating│
│  │ Copy Field Value from:                │                    │
│  │     Block                             │                    │
│  │     Field                             │                    │
│  │ Default                               │                    │
│  │ Range Low                             │                    │
│  │      High                             │                    │
│  │ List of Values:                       │                    │
│  │     Table                             │                    │
│  │     Column                      my or Foreign Film Awards │
│  │ Help:                                 │                    │
│  │ Enter a unique title code for this film│                   │
│  │ title.                                │                    │
│  │  [Next Block] Synopsis   VIDEO QUEST RENTALS, Inc.   [Exit] Main Menu│
│  │  Form: title     Block: title    Page: 1   SELECT: 1  Char Mode: Replace│
└─────────────────────────────────────────────────────────────┘
```

Figure 7.17   The SPECIFY VALIDATION Window

The SPECIFY VALIDATION window lets you add a host of validation criteria. You will see examples of this criteria during the course of building the other forms. At present, add a help message, to be displayed whenever the operator presses the [Help] key.

6. Type in the help message text: `Enter a unique title code for this film title`.

The two lines of the help message text are concatenated; if you need both lines, type all the way to the end of the first line, splitting words if necessary.

Generating and Saving the Form

Save your work periodically. The changes you make on-line alter a copy of the form in memory, not disk. Computer memory is volatile and obviously not the safest place to store data for any length of time. When you generate a form, SQL*Forms takes the .INP file you are creating and compiles it, adding the suffix .FRM to the executable file. A copy of your latest .INP file is also maintained in the current directory on disk. When you save a form, SQL*Forms writes the .INP file in memory out to the database.

In every ORACLE environment except Professional ORACLE V5.1A and earlier versions, forms can be generated and run from within the SQL*Forms (Design). On the PC, hardware limitations force you to generate and run your forms directly from the operating system. Building a form is an iterative process involving continuous trial-and-error testing. Logging in and out of SQL*Forms to run your form can get tedious, particularly if you save it to the database every time. To shortcut this procedure, we suggest you forgo saving your forms to the database. Ignore the SAVE option each time you exit SQL*Forms. You can protect your forms by keeping a backup copy of your .INP files on disk rather than in the ORACLE database.

When you exit SQL*Forms to generate your form, choose DISCARD from the FILE menu (not the SAVE item). This discards the copy in memory and exits you to the operating system. To work with the form again, invoke SQL*Forms, then simply reload the form from the .INP file on disk by choosing the LOAD option. This is much quicker than using the MODIFY option, which would retrieve your form from the database had you saved it to the database.

The TITLE Fields

The following chart identifies the field attributes and validation criteria that you will define for each field in the TITLE block. Take the time to enter this information now.

The field attributes listed are those *added* to the default attributes generated by the DEFAULT BLOCK option. There are two exceptions to this rule: the two description fields you created from scratch, CATDESC and XTDESC. These are nondatabase fields which merely *display* data. Consequently, these fields are given a single field attribute—Displayed. When you first created them, SQL*Forms automatically assigned the fields normal default attributes—Database Field, Displayed, Input Allowed, Query Allowed, and Update Allowed. Be sure to deselect all default attributes *except* Displayed.

Note that the field list is sorted by sequence number. The sequence number, located on the upper righthand corner of the DEFINE FIELD window of each field, determines the order in which the cursor navigates from field to field when you run a form. Be sure to update the sequence numbers on your form to match those below.

Table 7.1   TITLE Field Definitions

Seq#	Field Name	Label	Field Type
#1	*TITLECD*	*Title Code*	CHAR
	Attributes:	Primary Key	
		Uppercase	
	Validation:	Help: "Enter unique title code for this film title."	
#2	*TITLE*	*Title*	CHAR
	Attributes:	(Default)	
	Validation:	Help: "Title of this film."	
#3	*CATEGORY*	*Film Category*	CHAR
	Attributes:	Uppercase	
	Validation:	Default Value: 999	
		List of Values: Table—Category	
		Column—Category	
		Help: "Category code to identify film category, e.g., **100** = Adventure . . ."	
#4	*CATDESC*	*(None)*	CHAR
	Attributes:	Displayed (only)	
	Validation:	(None)†	
#5	*RELEASE*	*Released*	CHAR
	Attributes:	(Default)	
	Validation:	Help: "Year film was released. Enter the year only, e.g., 1987."	
#6	*STUDIO*	*Studio*	CHAR
	Attributes:	(Default)	
	Validation:	Help: "Studio that distributes the film."	
#7	*COLOR_BW*	*Color/B&W*	CHAR
	Attributes:	(Default)	
	Validation:	Help: "Enter 'Color' or 'B&W'."	
#8	*RUNTIME*	*Running Time*	RNUMBER type††
	Attributes:	Automatic Help (Displays help message on entry into field)	
	Validation:	Help: "Running time of the film, e.g., '120 mins.'."	

Table 7.1   *(continued)*

Seq#	Field Name	Label	Field Type
#9	*CENSORRTG*	*Censor Rating*	CHAR
	Attributes:	Uppercase	
	Validation:	Help: "Censorship rating of the film, e.g., 'G = General', 'PG = Parental Guidance."	
#10	*STARRTG*	*Star Rating*	CHAR
	Attributes:	(Default)	
	Validation:	Help: "Star rating for this title, e.g., *, **, ***, ****, ***** (5 Stars is tops!)"	
#11	*DIRECTORS*	*Directors*	CHAR
	Attributes:	(Default)	
	Validation:	Help: "Names of directors for this title."	
#12	*PRODUCERS*	*Producers/Co-Producers*	CHAR
	Attributes:	(Default)	
	Validation:	Help: "Names of producers and co-producers for this film."	
#13	*ACTORS*	*Actors/Actresses*	CHAR
	Attributes:	(Default)	
	Validation:	Help: "Names of starring actors and actresses for this film."	
#14	*SCREENPLAY*	*Screenplay*	CHAR
	Attributes:	(Default)	
	Validation:	Help: "Names of screen writers for this film."	
#15	*AWARDS*	*Academy or Cannes Festival Awards*	CHAR
	Attributes:	(Default)	
	Validation:	Help: "List of awards for this title, if any."	
#16	*XTDESC*	*Synopsis for Title*	CHAR
	Attributes:	Displayed (only)	
	Validation:	(None)†	

†Nonenterable fields do not need added validation logic.
††Right-justified number

Creating the SYNOPSIS Block

The SYNOPSIS block displays synopsis text for the title appearing on the TITLE block. You will not use the DEFAULT BLOCK Option to create the SYNOPSIS fields. You will use the CREATE FIELD function instead to create each field individually in the screen painter. Your completed SYNOPSIS block should look like the one in Figure 7.18.

The SYNOPSIS block is based on columns derived from the SYNOPSIS table. These are

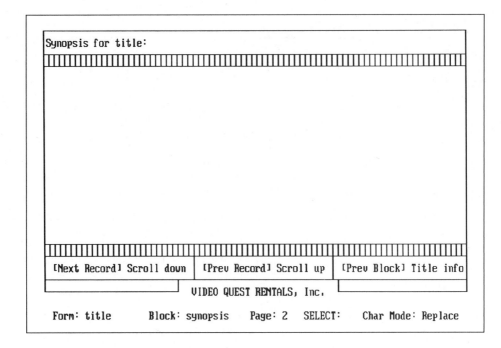

Figure 7.18   The Completed SYNOPSIS Block

Column	Column Definition
Titlecd	Char(15)
Lineno	Number
Description	Char(78)

Only one of these columns, however, is displayed on the SYNOPSIS screen. This is the *description* column, which stores a single line of synopsis text for every row in the SYNOPSIS table. A film synopsis may require several lines of text. Each line must be identified by title code, titlecd, and given a unique line number, *lineno*, to ensure that the appropriate text is displayed in the correct order.

The fields that correspond to the *titlecd* and *lineno* columns are nondisplayed fields. The application is solely responsible for maintaining these fields; no operator intervention is required. SQL*Forms places nondisplayed fields on Page 0 of the current block. For each block of the form, a separate Page 0 is maintained by SQL*Forms to control nondisplayed fields. You will define the *titlecd* and *lineno* fields on Page 0 of the SYNOPSIS block.

Here is a summary of the steps required to create the SYNOPSIS block:

1. Enter the block name SYNOPSIS on the CHOOSE BLOCK window.
2. Enter 2 for the Page Number and choose CREATE.
3. Use CREATE FIELD to create the DESCRIPTION field with the following field length, attributes, and validation information. (Place the DESCRIPTION field beneath the XTDESC field of the TITLE block as shown in Figure 7.18.)

Table 7.2   SYNOPSIS Field Definitions

Seq#	Field Name	Label	Length / Field Type
#1	DESCRIPTION	(None)	78 chars / CHAR
	Attributes:	Database Field	
		Displayed	
		Input Allowed	
		Query Allowed	
		Autoskip (Automatically skips cursor to the next row when text reaches the end of the line.)	
	Validation:	Help: "Text for film synopsis"	

The SYNOPSIS block is a multi-record block. You want to display as many rows of synopsis text as will fit on the screen. To control the number of rows displayed, you use the DEFINE BLOCK window.

4. Press [Select Block], then [Define] to display the DEFINE BLOCK window.
5. Choose OPTIONS to display the SPECIFY BLOCK OPTIONS window.
6. Enter 14 for Number of Rows displayed.
   Enter 50 for the Number of Rows buffered.
   Enter 1 for the Number of Lines per row.

If you designed the interface of the SYNOPSIS block exactly as it appears in Figure 7.18—ornamental lines and all—then you should have enough room on the screen to display at least 14 rows of text. (This number may vary with the terminal display you're using.)

When a synopsis is queried, the text must be retrieved in line number sequence. You can ensure this by specifying an ORDER BY clause for the entire block. From the DEFINE BLOCK window:

7. Choose ORDERING to display the SPECIFY DEFAULT ORDERING window.
8. Enter ORDER BY lineno.

You should now create the remaining two fields, TITLECD and LINENO on Page 0. Follow these steps:

9. From the CHOOSE BLOCK window, enter *0* for the Page Number. (*Be sure* the block name is SYNOPSIS.)

10. Use CREATE FIELD to create the TITLECD and LINENO fields with the following length, attributes and validation information. Label the fields accordingly.

Table 7.3   TITLECD and LINENO Field Definitions

Seq#	Field Name	Label	Length / Field Type
#2	*TITLECD*	*Titlecd*	*15 chars / CHAR*
	Attributes:	Database Field	
	Validation:	Copy Field Value From: BLOCK title	
		FIELD Titlecd	
#3	*LINENO*	*Lineno*	*4 chars / INT**
	Attributes:	Database Field	
	Validation:	(None)	

* Integer field

Note the copy field validation defined for the TITLECD field. The copy field instructs SQL*Forms to copy the primary key TITLECD over to this field whenever an operator moves into the SYNOPSIS block. A copy field is a first step to enforcing block coordination between the two blocks; an operator can only insert and query SYNOPSIS records associated with the film title displayed on the TITLE screen.

Defining Triggers

SQL*Forms triggers transform your application from the rudimentary to the fully functional. Triggers are packets of logic placed at various event points in the form. When a certain event occurs, a predefined trigger will fire, executing a set of instructions written to control processing for the event. For example, suppose an operator is entering the format of a new film title. The allowed values are either 'Color' or 'B&W', but an operator mistakenly enters the value 'Cartoon.' A trigger could be defined at this event point which would activate as soon as the operator attempted to move out of the field. The field trigger would immediately reject the value 'Cartoon' and issue an error message.

Triggers can be written with SQL statements or a variety of SQL*Forms commands. The latter include a macro language for reprogramming and augmenting the function of function keys, a CASE statement to perform if-then-else style logic, and global SQL*Forms commands to call other forms and to process information passed between forms in the application. Via user exits, programs written in natural languages can be called from within a form to perform highly specialized functions.

Triggers are associated with (or *triggered by*) five different events that occur during the processing of an application. These events are:

Entry	when an operator first runs a form or when the cursor *enters* a new block, record, or field.
Query	before or after records are fetched from the database.
Change	after the operator changes a value, or before or after inserted, updated, or deleted records are committed to the database.
Exit	when the operator leaves a form or when the cursor leaves a block, record, or field.
Keystrokes	when the operator presses a function key

Triggers can be defined to control these events at three different *levels* of the form—the form, block, and field levels. In hierarchical fashion, the *trigger scope*, or the range of a trigger depends on the level for which it is defined. A trigger defined at the broadest level, the form level, affects every block of the form unless it is redefined for a specific block. A block level trigger—the next level down the hierarchy—affects only the events and perhaps fields within the block for which it is defined. The lowest trigger level, the field level, affects only the individual trigger field.

Field Triggers

At the field level, SQL*Forms provides three types of triggers—*Pre-Field*, *Post-Field*, and *Post-Change*. These field triggers are appropriately named after the events they control:

Pre-Field	Executes when the cursor moves *into* a field.
Post-Field	Executes when the cursor moves *out* of the field.
Post-Change	Executes when the cursor moves out a field whose value has changed. Also executes when a record is fetched by a query because the field is then *changed* by the displayed data.

The Trigger Objective

To be successful with triggers, you must clarify the objective of each trigger succinctly. Know precisely what you want the trigger to do before you write a single trigger step. Absolute clarity of the trigger objective makes it easier to determine which type of trigger to use and where to place it.

The first trigger you will define for the TITLE block is on the COLOR_ BW field. The trigger objective is as follows:

"Define a trigger to verify that an operator enters only the values 'Color' or 'B&W' for the format of the film title."

Given the three trigger types, which one would you use to define this trigger? Clearly, the trigger must check against a value entered by an operator, so this rules out the Pre-Field trigger. A Post-Field trigger fires only when the cursor leaves the field, but says nothing about a value being *changed* in the field. The Post-Change trigger is the correct choice.

The following summarizes the steps required to write this Post-Change trigger.

1. Press [Define] to display the DEFINE FIELD window for the COLOR_ BW field.

2. Choose the TRIGGER action item.

3. Type POST-CHANGE and select CREATE.

You are now peering into the TRIGGER STEP window where you will write the Post-Change trigger. As shown in Figure 7.19, you will write a simple SQL SELECT statement trigger to validate data entry on the COLOR_ BW field; this trigger step will be labelled "Chk-entry." A trigger can contain a single step or span many steps. While not mandatory, it is advisable to get into the habit of labelling trigger steps for mnemonic reasons.

4. Write the SELECT statement trigger, label it and add the error message as follows:

```
Seq #1                        Label: Chk-Entry

SELECT color_bw
  FROM title
 WHERE title.color_bw = :title.color_bw

Message if trigger step fails:

Valid choices are 'Color' or 'BW'. Please reenter . . .
```

```
┌──────────────────────────────────────────────────────────────────────┐
│  ┌─ Video Quest TITLE Search ─────────────────────────────────────┐   │
│  │                                                                 │   │
│  │   ┌─────────────────────────────────────┐                      │   │
│  │   │    DEFINE FIELD        Seq # 7       │                      │   │
│  │   │ Name color_bw                                               │   │
│  │   │   ┌──────────────────────────────┐                         │   │
│  │   │   │    CHOOSE TRIGGER            │ ning Time  Censor Rating  Star Rating│
│  │   │   │ Name                         │                          │   │
│  │   │   │ POST-CHANGE                  │                          │   │
│  │   │   └──────────────────────────────┘                         │   │
│  │   ┌───────────────────────────────────────────────────────┐    │   │
│  │   │ Seq # 1           TRIGGER STEP        Label Chk-entry  │    │   │
│  │   │ SELECT color_bw                                        │    │   │
│  │   │   FROM title                                           │    │   │
│  │   │  WHERE title.color_bw = :title.color_bw                │    │   │
│  │   │                                                        │    │   │
│  │   │                                                        │    │   │
│  │   │ Message if trigger step fails:                         │    │   │
│  │   │ Valid choices are 'Color' or 'B&W'.  Please re-enter...│    │   │
│  │   │ Actions:                                               │    │   │
│  │   │    CREATE      COPY       DROP       ATTRIBUTES   COMMENT│   │   │
│  │   │    FORWARD     BACKWARD   PREV STEP  NEXT STEP          │    │   │
│  │   └───────────────────────────────────────────────────────┘    │   │
│  │              ┴┴┴                             ┴┴┴                 │   │
│  └─────────────────────────────────────────────────────────────────┘  │
│   Form: title      Block: title      Page: 1   SELECT: 1  Char Mode: Replace│
└──────────────────────────────────────────────────────────────────────┘
```

Figure 7.19   Post-Change Trigger on the COLOR_BW Field

SQL*Forms requires special syntax when you reference a form field in the WHERE clause of a SQL statement trigger. A field reference must be preceded by a colon (:) to distinguish it from a table reference of the same name. One exception to this rule is with the SQL*Forms extension to SQL, the SELECT INTO statement, which we'll discuss in a moment.

Observe what this trigger is actually doing. The WHERE clause compares the value entered in the COLOR_BW field (*:title.color_bw*) by the allowed values stored in the corresponding *color_bw* column in the TITLE table (*title.color_bw*). If there is a match, then the SELECT statement trigger returns a row from the table, and the trigger is said to *succeed*. If no values match, then the SELECT statement fails; ergo, the trigger is said to *fail*. When it does, SQL*Forms displays the error message you've defined.

Note: There are performance implications with this trigger. Since the trigger must scan all *color_bw* column values in the TITLE table, the trigger will perform worse as the TITLE table grows. There are ways to redesign the trigger to improve performance, such as with the following SELECT statement:

```
SELECT 'x'
  FROM dual
 WHERE :title.color_bw IN ('BW', 'Color')
```

You will investigate these techniques in a moment.

You should now test your trigger yourself. Save, generate, then run the form (after you've written the trigger, naturally). Query a title record, then update the COLOR_BW field by entering garbage data into it. The trigger will not let you get by—that is, the trigger fails—unless, of course, you committed a typographical error when entering the trigger step. If you've erred, return to SQL*Forms (Design) and correct the trigger step. Retest the trigger as many times as necessary.

Defining a Trigger to Display Data

Triggers are useful for displaying data that is related to a form field but is not stored in the base table of the form. By displaying related data, the form automatically validates operator input as well. A related value cannot be displayed unless it *relates* exclusively to the compared value.

Trigger Objective:
Display a description of the film category code entered by the operator.

Solution:
Define a Post-Change trigger on the CATEGORY field which selects the film category *description* matching the category code entered by the operator. This SELECT statement trigger performs a table look-up in the CATEGORY table. Any value returned by the SELECT statement is displayed in the temporary field, CATDESC, which you added to the TITLE form for this very reason.

Enter the following Post-Change trigger for the CATEGORY field:

```
Seq #1                    Label: Get-catdesc

SELECT description
  INTO catdesc
  FROM category
 WHERE category.category = :title.category

Message if trigger step fails:

Invalid film category. Use [List Values] to see valid choices.
```

The trigger you just entered should appear on the TRIGGER STEP Window as in Figure 7.20.

```
┌──────────────────────────────────────────────────────────────────────┐
│  ┌─ Video Quest TITLE Search ─────────────────────────────────────┐   │
│  │                                                                 │   │
│  │  ┌──────────────────────────────────────────────┐              │   │
│  │  │     DEFINE FIELD        Seq # 3               │              │   │
│  │  │ Name category                                 │              │   │
│  │  │  ┌──────────────────────────────────────────┐ │             │   │
│  │  │  │      CHOOSE TRIGGER                       │ │             │   │
│  │  │  │ Name                         ning Time  Censor Rating  Star Rating
│  │  │  │ POST-CHANGE                              │ │             │   │
│  │  │  └──────────────────────────────────────────┘ │             │   │
│  │  ┌────────────────────────────────────────────────────────────┐│   │
│  │  │ Seq # 1            TRIGGER STEP          Label Get_cat      ││   │
│  │  │ SELECT description                                         ││   │
│  │  │   INTO cdesc                                               ││   │
│  │  │   FROM category                                           ││   │
│  │  │ WHERE category.category = :title.category                 ││   │
│  │  │                                                            ││   │
│  │  │ Message if trigger step fails:                            ││   │
│  │  │ Invalid category. Use [List Values] to see valid choices. ││   │
│  │  │ Actions:                                                   ││   │
│  │  │     CREATE      COPY        DROP        ATTRIBUTES   COMMENT││   │
│  │  │     FORWARD     BACKWARD    PREV STEP   NEXT STEP          ││   │
│  │  └────────────────────────────────────────────────────────────┘│   │
│  └─────────────────────┴┴┴─────────────────────────┴┴┴───────────┘   │
│                                                                        │
│   Form: title      Block: title      Page: 1    SELECT: 1  Char Mode: Replace
└──────────────────────────────────────────────────────────────────────┘
```

Figure 7.20   Post-Change Trigger on the CATEGORY Field

The SELECT INTO Statement

The SELECT INTO statement is a SQL extension peculiar to ORACLE tools, such as SQL*Forms, that store values returned by SELECT statements. SELECT INTO is required whenever you retrieve a value from a SELECT statement and display it in a form field. You must use SELECT INTO whether you are retrieving a value from a database table or simply selecting a value from one form field to be displayed in another field.

Converting Date Formats in Triggers

Converting date formats in triggers appears tricky at first. In reality, it is no more difficult than converting date formats within SQL*Plus. Walk through the following trigger to see how this is done.

Trigger Objective:
Prevent an operator from entering a release date for a title which is later than the current date.

Solution:
Define a Post-Change trigger on the RELEASE field to compare the entered value to the current date (*sysdate*). This Post-Change trigger involves a date

format conversion of the RELEASE value (which is a CHAR field) to a date value in the 'YYYY' format mask.

Enter the following Post-Change trigger for the RELEASE field (the syntax will be explained in the following sections):

```
Seq #1                          Label: Chk-release


SELECT 'x'
  FROM dual
 WHERE to_date(:release, 'YYYY') <= sysdate


Message if trigger step fails:

You cannot enter a release date that is later than today!
```

The trigger you just entered should appear on the TRIGGER STEP Window as in Figure 7.21.

The secret of converting dates in triggers is that SQL*Forms converts all data on the screen to character values. Any data displayed on the screen is treated as a character string whether it is a number, a date, or a character value in the database. SQL*Forms ultimately converts all character

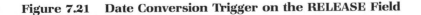

Figure 7.21   Date Conversion Trigger on the RELEASE Field

values on screen back to their appropriate datatype formats when committing the data to the database.

When you want to change the format of a "date" within SQL*Forms, you must first convert the on-screen character value to a *date* value. New SQL*Forms users often have trouble with this concept. Within SQL*Plus, a date value must be converted to a character string to alter the date format. Within SQL*Forms, however, the direction of the conversion is reversed.

Since every value is treated as a character in SQL*Forms, you must always convert to a date value no matter what datatype you are working with. This rule applies to fields defined as *date fields* as well. If you remember that a date field datatype refers to the *database* format in SQL*Forms, not the format displayed on screen, the concept is easier to grasp.

The DUAL Table in SQL*Forms

Another twist to this trigger is the use of the DUAL table. DUAL is the dummy table supplied by ORACLE—a one-row, one-column table. You will rely on DUAL when building SELECT triggers that compare field values or propagate values derived from other screen fields. If you do not need to select a value from a specific table, use DUAL. The law of SQL syntax demands that you SELECT FROM some table or another. For performance reasons, use the smallest conceivable table, DUAL.

Block Triggers

Block triggers cover a much wider territory than field triggers and control many more events. SQL*Forms provides twelve types of block triggers, which can be classified either as *query triggers*, *commit triggers*, *block navigation triggers*, or *record triggers*. The block triggers are summarized as follows:

Query Triggers
These are activated during query processing.

Pre-Query	Executes after an operator presses [Execute Query] or [Count Query Hits] (or when another trigger executes these query functions); this trigger executes *once* per query.
Post-Query	Executes once for each record retrieved by the query, just after the record is displayed.

Commit Triggers

These are activated during the commit of a transaction.

Pre/Post-Delete	Executes once for each deleted record, just *before* or *after* the corresponding row is deleted from the database.
Pre/Post-Insert	Executes once for each inserted record, just *before* or *after* the corresponding row is inserted into the database.
Pre/Post-Update	Executes once for each updated record, just *before* or *after* the corresponding row is updated in the database.

Block Navigation Triggers

These are activated while moving through a block.

Pre-Block	Executes when the cursor moves into a block.
Post-Block	Executes when the cursor is about to leave the block; this trigger fires *after* the Post-Field and Post-Record triggers have fired.

Record Triggers

These are activated during processing of a record.

Pre-Record	Executes when the cursor is about to move into any record in the block; this trigger fires *after* the Pre-Block trigger (if the cursor is just moving into the block), but *before* a Pre-Field trigger defined for the first field the cursor moves into.
Post-Record	Executes when the cursor is about to leave the record; this trigger fires *after* the post-field trigger of the current field, but *before* the post-block trigger (if the cursor is moving out of the block as well).

In addition to these block triggers, the field triggers can be defined at the block level. You can also define *user-named triggers* at both the block and field levels. User-named triggers are ordinary triggers that can be called from another trigger by name. User-named triggers are frequently used to save the designer from having to retype triggers issued repeatedly.

Defining the TITLE Block Triggers

Only two block triggers are defined for the TITLE block. One trigger represents the *commit trigger* class, while the other is a *program trigger* which uses a macro function to augment the processing of a function key.

Commit Trigger Objective:

Prevent an operator from deleting a title record if there is also a synopsis for the title.

Solution:

Define a Pre-Delete commit trigger on the TITLE block. The trigger objective clearly described a delete operation, and the *pre*-delete event point was intimated by the wording of the objective. The trigger must check whether a synopsis exists for the title record *before* the delete operation is transacted.

Enter the following Pre-Delete trigger text for the TITLE block (you will do so from the DEFINE BLOCK window, choosing the TRIGGER item):

```
Seq #1                     Label: No-del-if-synopsis

SELECT 'x'
  FROM synopsis
 WHERE synopsis.titlecd = :title.titlecd


Message if trigger step fails:

You cannot delete title as synopsis exists! Delete
synopsis first . . .
```

The trigger you just entered should appear on the BLOCK TRIGGER STEP Window as in Figure 7.22.

Examine the WHERE clause of this SELECT statement trigger. The title displayed on the screen (represented by the primary key *titlecd*) is compared to the foreign key *titlecd* column in the SYNOPSIS table. If there is a matching row in the SYNOPSIS table, then the trigger succeeds. But observe how the error message is worded—the message implies that the trigger *did* find a matching value, that is, a synopsis does exist for the title an operator is trying to delete. To display a "failure" message when a trigger actually succeeds, you must reverse the return code of the message. You do this on the TRIGGER STEP ATTRIBUTES window:

1. Choose the ATTRIBUTES item on the BLOCK TRIGGER STEP window.

2. Select the Reverse Return Code option.

The TRIGGER STEP ATTRIBUTES window for your Pre-Delete trigger is shown in Figure 7.23.

A trigger step defaults to the Abort trigger when step fails attribute. This ensures that if an individual trigger step fails, the entire trigger

```
┌─────────────────────────────────────────────────────────────────┐
│  ┌─ Video Quest TITLE Search ──────────────────────────────────  │
│  │                                                                │
│  │ ┌──────────────────────────────────────────┐                  │
│  │ │       DEFINE BLOCK          Seq # 1       │                  │
│  │ │  Name   title                             │                  │
│  │ │ ┌──────────────────────────────┐          │                  │
│  │ │ │      CHOOSE TRIGGER          │          │                  │
│  │ │ │ Name                         │ Time  Censor Rating  Star Rating │
│  │ │ │ PRE-DELETE                   │                       │
│  │ │ └──────────────────────────────┘          │                  │
│  │ ┌────────────────────────────────────────────────────────┐    │
│  │ │ Seq # 1           TRIGGER STEP        Label Chk-synopsis│    │
│  │ │ SELECT 'x'                                              │    │
│  │ │   FROM synopsis                                         │    │
│  │ │  WHERE synopsis.titlecd = :title.titlecd               │    │
│  │ │                                                        │    │
│  │ │                                                        │    │
│  │ │ Message if trigger step fails:                         │    │
│  │ │ You cannot delete title as synopsis exists!  Delete synopsis first...│
│  │ │ Actions:                                               │    │
│  │ │     CREATE        COPY         DROP       ATTRIBUTES    COMMENT │
│  │ │     FORWARD       BACKWARD     PREV STEP  NEXT STEP     │    │
│  │ └────────────────────────────────────────────────────────┘    │
│  │                                                                │
│  Form: title      Block: title      Page: 1   SELECT: B Char Mode: Replace │
└─────────────────────────────────────────────────────────────────┘
```

Figure 7.22   Pre-Delete Trigger on the TITLE Block

```
┌─────────────────────────────────────────────────────────────────┐
│  ┌─ Video Quest TITLE Search ──────────────────────────────────  │
│  │                                                                │
│  │ ┌──────────────────────────────────────────┐                  │
│  │ │       DEFINE BLOCK          Seq # 1       │                  │
│  │ │  Name   title                             │                  │
│  │ │ ┌──────────────────────────────┐          │                  │
│  │ │ │      CHOOSE TRIGGER          │          │                  │
│  │ │ │ Name                         │ Time  Censor Rating  Star Rating │
│  │ │ │ PRE-DELETE                   │                       │
│  │ │ └──────────────────────────────┘          │                  │
│  │ ┌────────────────────────────────────────────────────────┐    │
│  │ │ Seq # 1           TRIGGER STEP        Label Chk-synopsis│    │
│  │ │ SELECT 'x'       ┌──────────────────────────────────┐  │    │
│  │ │   FROM synopsis  │       TRIGGER STEP ATTRIBUTES     │  │    │
│  │ │  WHERE synopsis.titlecd = : │                        │  │    │
│  │ │                  │   Abort trigger when step fails   │  │    │
│  │ │                  │  *Reverse return code             │  │    │
│  │ │ Message if trigger step fai│ Return success when aborting trigger │
│  │ │ You cannot delete title as │ Separate cursor data area │  │  │
│  │ │ Actions:         │                                   │  │    │
│  │ │     CREATE        COPY      │ Success label           │  │    │
│  │ │     FORWARD       BACKWARD  │ Failure label           │  │    │
│  │ │                  └──────────────────────────────────┘  │    │
│  │ └────────────────────────────────────────────────────────┘    │
│  │                                                                │
│  Form: title      Block: title      Page: 1   SELECT: B Char Mode: Replace │
└─────────────────────────────────────────────────────────────────┘
```

Figure 7.23   TRIGGER STEP ATTRIBUTES Window

aborts. If the trigger contains additional trigger steps, none of them are executed. By adding the Reverse Return Code, you instruct SQL*Forms to display a "failure" message when the trigger succeeds.

When the Reverse return code attribute is combined with the default Abort Trigger attribute, the trigger aborts even though the result of trigger step is true (or *succeeds*). The trigger step is said to fail if the "failure" message displays. However, if you were to select *only* the Reverse Return code attribute, the "failure" message would indeed display if the trigger statement were true—but SQL*Forms would cause the trigger step to *succeed* and the operator would be allowed to delete the record anyway. This would of course defeat the purpose of the trigger.

Using Macros in Triggers

Movement between the TITLE and SYNOPSIS blocks must be carefully controlled. A synopsis only has meaning if tied to a film title. The application would look rather sloppy if an operator were to query a synopsis against the *Ghostbusters* title and see the synopsis text for *Citizen Kane* instead.

Macro functions in triggers are a powerful technique for controlling cursor navigation and coordinating related blocks. Macros are often used in the context of *event triggers* such as the Pre-Delete or the Post-Change triggers studied in the preceding examples. Event triggers execute during processing of normal SQL*Forms events—entries, exits, queries and so forth.

Macros also play a role in *program triggers*, triggers that execute independently of normal SQL*Forms processing. Function key triggers, like the one you are about to define, are the most common application of program triggers.

Trigger Objective:
Automatically query the synopsis text for the current title when the operator wants to see it.

Solution:
Define a Key-Nxtblk key trigger to augment the functionality of the [Next Block] key. An operator normally presses [Next Block] to move into the SYNOPSIS block. Your Key-Nxtblk trigger will automatically query a synopsis of the title by executing the EXEQRY macro function after the cursor moves into the SYNOPSIS block. (The EXEQRY macro acts as if the operator had pressed the [Execute Query] function key.)

Enter the Key-Nxtblk trigger for the TITLE block:

```
Seq #1                          Label: autoqry-nxtblk

#EXEMACRO nxtblk; exeqry;

Message if trigger step fails:

Program error occurred while querying synopsis. Call your
supervisor.
```

The trigger you just entered should appear on the BLOCK TRIGGER STEP Window as in Figure 7.24.

```
 ┌─ Video Quest TITLE Search ──────────────────────────────────────┐
 │                                                                  │
 │   ┌─────────────────────────────────────────┐                    │
 │   │       DEFINE BLOCK        Seq # 1        │                    │
 │   │  Name   title                            │                    │
 │   │   ┌──────────────────────────────┐       │                    │
 │   │   │       CHOOSE TRIGGER          │       │                    │
 │   │  Name                            │  Time  Censor Rating  Star Rating
 │   │  Key-nxtblk                      │                            │
 │   ├──────────────────────────────────────────────────────────┐   │
 │   │ Seq # 1          TRIGGER STEP        Label get_nxtblk     │   │
 │   │ #EXEMACRO nxtblk;exeqry;                                  │   │
 │   │                                                          │   │
 │   │                                                          │   │
 │   │                                                          │   │
 │   │ Message if trigger step fails:                           │   │
 │   │ Program error occurred while querying synopsis.  Call your supervisor.
 │   │ Actions:                                                 │   │
 │   │     CREATE      COPY       DROP      ATTRIBUTES  COMMENT  │   │
 │   │     FORWARD     BACKWARD   PREV STEP NEXT STEP            │   │
 │   └──────────────────────────────────────────────────────────┘   │
 │                                                                  │
 │   Form: title      Block: title     Page: 1   SELECT: B  Char Mode: Replace
 └──────────────────────────────────────────────────────────────────┘
```

Figure 7.24   Key-Nxtblk Trigger on the TITLE Block

Defining the SYNOPSIS Block Triggers

You will define three block-level triggers for the SYNOPSIS block. The first two, Key-Nxtblk and Pre-Update, show you how to disable function keys and prevent commit processing for the block. The third example, Pre-Insert, demonstrates how to define a three-step trigger to generate line numbers for rows of synopsis text.

Disabling Function Keys

When an operator reaches the last block of a form, SQL*Forms causes [Next Block] to loop to the first block. Since the TITLE and SYNOPSIS blocks must be carefully coordinated, you should only allow monodirectional movement between the blocks. Pressing [Previous Block] to return to the TITLE block is quite sufficient.

Trigger Objective:
Prevent an operator from using [Next Block] to return to the TITLE block.

Solution:
Disable the [Next Block] function in the SYNOPSIS block. The Key-Nxtblk key trigger employs the NULL (or NOOP) macro function to do this. In the TITLE block, the [Next Block] function has a special function, while in the SYNOPSIS block, the same function is disabled. This is one example of trigger scope. Enter the trigger:

```
Seq #1                    Label: no-nxtblk


#EXEMACRO null;


Message if trigger step fails:

Press Previous Block to return to the TITLE page.
```

Under normal conditions, the failure message displays only when the trigger step fails. When disabling a function key, however, you must reverse the return code of the failure message to display the message text. Even though the result of the trigger disables the function key (or causes it to fail), the trigger step has *succeeded*. Thus, the failure message wouldn't display unless you specify the reverse return code attribute, causing the message to display upon *success* of the trigger step.

Generating Line Numbers

When a new line of synopsis text is inserted into the database, a unique line number must be stored with it. The challenge is to generate a line number for the first record and each successive line number in sequence.

Trigger Objective:
Automatically generate a unique, sequential line number for every synopsis record inserted into SYNOPSIS table.

Solution:
Define a Pre-Insert trigger consisting of three separate steps. The first trigger step must verify whether the record is the first record being inserted

into the table. If it is, then a separate trigger step must be executed to generate line number 1 for this record; if it is not the first record, then the remainder of the trigger steps are allowed to execute. This is an example of *conditional branching* logic in SQL*Forms triggers.

To summarize these steps, the trigger you will write performs the following logic conditionally.

Seq #1   Add-lineno

Generate the next sequential line number if the record is not the first one inserted into the table. Select this number into the LINENO field, then GO TO trigger step labelled: Okay-lineno.

If it is the first row, GO TO a trigger step labelled Line1.

Seq #2   Line1

Select the number 1 into the lineno *column and the corresponding TITLECD into the SYNOPSIS field, then GO TO next trigger step in sequence.*

Seq #3   Okay-lineo

Forces success of the entire trigger, allowing a graceful exit.

Enter the following three-step, Pre-Insert trigger for the SYNOPSIS block:

Trigger Step #1

Seq #1   Label: Add-lineno

```
SELECT nvl(max(lineno), 0) + 1
  INTO lineno
  FROM synopsis
 WHERE synopsis.titlecd = :synopsis.titlecd
```

To control the success or failure branching of this trigger, you use the TRIGGER STEP ATTRIBUTES window. Figure 7.25 shows how these labels must be defined for this first trigger step.

If this trigger step succeeds—if it is *not* the first row to be inserted—then SQL*Forms will jump immediately to the trigger step labelled *Okay-lineno* (the third step in sequence). If this step fails, SQL*forms branches to the step labelled *Line1* (the next step in sequence) and executes that step instead. Observe that there are no trigger attributes for this step.

```
┌─────────────────────────────────────────────────────────────────────┐
│ Synopsis for title:                                                   │
│  ┌──────────────────────────────────────┬─────────────────────────┐  │
│  │        DEFINE BLOCK        Seq # 2    │ ▌▌▌▌▌▌▌▌▌▌▌▌▌▌▌▌▌▌▌▌▌▌▌▌ │  │
│  │   Name   synopsis                     │                         │  │
│  │  ┌──────────────────────┐             │                         │  │
│  │  │     CHOOSE TRIGGER    │             │                         │  │
│  │  │ Name                 │             │                         │  │
│  │  │ PRE-INSERT           │             │                         │  │
│  └──┴──────────────────────┴─────────────┴─────────────────────────┘  │
│  ┌────────────────────────────────────────────────────────────────┐  │
│  │ Seq # 1          TRIGGER STEP          Label Add-lineno          │  │
│  │ SELECT nvl(max(lineno),0) +┌──────────────────────────────────┐ │  │
│  │   INTO lineno              │    TRIGGER STEP ATTRIBUTES        │ │  │
│  │   FROM synopsis            │                                  │ │  │
│  │   WHERE synopsis.titlecd = :│   Abort trigger when step fails │ │  │
│  │                            │   Reverse return code           │ │  │
│  │ Message if trigger step fai│   Return success when aborting trigger│ │
│  │                            │   Separate cursor data area      │ │  │
│  │ Actions:                   │                                  │ │  │
│  │     CREATE      COPY       │  Success label Okay-lineno       │ │  │
│  │     FORWARD     BACKWARD   │  Failure label Line1             │ │  │
│  └────────────────────────────┴──────────────────────────────────┘  │
│  └──────────────────────────┘ VIDEO QUEST RENTALS, Inc. └──────────┘  │
│                                                                       │
│  Form: title       Block: synopsis    Page: 2   SELECT: B  Char Mode: Replace │
└─────────────────────────────────────────────────────────────────────┘
```

Figure 7.25   Success/Failure Labels for Pre-Insert Trigger

Trigger Step #2

Seq #2   **Label:** Line1

```
SELECT 1, :title.titlecd
  INTO lineno, synopsis.titlecd
  FROM dual
```

Message if trigger step fails:

Pre-insert error. Problem inserting 1st line number. Call your supervisor.

This step defaults to the Abort trigger when step fails attribute. If the trigger cannot insert the first line number, nothing should be inserted into the database. Upon success of this trigger step, SQL*Forms automatically executes the next step in sequence. No branch labels are required.

Now add the final trigger step:

Trigger Step #3

Seq #3   **Label:** Okay-lineno

```
SELECT 'x'
  FROM dual
 WHERE 1 = 1
```

The purpose of this trigger step is to force success and exit the trigger gracefully. If you define a success branch, a failure branch must also be defined, and vice versa. Since Trigger Step #1 has a failure branch, this step is its counterpart branch. The entire trigger will be repeated for the next row of text to be inserted into the SYNOPSIS table, until there are no more rows to be inserted.

Form Triggers

Triggers defined at the form level guard the entrance and exit to a form and control the processing events of every block and every field within the form. Specifically, there are two types of form triggers:

Pre-Form   Executes when a form is run or entered.

Post-Form   Executes when the operator is about to leave the form, *after* committing all changes and executing the Post-Field, Post-Record, and Post-Block triggers for the current field, record, and block.

In addition, you can define field, block, key, and user-named triggers at the form level. These affect all fields and blocks in the form unless a field or block-level trigger overrides them.

The Key-Startup Trigger

The Key-Startup program trigger is a clever device often used to design a form that runs without operator input. You will create such a form shortly. For the moment, study a less ambitious application of this trigger defined at the form level.

Trigger Objective:
Display a descriptive help message on the status line of the form as soon it starts up.

Solution:

A Key-Startup form trigger is used to force trigger success, displaying the help message. You define the help text as a "failure" message, and choose the Reverse Return Code attribute. (Version 2.3 of SQL*Forms offers a new MESSAGE function code that allows you to display messages conditionally, which is perhaps a cleaner way of doing this. Version 2.0 users, however, must be content with the Key-Startup approach.)

Form triggers are defined by executing the following steps:

1. Choose DEFINE from the CHOOSE FORM Window to display the DEFINE FORM window.

2. Choose TRIGGER to display the CHOOSE TRIGGER window.

3. Define the form trigger as you would any other.

Enter the following Key-Startup trigger text for the TITLE form:

```
Seq #1                    Label: Display-msg

SELECT 'x'
  FROM dual
 WHERE 1 = 1

Message if trigger step fails:

Add title or update one. To query: [Enter], type query,
[Execute Query].
```

Building the CUSTOMER Form

The theme for building the CUSTOMER form is Master-Detail block coordination. Although the blocks of the TITLE form require careful coordination, the design of the CUSTOMER form necessitates even tighter block control. The application must coordinate the CUSTOMER blocks for both query and modification operations *automatically*. When a master CUSTOMER record is queried, for example, any detail CUSTNAME records are automatically displayed. When a CUSTOMER record is deleted, the detail CUSTNAME records are deleted automatically.

Creating the CUSTOMER Block

The CUSTOMER block is created with the DEFAULT BLOCK Option. After you generate the default form, rearrange the fields in the screen painter. Your field placement should mirror the locations shown in Figure 7.26, the completed CUSTOMER form. Be sure to move all fields generated on Page 2 of this block and to erase the title text on this page.

Only one field must be resized to fit your screen. Resize the MEM-BERID field with the Resize Field function as follows:

```
Field Name   New Field Length
----------   -----------------------------
MEMBERID     7 characters  7 Query Length
```

Before defining the field attributes, create the following nondatabase fields. These are nonenterable fields displaying related data. They are shaded on Figure 7.26 to mark their placement.

```
Field Name   Field Length    Field Type    Related Field
----------   -------------   ----------    -----------------
CREDITDESC   20 characters   CHAR type     Creditcard field
FDESC        15 characters   CHAR type     Format field
```

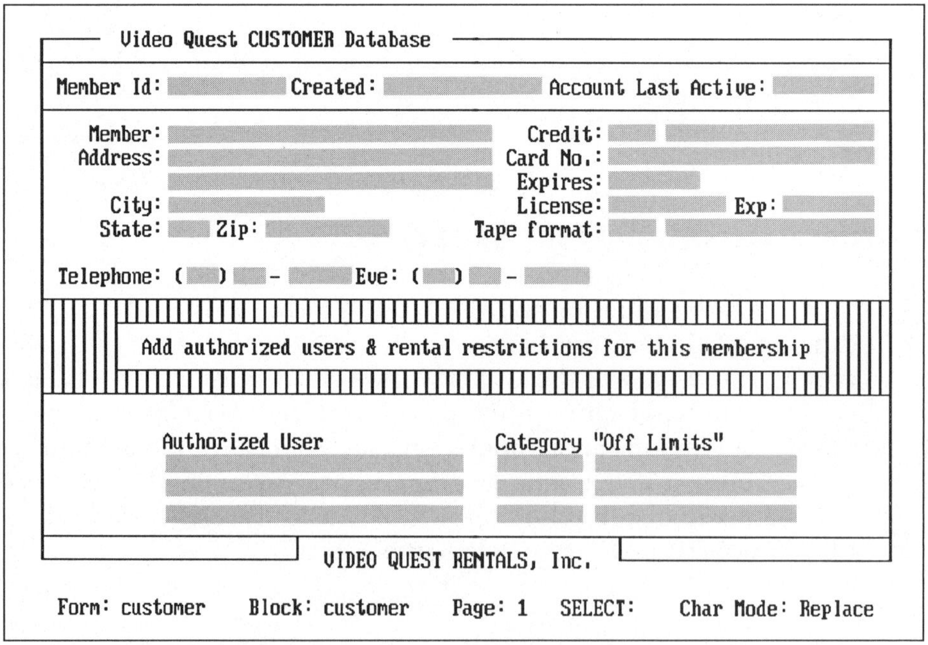

Figure 7.26   The Completed CUSTOMER Form

Define the attributes and default validation for the CUSTOMER fields according to the list of definitions in Table 7.4. The attributes listed are those *added* to the default attributes generated by DEFAULT BLOCK. Exceptions to this rule are the MEMBERID, CREDITDESC, FDESC and LAST_ACT fields. Define only the attributes listed for these fields.

Table 7.4   CUSTOMER Field Definitions

Seq#	Field Name	Label	Field Type
#1	MEMBERID	Member ID†	INT
	Attributes:	Database Field	
		Displayed	
		Query Allowed	
		(Define only these attributes)	
	Validation:	Help: "Memberid of primary member (system generated)."	
#2	NAME	Member:	CHAR
	Attributes:	Automatic help	
	Validation:	Help: "Primary member must be entered to establish membership."	
#3	AD1	Address:	CHAR
	Attributes:	(Default)	
	Validation:	Help: "Street address of customer."	
#4	AD2		CHAR
	Attributes:	(Default)	
	Validation:	Help: "Additional line for address, if necessary."	
#5	CITY	City:	CHAR
	Attributes:	(Default)	
	Validation:	Help: "City of customer's address."	
#6	STATE	State:	CHAR
	Attributes:	Uppercase	
	Validation:	Default Value: CA	
		Help: "State of customer's address."	
#7	ZIP	Zip:	CHAR
	Attributes:	Uppercase	
	Validation:	Help: "Zip code of customer's address."	
#8	DAY_AREA	Telephone:	CHAR
	Attributes:	Fixed Length	
		Autoskip	
	Validation:	Help: "Area code for daytime phone number."	
#9	DAY_PREFIX		CHAR
	Attributes:	Fixed Length	
		Autoskip	
	Validation:	Help: "Prefix for daytime phone number."	
#10	DAY_SUFFIX		CHAR
	Attributes:	Fixed Length	
		Autoskip	
	Validation:	Help: "Suffix for daytime phone number."	

†*Memberid* is nonenterable; the system will generate the unique Member ID with a Pre-Insert trigger.

Table 7.4 *(continued)*

Seq#	Field Name	Label	Field Type
#11	*EVE_AREA*	*Evening:*	*CHAR*
	Attributes:	Fixed Length	
		Autoskip	
	Validation:	Help: "Area code for evening phone number."	
#12	*EVE_PREFIX*		*CHAR*
	Attributes:	Fixed Length	
		Autoskip	
	Validation:	Help: "Prefix for evening phone number."	
#13	*EVE_SUFFIX*		*CHAR*
	Attributes:	Fixed Length	
		Autoskip	
	Validation:	Help: "Suffix for evening phone number."	
#14	*CREDITCARD*	*Credit:*	*CHAR*
	Attributes:	Mandatory	
		Uppercase	
	Validation:	List of Values: Table Paymethod	
		Column Paymethod	
		Help: "Credit card code, e.g., VI, MC, DI. Use [List Values] . . ."	
#15	*CREDITDESC*		*CHAR*
	Attributes:	Displayed	
	Validation:	(None)	
#16	*CREDCDNO*	*Card No.:*	*CHAR*
	Attributes:	Mandatory	
		Uppercase	
	Validation:	Help: "Credit card number."	
#17	*CARDEXP**	*Expires:*	*DATE*
	Attributes:	Mandatory	
		Uppercase	
		Autoskip	
	Validation:	Help: "Credit card expiration date, e.g., "31-DEC-89"."	
#18	*CDLNO*	*License:*	*CHAR*
	Attributes:	Mandatory	
		Uppercase	
	Validation:	Driver's license or ID number.	
#19	*CDLEXP**	*Exp:*	*DATE*
	Attributes:	Mandatory	
		Uppercase	
		Autoskip	
	Validation:	Help: "Driver's license expiration date, e.g., "25-NOV-89"."	
#20	*FORMAT*	*Tape format:*	*CHAR*
	Attributes:	Uppercase	
	Validation:	Default: V	
		Help: "Tape format. Choices: V = VHS, B = Beta, VB = Both VHS/Beta."	
#21	*FDESC*		*CHAR*
	Attributes:	Displayed (Only)	
	Validation:	(None)	

Table 7.4   (*continued*)

Seq#	Field Name	Label	Field Type
#22	*DATE_CREATED** Attributes: Validation:	*Created:* (Default) Default: $$date$$(Displays current date derived from *sysdate*) Help: "Date membership first created. Default is today's date."	*DATE*
#23	*LAST_ACT* Attributes: Validation:	*Account last active:* Database Field Displayed Query Allowed (Define only these attributes) Help: "Date account last activated for either rental, return, sale, or reservation."	*DATE*

Creating the CUSTNAME Block

The CUSTNAME block is based on the CUSTNAME table, allowing queries and modifications of authorized member records. You will create and place the CUSTNAME fields individually on the form.

The link between the CUSTNAME and the CUSTOMER blocks is the MEMBERID field. A copy field, MEMBERID is maintained by the system in the detail CUSTNAME block. MEMBERID is a nondisplayed database field, corresponding to the foreign key column, *memberid*.

Create the following CUSTNAME fields on their respective form pages:

Page	Field Name	Field Length	Field Type	Related Field
0	MEMBERID	7 characters	INT	
1	NAME	30 characters	CHAR	
1	RESTRICT_CAT	3 characters	CHAR	
1	CATDESC	20 characters	CHAR	Restrict_cat

Define the CUSTNAME fields with the field attributes and default validation information listed in Table 7.5.

Table 7.5   CUSTNAME Field Definitions

Seq#	Field Name	Label
#1	*MEMBERID*	*Memberid*
	Attributes:	Database Field (Only)
	Validation:	Copy Field: Block: CUSTOMER
		Field: MEMBERID
#2	*NAME*	*Authorized Member*
	Attributes:	(Default)
	Validation:	Help: "Name of authorized user for this membership."
#3	*RESTRICT_CAT*	*Category "Off Limits"*
	Attributes:	(Default)
	Validation:	List of Values: Table: Category
		Column: Category
		Help: "Restricted category code for authorized member. Use [List Values]."
#4	*CATDESC*	
	Attributes:	Displayed (Only)
	Validation:	(None)

Defining the Triggers

You will define triggers at strategic event points throughout the CUS-TOMER form. Some of these triggers are designed to meet specific functionality requirements; however, the lion's share meet the overriding tactical objective of the form—ensuring block coordination.

Defining the Field Triggers

The field triggers for both CUSTOMER and CUSTNAME blocks fall into two categories—triggers that display related data and triggers that validate a customer's credit card and driver's license.

Displaying Related Customer Information

You've discovered that the dual advantages of displaying related data are to assist operator entry and to prevent garbage from being entered into the database. Apply this knowledge to creating validation triggers for the CREDITCARD and FORMAT fields in the CUSTOMER form and the CATEGORY field in the CUSTNAME form.

CREDITCARD Trigger Objective:
Verify that an operator has entered a credit card honored by Video Quest.

Solution:
Define a Post-Change trigger on the CREDITCARD field that performs a look-up in the PAYMETHOD table. Enter the trigger:

```
Seq: 1      Label: Get-desc

SELECT paymethod.description
  INTO creditdesc
  FROM paymethod
 WHERE paymethod.paymethod = :customer.creditcard
```

Message if trigger step fails:

```
Invalid credit card code, e.g., VI, MC, AX . . . Use
[List Values].
```

FORMAT Trigger Objective:
Verify that an operator has entered an allowed format choice for the customer's default tape format.

Solution:
Define a Post-Change trigger on the FORMAT field that tests operator entry against the allowed format codes and uses the DECODE function to expand the code into English. Enter the trigger:

```
Seq: 1       Label: Get-format

SELECT DECODE(:format, 'V', 'VHS', 'B', 'Beta', 'VB', 'Both
       VHS/Beta')
   INTO fdesc
   FROM dual
  WHERE :format in ('V', 'B', 'VB')
```

Message if trigger step fails:

```
Invalid tape format. V = VHS, B = Beta, VB = Both VHS/Beta.
```

RESTRICT_CAT Trigger Objective:
Verify that the operator has entered a valid film category when adding a viewing restriction for an authorized member.

Solution:
Define a Post-Change trigger on the RESTRICT_CAT field in the CUST-NAME block. The trigger performs a table look-up in the CATEGORY table. Enter the trigger:

```
Seq #1      Label: Get-catdesc

SELECT category.description
  INTO catdesc
  FROM category
 WHERE category.category = :custname.restrict_cat
```

Message if trigger step fails:

```
Invalid film category code. Use [List Values].
```

Verifying Card Expiration Dates

A valid credit card and driver's license are required pieces of identification for membership at Video Quest. The operator cannot be counted on to verify this information manually. Validation triggers must be defined on both the CARDEXP and CDLEXP fields.

CARDEXP Trigger Objective:
Validate that the credit card entered by the operator has not expired.

Solution:
Write a Post-Change trigger on the CARDEXP field that compares the entered date to *sysdate*. Enter the trigger:

```
Seq #1              Label: Chk-cardexp

SELECT 'x'
  FROM dual
 WHERE to_date(:cardexp) >= sysdate
```

Message if trigger step fails:

```
Credit card has expired! If entered incorrectly, try
again . . .
```

Write the same trigger for the CDLEXP field, but change the failure message to reflect the new context—driver's license expiration as opposed to credit card expiration.

Defining the Block Triggers

The block triggers defined for the CUSTOMER form meet two major objectives of the application: enforcing block coordination and generating unique membership IDs for new Video Quest customers.

Enforcing Block Coordination

Automatic block coordination is a three-fold challenge. You must first determine what operations affect both blocks simultaneously, then break these operations down into their respective processing events. Once you've identified the event points, defining the triggers is a formality.

Block coordination typically affects block navigation, query, insert and delete operations. By breaking these functions down, you would see the following events and associated triggers:

Block Navigation	*Trigger*
[Next Block]	Key-Nxtblk
[Previous Block]	Key-Prvblk

Queries	*Trigger*
[Exeqery]	Key-Exeqery
[Entqry]	Key-Entqry
[Next Record]	Key-Nxtrec
[Previous Record]	Key-Prvrec

Inserts	*Trigger*
[Create Record]	Key-Crerec

Deletes	*Trigger*
[Delete]	Key-Delrec
	Pre-Delete

Let's explore the triggers you will define for each of these operations.

Block Navigation Triggers

Key-Nxtblk Objective:

Prevent an operator from moving into the detail block unless a master CUSTOMER record is displayed.

Solution:

Define a Key-Nxtblk trigger to test whether a master record is displayed and, if so, allow the Next Block function to be executed. This trigger requires two steps. Enter

```
Seq #1        Label: Chk-master

SELECT 'x'
  FROM dual
 WHERE :customer.name is null
```

continued

```
Message if trigger step fails:
```

```
You must enter customer information before going to the
next block.
```

Select both the Abort Trigger and the Reverse Return Code attributes. You want the error message to display if the result is true, but you also want to abort this step to prevent the operator from moving to the next block until a value has been entered. Now enter the last trigger step:

```
Seq: 2          Label: Ok-nxtblk
```

```
#EXEMACRO nxtblk;
```

```
Message if trigger step fails:
```

```
Program error: Problem executing Next Block. See your
supervisor.
```

Key-Prvblk Objective:
Prevent an operator from using [Previous Block] in the CUSTOMER block to move into the detail block.

Solution:
Disable the [Previous Block] function. Unless you do, the operator can bypass the copy field control and operate on random CUSTNAME records. Enter the Key-Prvblk trigger text:

```
Seq #1     Label: No-prvblk
```

```
#EXEMACRO null;
```

```
Message if trigger step fails:
```

```
Nowhere to go from here! You're in the Master block . . .
```

Be sure to specify the reverse the return code attribute.

Query Coordination Triggers

One tedious aspect of defining the query triggers for coordinated blocks is that block navigation must be built into each query function. Fortunately there's a shortcut. You can define a user-named trigger to perform this repetitive task, and call it from the query triggers with the EXETRG macro function. You will define the Query_Details user-named trigger to do the grunt work.

Query_Details Objective:
Automatically coordinate query execution between blocks.

Solution:
Define a user-named trigger on the CUSTOMER block that employs the CASE statement macro. The CASE statement executes conditionally, testing whether a master record exists before executing the coordinated query.

Enter the Query_Details trigger text:

```
Seq #1      Label: Query-details

#EXEMACRO CASE customer.memberid is
    WHEN '' then null;
    WHEN others THEN goblk custname; exeqry;
        goblk customer;
END CASE;
```

Message if trigger step fails:

Program error: Problem querying coordinated blocks.

The sole reason you are testing for a null value in the Query-Details trigger is to avoid a bizarre block coordination problem with SQL*Forms. When SQL*Forms reaches the end of a set of queried records, a blank (or null) record is inserted into the master block. Because navigation between the blocks is automatically coordinated, SQL*Forms then moves into the detail block, but without copying a copy value. This violates block coordination, causing SQL*Forms to display unrelated data in the detail block. (SQL*Forms will actually fetch *all* records for the detail block as though [Execute Query] had been pressed on this block alone.)

You can now define the individual query key-triggers to call these user-named triggers where appropriate.

Key-Entqry
For this, you enter

```
Seq #1    Label: Coord-entqry

#EXEMACRO entqry; exetrg query_details;
```

Message if trigger step fails:

Program error: Problem executing [Enter Query] in coordinated blocks.

When the operator presses the [Enter Query] key and enters normal query conditions, the user-named trigger Query_Details will fire to enforce master-detail block coordination.

Since the EXECUTE QUERY function has been defined to operate in the Query_Details trigger, disable the [Execute Query] function key and select [Reverse Return Code] to display the failure message:

Key-Exeqry
For this, you enter

```
Seq #1      Label: No-exeqry

#EXEMACRO null;

Message if trigger step fails:

You must enter specific customer information to query.
Press [Enter Query].
```

Key-Nxtrec
To create this, enter

```
Seq #1      Label: Coord-nxtrec

#EXEMACRO nxtrec; exetrg query-details;

Message if trigger step fails:

Program error: Problem executing [Next Record] in
coordinated blocks.
```

Key-Prvrec
To create this trigger, you enter

```
Seq #1      Label: Coord-prvrec

#EXEMACRO prvrec; exetrg query-details;

Message if trigger step fails:

Program error: Problem executing [Previous Record] in
coordinated blocks.
```

Inserting Records with Coordinated Blocks

As in querying coordinated blocks, inserting records with coordinated blocks requires repetitive typing to perform block navigation. You can define the user-named trigger Clear_Details to handle this task.

Clear_Details Objective:

Automatically clear all previously displayed records in the detail block before creating new records.

Solution:

Write the same CASE statement trigger as in the Query_Details user-named trigger, but substitute the CLRBLK macro for the EXEQRY function. You must test for a null value in the master block prior to clearing the detail block. Enter the Clear_Details trigger text:

```
Seq #1     Label: Clr-details

#EXEMACRO CASE customer.memberid is
    WHEN '' then null;
     WHEN others THEN goblk custname; clrblk;
          goblk customer;
END CASE
```

You can now call Clear_Details from the insert key-trigger, Key-Crerec, which redefines the [Create Record] function key for the CUSTOMER block.

Key-Crerec / CUSTOMER Block

To perform this, enter

```
Seq #1     Label: Coord-crerec

#EXEMACRO EXETRG clear_details; crerec;

Message if trigger step fails:

Program error: Problem executing [Create Record] in
coordinated blocks.
```

Deleting Records From Coordinated Blocks

Enforcing block coordination with deletes is a bit trickier. You will redefine the [Delete Record] key to clear detail records and simultaneously delete the master record. In addition, you must define a Pre-Delete commit trigger to physically delete the detail records in the database. SQL*Forms permits data modification commands (INSERTS, UPDATES, DELETES) to be used only in commit triggers.

Key-Delete Objective:
Delete the master record, but clear the display of any associated detail records at the same time.

Solution:
Synchronize the Clear_Details and Query_Details triggers with the DELREC function. Use Clear_Details to clear the details records, then execute DELREC. As a precaution, call Query_Details to validate that the master record has been deleted from the screen, then enter the Key-Delrec trigger text.

Key-Delrec
The text for this trigger is

```
Seq #1     Label: Coord-delete

#EXEMACRO exetrg clear_details; delrec; exetrg query_details;

Message if trigger step fails:

Program error: Problem executing [Delete Record] in
coordinated blocks.
```

Now define the Pre-Delete commit trigger for the CUSTOMER block. This trigger has two steps.

Pre-Delete

```
Seq #1     Label: Lock-custname

LOCK TABLE custname IN SHARE UPDATE MODE

Message if trigger step fails:

Problem locking CUSTNAME table to delete detail records.
See supervisor.

Seq #2     Label: Del-details

DELETE FROM custname
  WHERE custname.memberid = :customer.memberid
```

Message if trigger step fails:

```
Pre-Delete error: Problem deleting detail members when
deleting master . . .
```

SQL*Forms (Runform) automatically manages locking for data queried or modified in the *base* tables of your form. SQL*Forms (Runform) does not, however, execute lock statements for triggers. If your trigger includes a write statement (an INSERT, UPDATE, or DELETE) to a table which is *not* the base table of that block, then you must explicitly define the locking mode in the trigger.

The Video Quest application is a multi-user application. The Pre-Delete trigger explicitly locks the CUSTNAME table in SHARE UPDATE MODE, allowing other application users to simultaneously query and update data from shared tables.

Generating Unique Sequence Numbers

Via SQL*Forms, the Video Quest application, generates a membership ID number for every new membership account. The appropriate time to generate this ID is at commit, just before the new membership record is inserted into the database.

Trigger Objective:
Have the system generate a unique membership Id and be sure each number is generated in sequence.

Solution:
Define a three-step Pre-Insert trigger. You will need a separate control table to generate the number. (The CNTL table contains the *next_memberid* column to handle this procedure.) A separate trigger step then selects the number into the MEMBERID field of the master block. To enforce uniqueness, the sequence number must be created with an update operation. Enter the Pre-Insert trigger:

Seq #1   Label: Lock-cntl

```
LOCK TABLE cntl in SHARE UPDATE MODE
```

Message if trigger step fails:

```
Program error: Problem locking CNTL table to generate new
memberid.
```

The second trigger step generates the next number in sequence with an UPDATE statement:

```
Seq #2      Label: New-memberid

UPDATE cntl
   SET last_memberid = nvl(last_memberid, 0) + 1
```

Message if trigger step fails:

Program error: Problem updating CNTL table to generate new memberid.

The final step executes a SELECT statement to retrieve the new number:

```
Seq #3      Label: Get-newid

SELECT last_memberid
  INTO customer.memberid
  FROM cntl
```

Message if trigger step fails:

Pre-insert error: Problem inserting new memberid. See your supervisor.

If you were building a single-user application, the above sequence number routine could be simplified. The following single-step SELECT statement trigger would do:

```
SELECT MAX(customer.memberid) + 1
  INTO customer.memberid
  FROM customer
```

Multi-user applications require locking protection to prevent users from inadvertently overwriting each other's changes, thus preserving the integrity of your data. This trigger does not provide such protection. To increase concurrency and transaction throughput, the designers of ORACLE decided against using locks for read operations (queries). Two operators fetching records concurrently from the CUSTOMER table may compete for the same sequence number. An UPDATE statement, however, puts an exclusive lock on the table, guaranteeing uniqueness in multi-user environments. In ORACLE Version 6 with the Transaction Processing Subsystem (TPS) Option, ORACLE supports *row-level* locking, a much smaller locking granularity for maximum concurrency and throughput.

Additionally, ORACLE Version 6 introduces a feature that enables it to generate unique sequence numbers automatically, storing them as objects in the database. Maintained in the database, the SEQUENCE function is created independently of transactions and avoids the serialization and extra work caused by generating them at the application level. This approach may greatly improve transaction throughput.

Building the RENTALS Form

Video tape rental transactions are managed from the RENTALS form. A three-block form, RENTALS interfaces the RENTALS transaction table and the INVOICE table, using a header, or *control block* to generate an invoice number and display the current transaction date.

The MEMBERID copy field coordinates all three blocks, ensuring that a rental transaction is charged to only one customer. As an operator moves into the RENTALS block to enter the details of a rentals transaction, the MEMBERID value is copied from the control block to a hidden database field in this block. The same value is copied when the operator moves into the INVOICE block to record the payment details. When the entire rental transaction is committed, the form inserts a record into the RENTALS table and another into the INVOICE table, both charged to the current member.

The RENTALS form adds a few bells and whistles. Certain function keys have been reprogrammed to perform special processing. Pressing the [Enter Query] key jumps you immediately into the CUSTOMER form so you can look up customer data without interrupting your rentals transaction. Pressing [Execute Query] jumps you into a form which displays the outstanding rentals for the current customer. Pressing [Duplicate Record] generates a printed invoice for the current rental transaction. A function key legend on the bottom of the RENTALS forms reminds the user that these automatic functions are available.

Creating the CUSTOMER Control Block

By definition, the CUSTOMER control block does not refer to a base table. While it doesn't update the database directly, the CUSTOMER block passes control information to both the RENTALS and the INVOICE blocks. You will create the fields for this block—and for the other two blocks—by hand.

Create and define the CUSTOMER fields, placing them in the upper portion of the screen as shown in Figure 7.27. Since all fields are created by hand, you only need to define the listed attributes.

Table 7.6   CUSTOMER Field Definitions

Seq#	Page	Field Name	Label	Length/Field Type
#1	0	XSLSTAXPCT	Xslstaxpct	10 chars/CHAR
		Attributes:	(None)	
		Validation:	(None)	
#2	1	INVNO	Invoice Number	7 chars/RINT
		Attributes:	Displayed	
		Validation:	(None)	
#3	1	DAY		9 chars/CHAR
		Attributes:	Displayed	
		Validation:	(None)	
#4	1	XDATEOUT		9 chars/DATE
		Attributes:	Database Field	
			Displayed	
		Validation:	Default: $$date$$	
#5	1	TIME		9 chars/CHAR
		Attributes:	Displayed	
		Validation:	(None)	
#6	1	MEMBERID	Member ID:	7 chars/INT
		Attributes:	Database Field	
			Displayed	
			Input Allowed	
		Validation:	Help: "Enter membership ID."	
#7	1	NAME		28 chars/CHAR
		Attributes:	Displayed	
		Validation:	(None)	
#8	1	OUTRENT	Tapes currently out:	3 chars/RINT
		Attributes:	Displayed	
		Validation:	(None)	

Creating the RENTALS Block

Create and define the RENTALS block fields, placing them in the middle block of the screen. Figure 7.28 illustrates proper field placement. Be sure to define every non-displayed field; there are quite a few for this and the INVOICE block.

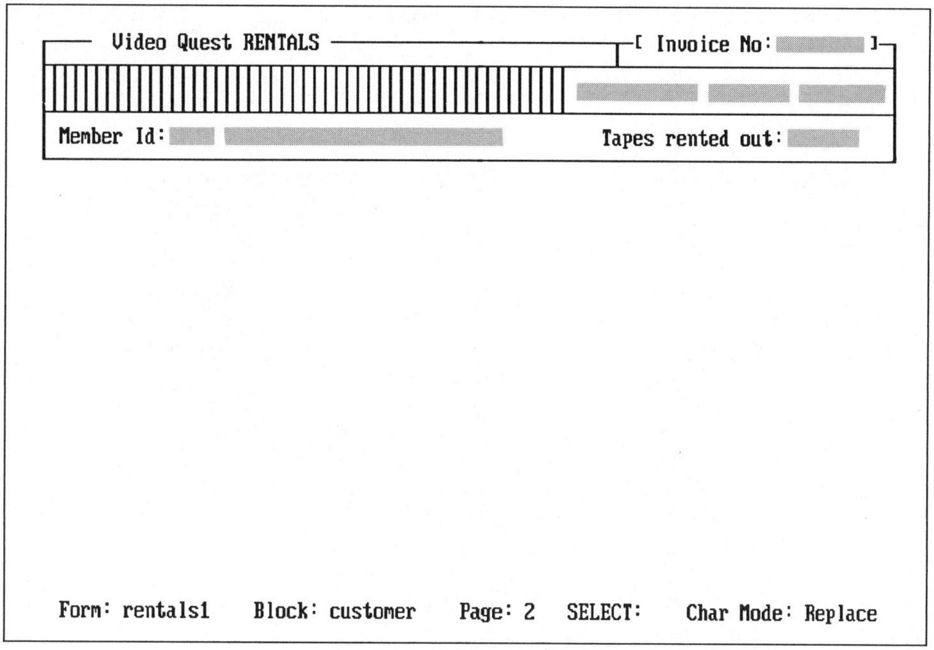

```
 ┌─ Video Quest RENTALS ──────────────┐ [ Invoice No:▓▓▓▓▓▓ ]─┐
 │ ┌┬┬┬┬┬┬┬┬┬┬┬┬┬┬┬┬┬┬┬┬┬┬┬┬┬┬┬┬┬┬┬┐  ▓▓▓▓▓▓ ▓▓▓▓ ▓▓▓▓        │
 │ Member Id:▓▓▓▓ ▓▓▓▓▓▓▓▓▓▓▓       Tapes rented out:▓▓▓▓▓▓  │
 │                                                            │
 │                                                            │
 │ Form: rentals1   Block: customer   Page: 2   SELECT:   Char Mode: Replace │
 └────────────────────────────────────────────────────────────┘
```

Figure 7.27   Field Placement for the CUSTOMER Block

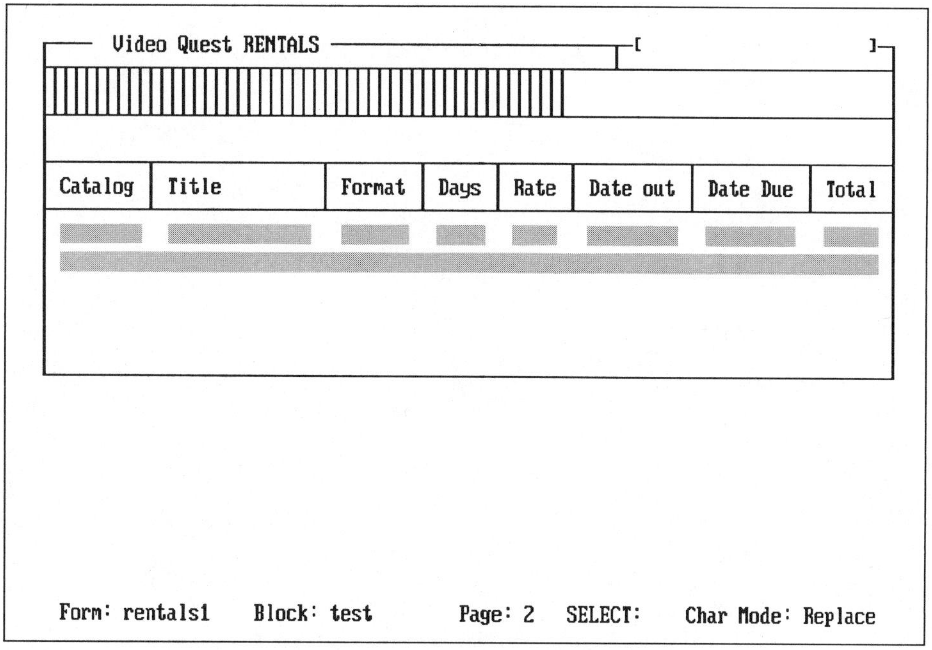

Catalog	Title	Format	Days	Rate	Date out	Date Due	Total

```
 ┌─ Video Quest RENTALS ──────────────┐ [                    ]─┐
 Form: rentals1   Block: test   Page: 2   SELECT:   Char Mode: Replace
```

Figure 7.28   Field Placement for the RENTALS Block

Table 7.7   RENTALS Field Definitions

Seq#	Page	Field Name	Label	Length/Field Type
#1	0	MEMBERID	Memberid	7 chars/INT
		Attributes:	Database Field	
		Validation:	Copy Field: Block: CUSTOMER	
			Field: MEMBERID	
#2	0	INVNO	Invno	7 chars/INT
		Attributes:	Database Field	
		Validation:	Copy Field: Block: CUSTOMER	
			Field: INVNO	
#3	0	XPRODNO	Xprodno	25 chars/CHAR
		Attributes:	(None)	
		Validation:	(None)	
#4	0	XSTORENO	Xstoreno	3 chars/INT
		Attributes:	(None)	
		Validation:	(None)	
#5	0	ACTRTN	Actrtn	9 chars/DATE
		Attributes:	Database Field	
		Validation:	(None)	
#6	0	XCATEGORY	Xcategory	3 chars/INT
		Attributes:	(None)	
		Validation:	(None)	
#7	1	CATNUM	Catalog	10 chars/CHAR
		Attributes:	Database Field	
			Displayed	
			Input Allowed	
		Validation:	Help: "Enter catalog number of rental tape."	
#8	1	TITLECD	Title	15 chars/CHAR
		Attributes:	Displayed	
		Validation:	(None)	
#9	1	FDESC	Format	4 chars/CHAR
		Attributes:	Displayed	
		Validation:	(None)	
#10	1	RENTDAYS	Days	3 chars/RINT
		Attributes:	Database Field	
			Displayed	
			Input Allowed	
			Mandatory	
		Validation:	Help: "Number of days customer will rent this tape."	
#11	1	RATEPDY	Rate	7 chars/RMONEY
		Attributes:	Default (Database, Displayed, etc.)	
		Validation:	Help: "Rate per day. You may overwrite displayed	
			(default) value."	
#12	1	DATEOUT	Date Out	9 chars/DATE
		Attributes:	Database Field	
			Displayed	
		Validation:	Default: $$date$$	
#13	1	SCHDRTN	Date Due	9 chars/DATE
		Attributes:	Database Field	
			Displayed	
		Validation:	(None)	

Table 7.7   *(continued)*

Seq#	Page	Field Name	Label	Length/Field Type
#14	*1*	*LINETTL*	*Total*	*7 chars/RMONEY*
		Attributes:	Displayed	
		Validation:	(None)	
#15	*1*	*TITLE*		*76 chars/CHAR*
		Attributes:	Displayed	
		Validation:	(None)	

Creating the INVOICE Block

Create and define the INVOICE block fields individually, placing them on the bottom block of the screen. Figure 7.29 illustrates proper field placement.

Table 7.8   INVOICE Field Definitions

Seq#	Page	Field Name	Label	Length/Field Type
#1	*0*	*MEMBERID*	*Memberid*	*7 chars/INT*
		Attributes:	Database Field	
		Validation:	Copy Field: Block: CUSTOMER	
			Field: MEMBERID	
#2	*0*	*INVNO*	*Invno*	*7 chars/INT*
		Attributes:	Database Field	
		Validation:	Copy Field: Block: RENTALS	
			Field: INVNO	
#3	*0*	*TRANTYPE*	*Trantype*	*1 char/CHAR*
		Attributes:	Database Field	
		Validation:	Default Value: R	
#4	*0*	*TRANDATE*	*Trandate*	*9 chars/DATE*
		Attributes:	Database Field	
		Validation:	Copy Field: Block: RENTALS	
			Field: DATEOUT	
#5	*0*	*TRANTIME*	*Trantime*	*8 chars/CHAR*
		Attributes:	Database Field	
		Validation:	(None)	
#6	*1*	*PAYMETHOD*	*Paymethod:*	*2 chars/CHAR*
		Attributes:	Database Field	
			Displayed	
			Input Allowed	
			Mandatory	
			Uppercase	
			Automatic Help	
		Validation:	List of Values: Table: PAYMETHOD	
			Column: PAYMETHOD	
			Help: "Enter pay method. CAsh, VI, MC, etc. Use [List Values] . . ."	

Table 7.8 *(continued)*

Seq#	Page	Field Name	Label	Length/Field Type
#7	*1*	*PAYDESC*		*20 chars/CHAR*
		Attributes:	Displayed	
		Validation:	(None)	
#8	*1*	*CASHTEND*	*Cash given:*	*7 chars/RMONEY*
		Attributes:	Displayed	
			Input Allowed	
		Validation:	Default: 0	
			Help: "If cash, enter amount received from customer."	
#9	*1*	*CHANGE*	*Change:*	*7 chars/RMONEY*
		Attributes:	Displayed	
		Validation:	Default: 0	
#10	*1*	*TOTAL*	*Total:*	*7 chars/RMONEY*
		Attributes:	Database Field	
			Displayed	
		Validation:	(None)	
#11	*1*	*TAX*	*Tax:*	*7 chars/RMONEY*
		Attributes:	Database Field	
			Displayed	
		Validation:	(None)	
#12		*GRAND_TOTAL*	*Pay this amount:*	*7 chars/RMONEY*
		Attributes:	Displayed	
		Validation:	(None)	

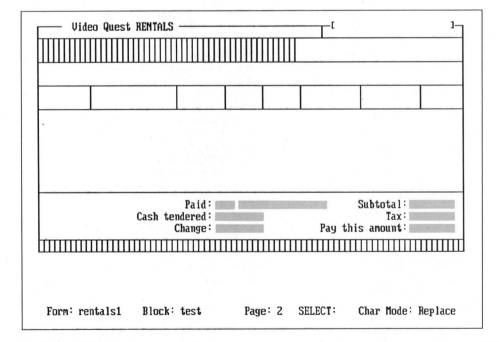

Figure 7.29   Field Placement for the INVOICE Block

Defining the Triggers

A host of triggers operate behind the scenes of the RENTALS form to control rentals transaction processing and perform complex validation. Figure 7.30 illustrates some of the triggers you will define and the events that trigger them.

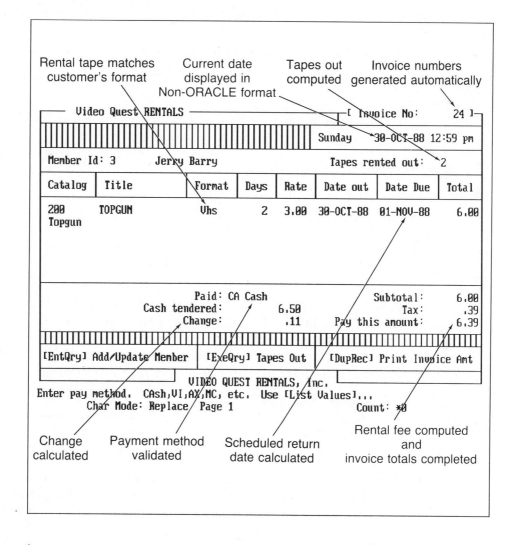

Figure 7.30   RENTALS Form Triggers

In the CONTROL block, for example,

> invoice numbers are generated automatically
>
> the current date is displayed in an intuitive format

a table look-up computes the number of tapes currently checked out by the customer

In the RENTALS block, the system

validates the rental tape entered by an operator

ensures that the rental tape matches the customer's default tape format

prevents rentals to a customer who has exceeded the rental limit

prevents an authorized member from renting a restricted tape

automatically calculates the scheduled return date

automatically computes rental fees for each rental record and computes invoice totals for the rental transaction

In the INVOICE block, the system

validates the payment method entered

computes the proper change due for cash transactions

The CUSTOMER Block Triggers

You will define field triggers on both the XDATEOUT and MEMBERID fields for this block. The XDATEOUT trigger performs a date format conversion and retrieves sales tax information. On the MEMBERID field, two triggers are defined. One trigger validates data entry and computes the outstanding rentals for this account, and the other controls cursor navigation.

XDATEOUT Trigger Objectives:
Display the current date in a more useful format and get the sales tax percentage to be used in computing tax amounts for invoicing.

Solution:
Define a Post-Change trigger on XDATEOUT. The trigger converts and displays *sysdate* in the displayed DAY and TIME fields, and also selects the sales tax percentage from the CNTL table into the SLSTAXPCT field hidden on Page 0. Enter this trigger:

```
Seq #1              Label: Convert-get-info

SELECT to_char(to_date(:xdateout), 'Day')
       to_char(sysdate, 'hh:mi am'), slstaxpct
  INTO day, time, xslstaxpct
  FROM cntl
```

```
Message if trigger step fails:
```

Program error: Problem converting date formats. See your
supervisor.

MEMBERID Trigger Objectives:

Validate the customer's Member ID, and let the operator know how many
tapes this member still has not returned. Also, enhance navigation so that
pressing [Next Field] moves the cursor automatically into the RENTALS
block.

Solution:

To solve the first problem, define a two-step Post-Change trigger on MEM-
BERID. Step 1 validates the value entered for MEMBERID. Step 2 employs a
group function to compute the number of outstanding tapes charged to
this customer and selects this value into the OUTRENT display field. Enter
the following two-step trigger:

```
Seq #1      Label: Get-name

SELECT name
  INTO name
  FROM customer

 WHERE customer.memberid = :customer.memberid
```

```
Message if trigger step fails:
```

Invalid Id. Verify card, or clear block & [Execute Query]
to query customer.

```
Seq #2      Label: Get-outrent

SELECT count(*)
  INTO outrent
  FROM rentals
 WHERE rentals.memberid = :customer.memberid
   AND rentals.actrtn is null
```

```
Message if trigger step fails:
```

Program Error: Problem computing outstanding rentals for
this customer.

To solve the cursor navigation problem, you define the Key-Nxtfld key-trigger on MEMBERID. This key-trigger redefines [Next Field] to execute the NXTBLK function so that the operator simply presses [Return] to glide into the RENTALS block. Enter the Key-Nxtfld trigger text:

```
Seq #1      Label: go-nxtblk

#EXEMACRO nxtblk;

Message if trigger step fails:

Program Error: Problem executing nxtblk on MEMBERID. See
your supervisor.
```

The RENTALS Block Triggers

The RENTALS block is the focal point of this form. The triggers you define here shoulder most of the responsibility for controlling rentals processing.

The Field Triggers

Triggers at the field level perform multi-statement validation or field arithmetic when an operator enters three key points: 1) a catalog number on the CATNUM field (labelled "Catalog"); 2) the number of days rented on RENTDAYS (labelled "Days") and 3) the rental rate on the RATEPDY field (labelled "Rate").

CATNUM Trigger Objectives:
The CATNUM trigger (on the field labelled "Catalog") is ambitious. It will

1. Validate the catalog number entered by an operator
2. Display the related title code, title and default rate per day for the catalog number
3. Warn the operator that the film being rented has a viewing restriction attached to it for this account
4. Prevent the rental of a tape which does not match the customer's default tape format

All objectives are solved by defining a six-step Post-Change trigger on the CATNUM field. Walk through the construction of this trigger.

Steps #1 and #2

Two steps are necessary to validate the catalog number. You must check
not only that the catalog number exists, but also that the catalog number
is not that of a rental tape currently checked out.

Step 1 retrieves the related product number and store number, temporarily storing the values in their respective hidden fields on Page 0. In
effect, the trigger joins the RENTALS and TAPE tables to validate the catalog number.

Seq #1   Label: Get-prodno

```
SELECT prodno, storeno
  INTO xprodno, xstoreno
  FROM tape
 WHERE tape.catnum = :rentals.catnum
```

Message if trigger step fails:

```
Invalid catalog number. Please re-enter.
```

Step 2 tests this catalog number against outstanding rentals.

Seq #2   Label: Chk-if-rented

```
SELECT 'x'
  FROM rentals
 WHERE rentals.catnum = :rentals.catnum
   AND rentals.actrtn is null
```

Message if trigger step fails:

```
Rental with this catalog number is already checked out.
Please re-enter.
```

Select both the Abort and Reverse Return Code attributes for this trigger step.

Step #3

This step uses the *prodno* and *storeno* fetched by Step 1 as join conditions
to retrieve the Title Code, Format, and Rate Per Day from the PRODUCT
and RENTCLASS tables. This step also verifies that the rental tape is a valid
rental product. It is not uncommon for a clerk to pull a sale-only tape from
the wrong shelf.

Seq #3   Label: Get-titlecd

```
SELECT titlecd, ratepdy,
       decode(product.format, 'V', 'VHS', 'B', 'Beta', null)
  INTO titlecd, ratepdy, fdesc
  FROM product, rentclass
 WHERE product.prodno = :xprodno
   AND product.storeno = :xstoreno
   AND product.rentclass = :rentclass.rentclass
   AND product.prodtype in ('R', 'RS')
```

Message if trigger step fails:

Invalid product number OR product is not a rental item. Please re-enter.

Step #4

With the title code on screen, Step 4 can now retrieve the associated title and film category of this rental tape from the TITLE table. Selected into the hidden field, XCATEGORY, the film category value will be used in Step 5 to check viewing restrictions.

Seq #4   Label: Get-title

```
SELECT title, category
  INTO title, xcategory
  FROM title
 WHERE title.titlecd = :titlecd
```

Message if trigger step fails:

Invalid title or category not fetched for this title. See your supervisor.

Step #5

This step uses the film category of this rental tape and the current *memberid* to test the CUSTNAME table for viewing restrictions. If any authorized members are restricted from viewing a tape that matches this category, the trigger succeeds.

```
Seq #5     Label: Chk-restrict

SELECT 'x'
  FROM custname
 WHERE custname.memberid = :customer.memberid
   AND custname.restrict_cat = :xcategory
```

Message if trigger step fails:

```
Authorized user(s) restricted from viewing this tape.
Consult key member.
```

Select the Abort and Reverse Return Code attributes.

Step #6

In this step you verify that the tape rented out to this customer is in a format compatible with the default tape format which is recorded in their customer file. As search criteria, the trigger step uses the expanded tape format displayed in the FDESC field and uses reverse DECODE to make the comparison.

```
Seq #6     Label: Chk-custformat

SELECT 'x'
  FROM customer
 WHERE customer.memberid = :customer.memberid
   AND (customer.format = DECODE(:fdesc, 'VHS', 'V', 'Beta',
       'B') OR customer.format = 'VB')
```

Message if trigger step fails:

```
Format of this tape doesn't match customer's default tape
format. Check it.
```

RENTDAYS Trigger Objective:

Calculate the scheduled return date for the rental tape entered by the operator.

Solution:

Define a Post-Change trigger on the RENTDAYS field (labelled "Days") that performs date arithmetic. When the operator enters the number of days rented, the trigger adds this number to *sysdate*, selecting the resulting date into the SCHDRTN field. Notice that the value in RENTDAYS must be converted to a number value; remember, SQL*Forms stores all values as characters on the screen. (This changes in SQL*Forms Version 2.3; date values are stored as date values on screen in this version.) Enter the trigger:

Seq #1   Label: Calc-schdrtn

```
SELECT sysdate + to_number(:rentdays)
   INTO schdrtn
   FROM dual
```

Message if trigger step fails:

```
Program error: Problem calculating scheduled return date.
See supervisor.
```

RATEPDY Trigger Objective:
Calculate the rental fee and sales tax totals to generate an invoice for each rental transaction.

Solution:
Define a Post-Change trigger on the RATEPDY field (labelled "Rate") in three steps to perform the line total and grand total calculations. Briefly, these steps will

1. Calculate the line total for each rental tape record and select this amount into the displayed LINETTL field

2. Calculate the accumulated rental and sales tax totals of all rental records for this transaction. These totals are accumulated in the TOTAL and TAX fields in the INVOICE block. The corresponding INVOICE base table stores the total rental fees and total tax values for each rental transaction in the *total* and *tax* columns.

3. Combine the rental fee total and the total sales tax to generate the grand total for the invoice. The resulting value is stored in the display-only field, GRAND_TOTAL. (Since the TOTAL and TAX values are both stored in the INVOICE table, it would be redundant to store the grand total as well.)

Step #1
To calculate the line total, enter

Seq #1   Label: Calc-total

```
SELECT (nvl(:rentals.rentdays, 0) * nvl(:rentals.ratepdy, 0))
   INTO rentals.linettl
   FROM dual
```

Message if trigger step fails:

Program error: Can't calculate line total on RATEPDY. See your
supervisor.

Step #2
To calculate the accumulated TOTAL and TAX amounts, Step 2 uses the
sales tax percentage stored in a hidden field in the CUSTOMER block. This
value was retrieved by the XDATEOUT field trigger. To create this trigger,
you enter

Seq #2   Label: Calc–subtotals

```
SELECT nvl(:invoice.total, 0) + nvl(:rentals.linettl, 0),
       round(nvl(:invoice.tax, 0) +
       nvl(:rentals.linettl, 0) *(nvl(customer.xslstaxpct,
                                 0)100),2)
  INTO invoice.total, invoice.tax
  FROM dual
```

Message if trigger step fails:

Program error: Can't calculate subtotals on RATEPDY. See
your supervisor.

When multiplying percent values, you must divide the entire expression by 100 to get the correct result; when money values are computed
with percent values, round the expression to two decimal places.

Step #3
To calculate the grand invoice total, enter

Seq #3   Label: Calc–grandtotals

```
SELECT nvl(:invoice.total, 0) + nvl(:invoice.tax, 0))
  INTO invoice.grand_total
  FROM dual
```

Message if trigger step fails:

Program error: Can't calculate grand total on RATEPDY.
See your supervisor.

The Block Triggers

The two block-level triggers you define must answer the crucial question: "What happens just *before* and just *after* a rental transaction is inserted into the database?"

Pre-Insert Trigger Objectives:
Two things must be accomplished before any rentals records can be inserted successfully. The system must

1. Prevent the customer from renting out a tape if the customer has exceeded the maximum rental limit set by Video Quest.
2. Generate a unique invoice number for the transaction.

Solution:
Define a Pre-Insert trigger with no less than six steps. The first trigger step performs the maximum rental validation, and the other steps are required to solve the invoice number problem.

When generating the sequence number, you must first test whether the INVNO field in the CUSTOMER block currently displays a value; if so, the trigger will branch to a separate trigger step to initialize this and other control fields in the rentals block. This conditional test prevents a new invoice number from being generated for each rentals record, because a Pre-Insert trigger fires for *every* record inserted into a table.

Step #1
In checking maximum rentals, Step #1 counts the number of rentals outstanding for this member and compares it against the maximum allowed value, *maxrent*, stored in the CNTL table. Reverse the return code for this trigger.

```
Seq #1              Label: Check-maxrent

  SELECT count(*)
    FROM rentals
   WHERE rentals.memberid = :rentals.memberid
     AND actrtn is null
   GROUP BY rentals.memberid
  HAVING count(*) >=
         (SELECT maxrent FROM cntl)
```

Message if trigger step fails:

Customer exceeded rental limit! Please have customer
return tapes.

Steps #2-6
These steps conditionally generate an invoice number.

Seq #2   **Label:** Chk-custinvno

```
SELECT 'x'
  FROM dual
 WHERE :customer.invno is null
```

Success label: Lock-cntl   (The next step in sequence)
Failure label: Init-rental (The last step in sequence)

Seq #3   **Label:** Lock-cntl

```
LOCK TABLE cntl IN SHARE UPDATE MODE
```

Message if trigger step fails:

Program error: Problem locking CNTL table to generate new
invoice number.

Seq #4   **Label:** New-invno

```
UPDATE cntl
   SET last_invoice = nvl(last_invoice, 0) + 1
```

Message if trigger step fails:

Program error: Problem updating CNTL table to generate new
invoice number.

Seq #5   **Label:** Get-newinvno

```
SELECT last_invoice
  INTO customer.invno
  FROM cntl
```

Message if trigger step fails:

Program error: Problem inserting new invoice number. See your
supervisor.

continued

```
Seq #6       Label: Init-rental

SELECT null, :customer.xdateout, :customer.invno
  INTO actrtn, dateout, rentals.invno
  FROM dual
```

Message if trigger step fails:

Program error: Problem initializing rental fields. See your
supervisor.

Post-Insert Trigger Objective:

Have the system automatically decrement the On Hand position in the
PRODUCT table after the rentals transaction records have been inserted.
Also, update the *last_act* column in the CUSTOMER table to record this
transaction as the latest activity for the account.

Solution:

Define two separate UPDATE statements in this Post-Insert trigger. Be sure
to lock each referenced table in SHARE UPDATE mode. Enter the trigger:

```
Seq #1       Label: Lock-product

LOCK TABLE product IN SHARE UPDATE MODE
```

Message if trigger step fails:

Program error: Problem locking PRODUCT table to decrement
qtyoh. See supervisor.

```
Seq #2       Label: Update-product

UPDATE product
   SET qtyoh = qtyoh - 1
 WHERE product.prodno = :xprodno
   AND product.storeno = :xstoreno
```

Message if trigger step fails:

Program error: Problem decrementing qtyoh in PRODUCT
table to reflect rental.

```
Seq #3      Label: Lock-customer

LOCK TABLE customer IN SHARE UPDATE MODE
```

Message if trigger step fails:

Program error: Problem locking CUSTOMER table to update last-act. See supervisor.

```
Seq #4      Label: Update-customer

UPDATE customer
   SET last_act = sysdate
 WHERE customer.memberid = :rentals.member
```

Message if trigger step fails:

Program error: Problem updating last_act in CUSTOMER table. See supervisor.

The INVOICE Block Triggers

The triggers defined for the INVOICE block preserve the integrity of the INVOICE table against unlawful data entry. Additionally, a block-level trigger ensures that each committed INVOICE record is tied to a single invoice number and is charged to the appropriate customer.

The Field Triggers

Although invoice totals are not calculated on this block, an operator accepts payment from here. An interesting trigger on the CASHTEND field (labelled "Cash Tendered:") calculates change due a customer. A trigger should also be defined on the PAYMETHOD field (labelled "Paid:") to validate payment. Create this trigger yourself. If you need guidance, refer to a similar trigger defined on the CREDITCARD field in the CUSTOMER form.

CASHTEND Trigger Objective:
Calculate the change due a customer for a cash transaction.

Solution:
Define a two-step Post-Change trigger to perform the following routine:

1. Test whether this is a cash transaction (that is, the value in PAY-METHOD is 'CA'). If so, calculate the change and display the result in

the CHANGE field. You will use the DECODE function to manage the true/false test and to calculate the change due.

2. If the operator inadvertently attempts to make change for a noncash transaction, issue an error message.

Here is what to enter:

Seq # 1   **Label:** Change-if-cash

```
SELECT DECODE(:paymethod, 'CA',
              nvl(:cashtend, 0) - nvl(:grand_total, 0), 0)
  INTO change
  FROM dual
```

Message if trigger step fails:

```
Program error: Problem calculating change. See your
supervisor.
```

Observe how DECODE manipulates the true/false test. The statement translates to "If the value in PAYMETHOD is 'CA', then calculate the change. BUT, If the value is not 'CA', write the value 0."

The second trigger step explains the error to the operator:

Seq # 2   **Label:** Alert-no-change

```
SELECT 'xs'
  FROM dual
 WHERE :paymethod = 'CA'
```

Message if trigger step fails:

```
Change given only with cash transactions. Clear field and
commit, please . . .
```

The Block Triggers

You've coordinated the three blocks of the RENTALS form with the MEM-BERID copy value, and you've used the INVNO copy value to tie the knot between the RENTALS and INVOICE blocks. Before you finally insert the INVOICE record, however, you might want to play it safe and initialize the critical INVOICE fields. With complex forms applications, one can never predict when incorrect data might land in a database field and get committed by mistake.

Pre-Insert Trigger Objectives:
Prevent erroneous data from being inadvertently written to the INVOICE table.

Solution:
Initialize the corresponding INVOICE fields just prior to inserting a new invoice record. Enter the trigger:

```
Seq # 1         Label: Init-invoice

SELECT to_number(:customer.invno), 'R',
       to_date(:customer.xdateout),
       to_char(sysdate, 'hh:mi am'), :customer.memberid
  INTO invoice.invno, trantype, invoice.trandate,
       invoice.trantime, invoice.memberid
  FROM dual
```

```
Message if trigger step fails:

Program error: Problem initializing the INVOICE fields.
See your supervisor.
```

Defining the Form Triggers

The form-level triggers reprogram certain function keys to perform enhanced SQL*Forms processing. You will redefine the [Enter Query], [Execute Query], and [Duplicate Record] functions with key-triggers. Defined at the form-level, these function keys operate with the new functionality from any block or field in the form.

Key-Entqry Trigger Objective:
Permit an operator to jump into the CUSTOMER form to look up customer information without interrupting a rentals transaction.

Solution:
Redefine the [Enter Query] function key to call the CUSTOMER form. The Key-Entqry key-trigger will use the SQL*Forms CALL macro function. When you call the CUSTOMER form, SQL*Forms temporarily suspends processing of the RENTALS form, jumps you into CUSTOMER, and returns to the RENTALS form when you press [Exit]. Enter the trigger:

```
Seq # 1     Label: Call-customer

#EXEMACRO call customer;

Message if trigger step fails:
```

Program error: Problem calling CUSTOMER form. See your
supervisor.

Key-Exeqry Trigger Objective:
Automatically query the outstanding rentals for the current customer
when an operator presses the [Execute Query] function.

Solution:
Define a Key-Exeqry key-trigger to call a form entitled OUTRENT, which is
based on the PRODUCTS_RENTED view created in the section on creating
views in Chapter 6, Advanced SQL Capabilities. Key-Exeqry uses the
SQL*Forms COPY command to copy the current *memberid* and *name* values (called *field variables*) to the OUTRENT form. Once copied from the
source fields, or field variables, to *global variables*, these values hang in
limbo, waiting to be copied somewhere in the called OUTRENT form. At
the receiving OUTRENT form (called the *destination*), a Key-Startup trigger
is defined to start up the form and execute the COPY command, copying
these global variables into the designated fields.

     Enter the Key-Exeqry key-trigger:

```
Seq # 1     Label: Chk-null

SELECT 'x'
  FROM dual
 WHERE :customer.memberid is not null

Message if trigger step fails:
```

You must enter a member ID to query outstanding rentals.
Please do so . . .

```
Seq # 2     Label: Copy-memberid

#COPY :customer.memberid global.memberid

Seq # 3     Label: Copy-name

#COPY :customer.name global.name
```

```
Seq # 4     Label: Auto-query
```

`#EXEMACRO callqry outrent;`

Message if trigger step fails:

Program error: Problem calling OUTRENT to auto-query. See supervisor.

You must now define the Key-Startup trigger at the form level of the OUTRENT form to provide the other half of this automatic query equation:

Key-Startup Trigger / OUTRENT Form

```
Seq # 1     Label: Copy-memberid
```

`#COPY global.memberid :customer.memberid`

```
Seq # 2     Label: Copy-name
```

`#COPY global.name :customer.name`

```
Seq # 4     Label: Auto-query
```

`#EXEMACRO nxtblk; exeqry;`

Message if trigger step fails:

Program error: Problem moving to NXTBLK and executing query. See supervisor.

OUTRENT is a two-block form. The first block, CUSTOMER, is simply a control block containing two fields—MEMBERID and NAME—to capture the global *memberid* and *name* values copied into the form. The second block is based on the PRODUCTS_RENTED view which joins the TAPES, RENTALS, and PRODUCTS tables and allows you to query rental and product information by Member ID for all outstanding rental tapes. To create OUTRENT, refer to the complete program listing, the OUTRENT.INP file, appearing in Appendix B.

Key-Duprec Trigger Objective:
Print an invoice of the completed rental transaction.

Solution:
One method is to redefine the [Duplicate Record] key (a function key that

would least likely be used in this application) to execute the PRINT macro function. You could also define any one of key triggers KEY-F0 through KEY-F9 to avoid interfering with existing SQL*Forms functionality. In Professional ORACLE, the PRINT function invokes the DOS Print command. This trigger should verify that an invoice has been generated before attempting to print one. Enter the trigger:

Seq # 1   Label: Chk-rental

```
SELECT 'x'
  FROM dual
 WHERE :customer.memberid is not null
   AND :rentals.invoice is not null
   AND :invoice.paymethod is not null
```

Message if trigger step fails:

Why print a blank invoice? Enter ALL rental information and try again . . .

Seq # 2   Label: Ok-print

```
#EXEMACRO print; redisp;
```

Message if trigger step fails:

Program error: Problem printing screen or refreshing screen after print.

Summary

The importance of forms to fourth-generation applications cannot be underestimated. Forms are the traditional interface of most fourth-generation applications, allowing users to interact with the database quickly and efficiently. This chapter introduced you to ORACLE's forms-based application development tool, SQL*Forms. It walked you through the SQL*Forms design phases within the Video Quest environment, covering many useful—and transferable—methods in depth. Using SQL*Forms, you created the three major Video Quest forms:

- ▶ The TITLE Form
- ▶ The CUSTOMER Form
- ▶ The RENTALS Transaction Form

The forms you have yet to build are the PRODUCT form, the RETURNS form, and the default-generated Code Maintenance forms—CATEGORY, CATALOG, RENTAL CLASS, and PAYMENT. Appendix B contains the complete program listings for the more complicated forms—PRODUCT and RETURNS; consult it for assistance, if necessary. The Code forms are *not* listed in Appendix B, because they can be generated simply enough with the SQL*Forms DEFAULT BLOCK facility.

8

Generating Reports

8

Generating Reports

Chapter 8 discusses tips and techniques for generating reports with SQL*Plus and Oracle's newest reporting tool, SQL*ReportWriter. With SQL*Plus you will plan, design, and generate four reports that satisfy Video Quest's most pressing information needs:

▶ The Product Inventory report

▶ The Tapes Overdue report

▶ The Rentals Report—Detail and Summary information

▶ The Yearly Rental History Report

Previewing SQL*ReportWriter, you will work with a modified Tapes Overdue Report which demonstrates the added formatting control available with the more sophisticated reporting tool.

Fourth-Generation Environment Reporting Tools

An automated business requires various report outputs to perform everyday business functions or monitor current and historical trends of the business. A *report output* can be anything from a formal hard-copy report such as a monthly bank statement or a profit and loss statement for the business, to a conventional invoice or an address labelling report. Most data entered into a 4GE database application is destined to be recast into some meaningful report format.

SQL's query capabilities give interactive users immediate access to information with *ad hoc* queries. *Ad hoc* queries are useful for information center applications and decision support functions, such as trends analysis and posing *What If?* hypothetical questions to forecast needs and make predictions. But there are limits to what the SQL SELECT statement can do without the aid of dedicated reporting capabilities.

SQL*Plus's reporting extensions let you easily control the output format of *ad hoc* reports, including header and footer titles, line positioning, pagesize, and page numbering control. SQL*Plus provides much finer control of page formatting, margin, spacing, and column layout of the printed output than is otherwise possible with plain vanilla SQL. With SQL*Plus commands, you can design rather complex tabular reports, organizing groups of rows in the report on column, row, page, or report breaks, and computing subtotals on any combination of breaks.

Businesses often demand more sophisticated reports, such as a two-column newspaper format, a matrix format, or a summary report that merges the results of multiple queries into one report. For these and other highly formatted reports, SQL*Plus clearly does not have the horsepower. You must look to a tool like SQL*ReportWriter which has such flexibility and control—without the complexity of a procedural reporting language.

The Product Inventory Report

The Product Inventory Report captures current inventory positions for each product carried by the store (both film and nonfilm products) or for several stores in a distributed environment. At the close of each fiscal quarter, Video Quest personnel physically count the store inventory. The Product Inventory Report assists them in this effort, serving as a check and balance system to reconcile any discrepancies. The report details what the computer system *says* exists. One would expect the report to be accurate, for it is the responsibility of the application to control the flow of products through the system. Sigh, human error does enter the picture from time to time. Figure 8.1 illustrates the Product Inventory Report output.

The output in Figure 8.1 should look familiar to those who had worked through the view exercises in Chapter 6 in the section on creating views. It is based on the PRODUCTS_RENTED, QTY_RENTED, and INVENTORY views. To build the Product Inventory Report, you will augment the INVENTORY view created earlier and use SQL*Plus formatting functions to enhance the report's appearance. If you haven't created the PRODUCTS_RENTED and QTY_RENTED views, you should do so now. If you have, then you will have also created the INVENTORY view. Use the DROP TABLE command to drop the INVENTORY view from the database, because you are going to recreate it in this exercise.

```
Fri Jun 10                                                                    page   1


                                     Video Quest Movie Rentals
                                     CURRENT INVENTORY POSITIONS



                                         Qty   On  Qty   Qty    Actual
     Product Format Description Title    Cost Recvd Hand Sold Rented  Inventory <Variance>
     ------- ------ ----------- -------------------------------- ------ ------ ----- ----- ------- ---------- -----------
     P100    Vhs    Film        The Sound of Music     $19.95     2         1     1      2
     P200    Vhs    Film        Topgun                 $29.95     2               2      2
     P300    Beta   Film        Gone with the Wind     $59.95     2         1     1      2
     P300    Vhs    Film        Gone with the Wind     $59.95     2               2      2
     P450    Vhs    Film        Citizen Kane           $49.95     2               2      2
     P470    Beta   Film        Ghostbusters           $19.95     1    1                 1
     P470    Vhs    Film        Ghostbusters           $19.95     2    1          1      2
     P475    Vhs    Film        The Hitcher            $79.95     1    1                 1
     P480    Vhs    Film        The Shining            $69.95     2          1           1         1
     P500           Tape Case                          $2.99     30   20    10           30
                                                               ------ ----- ----- ------- ---------- -----------
                                                                 46   23    13     9      45         1



                                     Video Quest, Inc.
                                     Have A Good Day!
     10 records selected.
```

Figure 8.1   Sample Output of the Product Inventory Report

The original INVENTORY view produced these results:

Product	Description	Film Titles	Cost	Qty Recvd	Qty Oh	Qty Sold	Qty Rented
P100V	Film	The Sound of Music	19.95	2	1	1	
P200V	Film	Topgun	29.95	2	1		1
P300B	Film	Gone with the Wind	59.95	1		1	
P300V	Film	Gone with the Wind	59.95	2			2
P450V	Film	Citizen Kane	49.95	2	1	1	
P470B	Film	Ghostbusters	19.95	1	1		
P470V	Film	Ghostbusters	19.95	2	1		1
P475V	Film	The Hitcher	79.95	1	1		
P480V	Film	The Shining	69.95	2		1	1
P500	Tape Case		2.99	30	20	10	

Comparing the output of the original INVENTORY view to that of the newer version, you will notice that three informational fields were added:

1. Total (the column heading in the figure is Actual Inventory). This is a computed field which calculates the actual inventory position by totalling the values of *qtyoh*, *qtysold* and *qty_rented*.

2. Variance—a computed field which calculates the difference between *qtyrecvd* and the derived *total*.

3. Format—a virtual field displaying the product format when the SUBSTR function is applied to each returned *prodno* value.

The other significant addition to this report, aside from new formatting elements, is the display of summary totals computed for each printed inventory column. The SQL*Plus COMPUTE command is used to generate these totals.

Refining the INVENTORY View

To refine the INVENTORY view, enter the following CREATE VIEW statement:

```
CREATE VIEW inventory
       (prodno, description, title, cost, qtyrecvd, qtyoh,
       qtysold, qty_rented, total, variance)
AS
SELECT product.prodno, product.description, title, cost,
       qtyrecvd, qtyoh, qtysold, qty_rented
       (nvl(qtyoh, 0) + nvl(qtysold, 0) + nvl(qty_rented, 0)),
       (qtyrecvd - (nvl(qtyoh, 0) + nvl(qtysold, 0) +
             nvl(qty_rented, 0)))
  FROM product, title, qty_rented
 WHERE product.titlecd = title.titlecd (+)
   AND product.prodno = qty_rented.prodno (+)
```

Creating the INVENTORY view is the first stage in building the procedure for the Product Inventory Report. It would be a more productive use of your time to build the entire procedure from a command file rather than interactively. A good name for it would be INVENTOR.SQL. If you build the report procedure in structured fashion, you can enter SQL*Plus and test each component incrementally as you progress.

If you were to select from this view without any concern for its appearance, the following chaos would be displayed on your terminal:

```
PRODNO                         DESCRIPTION
------------------------------ ---------------------------------
TITLE
------------------------------------------------------------------------
       COST   QTYRECVD         QTYOH    QTYSOLD QTY_RENTED     TOTAL    VARIANCE
------------------------------------------------------------------------
P500                           Tape Case
       2.99         30            20         10                  30
P450V                          Film
Citizen Kane
      49.95          2             0          1          1        2
          :           :            :          :          :        :          :
          :           :            :          :          :        :          :
          :           :            :          :          :        :          :

10 records selected.
```

Defining the Page Format

Since you are designing a printed report, you must envision how the results of your query are going to appear in printed format as opposed to the terminal screen. The conceptual shift is from displaying queried data on a screen *page* to laying rows of text out on a printed *page*. The query may be the same, but the landscape in which the results are presented may dramatically change.

Your first task in making this shift is to reformat the query results to suit the physical dimensions of a printed page. This report attempts to squeeze several columns across the page, so you will expand the linesize from an 80-column width to a wide, 132-column printed output. To conserve as much space as possible, you will allow only 1 space between each column with the SPACE command.

The pagesize, which defines the number of lines per page, should be expanded to 54 lines for this report, allowing 6 lines each (or 1 inch for a standard 6-lines-per-inch printer setting) for the top and bottom margins. Enter these SQL*Plus commands:

```
SET LINESIZE 132
SET PAGESIZE 54
SET SPACE 1
```

Altering the Report Environment

You can alter the environment in which your report executes in several ways with SET command variables. With SET commands, for example, you can suppress the query output to your terminal, ensure that commands do not display on the screen as they execute (which is costly in terms of performance), and cause SQL*Plus to pause before displaying a page of data, thus giving the operator time to set up the printer.

Similar to the COLUMN command, a SET command endures for the life of your log-on session, until you redefine the command or toggle it off. Some environment commands, such as COMPUTE and BREAK commands, however, must be explicitly cleared from memory when you are finished, by using the CLEAR command. You may remember using this command to clear the SQL buffer before executing a new SQL command. As a rule of thumb, you will want to clear the SQL buffer and all COMPUTES or BREAKS at the outset of all report procedures, so that any new commands do not conflict with preceding ones.

Enter the following SET and CLEAR commands for this report:

```
CLEAR BREAKS
CLEAR COMPUTES

SET TERM OFF   (Suppresses output to terminal)
SET ECHO OFF   (Suppresses display of SQL*Plus commands)
SET PAUSE ON   (Pauses at end of each printed page)
```

Creating Top and Bottom Titles

The TTITLE and BTITLE commands are used to define your top and bottom (or, header and footer) page titles. Enter the following title commands:

```
TTITLE 'Video Quest Movie Rentals!Current Inventory Positions'
BTITLE CENTER 'Have a Good Day!' SKIP 1 CENTER 'Inventor.SQL'
```

Titles can span multiple lines. As shown in the TTITLE example, a new line is indicated by the '!' symbol. You can also use the SKIP *n* parameter, which skips *n* lines before printing the next line of the title. You cannot, however, mix the '!' symbol and SKIP *n* parameter in the same TTITLE or BTITLE statement.

Titles are centered on the page by default, unless you split them with the SKIP parameter. You can override the default by specifying the RIGHT or LEFT justification parameters. To specify an exact column position where the title should start, you use the COL *n* parameter. (You cannot mix the RIGHT or LEFT justification parameters with the COL parameter in the same format.) SQL*Plus automatically prints the current date on the left hand margin, above the top title. The page number is printed on the same line, but on the opposite margin.

You can force as many blank lines as you want between the bottom title of a page and the top title of the following page with the NEWPAGE command, by entering

```
SET NEWPAGE 0
```

SQL*Plus form feeds to the top of a fresh sheet of paper (line 0) at the end of the current page when printing a report.

Reformatting Columns

Reformatting columns is old hat to you. Define the column headings for this report in the following fashion, or experiment with other available column format options (refer to the *SQL*Plus Reference Guide* for the complete list of options):

```
COLUMN prodno        HEADING 'Product'            FORMAT A7
COLUMN description   HEADING 'Description'        FORMAT A12
COLUMN fmt           HEADING 'Format'             FORMAT A6
COLUMN title         HEADING 'Title'             FORMAT A35 TRUNC
COLUMN cost          HEADING 'Cost'              FORMAT $99.99
COLUMN qtyrecvd      HEADING 'Qty!Recvd'         FORMAT 99999
COLUMN qtyoh         HEADING 'Qty!On Hand'       FORMAT 99999
COLUMN qtysold       HEADING 'Qty!Sold'          FORMAT 99999
COLUMN qty_rented    HEADING 'Qty!Rented'        FORMAT 99999
COLUMN total         HEADING 'Actual!Inventory'  FORMAT 99999
COLUMN variance      HEADING '<Variance>'        FORMAT 99999
```

Specifying Report Breaks

You can organize rows of a report into groups with the BREAK command, and you can dictate special actions a query should take when the report *breaks* on these rows. For example, you can skip a line when the break occurs, start a new page, or compute subtotals on the rows organized by the break.

SQL*Plus lets you organize rows at the following BREAK points:

On a single column:	BREAK ON *column*
On more than one column:	BREAK ON *column* ON *column*
Whenever a row is retrieved:	BREAK ON ROW
At the end of a page:	BREAK ON PAGE
At the end of the report:	BREAK ON REPORT

Computing Totals at Breaks

The Product Inventory Report is used when there is a desire to reconcile the inventory positions for each product. However, management also wants to study the summary totals for each inventory category.

The COMPUTE command generates either totals or subtotals for the rows organized by a BREAK command. For example, if you create a BREAK at the end of the Product Inventory Report, you can use COMPUTE to calculate the totals on each inventory column (*qtyrecvd*, *qtyoh*, *qtysold*, *qty_rented*, *total*, and *variance*) for all the rows of the report.

Enter the BREAK and COMPUTE commands for this report:

```
BREAK ON REPORT
COMPUTE SUM OF qtyrecvd     ON REPORT
COMPUTE SUM OF qtyoh        ON REPORT
COMPUTE SUM OF qtysold      ON REPORT
COMPUTE SUM OF qty_rented   ON REPORT
COMPUTE SUM OF total        ON REPORT
COMPUTE SUM OF variance     ON REPORT
```

Defining the Report Query

The base query for this report is anything but elaborate. It needn't be, because most of your work went into building the views, setting up the report environment, and reformatting the columns in preparation for this query.

Enter the report query and spool the results of the query to the INVEN132.LIS file for output:

```
SPOOL Inven132.lis

SELECT SUBSTR(prodno, 1, 4) prodno,
       DECODE(SUBSTR(prodno,5,1), 'V','Vhs','B','Beta',null) fmt,
       description, title, cost, qtyrecvd, qtysold, qty_rented,
       total, variance
  FROM inventory
 ORDER BY prodno
/
SPOOL off
```

The Product Inventory Report Listing

Listing 8.1, the Product Inventory Report, includes the prerequisite PRODUCTS_RENTED and QTY_PRODUCTS_OUT views.

Listing 8.1   The Product Inventory Report

```
rem * ------------------------------------------------------------
rem * Product Inventory Report procedure
rem * Inven132.SQL
rem *
rem * Views Created:    PRODUCTS_RENTED
rem *                   QTY_PRODUCTS_OUT
rem *                   INVENTORY
rem *
rem * ------------------------------------------------------------
rem * Step #1 - Create PRODUCTS_RENTED View
rem * ------------------------------------------------------------

DROP VIEW products_rented
/

CREATE VIEW products_rented
(memberid, catnum, prodno, dateout, schdrtn)
AS
SELECT memberid, tape.catnum, prodno, dateout, schdrtn
  FROM rentals, tape
 WHERE rentals.catnum = tape.catnum
   AND actrtn is null
/


rem * ------------------------------------------------------------
rem * Step #2 - Create QTY_RENTED View
rem * ------------------------------------------------------------

DROP VIEW qty_rented
/

CREATE VIEW qty_rented
(prodno, qty_rented)
AS
SELECT prodno, count(catnum)
  FROM products_rented
 GROUP BY prodno
/
```

continued

Listing 8.1   *(continued)*

```
rem * ----------------------------------------------------------
rem * Step #3 - Create INVENTORY View
rem * ----------------------------------------------------------

DROP VIEW inventory
/

CREATE VIEW inventory
        (prodno, description, title, cost, qtyrecvd, qtyoh,
qtysold, qty_rented, total, variance)
AS
SELECT product.prodno, product.description, title, cost,
        qtyrecvd, qtyoh, qtysold, qty_rented
        (nvl(qtyoh, 0) + nvl(qtysold, 0) + nvl(qty_rented, 0)),
        (qtyrecvd _ (nvl(qtyoh, 0) + nvl(qtysold, 0) +
            nvl(qty_rented, 0)))
   FROM product, title, qty_rented
  WHERE product.titlecd = title.titlecd (+)
    AND product.prodno = qty_rented.prodno (+)
/


rem * ----------------------------------------------------------
rem * Step #4 - Generate Product Inventory Report
rem * ----------------------------------------------------------

CLEAR BREAKS
CLEAR COMPUTES

SET NEWPAGE 0
SET LINESIZE 132
SET PAGESIZE 54
SET SPACE 1
SET TERM OFF
SET ECHO OFF
SET PAUSE ON

TTITLE 'Video Quest Movie Rentals!Current Inventory Positions'
BTITLE CENTER 'Have a Good Day!' SKIP 1 CENTER 'Inventor.SQL'

COLUMN prodno        HEADING 'Product'        FORMAT A7
COLUMN description   HEADING 'Description'    FORMAT A12
```

```
COLUMN fmt          HEADING 'Format'             FORMAT A6
COLUMN title        HEADING 'Title'              FORMAT A35 TRUNC
COLUMN cost         HEADING 'Cost'               FORMAT $99.99
COLUMN qtyrecvd     HEADING 'Qty!Recvd'          FORMAT 99999
COLUMN qtyoh        HEADING 'Qty!On Hand'        FORMAT 99999
COLUMN qtysold      HEADING 'Qty!Sold'           FORMAT 99999
COLUMN qty_rented   HEADING 'Qty!Rented'         FORMAT 99999
COLUMN total        HEADING 'Actual!Inventory'   FORMAT 99999
COLUMN variance     HEADING '<Variance>'         FORMAT 99999

BREAK ON REPORT
COMPUTE SUM OF qtyrecvd ON REPORT
COMPUTE SUM OF qtyoh       ON REPORT
COMPUTE SUM OF qtysold     ON REPORT
COMPUTE SUM OF qty_rented ON REPORT
COMPUTE SUM OF total       ON REPORT
COMPUTE SUM OF variance    ON REPORT

SPOOL Inven132.lis

SELECT SUBSTR(prodno,1,4) prodno,
       DECODE(SUBSTR(prodno,5,1), 'V','Vhs','B','Beta',null) fmt,
       description, title, cost, qtyrecvd, qtysold, qty_rented,
       total, variance
  FROM inventory
 ORDER BY prodno
/

SPOOL OFF
CLEAR BREAKS
CLEAR COMPUTES
SET PAUSE OFF
TTITLE OFF
BTITLE OFF

rem * End Product Inventory report procedure
```

The Tapes Overdue Report

Video Quest does not lose direct revenue on overdue tapes. Customers are
charged one and one half times the daily rental rate for every late tape.

But if popular titles are continually returned late, the store stands to lose much more than direct revenue—customer satisfaction and loyalty. This is a delicate issue, one that Video Quest monitors closely with the aid of the Tapes Overdue Report.

Video Quest runs the Tapes Overdue report at least once a day, sometimes twice on busy days, and always twice on weekends. Figure 8.2 shows sample output of this report.

```
Fri Jun 10                                                                page    1

                                  Video Quest Movie Rentals
                                     TAPES OVERDUE REPORT


                        Catalog           Scheduled       Days Late   Member
Title                   Number   Format   Return Date     Late Charge  Name                    Phone
----------------------- -------  ------   ----------------  ---- --------  --------------------  ------------

Citizen Kane               451   Vhs          20 May , 88    22   $82.50  Jerry Barry            415-893-0050


Ghostbusters               470   Vhs          12 April, 88    60  $270.00  Daniel James Cronin   415-598-8125


Gone with the Wind         301   Vhs          14 April, 88    58  $217.50  Jerry Barry            415-893-0050

                           305   Beta         19 May , 88     23   $86.25  Daniel James Cronin   415-598-8125








                                     Have A Good Day!
                                       Overdue.SQL

4 records selected.
```

Figure 8.2   Sample Output of the Tapes Overdue Report

Laying Out the Report

The environment for the Tape Overdue Report is a carbon copy of the preceding Product Inventory Report. You must lay out the page format to accommodate the printed page, tune the environment with SET and

CLEAR commands to reduce processing overhead and procedural error, and add both top and bottom titles.

Enter these SQL*Plus commands into your Tapes Overdue Report procedure file:

```
CLEAR BREAKS
CLEAR COMPUTES

SET NEWPAGE 0
SET LINESIZE 132
SET PAGESIZE 54
SET SPACE 2

SET TERM OFF
SET ECHO OFF
SET PAUSE ON

TTITLE 'Video Quest Movie Rentals!TAPES OVERDUE REPORT'
BTITLE CENTER 'Have a Good Day!' SKIP 1 CENTER 'Overdue.SQL'
```

Constructing the Tapes Overdue Query

The Tapes Overdue Report provides a snapshot of all overdue rental tapes by title, catalog number, and the customer responsible for the tape. The report retrieves information from five tables—the RENTALS, TAPE, TITLE, PRODUCT, and CUSTOMER tables. It posts the scheduled return date, converting the date into a more readable format, and then it calculates the number of days late and the accrued late charge for each tape. The daytime phone number of the irresponsible customer is also printed to assist the Video Quest clerks in tracking the customer down.

Enter the Tapes Overdue report query:

```
 SPOOL Overdue.lis
SELECT title, rentals.catnum
       DECODE(product.format, 'V', 'Vhs', 'B', 'Beta', null) fmt,
       TO_CHAR(schdrtn, 'DD FMMonth, YY') due,
       ROUND(sysdate - schdrtn) dayslate,
       ROUND(sysdate - schdrtn) * (rentals.ratepdy * 1.5)
            latecharge, customer.name,
       day_area !!'-'!! day_prefix !!'-'!! day_suffix "Phone"
   FROM rentals, tape, title, product, customer
```

continued

```
   WHERE rentals.catnum = tape.catnum
     AND title.titlecd = product.titlecd
     AND tape.storeno = product.storeno AND
         tape.prodno= product.prodno
     AND rentals.memberid = customer.memberid
     AND actrtn is null
     AND trunc(sysdate - schdrtn) > 0
   ORDER BY title, schdrtn
 /
SPOOL OFF
```

Notice that the telephone number is derived by concatenating the three relevant daytime phone columns. An alias name ("Phone") is attached to the displayed column.

This report is logically organized by film title, so it would make sense to group the rows by film title on the printed page. You will break the rows of the report on the *title* column, and instruct SQL*Plus to skip a line at each break to make the rows stand out. When you break on a column, you must also ORDER BY the same column in the report query to ensure that the report is ordered properly. If you don't, breaks are apt to occur at apparently random points.

Using Table Alias Names

You can eliminate tedious typing by using alias names for the tables referred to in this 5-table join query. For example, a letter identifier could be substituted for each table name, eliminating dozens of keystrokes. An alias table name is defined in the FROM table statement and must be used consistently whenever the table appears in the query. An example of this approach appears in Listing 8.2, The Tapes Overdue Report.

Listing 8.2   The Tapes Overdue Report

```
rem *  -----------------------------------------------------
rem *      Tapes Overdue Report procedure
rem *      Overdue.SQL
rem *  -----------------------------------------------------

CLEAR BREAKS
CLEAR COMPUTES
SET NEWPAGE 0
SET LINESIZE 132
SET PAGESIZE 54
SET SPACE 2
```

```
SET TERM OFF
SET ECHO OFF
SET PAUSE ON

TTITLE 'Video Quest Movie Rentals!TAPES OVERDUE REPORT'
BTITLE CENTER 'Have a Good Day!' SKIP 1 CENTER 'Overdue.SQL'

COLUMN name        HEADING 'Name'                 FORMAT A20
COLUMN catnum      HEADING 'Catalog!Number'       FORMAT 9999
COLUMN title       HEADING 'Title'                FORMAT A40 TRUNC
COLUMN fmt         HEADING 'Format'               FORMAT A6
COLUMN due         HEADING 'Scheduled!Return Date' FORMAT A16
COLUMN dayslate    HEADING 'Days!Late'            FORMAT 999
COLUMN latecharge  HEADING 'Late!Charge'          FORMAT $999.99

BREAK ON title SKIP 1

SPOOL Overdue.lis

SELECT title, a.catnum
       DECODE(d.format, 'V', 'Vhs', 'B', 'Beta', null) fmt,
       TO_CHAR(schdrtn, 'DD FMMonth, YY') due,
       ROUND(sysdate - schdrtn) dayslate,
       ROUND(sysdate - schdrtn) * (a.ratepdy * 1.5)
           latecharge, name,
       ROUND(sysdate - schdrtn) * (a.ratepdy * 1.5)
  FROM rentals a, tape b, title c, product d, customer e
 WHERE a.catnum     = b.catnum
   AND c.titlecd    = d.titlecd
   AND b.storeno    = d.storeno AND
       b.prodno     = d.prodno
   AND a.memberid   = e.memberid
   AND actrtn is null
   AND TRUNC(sysdate - schdrtn) > 0
 ORDER BY title, schdrtn

SPOOL OFF
CLEAR BREAKS
CLEAR COMPUTES
SET PAUSE OFF
BTITLE OFF
TTITLE OFF

rem * End Tapes Overdue Report procedure
```

The Daily Rentals Report

Video Quest is a mob scene on weekends. Tallies of 300 to 400 rental transactions on a Friday or Saturday are not uncommon. Management at Video Quest has demanded a daily record of the titles that have moved, and of precisely how many copies of each left the store. It has become a nightly ritual of Video Quest personnel to generate this Daily Rentals Report, incorporating the task into store closing procedures.

The Daily Rentals Report is divided into two parts, a detailed report linking tapes and customers, and a summary report returning quantity and revenue totals by title (Listing 8.3). Figures 8.3 and 8.4 illustrate outputs of both reports.

```
Fri Jun 10                                                                page    1


                                    Video Quest Movie Rentals
                                    RENTALS JOURNAL - DETAILS


  Rental                                    Catalog  Film          Member
  Date         Title              Format    Number   Category      Name                   Phone
  ---------    -----------------  ------    -------  ------------  --------------------    ------------
  10-JUN-88    Citizen Kane       Vhs          450   Classics      Martha Kent             453-392-4457

               Ghostbusters       Beta         473   Comedy        Jerry Barry             415-893-0050

               Gone with the Wind Vhs          300   Classics      Martha Kent             453-392-4457

               The Shining        Vhs          481   Horror        Martha Kent             453-392-4457
```

```
                                          Have a Good Day!
                                          Dayrent.SQL
```

Figure 8.3   Sample Output of the Daily Rentals Report—Details

The Detail Report

The detailed portion of the Daily Rentals Report itemizes the tapes rented out the day the report is run. Involving a 6-table join, the report is organized by film title, catalog number, and tape format. The report query selects other convenient information as well, such as the film category of the rental tape and both the name and phone number of the customer who rented it out.

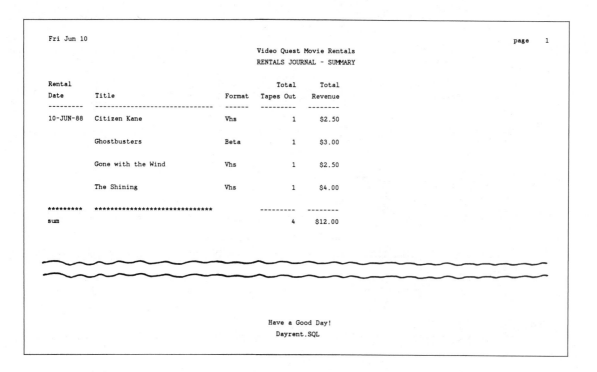

```
Fri Jun 10                                                                    page    1

                                    Video Quest Movie Rentals
                                    RENTALS JOURNAL - SUMMARY

Rental                                          Total       Total
Date        Title                    Format   Tapes Out    Revenue
---------   ------------------------ ------   ---------    --------
10-JUN-88   Citizen Kane             Vhs          1         $2.50

            Ghostbusters             Beta         1         $3.00

            Gone with the Wind       Vhs          1         $2.50

            The Shining              Vhs          1         $4.00

*********   ******************************      ---------    --------
sum                                              4         $12.00




                                    Have a Good Day!
                                    Dayrent.SQL
```

Figure 8.4   Sample Output of the Daily Rentals Report—Summary

Although initially designed to report the tapes rented out for the current date, the report procedure has been generalized to permit some flexibility. The report currently shows the date each tape was rented, *dateout*. This would be a superfluous piece of information if the report were hard-coded; the current date could just as easily be posted as a variable in the title of the report instead. By generalizing the procedure, however, you can broaden the Daily Rentals Report to provide rental trends over a user-specified period of time. We will look at this enhancement shortly.

Enter the detail report query, ordering the rows by date rented out and film title:

```
SELECT dateout, title,
       DECODE(d.format, 'V', 'Vhs', 'B', 'Beta', null) fmt,
       a.catnum, initcap(f.description), name,
       DECODE(d.format, 'V', 'Vhs', 'B', 'Beta', null) fmt,
  FROM rentals a, tape b, title c, product d, customer e,
       category f
 WHERE a.catnum    = b.catnum
   AND b.storeno   = d.storeno AND
```

continued

```
        b.prodno    = d.prodno
   AND  c.titlecd   = d.titlecd
   AND  c.category  = f.category
   AND  a.memberid  = e.memberid
   AND  dateout     = TRUNC(sysdate)
ORDER BY dateout, title
```

The Summary Report

The summary portion of the Daily Rentals Report is chiefly concerned with daily totals—the total number of tapes rented out for the day by title and format, and the total revenue generated for this group *and* for the entire day.

Enter the summary report query:

```
SELECT  dateout, title
        MAX(DECODE(d.format, 'V', 'Vhs', 'B', 'Beta', null) fmt,
        COUNT(a.catnum) ttltapes,
        SUM(ratepdy) revenue
   FROM rentals a, tape b, title c, product d
  WHERE a.catnum    = b.catnum
    AND b.storeno   = d.storeno AND
        b.prodno    = d.prodno
    AND c.titlecd   = d.titlecd
    AND dateout     = TRUNC(sysdate)
  GROUP BY dateout, title, d.format
```

This report returns summary information grouped by rental date, the titles rented for that date, and further, by tape format. The GROUP BY function is applied so that the *dateout* and *title* columns, which normally return individual results, can be conjoined with the summary tape and revenue totals to clearly identify the date and title to which these summary totals belong.

Remember that some titles, for example *Gone With the Wind*, may be rented out in either Beta or VHS format. Since the report groups totals by tape format, you need some way of selecting the individual format value in one and the same group query. The ploy used here is to turn the column into a group expression with the MAX group function. If you use the GROUP BY tape format and then the MAX format for each, the Beta group, for example, will of course be the value 'Beta', and it can then be displayed as 'Beta'.

The grand totals—the total number of tapes rented and the total revenue generated for the day—are computed on the *ttltapes* and *revenue* columns with the COMPUTE function. You must first define a break on the *dateout* column; in the same statement, you will define a break on the *title* column. To enhance readability of the report, use a BREAK clause to skip lines on these breaks. Observe:

```
BREAK ON dateout SKIP 2 title SKIP 1
COMPUTE SUM of ttltapes ON dateout
COMPUTE SUM of revenue ON dateout
```

Listing 8.3   The Daily Rentals Report

```
rem * ------------------------------------------------------------
rem * The Daily Rentals Report Procedure
rem * Dayrent.SQL
rem * ------------------------------------------------------------
CLEAR BREAKS
CLEAR COMPUTES

SET NEWPAGE 0
SET LINESIZE 132
SET PAGESIZE 54
SET SPACE 2

SET TERM OFF
SET ECHO OFF
SET PAUSE ON


rem * ------------------------------------------------------------
rem * Begin Detail Report
rem * ------------------------------------------------------------
TTITLE 'Video Quest Movie Rentals!DAILY RENTALS REPORT - DETAILS'
BTITLE CENTER 'Have a Good Day!' SKIP 1 CENTER 'Dayrent.SQL'
COLUMN name            HEADING 'Member!Name      FORMAT A20
COLUMN title           HEADING 'Title'           FORMAT A40 TRUNC
COLUMN catnum          HEADING 'Catalog!Number'  FORMAT 9999
COLUMN fmt             HEADING 'Format'           FORMAT A6
COLUMN dateout         HEADING 'Rental!Date'     FORMAT A9
COLUMN initcap(f.description)  HEADING 'Film!Category' FORMAT A12

SPOOL dayrent.lis
```

continued

Listing 8.3 *(continued)*

```
BREAK ON dateout SKIP 2 ON title SKIP 1

SELECT dateout, title,
       DECODE(d.format, 'V', 'Vhs', 'B', 'Beta', null) fmt,
       a.catnum, initcap(f.description), name,
       day_area ||'-'|| day_prefix ||'-'|| day_suffix "Phone"
  FROM rentals a, tape b, title c, product d, customer e,
       category f
 WHERE a.catnum      = b.catnum
   AND b.storeno     = d.storeno AND
       b.prodno      = d.prodno
   AND c.titlecd     = d.titlecd
   AND c.category    = f.category
   AND a.memberid    = e.memberid
   AND dateout       = TRUNC(sysdate)
 ORDER BY dateout, title
/


rem * -------------------------------------------------------------
rem * Begin Summary Report
rem * -------------------------------------------------------------
TTITLE 'Video Quest Movie Rentals│DAILY RENTALS REPORT - SUMMARY'
COLUMN ttltapes      HEADING 'Total│Tapes Out'     FORMAT 999
COLUMN revenue       HEADING 'Total│Revenue'       FORMAT $999.99

COMPUTE SUM of ttltapes ON dateout
COMPUTE SUM of revenue ON dateout

SELECT dateout, title
       MAX(DECODE(d.format, 'V', 'Vhs', 'B', 'Beta', null) fmt,
       COUNT(a.catnum) ttltapes,
       SUM(ratepdy) revenue
  FROM rentals a, tape b, title c, product d
 WHERE a.catnum   = b.catnum
   AND b.storeno  = d.storeno AND
       b.prodno   = d.prodno
   AND c.titlecd  = d.titlecd
   AND dateout    = TRUNC(sysdate)
 GROUP BY dateout, title, d.format
/
```

```
SPOOL OFF
TTITLE OFF
BTITLE OFF
CLEAR BREAKS
CLEAR COMPUTES
SET PAUSE OFF

rem * End Daily Detail/Summary Rental Report Procedure
```

Using Substitution Variables in the Procedure

The scope of the Daily Rentals Report can be expanded by making a slight modification to the procedure. By defining a substitution variable (a technique discussed in depth in Chapter 5, in the section *Using Parameters in a Command File*), you may report on rental activities over a different period of time in a way that takes advantage of the dynamic nature of SQL, *each time* the report is generated. For instance, to find out what tapes had been rented out over the past month or longer, you would replace the existing WHERE condition (`WHERE dateout = TRUNC(sysdate)`) with the following condition in both the detail and summary reports:

```
WHERE dateout BETWEEN ADD_MONTHS(sysdate, &1) AND sysdate
```

The operator may now limit the report to a specified number of months when starting the report. If today's date is 15-MAY-88, and the operator wanted to see the daily rentals over the past month, he or she would enter

```
START dayrent -1
```

and would see results similar to the reports shown in Figures 8.5 and 8.6.

Suppose you wanted to study the rental activity for a range of dates. You could alter the WHERE clause in both the detailed and summary procedures to substitute two variables like this:

```
WHERE dateout BETWEEN '&1' AND '&2'
```

The variables are enclosed in quotes just as if you had included constant date values in the expression. To generate a daily rental report for the period between 16-MAY-88 through 23-MAY-88, for example, an operator would enter the range

```
Fri Jun 10                                                                    page   1

                                    Video Quest Movie Rentals
                                    RENTALS JOURNAL - DETAILS
                                    By User-Specified Range


Rental                              Catalog  Film          Member
Date       Title            Format  Number   Category      Name                   Phone
---------  --------------------- ------  -------  ------------  --------------------   -----------
18-MAY-88  Citizen Kane     Vhs       450    Classics      Martha Kent            453-392-4457
                            Vhs       451    Classics      Jerry Barry            415-893-0050

           Gone with the Wind  Beta   305    Classics      Daniel James Cronin    415-598-8125
                            Vhs       300    Classics      Jerry Barry            415-893-0050

           The Sound of Music  Vhs    100    Musicals      Martha Kent            453-392-4457

           Topgun           Vhs       201    Adventure     Martha Kent            453-392-4457




                                        Dayrent1.SQL

   6 records selected.
```

**Figure 8.5   Sample Output of the Daily Rentals for One Month—
Detail Report**

```
START dayrent 16-MAY-88 23-MAY-88
```

and see only the titles rented through that week.

The Year-to-Date Rental History Report

In the past, management had only the vaguest sense of rentals activity trends over the year or even fiscal quarter. Management could determine gross revenue figures for a given period based on rentals receipts, but didn't have access to tools that could present rental trends in any meaningful way. What categories of films moved the best in the summertime? Did comedies do well in the Christmas season? What new titles were the most popular their first two weeks on the shelf? Were horror and slasher films on an upswing, or was the fad fading toward the end of the year?

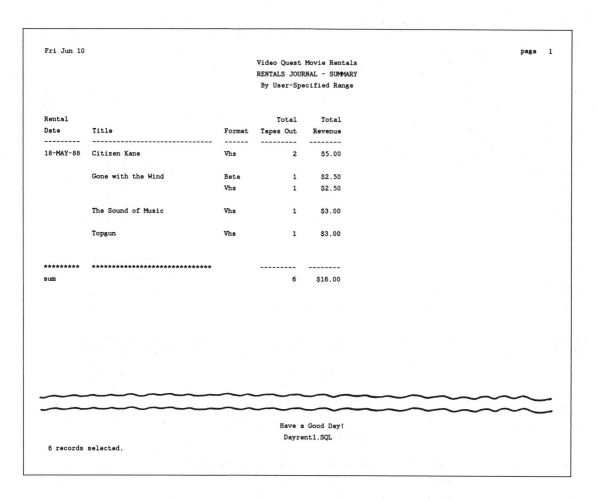

```
Fri Jun 10                                                              page   1

                              Video Quest Movie Rentals
                              RENTALS JOURNAL - SUMMARY
                              By User-Specified Range


Rental                                      Total        Total
Date       Title                  Format    Tapes Out    Revenue
---------  -----------------------------    ------    ---------    --------
18-MAY-88  Citizen Kane           Vhs           2        $5.00

           Gone with the Wind     Beta          1        $2.50
                                  Vhs           1        $2.50

           The Sound of Music     Vhs           1        $3.00

           Topgun                 Vhs           1        $3.00


*********  ******************************            ---------    --------
sum                                               6       $16.00
```

Have a Good Day!
Dayrent1.SQL

6 records selected.

**Figure 8.6   Sample Output of the Daily Rentals for One Month—
Summary Report**

One can answer analytical questions like these with a Year-to-Date
Rental History Report. Such a report would help management better understand the tastes of their customers and sharpen their forecasting skills
in order to make more accurate purchasing decisions. Figure 8.7 illustrates
sample output from the Year-to-Date Rental History Report.

Creating the YEAR_RENTALS View

The Year-to-Date Rental History Report requires a small amount of preparation. A view must first be created to summarize the rentals activity for
each calendar month, grouping the summary totals by film title and format. You will use the DECODE function in conjunction with the SUM

```
Fri Jun 10                                                                    page   1
                              Video Quest Movie Rentals
                             RENTAL ACTIVITY FOR CURRENT YEAR
                               Ranked By Rental Quantity

                                                                           Yearly
YR Title                   F    Jan Feb Mar Apr May Jun Jul Aug Sep Oct Nov Dec Total
-- ----------------------- ---- ---- ---- ---- ---- ---- ---- ---- ---- ---- ---- ---- -------
88 Gone with the Wind      Vhs          1    2    1    1                              5

   Citizen Kane            Vhs                    2    1                              3

   The Shining             Vhs               1         1                              2

   The Sound of Music      Vhs          1         1                                  2

   Topgun                  Vhs               1    1                                  2

   Ghostbusters            Beta                        1                              1
                           Vhs               1                                       1

   Gone with the Wind      Beta                   1                                   1

** *********************************** ---- ---- ---- ---- ---- ---- ---- ---- ---- ---- ---- -------
sum                                     2    5    6    4                             17
```

```
                              Have a Good Day!
                                Rentytd.SQL

8 records selected.
```

**Figure 8.7   Sample Output of the Year-to-Date Rental History
Report**

group function to summarize this data. Create the YEAR_RENTALS view
as shown:

```
CREATE VIEW year_rentals
(titlecd, format,
jan, feb, mar, apr, may, jun, jul,
aug, sep, oct, nov, dec, yr_total)
AS
SELECT product.titlecd, product.format,
       SUM(DECODE(TO_CHAR(dateout, 'MM'), '01', 1, 0),
       SUM(DECODE(TO_CHAR(dateout, 'MM'), '02', 1, 0),
       SUM(DECODE(TO_CHAR(dateout, 'MM'), '03', 1, 0),
       SUM(DECODE(TO_CHAR(dateout, 'MM'), '04', 1, 0),
       SUM(DECODE(TO_CHAR(dateout, 'MM'), '05', 1, 0),
       SUM(DECODE(TO_CHAR(dateout, 'MM'), '06', 1, 0),
       SUM(DECODE(TO_CHAR(dateout, 'MM'), '07', 1, 0),
```

```
        SUM(DECODE(TO_CHAR(dateout, 'MM'), '08', 1, 0),
        SUM(DECODE(TO_CHAR(dateout, 'MM'), '09', 1, 0),
        SUM(DECODE(TO_CHAR(dateout, 'MM'), '10', 1, 0),
        SUM(DECODE(TO_CHAR(dateout, 'MM'), '11', 1, 0),
        SUM(DECODE(TO_CHAR(dateout, 'MM'), '12', 1, 0),
        SUM(1)
  FROM  rentals, tape, product
 WHERE  (rentals.catnum   = tape.catnum)
   AND  (tape.storeno      = product.storeno AND
         tape.prodno       = product.prodno)
   AND  TO_CHAR(dateout, 'YY') = TO_CHAR(sysdate, 'YY')
 GROUP  BY product.titlecd,  product.format
```

The compound SUM and DECODE function statement uses true/false logic to test whether any rentals have occurred for a given month before the group function is performed. The statement

```
SUM(DECODE(TO_CHAR(dateout, 'MM'), '01', 1, 0)
```

can be translated as:

1. Convert any date value in *dateout* to month format ('MM'). (January = '01', February = '02', March = '03', etc.)

2. If any *dateout* value exists for the month of January ('01', the first argument), then return 1 (the second argument), and perform the SUM computation for all returned values.

3. If no *dateout* values exist for January, return 0 (the third argument).

Notice the last column that is selected—SUM(1). What this expression does is count the values in every row returned by the query, counting column values *across* the row. This count represents the total rental transactions for the title over the year, and is stored in the view column, *yr_total*.

In order to be effective, the YEAR_RENTALS view must ensure that only the films rented for the current year-to-date are picked up. The WHERE condition

```
AND  TO_CHAR(dateout, 'YY') = TO_CHAR(sysdate, 'YY')
```

converts *sysdate* to a year format and compares this to the *dateout* column in the RENTALS table to select only those transactions processed in the same year.

Generating the Year-to-Date Report

With YEAR_RENTALS as the foundation, your Year-to-Date report can now be generated with a simple query. You will retrieve the values for each month, the summary *yr_total* value, and perform an elementary join to extract the film title for the *titlecd* that identifies each row in YEAR_RENTALS. Enter the report query:

```
SELECT TO_CHAR(sysdate, 'YYYY') year, title,
       DECODE(format, 'V', 'Vhs', 'B', 'Beta', null) fmt,
       jan, feb, mar, apr, may, jun, jul, aug, sep, oct, nov,
       dec, yr_total
  FROM year_rentals, title
 WHERE year_rentals.titlecd = title.titlecd
 ORDER BY yr_total desc, title, format
```

The *year* column, derived from *sysdate* converted to the 'YYYY' format, or 1988, has been added to the report. This virtual column enables you to compute yearly rentals totals by calendar month with the COMPUTE function. To do this, of course, you must first define a BREAK on the *year* column.

Listing 8.4   The Year-to-Date Rental History Report

```
rem * --------------------------------------------------------
rem * The Year-to-Date Rental History Report Procedure
rem * Rentytd.SQL
rem * --------------------------------------------------------

rem * --------------------------------------------------------
rem * Step #1 - Create the YEAR_RENTALS View
rem * --------------------------------------------------------

DROP VIEW year_rentals
/

CREATE VIEW year_rentals
(titlecd, format,
jan, feb, mar, apr, may, jun, jul,
aug, sep, oct, nov, dec, yr_total)
AS
SELECT product.titlecd, product.format,
       SUM(DECODE(TO_CHAR(dateout, 'MM'), '01', 1, 0),
       SUM(DECODE(TO_CHAR(dateout, 'MM'), '02', 1, 0),
```

```
          SUM(DECODE(TO_CHAR(dateout, 'MM'), '03', 1, 0),
          SUM(DECODE(TO_CHAR(dateout, 'MM'), '04', 1, 0),
          SUM(DECODE(TO_CHAR(dateout, 'MM'), '05', 1, 0),
          SUM(DECODE(TO_CHAR(dateout, 'MM'), '06', 1, 0),
          SUM(DECODE(TO_CHAR(dateout, 'MM'), '07', 1, 0),
          SUM(DECODE(TO_CHAR(dateout, 'MM'), '08', 1, 0),
          SUM(DECODE(TO_CHAR(dateout, 'MM'), '09', 1, 0),
          SUM(DECODE(TO_CHAR(dateout, 'MM'), '10', 1, 0),
          SUM(DECODE(TO_CHAR(dateout, 'MM'), '11', 1, 0),
          SUM(DECODE(TO_CHAR(dateout, 'MM'), '12', 1, 0),
          SUM(1)
   FROM rentals, tape, product
  WHERE rentals.catnum      = tape.catnum
    AND tape.storeno        = product.storeno AND
        tape.prodno         = product.prodno
    AND TO_CHAR(dateout, 'YY') = TO_CHAR(sysdate, 'YY')
  GROUP BY product.titlecd, product.format
/


rem * ------------------------------------------------------
rem * Generate Year-to-Date Rental History Report
rem * ------------------------------------------------------

CLEAR BREAKS
CLEAR COMPUTES

SET NEWPAGE 0
SET LINESIZE 132
SET PAGESIZE 54
SET SPACE 1

SET TERM OFF
SET ECHO OFF
SET PAUSE ON

TTITLE CENTER 'Video Quest Movie Rentals SKIP 1 CENTER
        RENTAL ACTIVITY FOR CURRENT YEAR - DETAILS' SKIP
        1 CENTER 'Ranked by Rental Quantity'
BTITLE CENTER 'Have a Good Day!' SKIP 1 CENTER 'Rentytd.SQL'
COLUMN title      HEADING 'Film!Title      FORMAT A35 TRUNC
COLUMN fmt        HEADING 'Format'         FORMAT A6
COLUMN year       HEADING 'Year'           FORMAT A4
COLUMN jan        HEADING 'Jan'            FORMAT 9999
COLUMN feb        HEADING 'Feb'            FORMAT 9999
COLUMN mar        HEADING 'Mar'            FORMAT 9999      continued
```

Listing 8.4 *(continued)*

```
COLUMN apr        HEADING 'Apr'           FORMAT 9999
COLUMN may        HEADING 'May'           FORMAT 9999
COLUMN jun        HEADING 'Jun'           FORMAT 9999
COLUMN jul        HEADING 'Jul'           FORMAT 9999
COLUMN aug        HEADING 'Aug'           FORMAT 9999
COLUMN sep        HEADING 'Sep'           FORMAT 9999
COLUMN oct        HEADING 'Oct'           FORMAT 9999
COLUMN nov        HEADING 'Nov'           FORMAT 9999
COLUMN dec        HEADING 'Dec'           FORMAT 9999
COLUMN yr_total   HEADING 'Yearly!Total'  FORMAT 99999

SPOOL Rentytd.lis

BREAK ON year ON title SKIP 1
COMPUTE SUM of jan        ON year
COMPUTE SUM of feb        ON year
COMPUTE SUM of mar        ON year
COMPUTE SUM of apr        ON year
COMPUTE SUM of may        ON year
COMPUTE SUM of jun        ON year
COMPUTE SUM of jul        ON year
COMPUTE SUM of aug        ON year
COMPUTE SUM of sep        ON year
COMPUTE SUM of oct        ON year
COMPUTE SUM of nov        ON year
COMPUTE SUM of dec        ON year
COMPUTE SUM of yr_total   ON year
/

SELECT TO_CHAR(sysdate, 'YYYY') year, title,
       DECODE(format, 'V', 'Vhs', 'B', 'Beta', null) fmt,
       jan, feb, mar, apr, may, jun, jul, aug, sep, oct, nov,
       dec, yr_total
  FROM year_rentals, title
 WHERE year_rentals.titlecd = title.titlecd
 ORDER BY yr_total desc, title, format

SPOOL OFF
CLEAR COMPUTES
CLEAR BREAKS
TTITLE OFF
BTITLE OFF

rem * End Year-to-Date Rental History Report procedure
```

SQL*ReportWriter

SQL*ReportWriter is a comprehensive reporting tool which meets virtually all of your production reporting needs. With SQL*ReportWriter, you can develop the full range of business reports, from a simple table listing or mailing labels to sophisticated multi-query, multi-page production reports. SQL*ReportWriter's nonprocedural approach enables developers to build even the most demanding reports quickly and efficiently. Simply enter one or more SELECT statements and SQL*ReportWriter generates a default report—complete with column headings, details, and page layout—which can be easily expanded via a spreadsheet style, fill-in-the forms interface.

SQL*ReportWriter's real power is its breadth of formatting control. You can create

▶ Versatile tabular and control break reports. You can display headers and footers and insert control breaks at the data, page *and* report boundaries. Data, boilerplate text, and computed functions such as fixed and running sums, averages, percents, subtotals, and totals, can be placed (or repeated) anywhere in the report—even within headers, footers, and breaks.

▶ Multi-section reports. You can create reports containing the results of multiple queries and place the results anywhere, including side by side, on the page. Multi-section reports such as Master/Detail, Master/Detail/Detail, and Master/Detail/Summary reports are much too advanced for a tool like SQL*Plus to handle.

▶ Matrix reports. You can build matrix reports (also known as *across* or *crosstab* reports) which contain a cross-tabulation of data laid out in a spreadsheet-style format. An example of a maxtrix report is the Year-to-Date Rentals Report you constructed earlier in the chapter with SQL*Plus.

▶ Wide reports with repeated columns. You can spread reports that are wider than a page onto multiple pages automatically. Additionally, you can retain full control over which label fields are repeated on each overflow page.

Building a Master-Detail Report

To appreciate the power of SQL*ReportWriter and the ease with which you can build and maintain highly formatted reports, walk through the steps of creating a typical multi-query report—a Master-Detail report. The Master-Detail report output you will generate is shown in Figure 8.8.

```
Fri Jun 10                                                      page   1


                          Video Quest Movie Rentals
                            LATE CHARGES REPORT

Customer:  Daniel J. Cronin
   Phone:  (415)526-8877

                                      Scheduled               Late
                Title                 Return     Days Late    Charges
                --------------------  ---------  ----------   --------

                Ghostbusters          12-APR-88  60           $ 270.00
                Gone With the Wind     19-MAY-88  23           $  86.25
                Topgun                 20-MAY-88  22           $  99.00
                                                               --------

                Charges for current member                    $ 455.25
                Running Total                                  $ 455.25



Customer:  Jerry Barry
   Phone:  (415) 893-0050

                                      Scheduled
                Title                 Return     Days Late    Charges
                --------------------  ---------  ----------   --------

                Citizen Kane          20-MAY-88  22           $  82.50
                Gone With the Wind     14-APR-88  58           $ 217.50
                                                               --------

                Charges for current member                    $ 300.00
                Running total                                  $ 755.25



Customer:  Martha Kent
   Phone:  (453) 392-4457

                                      Scheduled               Late
                Title                 Return     Days Late    Charges
                --------------------  ---------  ----------   --------

                The Sound of Music    20-MAY-88  22           $  99.00
                Topgun                20-MAY-88  22           $  99.00
                                                               --------

                Charges for current member                    $ 198.00
                Running total                                  $ 953.25

                Total late charges                             $ 953.25

                          Video Quest, Inc.
                          Have A Good Day!

   3 records selected.
```

Figure 8.8   Sample Output of a Completed Master-Detail Report

A Master-Detail report is normally generated from two related queries—a master or *parent* query and a detail or *child* query. SQL*ReportWriter dynamically joins the results of these queries so that the report output organizes the data in master-detail fashion, that is, each master record is grouped with all associated detail records. The data for this Master-Detail report will look familiar to you, for it is a variation of the Tapes Overdue Report. However, it is far more attractive than the tabular format of the Tapes Overdue Report, as you no doubt soon will agree.

The Action Menu

SQL*ReportWriter's pull-down menu interface is familiar and easy to use intuitively. The Action Menu is automatically highlighted when you enter the SQL*ReportWriter environment, as shown in Figure 8.9.

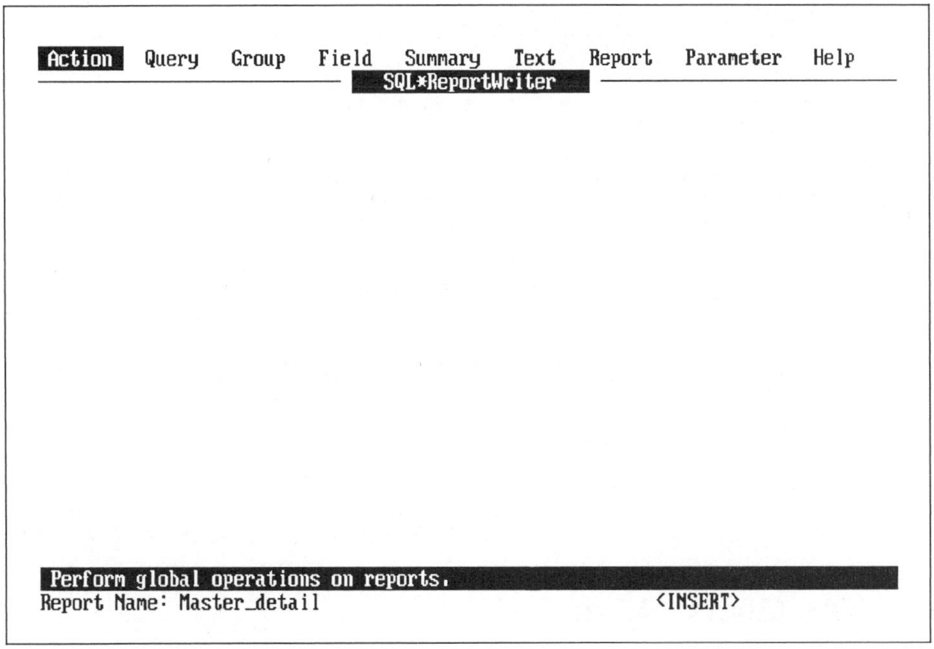

```
Action   Query   Group   Field   Summary   Text   Report   Parameter   Help
                          SQL*ReportWriter










 Perform global operations on reports.
 Report Name: Master_detail                            <INSERT>
```

Figure 8.9   The SQL*ReportWriter Top Menu

To navigate

1. Press [Enter] to select the Action Menu. The Action Menu is used to create a new report or open an existing one. Administrative functions, such as renaming, discarding, generating, and executing reports, are also performed from this menu.

2. Choose NEW ITEM to create a new report. You may use the [Up] or [Down] arrow keys to highlight the choice or enter the first letter of the choice.

3. Type the name *Master_Detail* and press [Enter].

4. Select the Query Menu from the menu bar. A blank Query screen appears as shown in Figure 8.10.

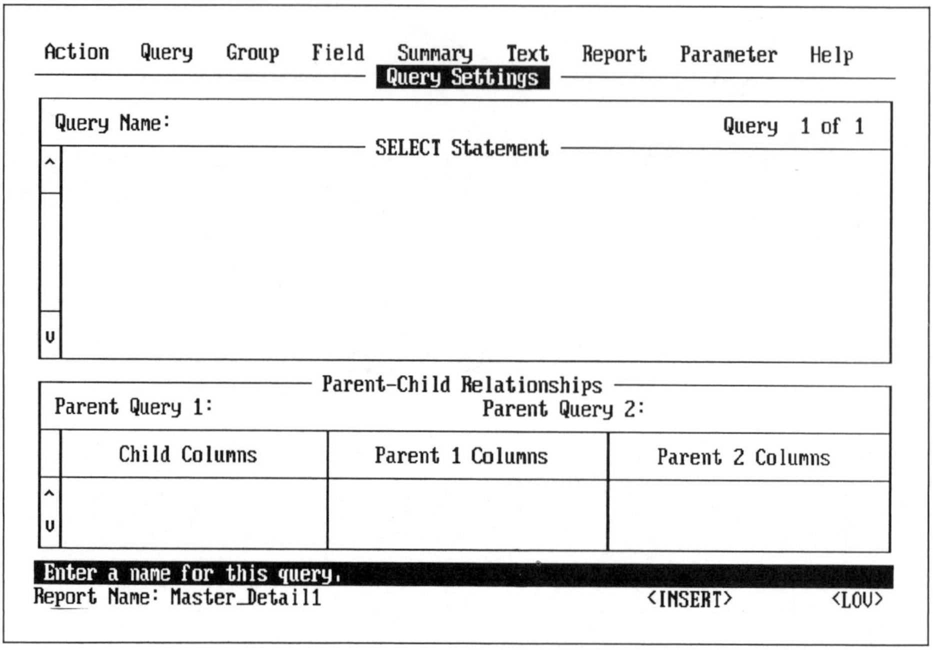

```
Action   Query   Group   Field   Summary   Text   Report   Parameter   Help
                              ▀Query Settings▀
Query Name:                                              Query  1 of 1
                          ── SELECT Statement ──
^



U

                      ── Parent-Child Relationships ──
   Parent Query 1:                    Parent Query 2:
        Child Columns         Parent 1 Columns         Parent 2 Columns
^
U

 Enter a name for this query.
Report Name: Master_Detail1                    <INSERT>         <LOU>
```

Figure 8.10   The Query Menu

The Query Menu

This screen is used to define the query or queries (for a multi-query report) which retrieve data for your report. You will build two distinct queries—a master or "Parent Query" which fetches the master records, and a detail or "Child Query" which fetches the associated detail records. When you define the primary key column, Member ID, SQL*ReportWriter knows to join the master and detail query records and display the results in the format you choose.

1. Type *Q_Master* for the name of the parent query.

2. Enter the following SELECT statement text for the *Q_Master* query.

```
SELECT memberid, name, day_area, day_prefix, day_suffix
   FROM customer
  WHERE memberid IN
(SELECT memberid
   FROM rentals)
```

SQL*ReportWriter provides several editing keys to facilitate data entry and cursor navigation. If you've entered an illegal SQL statement, SQL*ReportWriter notifies you immediately of any syntax errors.

Your entered query should look like the one in Figure 8.11.

```
 Action   Query   Group   Field   Summary   Text   Report   Parameter   Help
                             Query Settings
───────────────────────────────────────────────────────────────────────────
 Query Name: Q_Master                                        Query  1 of 2
 ^                          SELECT Statement
   SELECT memberid, name, day_area, day_prefix, day_suffix
      FROM customer
     WHERE memberid IN
           (SELECT memberid
               FROM rentals)
 U

                           Parent-Child Relationships
  Parent Query 1:                          Parent Query 2:
  ┌──────────────────────┬─────────────────────┬──────────────────────┐
  │    Child Columns     │   Parent 1 Columns  │   Parent 2 Columns   │
 ^│                      │                     │                      │
 U│                      │                     │                      │
  └──────────────────────┴─────────────────────┴──────────────────────┘
 Enter a name for this query.
 Report Name: Master_detail                      <INSERT>        <LOV>
```

Figure 8.11   The Q_Master Query

3. Press [Previous Field] to return to the Query Name field to enter the name of the second (or child) query.

SQL*ReportWriter automatically accepts your first query before returning you to the previous field. Notice that your screen still displays, that is, remembers, the text of the original query.

4. Press [Insert Record Below] to clear the screen and add the second query. (Overwriting the original SELECT statement simply updates it and does not insert a new query.)

5. Type *Q_Detail* for the name of the second query.

6. Enter the following SELECT statement for Q_Detail:

```
SELECT memberid, title.title, schdrtn,
       ROUND(sysdate-schdrtn) "Days Late",
       ROUND((sysdate-schdrtn) * ratepdy) "Charges"
  FROM rentals, tape, product, title
 WHERE rentals.catnum   = tape.catnum
   AND tape.prodno      = product.prodno
   AND product.titlecd  = title.titlecd
   AND actrtn is null
 ORDER BY memberid
```

7. Press [Tab] to move to the Parent-Child relationships block.

Here you will identify the associated parent query and the common column joining the two queries. Parent-child relationships are always defined on the detail queries in SQL*ReportWriter.

8. Type *Q_Master* as the name of the first Parent Query and press [Enter] twice.

9. Type *memberid* as the Child Columns and press [Enter].

10. Type *memberid* as the Parent 1 Columns and press [Enter]. *Memberid* is the column in the parent query that joins it to the current Q_Detail query.

Your Q_Detail query and parent-child relationships should be entered as shown on Figure 8.12.

11. Press [Ok] to save the changes and return to menu bar.

The Group Menu

To use this feature,

1. Select the Group Menu from the menu bar.

The Group Menu serves to define the report breaks and overall page layout of your report. A *group* is a SQL*ReportWriter term that refers to a distinct set of fields. With a group, you can single out a collection of fields (or isolate individual fields) and manipulate them as a single object on the report. All page-layout information, such as spacing around and between the text and data, can be applied equally to all fields of the group.

```
 Action   Query   Group   Field   Summary   Text   Report   Parameter   Help
                                  Query Settings
 ┌─────────────────────────────────────────────────────────────────────────┐
 │ Query Name: Q_Detail                                      Query  2 of 2   │
 │┌^┐───────────────────── SELECT Statement ──────────────────────────────┐ │
 │| | SELECT memberid, title.description, schdrtn,                        │ │
 │| |        round(sysdate-schdrtn) "Days Late",                          │ │
 │| |        round((sysdate-schdrtn) * ratepdy) "Charges"                 │ │
 │| |   FROM rentals, serialno, product, title                           │ │
 │| |  WHERE rentals.serialno = serialno.serialno                        │ │
 │| |    AND serialno.prodno  = product.prodno                           │ │
 │| |    AND product.titlecd  = title.titlecd                            │ │
 │|v|    AND actrtn is null                                               │ │
 │└─┘──────────────────────────────────────────────────────────────────── │
 │  ┌────────────────── Parent-Child Relationships ─────────────────────┐  │
 │  │ Parent Query 1: Q_Master            Parent Query 2:               │  │
 │  │ ┌──────────────────┬──────────────────┬──────────────────────────┐│  │
 │  │ │  Child Columns   │ Parent 1 Columns │    Parent 2 Columns       ││  │
 │  │^├──────────────────┼──────────────────┼──────────────────────────┤│  │
 │  ││ │ MEMBERID         │ MEMBERID         │                          ││  │
 │  │v└──────────────────┴──────────────────┴──────────────────────────┘│  │
 │  └────────────────────────────────────────────────────────────────────┘  │
 │ ▐ Enter a SQL SELECT statement defining data for this report. ▌          │
 │ Report Name: Master_detail                          <INSERT>             │
 └─────────────────────────────────────────────────────────────────────────┘
```

Figure 8.12   The Q_Detail Query

By default, all fields from a single query become a group. In our example, two groups have been automatically generated, "G_Master," referring to the "Q_Master" query, and "G_Detail," referring to the "Q_Detail" query. Certain default layout information has been applied to these groups.

2. Type in the following page layout information for both default groups by stepping through the spreadsheet-style form and filling in the blanks. (Only the information that you need to enter is listed below.)

Group	Query	Page Break	Relative Position	Lines Before	Spaces Before	Spacing Record	Label Position	Highlight Label
G_Master	Q_Master	Conditional				2	Left	Reverse
G_Detail	Q_Detail	Conditional	Below	2	3			

3. Create a third group, "G_Master1." This new group will place the three fields comprising the customer phone number (day_area, day_prefix, and day_suffix) below the customer name.

4. Position your cursor on the first record, "G_Master," and press [Insert Record Below].

5. Enter the following page layout information for G_Master1:

Group	Query	Page Break	Relative Position	Lines Before	Spaces Before	Spacing Record	Label Position	Highlight Label
G_Master1	Q_Master	Conditional	Below			1	Left	Reverse

The group information for this report should be entered as shown in Figures 8.13 through 8.15.

```
  Action    Query    Group    Field    Summary   Text    Report    Parameter   Help
 ───────────────────────────────── Group Settings ──────────────────────── 1 of 3

  ┌──────────────────────┬──────────────────┬───────────┬─────────┬─────────────┐
  │                      │                  │ Print     │ Matrix  │ Page        │
  │  Group Name          │ Query            │ Direction │ Group   │ Break       │
  ├──────────────────────┼──────────────────┼───────────┼─────────┼─────────────┤
^ │  G_Master            │ Q_Master         │ Down      │         │ Conditional │
  │  G_Master1           │ Q_Master         │ Down      │         │ Conditional │
  │  G_Detail            │ Q_Detail         │ Down      │         │ Conditional │
  │                      │                  │           │         │             │
  │                      │                  │           │         │             │
  │                      │                  │           │         │             │
  │                      │                  │           │         │             │
  │                      │                  │           │         │             │
U │                      │                  │           │         │             │
  └──────────────────────┴──────────────────┴───────────┴─────────┴─────────────┘

  Enter a name for this group.
  Report Name: Master_detail                              <OVERTYPE>        <LOV>
```

Figure 8.13   Group Information—First Panel

6. Press [Ok] to accept the changes and return to the top menu.

The Field Menu

The Field Menu is used to define field characteristics and positioning and to build computed fields for all fields of your report. Several default values are filled in by SQL*ReportWriter, such as the query source column name, group, label, data type, and field width. You may override these values at any time. To use this menu,

1. Select Field from the menu bar.

2. Enter the field information as follows for all fields of the Master-Detail report:

```
Action   Query   Group   Field   Summary   Text   Report   Parameter   Help
                          │ Group Settings │                          2 of 3
   ┌─────────────────────┬──────────┬──────┬───────┬─────────────┬────────┐
   │                     │ Relative │ Lines│ Spaces│   Spacing   │ Fields │
 ^ │ Group Name          │ Position │Before│ Before│Record  Field│ Across │
 │ ├─────────────────────┼──────────┼──────┼───────┼─────────────┼────────┤
 │ │ G_Master            │          │   2  │       │   2         │        │
 │ │ G_Master1           │ Below    │      │       │   1         │        │
 │ │ G_Detail            │ Below    │   2  │   3   │             │        │
 │ │                     │          │      │       │             │        │
 │ │                     │          │      │       │             │        │
 │ │                     │          │      │       │             │        │
 │ │                     │          │      │       │             │        │
 │ │                     │          │      │       │             │        │
 U │                     │          │      │       │             │        │
   └─────────────────────┴──────────┴──────┴───────┴─────────────┴────────┘
  ▐ Choose the position of this group in relation to the previous group. ▌
  Report Name: Master_detail                        <OVERTYPE>      <LOV>
```

Figure 8.14   Group Information—Second Panel

```
Action   Query   Group   Field   Summary   Text   Report   Parameter   Help
                          │ Group Settings │                          3 of 3
   ┌─────────────────────┬───────┬──────────┬─────────────────────────────┐
   │                     │ Multi-│ Label    │         Highlight           │
 ^ │ Group Name          │ Panel │ Position │ Field              Label    │
 │ ├─────────────────────┼───────┼──────────┼─────────────────────────────┤
 │ │ G_Master            │       │ Left     │            Reverse          │
 │ │ G_Master1           │       │ Left     │            Reverse          │
 │ │ G_Detail            │       │          │                             │
 │ │                     │       │          │                             │
 │ │                     │       │          │                             │
 │ │                     │       │          │                             │
 │ │                     │       │          │                             │
 │ │                     │       │          │                             │
 U │                     │       │          │                             │
   └─────────────────────┴───────┴──────────┴─────────────────────────────┘
  ▐ Keep all fields in a record on the same panel. ▌
  Report Name: Master_detail                        <OVERTYPE>
```

Figure 8.15   Group Information—Third Panel

Field Name	Source	Group	Label	Data Type	Width	Format	Align	Skip
MEMBERID	Q_Master.MEM..	G_Master	Memberid	NUM	10			X
NAME	NAME	G_Master	Name	CHAR	30		Left	
DAY_AREA	DAY_AREA	G_Master1	Phone	CHAR	3			
DAY_PREFIX	DAY_PREFIX	G_Master1		CHAR	3			
DAY_SUFFIX	DAY_SUFFIX	G_Master1		CHAR	3			
MEMBERID2	Q_Detail.MEM..	G_Detail	Memberid	CHAR	10			X
DESCRIPTION	DESCRIPTION	G_Detail	Title	CHAR	40			
SCHDRTN	SCHDRTN	G_Detail	Due	DATE	9			
Days_Late	Days Late	G_Detail	Days Late	NUM	10		Right	
Charges	Charges	G_Detail	Charges	NUM	10	$ZZ999.99	Right	

Notice that a few default values have been overridden and some field information added. Also note that the SKIP attribute for both occurrences of the *memberid* field has been marked. Since *memberid* is the join column determining the Master/Detail relationship for this report, you will suppress printing (or 'SKIP') this field.

The field information should be entered as shown in Figures 8.16 through 8.18.

Action	Query	Group	Field	Summary	Text	Report	Parameter	Help

—————————— Field Settings —————————— 1 of 3

Field Name	Source Column	Group	Label
MEMBERID	Q_Master.MEMBERI	G_Master	Memberid
NAME	NAME	G_Master	Customer
DAY_AREA	DAY_AREA	G_Master1	Phone
DAY_PREFIX	DAY_PREFIX	G_Master1	
DAY_SUFFIX	DAY_SUFFIX	G_Master1	
MEMBERID2	Q_Detail.MEMBERI	G_Detail	Memberid
DESCRIPTION	DESCRIPTION	G_Detail	Title
SCHDRTN	SCHDRTN	G_Detail	Due
Days_Late	Days Late	G_Detail	Days Late
Charges	Charges	G_Detail	Charges

Enter a name for this field.
Report Name: Master_detail   <INSERT>   <LOV>

Figure 8.16   Field Information—First Panel

3. Press [Ok] to save the changes and return to the menu bar.

4. Run the report built thus far by choosing the EXECUTE item on the Action Menu and pressing [Enter] through the Parameter value items.

```
Action   Query   Group   Field   Summary   Text   Report   Parameter   Help
                          Field Settings                                2 of 3
```

Field Name	Data Type	Field Width	Display Format	Relative Position	Lines Before	Spaces Before
MEMBERID	NUM	10				
NAME	CHAR	30				
DAY_AREA	CHAR	3				
DAY_PREFIX	CHAR	3				
DAY_SUFFIX	CHAR	4				
MEMBERID2	NUM	10				
DESCRIPTION	CHAR	40				
SCHDRTN	DATE	9				
Days_Late	NUM	10				
Charges	NUM	10	$ZZ999.99			

```
Enter the width of this field in spaces.
Report Name: Master_detail                              <INSERT>
```

Figure 8.17   Field Information—Second Panel

```
Action   Query   Group   Field   Summary   Text   Report   Parameter   Help
                          Field Settings                                3 of 3
```

Field Name	Align	Skip	Repeat	Computed Value Function	Reset Group
MEMBERID		X			
NAME	Left				
DAY_AREA					
DAY_PREFIX					
DAY_SUFFIX					
MEMBERID2		X			
DESCRIPTION					
SCHDRTN					
Days_Late	Right				
Charges	Right				

```
Choose the justification for this field.
Report Name: Master_detail                              <INSERT>        <LOU>
```

Figure 8.18   Field Information—Third Panel

You can browse the report interactively on screen by pressing [Window]. Browse mode is indicated by the blinking cursor on the lower right-hand corner of the screen. [Up], [Down], [Left] and [Right] arrow keys allow you to scroll in every direction.

The Summary Menu

The Summary screens let you define periodic and running summary totals for designated fields. You can create subtotals at any number of group levels or print grand totals and other high level summaries. You control the summary totals by specifying a reset value, termed a *reset group*. The reset group resets the totals cumulator back to zero after every record in the reset group has ben processed—which could be at the end of all records in a designated group of fields, or perhaps it could be at the end of the entire report.

Summary information can be printed anywhere on the report. You can manipulate the printing of summary information by controlling what is called the print group. The print group prints the current value for every record in the designated group; running subtotals, for example, can be placed after the appropriate field levels, and grand totals can be placed at the end of the report or at the beginning of the report—or both.

To navigate through this menu,

1. Select the Summary Menu from the menu bar.

2. Define the following summary information on the CHARGES field:

Summary Name	Field	Function	Data Type	Width	Format	Print Group	Reset Group
Subtotal_charges	Charges	SUM	NUM	9	$ZZ999.99	G_Detail	G_Detail
Running_charges	Charges	R_SUM	NUM	9	$ZZ999.99	G_Detail	Report
Report_to_charges	Charges	SUM	NUM	9	$ZZ999.99	Report	Report

The summary information should be entered as shown in Figures 8.19 and 8.20.

The Text Menu

The Text screen allows you to edit boilerplate text for page, report, and group objects. Use this screen to create headers and footers for each object, control the alignment of text, embed data within boilerplate text, and decide whether text should be repeated if the text overflows to another page.

```
 Action   Query   Group   Field   Summary   Text   Report   Parameter   Help
 ──────────────────────────── Summary Settings ──────────────────── 1 of 2

  ┌─┬───────────────────┬─────────────────┬─────────────┬──────┬───────┬──────────┐
  │ │                   │                 │             │ Data │       │ Display  │
  │ │  Summary Name     │  Field          │  Function   │ Type │ Width │ Format   │
  │^│                   │                 │             │      │       │          │
  │ │  Subtotal_charges │  Charges        │  Sum        │ NUM  │  10   │ $ZZ999.9 │
  │ │  Running_charges  │  Charges        │  R_Sum      │ NUM  │  10   │ $ZZ999.9 │
  │ │  Report_tot_charg │  Charges        │  Sum        │ NUM  │  10   │ $ZZ999.9 │
  │ │                   │                 │             │      │       │          │
  │ │                   │                 │             │      │       │          │
  │ │                   │                 │             │      │       │          │
  │ │                   │                 │             │      │       │          │
  │ │                   │                 │             │      │       │          │
  │ │                   │                 │             │      │       │          │
  │U│                   │                 │             │      │       │          │
  └─┴───────────────────┴─────────────────┴─────────────┴──────┴───────┴──────────┘
 ▐Enter a name for this summary field.                                        ▌
  Report Name: Master_detail                          <INSERT>        <LOV>
```

Figure 8.19   Summary Information—First Panel

```
 Action   Query   Group   Field   Summary   Text   Report   Parameter   Help
 ──────────────────────────── Summary Settings ──────────────────── 2 of 2

  ┌─┬───────────────────┬─────────────────┬──────────────────────────────────┐
  │ │                   │                 │                                  │
  │ │  Summary Name     │  Print Group    │  Reset Group                     │
  │^│                   │                 │                                  │
  │ │  Subtotal_charges │  G_Master1      │  G_Master1                       │
  │ │  Running_charges  │  G_Master1      │  REPORT                          │
  │ │  Report_tot_charg │  REPORT         │  REPORT                          │
  │ │                   │                 │                                  │
  │ │                   │                 │                                  │
  │ │                   │                 │                                  │
  │ │                   │                 │                                  │
  │ │                   │                 │                                  │
  │ │                   │                 │                                  │
  │U│                   │                 │                                  │
  └─┴───────────────────┴─────────────────┴──────────────────────────────────┘
 ▐Enter the name of the group where this summary is displayed.                ▌
  Report Name: Master_detail                          <INSERT>        <LOV>
```

Figure 8.20   Summary Information—Second Panel

You can also use this screen to customize the appearance of the detail lines or body text of any group. To use this feature,

1. Select the Text menu from the menu bar.

2. Browse the page, report, and group objects. All objects are stored in the database and are queryable. To browse the objects on screen, press [Select] to enter the query information, then press [Find] to fetch the queried objects. Using [Arrow Down] scrolls the fetched objects sequentially.

3. Fetch the Page object and enter the following header information:

   Type *1* for the Lines Before field.

   Type *Center* for the Justification field.

   Type *Video Quest Late Charges Report* as the boilerplate text.

4. Press [Next Record] to accept the changes of the header object and move to the Page Footer object.

5. Type the following page footer information:

   Type *2* for the Lines Before field.

   Type *Center* for the Justification field.

   Type *SQL*ReportWriter Master/Detail Example* as the boilerplate text.

   The boilerplate text for the Page Header and Page Footer objects should be entered as shown in Figures 8.21 and 8.22.

6. Edit the boilerplate text of the remaining *Master_Detail* objects as follows:

```
Object:    Type:             Text:
G_Master   Body              Customer:   &NAME

           Footer            Total Late Charges           &Report_tot_charges

G_Detail   Column Heading                       Scheduled           Late
                             Title               Return    Days Late Charges
                             --------------------- --------- --------- -------
           Body              <Accept Defaults>
           Footer            Charges for current member     &Subtotal_charges
                             Running total                  &Running_charges

G_Master1  Body              Phone:   (&DAY_AREA) &DAY_PREFIX-&DAY_SUFFIX
```

```
Action    Query    Group    Field    Summary    Text    Report    Parameter    Help
                                   Text Settings

  ┌────────────────────────────────────────────────────────────────────────────┐
  │ Object:  PAGE                    Type:  Header          Status:  Edited     │
  ├────────────────────────────────────┬───────────────────────────────────────┤
  │ Relative Position:                 │ Repeat On Page Overflow:               │
  │     Lines Before:  1               │            Justification:  Center      │
  │     Spaces Before:                 │               Frequency:               │
  └────────────────────────────────────┴───────────────────────────────────────┘

                                   ──── Text ────
  ┌────────────────────────────────────────────────────────────────────────────┐
  │ Panel Number:  1                                      Panels Defined: 1     │
  ├──┬─────────────────────────────────────────────────────────────────────────┤
  │^ │ Video Quest Late Charges Report                                          │
  │  │                                                                          │
  │  │                                                                          │
  │  │                                                                          │
  │  │                                                                          │
  │v │                                                                          │
  └──┴─────────────────────────────────────────────────────────────────────────┘
  Choose the position of this text in relation to the previous text.
  Report Name: Master_detail                          <INSERT>            <LOV>
```

Figure 8.21   Page Header Text

```
Action    Query    Group    Field    Summary    Text    Report    Parameter    Help
                                   Text Settings

  ┌────────────────────────────────────────────────────────────────────────────┐
  │ Object:  PAGE                    Type:  Footer          Status:  Edited     │
  ├────────────────────────────────────┬───────────────────────────────────────┤
  │ Relative Position:                 │ Repeat On Page Overflow:               │
  │     Lines Before:  2               │            Justification:  Center      │
  │     Spaces Before:                 │               Frequency:               │
  └────────────────────────────────────┴───────────────────────────────────────┘

                                   ──── Text ────
  ┌────────────────────────────────────────────────────────────────────────────┐
  │ Panel Number:  1                                      Panels Defined: 1     │
  ├──┬─────────────────────────────────────────────────────────────────────────┤
  │^ │ SQL*ReportWriter Master/Detail Example                                   │
  │  │                                                                          │
  │  │                                                                          │
  │  │                                                                          │
  │  │                                                                          │
  │v │                                                                          │
  └──┴─────────────────────────────────────────────────────────────────────────┘
  Choose the position of this text in relation to the previous text.
  Report Name: Master_detail                          <INSERT>            <LOV>
```

Figure 8.22   Page Footer Text

Summary

Automated businesses require various reports to perform everyday business functions and monitor business trends. This chapter taught you how to use SQL*Plus, ORACLE's report-formatting SQL language extensions, to design interesting tabular reports. The chapter also provided a sneak preview of SQL*ReportWriter, Oracle's newest report tool, which picks up where SQL*Plus leaves off in formatting control and power.

With SQL*Plus, you built the following reports:

► The Product Inventory Report

► The Tapes Overdue Report

► The Rentals Reports—Detail and Summary information

► The Yearly Rental History Report

With SQL*ReportWriter, you constructed a typical multi-section report derived from two related queries—a Master-Detail report.

Creating Integrated Menus

9

Creating Integrated Menus

Chapter 9 examines the process of creating integrated application menus. Although you can design a simple front-end menu with SQL*Forms, a more robust menuing tool is necessary for larger multi-user applications. This chapter demonstrates how to build a simple menu with SQL*Forms and an integrated menuing environment with ORACLE's non-procedural tool, SQL*Menu. SQL*Menu lets you build *dynamic* menus that change according to the privileges of the user accessing the system.

The Menuing Environment

An effective menuing system unifies all screens of the application—the master data entry screens, the maintenance and transactions screens, and those controlling report generation—as though they live under the same roof. User navigation and access to the application screens and reports is carefully controlled via the menuing interface.

With SQL*Forms, you can design a simple front-end menu suitable for smaller applications or prototypes. The SQL*Forms technique is quick but inflexible. It is handy in the early development cycles, however, when you are prototyping a few scattered forms and need to access them quickly to hasten interactive debugging. Larger applications require a more robust menuing tool. Although perfectly suitable for small, single-user applications, SQL*Menu has the flexibility and horsepower to integrate much larger applications supporting dozens of users accessing many screens.

SQL*Menu is based on the SQL*Forms technology and is nonprocedural. Using SQL*Menu, you can build a menu that lets a user point to and select the menu choices—using the [Up] or [Down Arrow] keys to highlight choices—or simply enter the number of the menu choice. The menuing environment can be customized for different groups, or *work classes*, of users, and several menu commands and macros are available to control menu navigation. SQL*Menu can be linked with the SQL*Plus and SQL*Forms tools for fast execution of forms and reports.

Designing a Simple Menu with SQL*Forms

The SQL*Forms technique for designing a quick and dirty menu employs the macro CASE statement. A separate form is used as a front-end menu, and the CASE statement tests menu choices entered by the operator on the screen. When a valid menu choice is entered, the CASE statement calls the appropriate form. Figure 9.1 illustrates a simple menu integrating the screens of the Video Quest application.

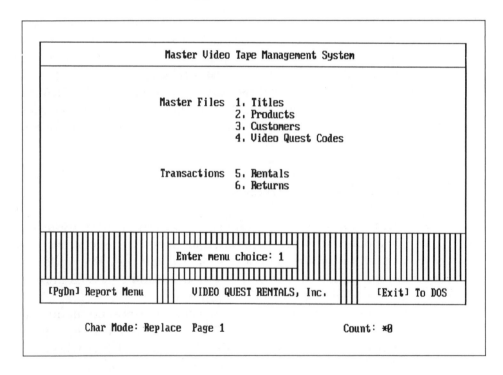

Figure 9.1   Video Quest Menu with SQL*Forms

VDOMENU is the simplest kind of form, a single-block, single-field form. As shown in Figure 9.1, there is only one enterable field, MENU_CHOICE. MENU_CHOICE is a CHAR field type, only 2 characters long. Its *raison d'être* is to accept input of the menu selection and to execute the macro CASE statement.

The macro CASE statement is defined as a Post-Change trigger on the MENU_CHOICE field. In this two-step trigger, the first step is as follows:

```
Seq #1        Label: Chk-choice

#EXEMACRO CASE menu_choice is
WHEN '1'    THEN CALL title
WHEN '2'    THEN CALL product
WHEN '3'    THEN CALL customer
WHEN '4'    THEN CALL tape
WHEN '5'    THEN CALL rental_class
WHEN '6'    THEN CALL category
WHEN '7'    THEN CALL payment
WHEN '8'    THEN CALL rentals
WHEN '9'    THEN CALL returns

Invalid menu choice. Please reenter . . .
```

The field variable after the WHEN clause refers to the menu choice that appears on the form screen. The second trigger step clears the field in preparation for the next time an operator attempts to access a form from this menu.

```
Seq #2        Label: Clear-field

SELECT null
  INTO menu_choice
  FROM dual

Program error: Problem clearing menu_choice field. See
your supervisor.
```

Building Dynamic Menus with SQL*Menu

SQL*Menu lets you define a complete menuing environment that changes dynamically for each user. Users are assigned work classes and are identified to SQL*Menu by log-on ID and password. The application designer predefines access privileges to the various work classes. At log-on, SQL*Menu displays only those menus and options available to the user by virtue of his or her work class.

With SQL*Menu Version 4.1, you are limited to a hierarchical menu interface, but there are no restrictions on the number of menu levels, or *submenus*, you can define. (Version 5.0 will support several other menu types, including a Macintosh-like pull-down bar menu and Lotus-style ring menus.)

Planning the Menus

It pays to build a model of the various menus, submenus, and options required to knit the screens and reports of your application together. Video Quest's menu structure is rather simplistic, so you could conceivably design and model the system interactively within SQL*Menu when building menus for similar applications. Larger applications are normally too complex to do this effectively; the menu structure is often multi-dimensional and demands more of a designer's time up front to design an appropriate menu navigation strategy.

Video Quest's application screens are organized by functionality—Master Tables, Transactions, Code Maintenance, and Reports. A schema diagram of the Video Quest menu environment appears in Figure 9.2.

MENU 1

MAIN MENU
1. Master Tables Menu
2. Transactions Menu
3. Code Maintenance Menu
4. Business Reports Menu
Video Quest Rentals, Inc.

Submenu 1	Submenu 2	Submenu 3	Submenu 4
Video Quest Master Tables Menu	Video Quest Transactions Menu	Video Quest Code Maintenance Menu	Video Quest Business Reports Menu
1. Titles 2. Products 3. Customers	1. Rentals Transactions 2. Rentals Transactions	1. Film Category Codes 2. Rental Class Codes 3. Payment Codes 4. Catalog Numbers	1. Tapes Overdue Report 2. Daily Rentals Report 3. Year-to-Date Rental History Report 4. Product Inventory Report
Video Quest Rentals, Inc.	Video Quest Rentals, Inc.	Video Quest Rentals, Inc.	Video Quest Rentals, Inc.

Figure 9.2   Fundamental Video Quest Menu Model

The model in Figure 9.2 plots the menu options derived from the forms and reports of the Video Quest application. Basic hierarchical navigation between the Main Menu and the second tier in the hierarchy is also represented.

At this point, you should analyze your model, thinking of ways to refine it. Consider any menu options that might facilitate operator movement between screens. One example might be allowing lateral movement between frequently used submenus. Figure 9.3 illustrates a few refinements to the basic model.

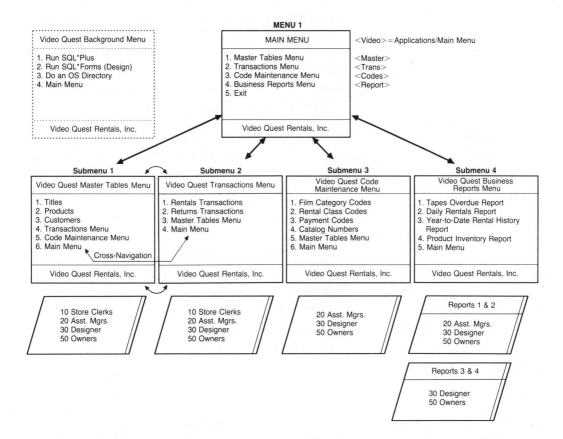

Figure 9.3 Refined Video Quest Menu Model

Setting Up Work Classes for Users

Video Quest personnel is divided into four primary classes of users—store clerks, assistant managers, store owners, and you, the application designer. (Even you are barred from the application unless you allow yourself certain privileges.) These user groups are work classes to SQL*Menu, a distinction which bears on access privileges rather than social status. SQL*Menu manages work classes by codes which you define. Video Quest's codes are as follows:

Work Class   Description
10   Store Clerks
20   Assistant Managers
30   Application Designer
50   Store Owner(s)

The owners of Video Quest are sensitive to protecting key information, such as rental classes or film categories, from deliberate or accidental tampering. The owners also see no business justification for store clerks to generate reports, even though the information may not contain trade secrets. In fact, the store owners are reluctant to let assistant managers access the Year-to-Date Rentals and the Product Inventory Reports. You will restrict access to these menu options accordingly; a store clerk shall never see the Code Maintenance or Reports menus when logging on to the system, and assistant managers will have access to only two of the four business reports. (See Table 9.1.)

Table 9.1   User Profiles by Work Class for All Video Quest Personnel

Work Class	Description	Users	ORACLE User ID	Menu Privileges
10	Store Clerks	Bo Diddly	BDIDDLY	Master Tables Menu
		Buster Keaton	BKEATON	Transactions Menu
		Charles Chaplin	CCHAPLIN	
20	Assistant Mgr.	Sam Huston	SHUSTON	Master Tables Menu
		George Lucas	GLUCAS	Transactions Menu
				Code Maintenance Menu
				Reports Menu
				− #1 Tapes Overdue
				− #2 Daily Rentals
30	Designer	You . . .	OPS$VIDEO	All Menus & Options
50	Store Owner(s)	Rex Reed	REXREED	All Menus & Options
		Gene Siskel	GSISKEL	

Constructing the Menu Application

A menu system is considered an *application* to SQL*Menu. When you construct a menu application, you are actually working in the SQL*Forms environment using the SQL*Forms (Runform) function keys. You enter menu information through the SQL*Menu Dynamic Menu Utility (DMU), which is in fact an elaborate form. One of the advantages of using a fourth-generation development tool is that interface issues are standardized. The interface of the Dynamic Menu Utility represents the look and feel of the menus you eventually create with this tool.

The Video Quest menu is constructed in the same manner as other SQL*Menu applications. There are four basic steps to the procedure:

1. Specify the application.

2. Enter user information, including work classes and special privileges.

3. Define the menus and submenus individually, filling out a three-screen form for each menu:

> Enter menu name and title.
>
> Specify menu options.
>
> Provide help messages.

4. Generate the menus.

We will explain each of these steps, walking through the screens and identifying the information you enter to create the Video Quest Menu. Start by logging on to SQL*Menu and accessing the design branch of the SQL*Menu Application. By following the design trail (refer to the *SQL*Menu User's Guide* for details), you should wind up on the Menu Information Maintenance menu shown in Figure 9.4.

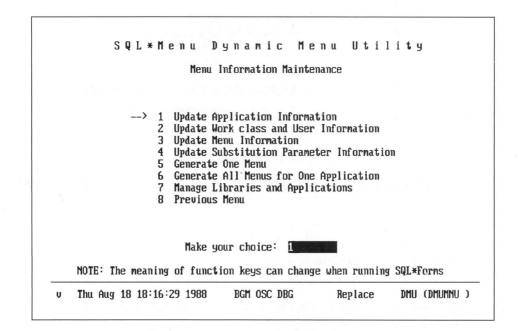

Figure 9.4   Menu Information Maintenance Menu

This is the SQL*Menu design branch. To create the Video Quest menu, you will use four of the selections from this menu:

1. Update application information

2. Update work class and user information

3. Update menu information

6. Generate all menus for one application

Specifying the Application

You begin by specifying the menu application to SQL*Menu. Select *Option 1: Update Application Information*, which displays the form shown in Figure 9.5.

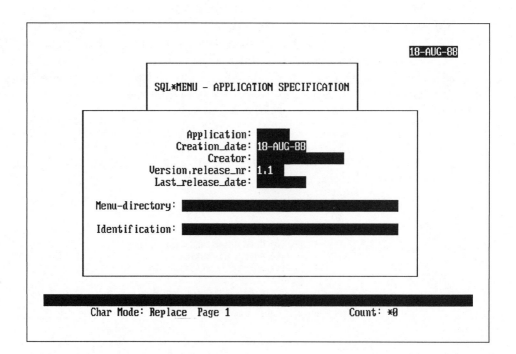

Figure 9.5   Application Specification Form

To specify the Video Quest application, fill in the fields with this information:

```
        Application:  VIDEO
      Creation_date:  [default]
            Creator:  [default]
 Version.release_nr:  [default]
  Last_release_date:  [Leave this blank]

Menu_directory: Your_current_disk_directory

Identification:  Video Quest Rentals Menu Application
```

Entering User Information

You now set up work classes for Video Quest personnel and enter user profile information. Select menu *Option 2: Update Work Class and User Information*. The form shown in Figure 9.6 should appear on the screen.

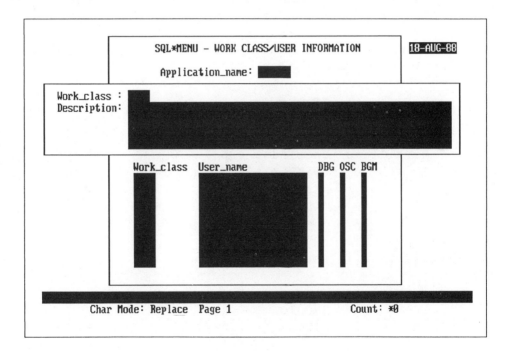

Figure 9.6   Update Work Class and User Information Form

In Table 9.1, you identified the Video Quest personnel and navigation rights by work class. Here you define the work classes and identify users to SQL*Menu by ORACLE user ID. You also define the following access privileges for each user:

1. DEBUG MODE (DBM). This privilege determines whether or not the user can run SQL*Menu in DEBUG MODE, a utility that isolates menu application problems by displaying the command line behind a menu option when it is chosen.

2. OPERATING SYSTEM COMMANDS (OSC). This privilege determines whether or not the user can run operating system commands within a SQL*Menu application.

3. BACKGROUND MENU (BGM). This determines whether or not the user can access the BACKGROUND Menu, a hidden menu that allows privileged users to run various ORACLE tools and reports, frequently used commands, and even non-ORACLE applications or programs from within the SQL*Menu application. The ability to run SQL*Forms (Design) or SQL*Plus within the SQL*Menu environment, for example, can save a designer valuable time while debugging forms and reports.

Enter the work class and user information for the Video Quest application as shown below:

```
Work_Class  :   10
Description :   Store Clerks

    Work_Class    User_name DBG       OSC       BGM
    10            BDIDDLY      N         N         N
    10            BKEATON      N         N         N
    10            CCHAPLIN     N         N         N

Work_Class  :   20
Description :   Assistant Managers

    Work_Class    User_name DBG       OSC       BGM
    20            SHUSTON      N         Y         N
    20            GLUCAS       N         Y         N

Work_Class  :   30
Description :   Application Designer

    Work_Class    User_name DBG       OSC       BGM
    30            OPS$VIDEO    Y         Y         Y
```

```
Work_Class  :   50
Description :   Store Owner(s)

    Work_Class   User_name DBG      OSC      BGM
    50           REXREED   Y        Y        Y
    50           GSISKEL   Y        Y        Y
```

Updating Menu Information

Menu *Option 3: Update Menu Information* invokes the first screen of the General Menu Information form. You use this three-screen form to define the Main Menu and submenus, the menu options, and help messages for your menu application. The General Menu Information form is the core of SQL*Menu's design branch. Figure 9.7 illustrates the first screen used to enter the name and titles of a menu or submenu:

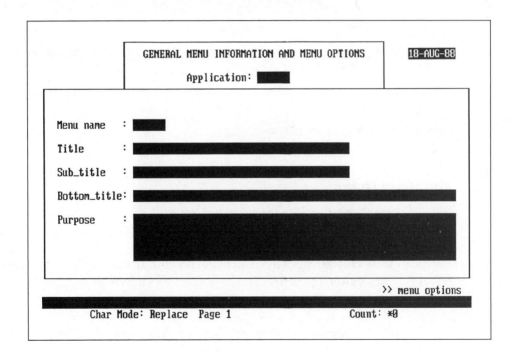

Figure 9.7   Menu Name and Titles

SQL*Menu requires that you give the Main Menu—the first menu you define—the same name as the application. The Main Menu for your Video Quest application is therefore named VIDEO after the application name.

Define the Main Menu by entering the name, titles and description as shown in Figure 9.8.

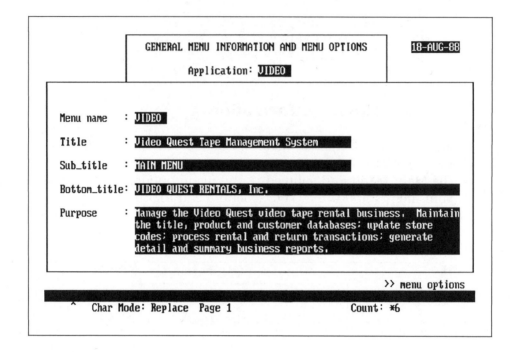

Figure 9.8   VIDEO Main Menu

The Menu Options

By selecting [Next Block], you invoke a second screen to define the menu options for the current menu. Figure 9.9 shows the first four menu options defined for the VIDEO Main Menu (there are five options on this menu, but only four can be displayed on the screen at one time). Step through the fields of *Option 1: Master Tables Menu*, as shown in Figure 9.9, and as explained below.

Option Number: 1:	The option number appearing on the menu.
Lower work class: 10:	The number of the lowest work class that can access this menu option. This field and the next define the *inclusive range* of work classes that are able to use the option.
Higher work class: 50:	The number of the highest work class that can use this option.

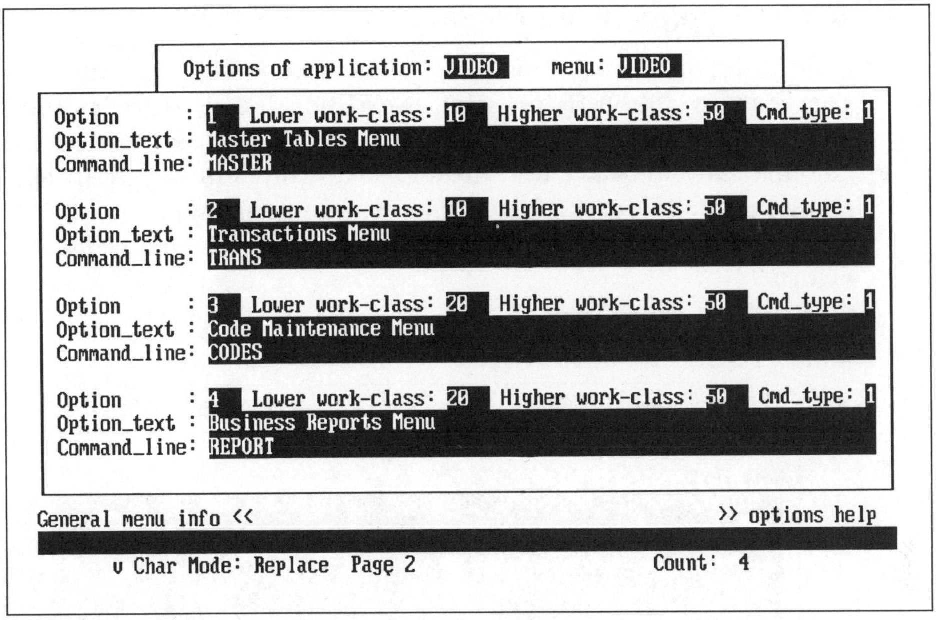

Figure 9.9   VIDEO Menu Options

Cmd_type: 1:   The action to be carried out by this option. This menu option invokes a submenu, so you specify command type 1. (See Table 9.2 below for a list of the six menu command types.)

Option_text: Master Tables Menu: The text appearing on the menu.

Command_line: MASTER: The command to initiate the action carried out by this option. This option invokes a submenu named MASTER.

Table 9.2   Menu Command Types

Command	Action
1	Invokes a submenu
2	Executes an operating system command
3	Executes an operating system command followed by a pause
4	Invokes SQL*Forms (Run Form) (Use this option if SQL*Forms is linked with SQL*Menu for fast execution of a form; otherwise use Command Type 2 or 3.)
5	Invokes SQL*Plus (Use this option if SQL*Plus is linked with SQL*Menu; otherwise use Command Type 2 or 3.)
6	Invokes a SQL*Menu macro command

Adding Help for Menu Options

After filling out information for any one option, you can enter a help message for that option by pressing [Next Block]. This displays the help text entry screen associated with the option. Sequence numbers are generated automatically for each line of help text; numbers skip 1 in sequence to allow lines to be inserted later and remain in sequence.

Enter the help message for *Option 1: Master Tables Menu* as shown in Figure 9.10:

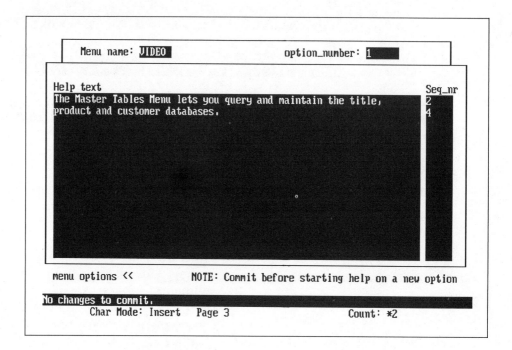

Figure 9.10   Help Message for Option 1: Master Tables Menu

Creating the Menus for the VIDEO Application

You have moved swiftly through the basic steps of creating the VIDEO Main Menu. This menu is not complete, however. Use the Video Menu Application system documentation in Tables 9.3 through 9.8 to verify that all menu options are specified and that a help message (if you choose to include one) is added to each option. Afterward, create the four submenus, MASTER, TRANS(actions), CODES, and BUSINESS REPORTS; then complete the Video Menu Application by creating the BACKGROUND Menu. Figures 9.11 through 9.16 show these completed menus.

Table 9.3   VIDEO Main Menu Documentation

Names and Titles

Title   : Video Quest Tape Management System
Subtitle   : MAIN MENU
Bottom title : VIDEO QUEST RENTALS, Inc.
Purpose   : Manage the Video Quest tape rental business. Maintain the title, product, and customer databases; update store codes; process rental and return transactions; generate detail and summary business reports.

Options

Option	Work Class Range	Command Type	Option Text	Command Line
1	10–50	1	Master Tables Menu	MASTER (submenu)
2	10–50	1	Transactions Menu	TRANS (submenu)
3	10–50	1	Code Maintenance Menu	CODES (submenu)
4	20–50	1	Business Reports Menu	REPORT (submenu)
5	10–50	6	Exit	exit; (macro)

Help Messages

Option	Text
1	The Master Tables Menu lets you query and maintain the title, product, and customer tables.
2	The Transactions Menu option lets you process rental and return transactions, automatically query rentals outstanding by member, update customer information, and print an invoice of a completed transaction.
3	The Code Maintenance Menu option lets management update store code information—film category codes, rental class codes, payment methods, and tape catalog numbers.
4	The Business Reports Menu option lets management generate detail and/or summary reports about overdue tapes, daily and year-to-date rental information, and current product inventory positions.
5	The Exit option boots you out to the operating system.

Generating Menus

Having defined the menus in your Video Quest application, you must now generate them. To do this, choose *Option 6: Generate All Menus for One Application* from the Menu Information Maintenance Menu. Enter VIDEO for the application name, and accept the default library module size of 128 (this allocates a library file large enough to store roughly 50 menus).

Table 9.4   MASTER Submenu Documentation

Names and Titles

Title   : Video Quest Master Tables Menu
Subtitle   : -
Bottom title : VIDEO QUEST RENTALS, Inc.
Purpose   : Query and maintain Master database tables, including film titles, products, and customers.

Options

Option	Work Class Range	Command Type	Option Text	Command Line
1	10–50	4	Titles	*RUNFORM title &UN/&PW*
2	10–50	4	Products	*RUNFORM product &UN/&PW*
3	10–50	4	Customers	*RUNFORM customer &UN/ &PW*
4	10–50	1	Transactions Menu	*TRANS*
5	10–50	1	Code Maintenance Menu	*CODES*
6	10–50	6	Main Menu	*mainmenu;* (macro)

Help Messages

Option Text

1   The Titles option lets you query and maintain the TITLES table.
2   The Products option lets you query and maintain the PRODUCTS table.
3   The Customers option lets you query and maintain the CUSTOMER and CUSTNAME tables.
4   The Transactions Menu option lets you process rental and return transactions; automatically query rentals outstanding by member, update customer information, and print an invoice of a completed transaction.
5   The Code Maintenance Menu option lets management update store code information—film category codes, rental class codes, payment methods, and tape catalog numbers.
6   The Main Menu option returns you to the Main Menu.

SQL*Menu maintains a separate library file for each menu application. When you generate a new application, SQL*Menu creates the library file for you, although you can create a library file separately. Your Video Quest application will be generated to the file named VIDEOMNU.DMM.

To use a newly generated application, you must exit from SQL*Menu, then reenter. Regenerated menus are available immediately. If you have made changes to only one or two menus in your application, you can cut corners by generating them individually. Choose *Option 5: Generate One Menu* to do this.

Table 9.5   TRANS(actions) Submenu Documentation

Names and Titles

Title   : Video Quest Transactions Menu
Subtitle   : -
Bottom title   : VIDEO QUEST RENTALS, Inc.
Purpose   : Process tape rental and return transactions.

Options

Option	Work Class Range	Command Type	Option Text	Command Line
1	10–50	4	Rentals Transactions	*RUNFORM rentals &UN/ &PW*
2	10–50	4	Returns Transactions	*RUNFORM returns &UN/ &PW*
3	10–50	1	Master Tables Menu	*MASTER*
4	10–50	6	Main Menu	*mainmenu;* (macro)

Table 9.6   CODES Submenu Documentation

Names and Titles

Title   : Video Quest Code Maintenance Menu
Subtitle   : -
Bottom title   : VIDEO QUEST RENTALS, Inc.
Purpose   : Query and maintain store codes—film categories, rental classes, payment methods, and catalog numbers.

Options

Option	Work Class Range	Command Type	Option Text	Command Line
1	20–50	4	Film Category Codes	*RUNFORM category &UN/&PW*
2	20–50	4	Rental Class Codes	*RUNFORM rental_class &UN/&PW*
3	20–50	4	Payment Codes	*RUNFORM payment &UN/&PW*
4	20–50	4	Catalog Numbers	*RUNFORM catalog &UN/ &PW*
5	20–50	1	Master Tables Menu	*MASTER*
6	20–50	6	Main Menu	*mainmenu;*

Table 9.7   BUSINESS REPORTs Submenu Documentation

Names and Titles

Title   : Video Quest Business Reports Menu
Subtitle   : ‾ ˜ ‾ ˜ ‾ ˜ ‾ ˜ ‾ ˜
Bottom title : VIDEO QUEST RENTALS, Inc.
Purpose   : Generate business reports—Tapes Overdue Report, Daily and Year-to-Date
               Rental Reports, and current Product Inventory status.

Options

Option	Work Class Range	Command Type	Option Text	Command Line
1	20–50	5	Tapes Overdue Report	*SQLPLUS &UN/&PW overdue*
2	20–50	5	Daily Rentals Report—Details/Summary	*SQLPLUS &UN/&PW dayrent*
3	30–50	5	Year-to-Date Rental History Report	*SQLPLUS &UN/&PW ytdrent*
4	30–50	5	Product Inventory Report	*SQLPLUS &UN/&PW inventor*
5	20–50	6	Main Menu	*mainmenu;*

Table 9.8   BACKGROUND Menu Documentation

Names and Titles

Title   : Video Quest Background Menu
Subtitle   : ‾ ˜ ˜ ‾ ˜ ‾ ˜ ‾ ˜
Bottom title : VIDEO QUEST RENTALS, Inc.
Purpose   : Make various tools available to authorized users. Background Menu is in-
               voked by entering 'BGM' in the selection box on *any menu* within the
               Video Quest Menu Application.

Options

Option	Work Class Range	Command Type	Option Text	Command Line
1	30–50	5	Run SQL*Plus	*SQLPLUS &UN/&PW*
2	30–50	2	Run SQL*Forms (Design)	*SQLFORMS &UN/&PW*
3	30–50	3	Do an OS Directory	*dir*
4	30–50	6	Main Menu	*mainmenu;*

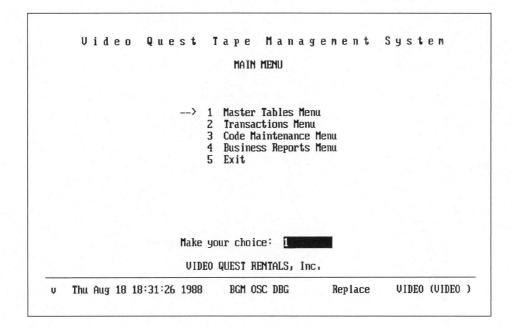

Figure 9.11   The Completed VIDEO Main Menu

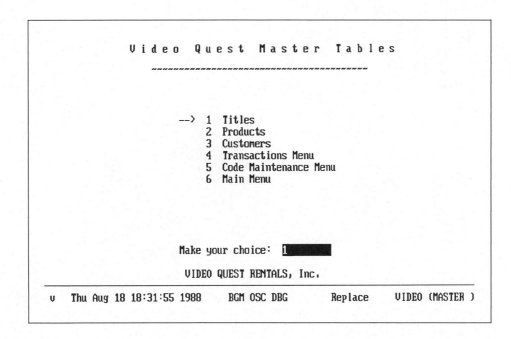

Figure 9.12   The Completed MASTER Submenu

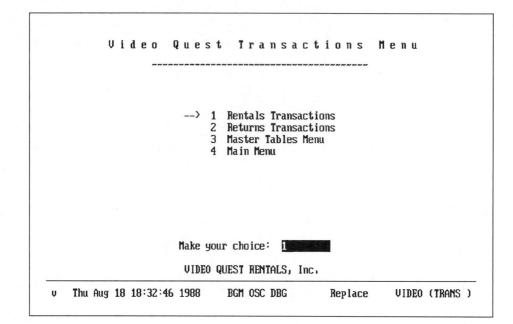

Figure 9.13   The Completed TRANS(actions) Submenu

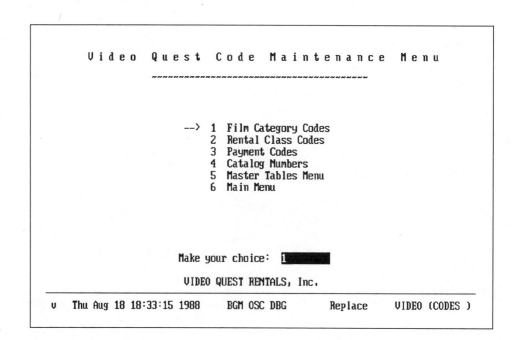

Figure 9.14   The Completed CODES Submenu

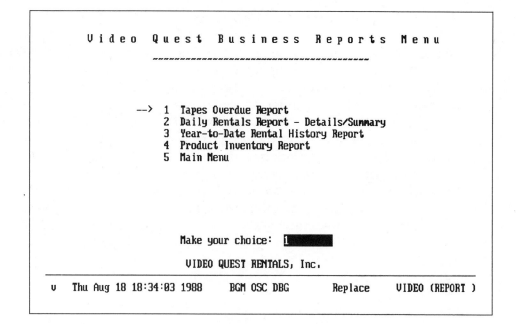

Figure 9.15   The Completed BUSINESS REPORTS Submenu

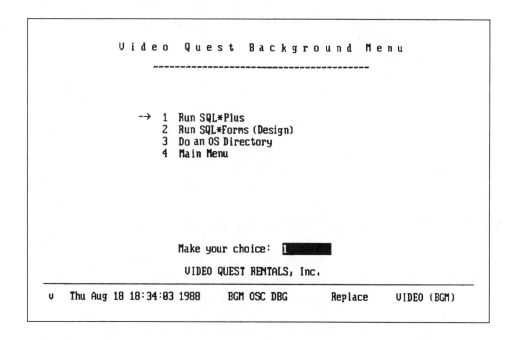

Figure 9.16   The Completed BACKGROUND Menu

Testing Your Menu Application

You, as the application designer (work class 30), have naturally granted yourself access to every component of the application. When you run the menu, every screen and menu option should be available to you. To put SQL*Menu's ability to respond to a dynamic environment to the test, you should impersonate a store clerk (either BDIDDLY, BKEATON, or CCHAPLIN of work class 10) and start the Video Quest menu application. Only the menus to which a store clerk has access should be visible to you.

The store clerk you decide to impersonate must be known to the database, or log-on to SQL*Menu will be denied. Log on to SQL*Plus as SYSTEM/MANAGER (or any other ORACLE user with DBA authority) and grant database access to the store clerk you choose. For example, you might enter

```
GRANT CONNECT
    TO BKEATON
IDENTIFIED BY COMEDY

    Grant succeeded.
```

You may now exit SQL*Plus and start up your SQL*Menu application as BKEATON. You can invoke the application from the SQL*Menu Dynamic Menu Utility, or you can start it directly from the operating system by issuing the following command:

```
SQLMENU video BKEATON COMEDY
```

If you are continually making changes to the application and running it for testing purposes, you are better off starting the application from within the SQL*Menu Dynamic Menu Utility.

Documenting the Menu Application

SQL*Menu provides system documentation facilities, saving you the trouble of having to produce the documentation manually for system maintenance. SQL*Menu produces two types of documentation:

▶ Application Information. This is a detailed report of all menus, menu options, work class definitions, users, help information, and substitution parameters.

▶ Summary Information. This lists only menus, menu options, work class definitions, and users.

Generating the Video Quest menu documentation couldn't be easier—simply choose the appropriate option from the Menu Documentation screen and SQL*Menu saves the generated documentation to a file named VIDEOAPL.DOC for the detailed version and VIDEOSUM.DOC for the summary version.

Summary

A dynamic menu environment unifies the screens and reports of your application, providing secure access and a uniform look and feel. This chapter taught you how to build a dynamic menuing environment with SQL*Menu. It covered

▶ Building a model of the menuing environment

▶ Setting up work classes for users

▶ Steps for constructing the menus

▶ Generating and testing your menus

▶ Documenting the menus

10

Advanced Concepts and Features

10

Advanced Concepts and Features

<hr />

Chapter 10 introduces advanced ORACLE concepts and features, ranging from application performance tuning tips to advanced techniques for controlling disk space, ensuring data integrity and data security, and documenting your completed application.

Application Performance Tuning

Up to now you have immersed yourself in the design and implementation phases of the application development life cycle. The endeavor has produced a fully integrated application that satisfies the fundamental functionality and reporting requirements of Video Quest. You are prepared now to move on to the final development phase—application performance tuning.

Tuning relational database applications is a complex discipline. Several performance factors are involved, such as the number of database users and the types of applications being run, the speed and capacity of the computer being used, general operating system considerations, database locking and concurrency issues, the effectiveness of the database design, the question of whether queries are written efficiently (or *optimized*), and of course, the performance capabilities of the underlying database management system. An entire book could be devoted to the subject of performance tuning relational database applications.

Within the confines of this book, the most we can do is highlight some of the performance tuning tools available to you and touch on various design alternatives to improve query retrieval speed and database performance.

Using Indexes

When you issue a simple SQL SELECT statement such as

```
SELECT title, actors, awards
  FROM title
 WHERE titlecd = 'TOPGUN'
```

ORACLE looks through every row in the database table sequentially to find the answer. In other words, ORACLE performs a *full table scan*. ORACLE reads the first row in the table, decides if the title code is TOPGUN, displays the row if it is, and moves on if not. ORACLE repeats this action until every row in the table has been read.

Another method ORACLE might use to speed up access to this data is via an *index*. Just as an index in a book helps you locate information quickly, an ORACLE index locates your data much faster than otherwise possible. A book index lets you find the exact page number of a word or topic without having to hunt through pages randomly. An ORACLE index works similarly, pointing to your data by storage location rather than by scanning every row in the table. An ORACLE index contains a key column value and the physical address, called the *ROWID*, of the record with that key value.

If you had created an index on the title code column in the above query, the index entries might look like this:

```
TITLECD            ROWID
-----------        ------------------
CKANE              00004C88.0003.0001
GHOSTBUSTERS       00004C88.0001.0001
GONEWIND           00004C88.0002.0001
HITCHER            00004C90.0002.0001
SHINING            00004C90.0003.0001
SOUNDMUSIC         00004C88.0004.0001
TOPGUN             00004C90.0001.0001
```

The ROWID is a hexadecimal representation of the record address. It contains three parts:

- ► the logical block number of the record
- ► the row sequence number of the value (a relative sequence number is generated for every row inserted into a table)
- ► the logical partition id.

Since our query is searching for every row with TOPGUN in the *titlecd* column, we know that based on the index entries, ORACLE will only return one row—the one with Row Sequence Number 1 of logical block address 4C90 of the first database partition. As shown, the index is sorted on the key value; if more than one row exists with the same key value, these rows are sorted on ROWID.

Enforcing Uniqueness

Another reason for creating an index is to guarantee that a column or a combination of columns is unique for every row in the table. When creating an index, you can add the keyword UNIQUE which thus prevents an operator from entering a duplicate value in the column or columns for which the index was created. For example, you can ensure that no two title codes are the same in the TITLE table by creating a UNIQUE index on the *titlecd* column.

Creating Indexes

Only the owner of a table (the original creator of the table) or a user who has been given INDEX access on the table can create indexes on it. ORACLE automatically maintains the indexes created. When data is changed in the table, ORACLE updates the corresponding indexes on the changed columns and resorts the values.

The syntax for the CREATE INDEX command is

```
CREATE [UNIQUE] INDEX index_name ON table_name
    column1_name [,column2_name, column3_name . . .}
[{SYSSORT ¦ NOSYSSORT}]
[PCTFREE = n]
[{COMPRESS ¦ NOCOMPRESS}]
```

The CREATE INDEX command used to create the index for previous TITLE table example is:

Enforces uniqueness

CREATE UNIQUE INDEX title0 ON title(titlecd);

index name   *table name*   *column name*

ORACLE would sort this index on the *titlecd* key values and on their associated ROWIDs, then load the B*tree structure, shown in Figure 10.1, that stores the index entries.

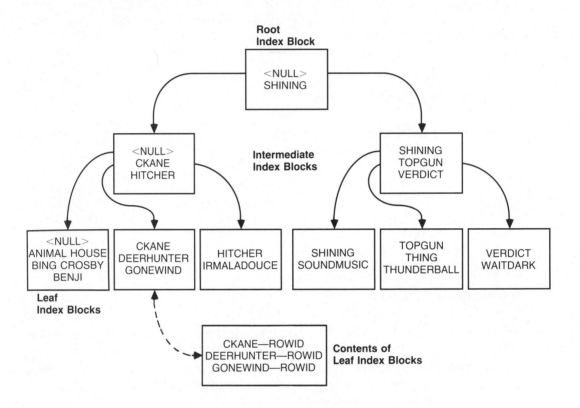

Figure 10.1   B*tree Index Structure

The B*tree structure consists of three levels of index blocks—the *root*, *intermediate*, and *leaf* blocks—chained together. The upper blocks contain index values used as pointers and address locations of the lower level index blocks. The lowest-level, or leaf blocks, contain index data values, that is, the index key values and associated ROWIDs.

Most database applications spend more time performing queries than manipulating data; the B*tree index structure is optimal for performing retrieval operations. All branches of the B*tree are the same depth, so retrieval of any record from the beginning or end of the table will take about the same time. Although some overhead is required to keep the B*tree index balanced, it is minimal compared to the savings in retrieval time.

ORACLE's B*tree indexes offer additional advantages. All nodes of the B*tree are kept more than half full, and storage space can be continually reclaimed and allocated. B*trees process record inserts and deletes efficiently, maintaining key value order for rapid interactive or batch retrieval.

One distinct advantage B*tree indexes have over many other access methods is that retrieval performance does not degrade as the table grows in size; performance always remains constant as the number of records managed by the indexes increases.

Concatenated Indexes

You can create a single index on more than one column in a table by *concatenating* the columns. A concatenated index is the only way of enforcing uniqueness in a table if it takes more than one column to uniquely identify a row. For example, to ensure that each rentals transaction is unique, you need to create the following concatenated index:

```
CREATE UNIQUE INDEX rentals0 ON rentals(memberid, catnum,
dateout)
```

Since a member can rent out the same tape more than once, the only way to enforce uniqueness is to nail down the date of the transaction. A tape is rented out for a minimum of one day, so a given tape cannot be rented out twice on the same day.

A concatenated index can improve query performance if defined on a combination of columns frequently used as criteria in a WHERE clause. For this reason, the following concatenated index might be built on the PRODUCT table:

```
CREATE UNIQUE INDEX product0 ON product(prodno, storeno)
```

Uniqueness is enforced by the *prodno* and *storeno* columns, but the added advantage is that queries referencing both columns are retrieved much faster than without the index (and only a single index need be used as opposed to two separate indexes). It would make sense to build a concatenated index if queries like the following were executed often:

```
SELECT *
  FROM product
 WHERE prodno = 'P500'
   AND storeno = '1'
```

It happens that our Video Quest application does indeed rely on several queries that reference both key columns.

The order in which you name columns in the CREATE INDEX command makes a difference when you set up concatenated indexes to speed retrieval. A concatenated index will speed retrieval on any query that uses the first columns of the index (these are also known as the *leading edge*). As a rule, therefore, you should name the columns used most often by your queries first in the CREATE INDEX command.

Because the previous query example referenced both columns in the index, the index can be used to speed retrieval. If only the product number is referenced, as in

```
SELECT * FROM product WHERE prodno = 'P500'
```

then the index will be used but it won't be as selective as when both are referenced. Now if the WHERE clause omits the index by omitting the first column used in the CREATE INDEX command, as in

```
SELECT *
  FROM product
 WHERE rentclass = 25
   AND storeno = 1
```

the concatenated index will not be used at all. This is true even though another column in the concatenated index is referenced.

Compressed and Noncompressed Indexes

ORACLE indexes are stored in compressed format by default. The compression algorithm uses both *forward compression* and *rear compression*. This means that it stores only a portion of an index value—the part of the value which makes it unique from adjacent index entries.

The benefit of compression is significantly reduced storage costs. A compressed index normally requires 50% less space than a noncompressed index. When you create additional indexes to make more access paths available to the ORACLE query optimizer, you may pay a premium in disk storage; as your tables grow, the space requirement can become significant. If you have created many indexes on a large database, it is not impossible for the space requirements of your indexes to be competitive with the data itself.

On the downside, the performance costs of index compression should be weighed. The initial processing costs of compressing the index can be a factor. Even greater are the cost of decoding the compressed value when data is retrieved or modified by inserts, updates, or delete operations, and the cost of resolving the query based on the decompressed value. ORACLE must search the table's actual data blocks to reconstruct the data values of the key that were stripped out during compression.

For certain queries, you can improve retrieval speed dramatically by creating an index without compressing it. Because a noncompressed index stores the entire index data value, table look-ups are avoided. Queries that leverage noncompressed indexes are those resolved directly in the indexes—that is, those that select only the data in the indexes themselves and do not have to look to the database to verify values. This is the case when *every* column referenced in the SQL statement appears in the noncompressed index *and* there is a WHERE clause. For example, the following query would speed retrieval considerably, because both columns referenced are part of a noncompressed, concatenated index:

```
SELECT catnum, storeno
  FROM tape
 WHERE catnum = 450
   AND storeno = 1
```

The index structure on this is a unique noncompressed index on *catnum* and *storeno*.

As a practical matter, however, there are few production queries that can be resolved with indexes alone.

To create a noncompressed index, you use the NOCOMPRESS option in the CREATE INDEX command as follows:

```
CREATE UNIQUE INDEX tape0 ON tape(catnum, storeno) NOCOMPRESS
```

The architecture of ORACLE Version 6, with the Transaction Processing Subsystem Option (TPS), has been redesigned to provide a five- to tenfold performance improvement over ORACLE Version 5, offering such performance advantages as row-level locking and deferred writes at commit. Index compression is not optional—it is built into Version 6; the performance losses due to compression are more than made up for by the new performance features, and the storage savings of compression are significant.

Restrictions on the Use of Indexes

An index is most effective when a query returns 25% or fewer rows of the table; more than this and a full table scan is preferable. Nine times out of ten, however, an indexed search will improve query performance to some degree over a full table scan, since most queries are designed to extract specific rows rather than all rows from a table.

An index *can* be used if an indexed column is referenced in the predicate of a WHERE clause. With compound expressions containing more than one predicate, an index may be used if it references at least one predicate. ORACLE's internal query optimizer often controls whether an index is appropriate to use based on the context of your query—and the preference of access paths available to the optimizer.

ORACLE imposes some practical restrictions on the use of indexes. An index *cannot* be used if

▶ there is no WHERE clause

▶ the predicate *modifies* the indexed column, either by a function or by an expression

▶ the predicate uses either the IS NULL or IS NOT NULL expression. (An index does not contain any references to records where the indexed value is null).

▶ the predicate tests for a NOT condition, such as '! = 10'. (In most "NOT = " queries, the number of rows returned is greater than the number skipped, so it is usually faster to ignore the index.)

In the following examples, an index would not be used because the WHERE predicate violates one of the above index usage rules:

```
1.   SELECT *
        FROM rentals
        WHERE to_char(dateout, 'DD Month, YYYY') = sysdate

2.   SELECT *
        FROM product
        WHERE substr(prodno,5,1) = 'V'

3.   SELECT invno
        FROM invoice
        WHERE (total * 6.5)/ 100 = 39.00

4.   SELECT description
        FROM category
        WHERE category is not null

5.   SELECT *
        FROM title
        WHERE titlecd != 'Ghostbusters'
```

You can often reword a query to ensure an index is used, even though the query may violate an index rule expressed another way. For example, you would get a much faster result if you reworded the following query:

```
SELECT *
  FROM product
 WHERE subst(prodno,5,1) = 'V'
```

to modify the constant, not the indexed column, like this:

```
SELECT *
  FROM product
 WHERE prodno like = '_ _ V'
```

You can also reword the following query:

```
SELECT invno
  FROM invoice
 WHERE total / 3.00 = 200
```

to modify the constant before the expression is compared, so it can still use the index on the *total* column:

```
SELECT invno
  FROM invoice
 WHERE total = 200 * 3.00
```

Deciding How Many Indexes to Create

Although indexes boost query performance, you pay a price in maintaining the indexes. Each time an insert, update, or delete operation changes a table, ORACLE must update the indexes on the affected columns. When deciding how many indexes to create, weigh the trade-offs—you give up increased retrieval speed for slower update processing. Update-intensive tables, such as the RENTALS and RETURNS transaction tables which change continuously throughout the day, should be created with just the minimum of indexes to provide acceptable query performance.

Tables that change infrequently, such as a firm's payroll records archived over the past few years, can support several indexes without compromising update processing. In the Video Quest application, the TITLE table, which we use primarily for queries, is a choice candidate for opening up several access paths to the ORACLE query optimizer. Table 10.1 shows a sampling of indexes you might create on this table.

Table 10.1   TITLE Table Indexes

UNIQUE		INDEX ON	*titlecd* (Primary Key)
NONUNIQUE		INDEX ON	*category* (Foreign Key)
NONUNIQUE	NONCOMPRESSED	INDEX ON	*titlecd-category*
NONUNIQUE	NONCOMPRESSED	INDEX ON	*actors-directors*
NONUNIQUE		INDEX ON	*actors-starrtg-awards*
NONUNIQUE		INDEX ON	*directors-starrtg-awards*
NONUNIQUE	NONCOMPRESSED	INDEX ON	*starrtg-runtime*
NONUNIQUE	NONCOMPRESSED	INDEX ON	*release-studio*

Using Multiple Indexes on a Single Table Query

A SQL statement with two or more predicates may use multiple indexes to expedite a search on a single table. The predicates must use equality comparisons; comparison operators such as GREATER THAN or LESS THAN are not allowed. The multiple indexes must also be nonunique. For example, the following query would use two indexes to perform the search:

```
SELECT prodno
  FROM product
 WHERE titlecd = 'TOPGUN'
   AND format = 'V'
```

The index structure on this is a nonunique index on *titlecd* and a nonunique index on *format*.

To use both indexes, the data in the indexes must be collated or merged (as in a join operation), to identify the records that satisfy the query criteria. ORACLE merges up to five indexes at a time for any given query. The fact that it sorts indexes on both key and ROWID minimizes the number of comparisons required to merge the indexes. Observe:

```
TITLECD      ROWID                            FORMAT   ROWID
----------   -------------------              ------   -------------------
CKANE        00004C88.0003.0001                 B      00004C88.0001.0001
GHOSTBUSTER  00004C88.0001.0001                 B      00004C88.0002.0001
GHOSTBUSTER  00004C89.0002.0001                 V      00004C88.0003.0001
GONEWIND     00004C88.0002.0001                 V      00004C89.0001.0001
GONEWIND     00004C89.0003.0001                 V      00004C89.0002.0001
HITCHER      00004C90.0002.0001                 V      00004C89.0003.0001
SHINING      00004C90.0003.0001          --->V         00004C90.0001.0001
SOUNDMUSIC   00004C89.0001.0001             !   V      00004C90.0002.0001
TOPGUN       00004C90.0001.0001<-----          B       00004C90.0003.0001
```

Multiple indexes *are not* used in queries that contain a nonequality predicate. For example, take a query like this, which mixes "bounded range" and "equality" predicates:

```
SELECT title
  FROM title
 WHERE directors = 'Orson Welles'
       and release < '1965'
```

The index structure on the above is a nonunique index on *directors* and a nonunique index on *release*.

This query is unable to leverage the multiple indexes. To optimize performance in this query, ORACLE would ignore the *release* index and use the index on the equality predicate to drive the query. This index then would be the *driving index*. ORACLE would find all records where 'Orson Welles' is the value for *director*, then check them manually to extract only those released after 1965.

Evaluating Multiple Indexes

When multiple indexes are available, but it is not clear which index has preference, ORACLE decides which index to use based on the index types available and on the column characteristics. For example, if a unique and nonunique index are available, ORACLE chooses the unique index to drive the query, ignoring the nonunique index. If two unique indexes are available and one of them is on a column defined as NOT NULL, then ORACLE will give preference to the NOT NULL column.

The ORACLE query optimizer ranks predicate clauses in the following order when selecting the driving index:

1. *ROWID* = constant
2. *Unique indexed column* = constant
3. *Entire unique concatenated key* = constant
4. *Entire cluster key* = *corresponding cluster key* in another table in same table (see the following section on Clustering Tables)
5. *Entire cluster key* = constant
6. *Entire nonunique, concatenated key* = constant
7. *Nonunique index* = constant
8. *Entire noncompressed, concatenated index* >= lower bound
9. *Entire compressed, concatenated index* >= lower bound

10. ***Most leading, noncompressed index*** $>=$ lower bound

11. ***Most leading, compressed index*** $>=$ lower bound

12. ***Unique indexed column*** BETWEEN low AND high
    OR
    Unique indexed column LIKE 'C%' (bounded range)

13. ***Nonunique indexed column*** BETWEEN low AND high
    OR
    Nonunique indexed column LIKE 'C%' (bounded range)

14. ***Unique indexed column*** $>$ constant
    OR
    Unique indexed column $<$ constant

15. ***Nonunique indexed column*** $>$ constant
    OR
    Nonunique indexed column $<$ constant

16. ***Sort/merge*** (Joins only)

17. If no indexes identified, then:
    WHERE MAX(column) $=$ constant
    OR
    WHERE MIN(column) $=$ constant

18. ***ORDER BY*** entire index

19. Full table scans

Using Indexes in Join Queries

Indexes are particularly important in queries that perform joins. If join queries are carelessly written or bereft of indexes they can cause multiple full-table scans resulting in poor performance. Usually the first indexes you create on a table are the primary and foreign key columns, often with joins in mind.

When designing join queries, you should first check that you have indexed both key columns of the join clause(s) that connect the tables. For example, the following simple join query:

```
SELECT prodno, title
  FROM product, title
 WHERE product.titlecd = title.titlecd
```

will perform well under most circumstances if you have created an index on the *titlecd* column in both the PRODUCT and the TITLE tables.

If an index exists on only one side of the join clause, then the table that is *not* indexed becomes the driving table and a full table scan must be performed. If no indexes are available on columns of the join clause—a type known as an *unindexed join*—then ORACLE uses the last table referenced in the FROM list as the driving table. The performance implications of this can be significant, because ORACLE Version 5 does a SORT-MERGE-JOIN join in the absence of indexes.

Be careful not to inadvertently suppress the key indexes when writing multi-table join queries. ORACLE merges only up to five multiple indexes in a query, remember. Any additional indexes are ignored, and the criteria is checked by a full table scan after the other results have been merged. This could undermine the performance benefits derived by using indexes. Be sure to create concatenated indexes and to design your join queries to leverage them whenever possible.

Clustering Tables

When ORACLE performs a join operation, much of the retrieval time is consumed by the repeated movement of the disk read/write drive heads from the physical disk location of one table to the storage locations of the other tables in the join. Access speed can be improved vastly when the join tables are stored physically close together on disk. ORACLE's table clusters allow you to do precisely this—that is, to reduce access time by storing tables frequently accessed together on common columns, such as join tables, in close physical proximity.

Table clustering has several advantages:

▶ It often reduces drive seek time by storing tables physically close together.

▶ It often reduces I/O for join operations by "pre-joining" queries.

▶ It can reduce storage requirements because the data common to clustered tables—the join column—is stored only once for the clustered block as opposed to once for each record in unclustered tables.

▶ It makes clusters transparent to users and applications.

Figures 10.2 and 10.3 show the frequently joined Video Quest tables, CUSTOMER and CUSTNAME, in both unclustered and clustered states.

```
       ★★ Block 00004C80 ★★                        ★★ Block 00004F88 ★★

CUSTOMER:  1  Daniel James Cronin  793 Vincente Avenue    CUSTNAME:  1  Duffy Cronin
CUSTOMER:  2  Martha Kent          100 First Street        CUSTNAME:  1  Eli Cronin
CUSTOMER:  3  Jerry Barry          1212 Broadway           CUSTNAME:  1  Ian Wilson



       ★★ Block 00004C88 ★★                        ★★ Block 00004F96 ★★

CUSTOMER:  49  Jimmy Jimereno  5219 Elm Drive             CUSTNAME:  2  Ken Kent
CUSTOMER:  50  Jack Clark      33 River Front             CUSTNAME:  3  Carrie Barry
CUSTOMER:  51  Sally Stanford  1883 Sausalito Street      CUSTNAME:  3  Chuck Barry
```

Figure 10.2   Unclustered CUSTOMER and CUSTNAME Tables

```
                  ★★ Block 00004F80 ★★
                     Cluster Key = 1

CUSTOMER:  Daniel James Cronin  793 Vincente Avenue
CUSTNAME:  Duffy Cronin         899
CUSTNAME:  Eli Cronin           899
CUSTNAME:  Ian Wilson           899



                  ★★ Block 00004F88 ★★
                     Cluster Key = 2

CUSTOMER:  Martha Kent  100 First Street
CUSTNAME:  Ken Kent     899



                  ★★ Block 00004F96 ★★
                     Cluster Key = 3

CUSTOMER:  Jerry Barry    1212 Broadway
CUSTNAME:  Carrie Barry   899
CUSTNAME:  Chuck Barry    140
```

Figure 10.3   Clustered CUSTOMER and CUSTNAME Tables

Improving Join Performance

A multi-way join query may need to retrieve data from several physical database blocks to satisfy the query. The performance goal of table clustering is to retrieve the data from the joined tables in a single physical block as opposed to one block for each table. Clustering effectively "pre-joins" queries so that all records from all tables referenced by the join criteria are in the same physical block, greatly reducing I/O. When the block is in memory, the information needed to satisfy the query is immediately available.

As Figure 10.3 shows, each value of the cluster key is stored in a separate block, "pre-joining" the records associated with the key. A word of caution, however, when choosing the cluster key: gauge in advance how many rows of data might be stored for each cluster key value. When the amount of data exceeds the block size, additional blocks are chained as required. Excessive chaining may negate the performance advantage of clustering. On the other hand, too little data stored for each key value may waste valuable storage space and earn nominal performance gains anyway. (You can adjust sizes of logical blocks to meet your storage requirements at the time you create the cluster. Refer to the *ORACLE Database Administrator's Guide* for details.)

Creating Clusters

Table clusters are created independently of your database tables. A cluster is *not* another table but an umbrella for your commonly accessed tables. Once you create a cluster based on a column common to the tables, you either create the tables *within* a cluster or move existing tables *into* a cluster. The syntax for the CREATE CLUSTER command is as follows:

```
CREATE CLUSTER cluster_name
   (cluster_key1 datatype, cluster_key2 datatype, . . .)
   [SPACE space_name]
   [SIZE logical_block_size]
   [COMPRESS | NOCOMPRESS]
```

Because the cluster key represents the join column (or columns) common to the clustered tables, it must be defined exactly as defined in the table columns. Both the datatype and size characteristics must match. If more than one column is common to both tables, concatenate the cluster key. At least one of the clustered columns in each table must be NOT NULL, however.

To create a cluster and move the existing CUSTOMER and CUSTNAME tables into the cluster, you perform these steps:

1. Create the cluster specifying the name and cluster key:

```
CREATE CLUSTER VDOCUSTOMERS
    (memberid number)
```

ORACLE automatically builds and maintains an index on the cluster key, although in ORACLE Version 6 this is not the case. ORACLE Version 5 users needn't worry about indexing the cluster key.

2. Verify that the cluster key column, *memberid*, is defined as NOT NULL in both the CUSTOMER and CUSTNAME clustered tables. If not, use the ALTER TABLE command to disallow NULLs on this column in both tables. (When you defined the Video Quest tables, you should have defined this column as NOT NULL in both tables.)

3. Create new tables in the cluster identical to the existing tables, except change the table names:

```
CREATE TABLE NEWCUSTOMER
    CLUSTER VDOCUSTOMERS(memberid)
    AS
    SELECT * FROM CUSTOMER

CREATE TABLE NEWCUSTNAME
    CLUSTER VDOCUSTOMERS(memberid)
    AS
    SELECT * FROM CUSTNAME
```

4. Drop the original tables and rename the clustered copies back to the original table names:

```
DROP TABLE CUSTOMER

RENAME NEWCUSTOMER TO CUSTOMER

DROP TABLE CUSTNAME

RENAME NEWCUSTNAME TO CUSTNAME
```

Caution: For performance reasons, it is preferable to create clusters from empty tables. When you move tables containing data into clusters, ORACLE is forced to physically load the rows from the current table blocks to the new cluster blocks, with all the overhead this implies. This can be regulated, however, with the judicious use of a WHERE in the CREATE TABLE AS SELECT statement.

A cluster is transparent to the user or application. A minor exception is that locking of one table of a cluster will lock *all* tables in the cluster. A query references tables by their original names, whether clustered or not. In fact, if you were to execute a query against the cluster

```
SELECT *
  FROM CUSTMEMBERS
```

the result would be

```
#ORA-942: table or view does not exist
```

Denormalizing Tables

Perhaps you weren't aware of it, but you were implementing the relational theory of *table normalization* while defining Video Quest's entity-relationship model. In lay terms, normalization is a data modelling technique that simplifies each table (that is, each table which describes an entity) in your database down to its key elements and attributes. The goal of normalization is to minimize data redundancy and to allow data to be easily managed and changed.

Pure normalization of data is not always practical in real-world applications. Normalization fosters many small tables, and this can increase the amount of I/O needed to retrieve certain information—particularly with join operations. A judicious use of *denormalization* is sometimes necessary to optimize performance of your applications. As the name implies, denormalization is the process of taking smaller, normalized tables and combining them into larger tables to reduce I/O overhead. Before rushing into this, however, the application designer must consider all the trade-offs denormalization implies. More on this in a moment.

By design, some tables are easier to update than others. Normalization theory ranks five different table designs according to the ease with which the stored data can be modified. These tables are called *normalized forms*, ranging from first normal form (abbreviated as 1NF) up to fifth normal form (5NF). When testing a table for ease of updatability—and determining whether a table is in first, second or third normal form—the normalization technique adheres to three firm rules:

> *First Normal Form:* A table is in first normal form if all nonkey columns are functionally dependent upon the unique (primary key) of a table.

Second Normal Form: A first normal form table is also in second normal form if its nonkey columns are dependent on the entire primary key, not merely a portion of it. If the primary key is concatenated (that is, if it uniquely identifies rows using multiple columns), a nonkey column must be dependent on the entire concatenated key, not just a portion of the key.

Third Normal Form: A second normal form is also in third normal form if no two nonkey columns are dependent upon each other, but are only bound to the primary key.

A table not represented in a normal form (known as an *unnormalized* table) stores data in a free form, unstructured fashion. Here is an example of an unnormalized table:

```
                                   Days
Catalog #  Date Out/Date Due       Rented     Member Information
---------  -------------------     ------     ------------------------------
100        15-Mar-88, 16-Mar-88    1 day      1 Will Clark     415-526-8888
300        28-Mar-88, 29-Mar-88    1 day      2 Jose Canseco   415-893-0000
200        09-Apr-88, 10-Apr-88    1 day      1 Will Clark     415-526-8888
451        18-May-88, 20-Apr-88    2 days     3 Mark McQuire   415-895-3331
300        21-May-88, 23-May-88    2 days     2 Jose Canseco   415-893-0000
```

First Normal Form

Compare the data in the unnormalized table to that of the same data in a first normal form table:

```
                                              Days                Scheduled
Catalog #  Memberid Name        Phone#        Rented Date Out     Return
---------  -------- ----------- ------------- ------ ---------    ---------
100             1 Will Clark    415-526-8888  1 day  15-Mar-88    16-Mar-88
300             2 Jose Canseco  415-893-0000  1 day  28-Mar-88    29-Mar-88
200             1 Will Clark    415-526-8888  1 day  09-Apr-88    10-Apr-88
451             3 Mark McQuire  415-895-3331  2 days 18-May-88    20-May-88
300             2 Jose Canseco  415-893-0000  2 days 21-May-88    23-May-88
```

A table in first normal form may appear logically cluttered, but it provides, nonetheless, a fundamental structure by storing only one value in a column for each row.

Though obscured, a primary key does exist in this table. As shown, the Catalog Number and Member ID columns are not sufficient to uniquely identify each transaction. A member can rent the same tape twice but on different days. The primary key requires the Date Out column as well. Thus the table's primary key is concatenated, consisting of the Catalog Number, Member ID, and Date Out columns. Every nonkey column depends on this primary key.

To test whether this table is also in second normal form, you must look at each nonkey column and analyze its relationship to *every* column in the primary key.

Q: Does the Days Rented column depend on only part of the key?

A: No. A value in Days Rented only has meaning when associated with a Catalog Number, Member ID, and Date Out.

Q: Does the Name column depend on only part of the key?

A: Yes. A member's Name only depends on the corresponding Member ID. You do not need to know a Catalog Number to know the Name.

This table violates the rule of second normal form. Values in the Name column depend only on a portion of the primary key, the Member ID. Forced to store data in first normal form, this table sacrifices the chief advantages relational databases offer. The major flaws in this design are

- ▶ Wasted space. Values for Name and Phone Number are stored redundantly for every transaction, wasting valuable storage space.

- ▶ Costly updates. What happens when a member's phone number has changed? The system must run through the table and change the phone number for every rental transaction charged to that member. Net result: the table is costly to update and difficult to maintain.

- ▶ Unreliability. Suppose that the only transaction containing the information for a particular member was deleted. The member information no longer exists anywhere in the system.

- ▶ Integrity problems. Since member information is stored redundantly, an error in update processing on specific rows could result in different member names or phone numbers being stored for a given *memberid*. The design exposes the database to serious integrity risks.

Second Normal Form

Notice that the table being used contains information about two separate entities—CUSTOMERS and RENTALS transactions. To rectify the design flaws of the first normal form, you must split the table into two separate tables like so:

RENTALS Transactions

Catalog #	Memberid	Days Rented	Date Out	Scheduled Return
100	1	1 day	15-Mar-88	16-Mar-88
300	2	1 day	28-Mar-88	29-Mar-88
200	1	1 day	09-Apr-88	10-Apr-88
451	3	2 days	18-May-88	20-May-88
300	2	2 days	21-May-88	23-May-88

CUSTOMER Information

Memberid	Name	Phone #
1	Will Clark	415-526-8888
2	Jose Canseco	415-893-0000
1	Will Clark	415-526-8888
3	Mark McQuire	415-895-3331
2	Jose Canseco	415-893-0000

Both tables are now in second normal form. The RENTALS table abides by the rule because both nonkey columns, Days Rented and Scheduled Return, owe their existence exclusively to the primary key columns. The CUSTOMER table is also in 2NF because the primary key is not concatenated, so the nonkey columns wholly depend on the single column key, Member ID.

Third Normal Form

The CUSTOMER table is automatically in third normal form. Neither of its nonkey columns depend on each other for anything; a value for a member Name could survive without the value for a Phone Number, and vice versa.

The RENTALS transaction violates the rule of third normal form, however. The Scheduled Return column is derived from the Date Out column, which is part of the primary key, and from the Days Rented column, which is a nonkey column. (SCHDRTN = DATEOUT * RENTDAYS.) You must know the number of days rented to calculate the scheduled return date; the dependency is clear.

Here is a case where a conscious decision was made to violate the rule of third normal form and *denormalize* the RENTALS table. Several queries in the Video Quest application depend on knowing the scheduled return date. Because this information is requested so frequently, it pays to store the value once with the transaction rather than compute it every time a query is executed. The performance gains of this approach outweigh the cost of disk space required to store the date value.

Fourth and Fifth Normal Forms

Tables simplified to the third normal form ensure minimal data redundancy. The structure is easy to understand, and the data is easy to query and modify. The simplicity of third normal form suits the requirements of most business models. Occasionally, however, a situation arises that demands further data simplification. The fourth and fifth normal forms accommodate these exceptional cases. The rules for testing fourth and fifth normal forms are

Fourth Normal Form: A third normal form is also in fourth normal form if it does not contain more than one attribute that admits multiple values for the entity described by the table.

Fifth Normal Form: A fourth normal form is in fifth normal form when its information cannot be reconstructed from several smaller tables not having the same key.

For more information about fourth and fifth normal forms and other intriguing aspects of relational database theory, refer to the bibliography at the end of this book.

Denormalization

After normalizing the data, you can evaluate the performance needs of your application more critically. At this point you might ask whether it makes sense, from the standpoint of performance and functionality, to duplicate any data elements stored in the normalized tables elsewhere in the database. If you see some candidates, be sure that the performance gains would clearly exceed the loss in disk space forced by the redundancy. You should also be willing to accept the consequences of any update problems or anomalies.

The more you understand the application and the usage trends of your tables, the more confident you can be in your decision regarding when to denormalize data. Ask yourself these questions: How often are the tables queried and how often are they changed? What portions of the tables are changed? What tables are accessed more frequently than others? How frequently are join queries performed on these tables?

We showed you an example of denormalization when we added the Scheduled Return column to the RENTALS table. Let's look at another case where it may be advantageous to denormalize the RENTALS transaction table further.

Rental information, particularly rental availability and overdue tapes, is queried constantly throughout the day. To determine the availability of a tape, you must know the actual date it was returned—if at all. In a purely normalized database, you would have to join the RENTALS and RETURNS tables to retrieve this information. Here is the current RENTALS and the normalized RETURNS table:

RETURNS

Catalog #	Memberid	Actual Return	Latecharge
100	1	19-Mar-88	13.50
300	2	30-Mar-88	4.50

RENTALS

Catalog #	Memberid	Days Rented	Scheduled Date Out	Return
100	1	1 day	15-Mar-88	16-Mar-88
300	2	1 day	28-Mar-88	29-Mar-88
200	1	1 day	09-Apr-88	10-Apr-88
451	3	2 days	18-May-88	20-May-88
300	2	2 days	21-May-88	23-May-88

Just as the Date Out column uniquely identifies a rentals transaction, the date in the Actual Return column uniquely identifies each returns transaction.

From a working knowledge of the application, you know that the tables must be joined frequently to verify rental status, and that the performance costs are exorbitant. To eliminate this join, you simply ensure that the RENTALS table contains all the required information—all that is missing is the date for the Actual Return column. The decision to denormalize in this case is quite clear-cut. The cost of inserting or deleting the date for actual return twice, once for each table, is negligible compared to the performance gains of eliminating the join.

If you study the Video Quest table design, you will find a few more isolated cases of denormalization. You are encouraged to review the table design with a view to understanding and justifying these violations.

Optimizing SQL*Forms

The essence of SQL*Forms is productivity—creating powerful applications without programming. Despite the "hands-off" approach, there are several tricks you can use to control SQL*Forms and enhance the performance of your SQL*Forms applications. Some of these tricks include

- Using the COPY command instead of SELECT INTO
- Default WHERE clause
- Enforcing uniqueness in the database not SQL*Forms
- Runform options

    Buffering Records

    Optimize SQL Processing

    Optimize Transaction Processing

Using the COPY Command

Occasionally you will define a trigger that copies the value from one screen field into another screen field, holding the value temporarily for later validation or processing. You've learned how to do this with the SELECT INTO statement. To improve performance, however, you can sometimes use the SQL*Forms COPY command instead.

For example, suppose you want to reinitialize the date field just before committing a rentals transaction on the RENTALS form. You define a *Pre-Insert* trigger that copies the system-generated date from the XDATEOUT field in the RENTALS block to the TRANSDATE field in the INVOICE block (see Figure 10.4).

```
┌──────────────────────────────────────────────────────────────────────────┐
│  ┌── Video Quest RENTALS ───────────────┐    ┌[ Invoice No:        ]┐      │
│  ┌╥╥╥╥╥╥╥╥╥╥╥╥╥╥╥╥╥╥╥╥╥╥╥╥╥╥╥╥╥╥╥╥╥┬╥╥╥┐                              │
│  │     DEFINE BLOCK        Seq # 2   │║║║│                              │
│  │  Name   rentals                   └╨╨╨┤  Tapes rented out:          │
│  │  ┌────────────────────────────────┐   ├────┬─────────┬──────────┬──────┤
│  │  │     CHOOSE TRIGGER             │   │Rate│ Date out│ Date Due │ Total│
│  │  │ Name                          │   │    │         │          │      │
│  │  │ PRE-INSERT                     │   │    │         │          │      │
│  │  └────────────────────────────────┘                                   │
│  ┌───────────────────────────────────────────────────────────────┐        │
│  │ Seq # 1         TRIGGER STEP         Label Init-date          │        │
│  │ #COPY :rentals.xdateout :invoice.transdate                    │        │
│  │                                                                │        │
│  │                                                                │        │
│  │ Message if trigger step fails:                                │        │
│  │                                                                │        │
│  │ Actions:                                                       │        │
│  │     CREATE       COPY       DROP        ATTRIBUTES    COMMENT   │        │
│  │     FORWARD      BACKWARD   PREV STEP   NEXT STEP              │        │
│  └───────────────────────────────────────────────────────────────┘        │
│  └──────────────────────┘ VIDEO QUEST RENTALS, Inc. └────────────┘         │
│   Form: rentals1   Block: rentals    Page: 1    SELECT: B  Char Mode: Replace│
└──────────────────────────────────────────────────────────────────────────┘
```

Figure 10.4   Copying a Value on the RENTALS Form

There are two ways to copy this value in SQL*Forms:

Solution 1—SELECT INTO

```
SELECT :rentals.xdateout
  INTO invoice.transdate
  FROM dual
```

Solution 2—COPY Command

```
#COPY :rentals.xdateout :invoice.transdate
```

Solution 2 offers a clear performance advantage in this case. A SQL statement must be parsed, whereas the COPY command needn't be, saving the parsing overhead. Additionally, a SQL statement trigger must obtain a cursor for processing, which means using an ORACLE memory space. A COPY command executes within SQL*Forms, eliminating the need for a cursor and the extra overhead of obtaining one. Since this trigger doesn't need to retrieve any table values for validation or display purposes, there is no reason to use the SELECT INTO syntax; use the COPY command instead.

The Default WHERE Clause

The SPECIFY DEFAULT ORDERING window is used to control which records are retrieved and the order in which they are displayed in a form block. You learned how to define a default ORDER BY clause on this window to sort the records. Another way to greatly improve performance is to use a default WHERE clause which forces the use of an index on the sort column. Since an index is already in sorted order, the end-user will immediately see an improvement in performance.

For example, recall the ORDER BY clause that you defined for the lineno column on the SYNOPSIS block, as shown in Figure 10.5.

```
Synopsis for title:

            DEFINE BLOCK        Seq # 2     |||||||||||||||||||||||||||||||
  Name    synopsis

                     SPECIFY DEFAULT ORDERING
  WHERE / ORDER BY clause for QUERY
  ORDER BY lineno




  Actions:          FORWARD       BACKWARD       DELETE




  |||||||||||||||||||||||||||||||||||||||||||||||||||||||||||||||||||||||||
  [Next Record] Scroll down | [Prev Record] Scroll up | [Prev Block] Title info
                     VIDEO QUEST RENTALS, Inc.
  Form: title      Block: synopsis     Page: 2    SELECT: B  Char Mode: Replace
```

Figure 10.5   Default ORDER BY for SYNOPSIS Block

To improve performance, first create an index on the *lineno* column in the SYNOPSIS table, then specify the following default WHERE clause to force the use of the index during retrieval:

```
WHERE lineno > ''
```

Be sure that the *lineno* column is defined as NOT NULL in the SYNOPSIS table. By deceit, the WHERE clause pushes SQL*Plus into using the

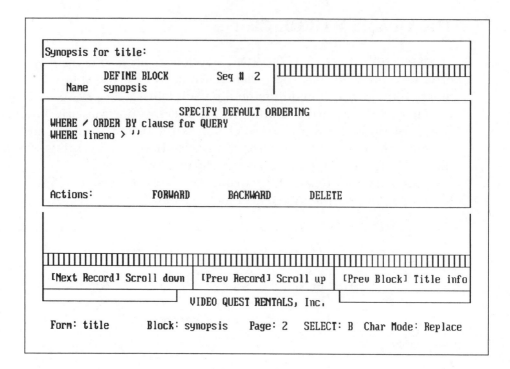

Figure 10.6 Default WHERE Clause for SYNOPSIS Block

lineno index because the criteria will retrieve every row in the column—
because any value is logically greater than a null (the absence of value)
and every row should contain a value.

Enforcing Uniqueness in the Database

SQL*Forms has a facility to prevent an operator from entering duplicate
rows into a table. Quite frankly, this facility is costly to use and should be
avoided. You realize better performance in enforcing uniqueness in the
database by creating a unique index on the primary key of your base
SQL*Forms tables.

Briefly, the SQL*Forms technique would have you define the Primary
Key attribute when defining attributes for key fields of the SQL*Forms
block, then selecting the *CHECK FOR UNIQUE KEY option for this block.

For example, to prevent an operator from entering a duplicate title
record into the TITLE table, you would first specify the Primary Key attribute on the TITLECD field as shown in Figure 10.7.

Then specify the CHECK FOR UNIQUE KEY option on the SPECIFY
BLOCK OPTIONS window (Figure 10.8).

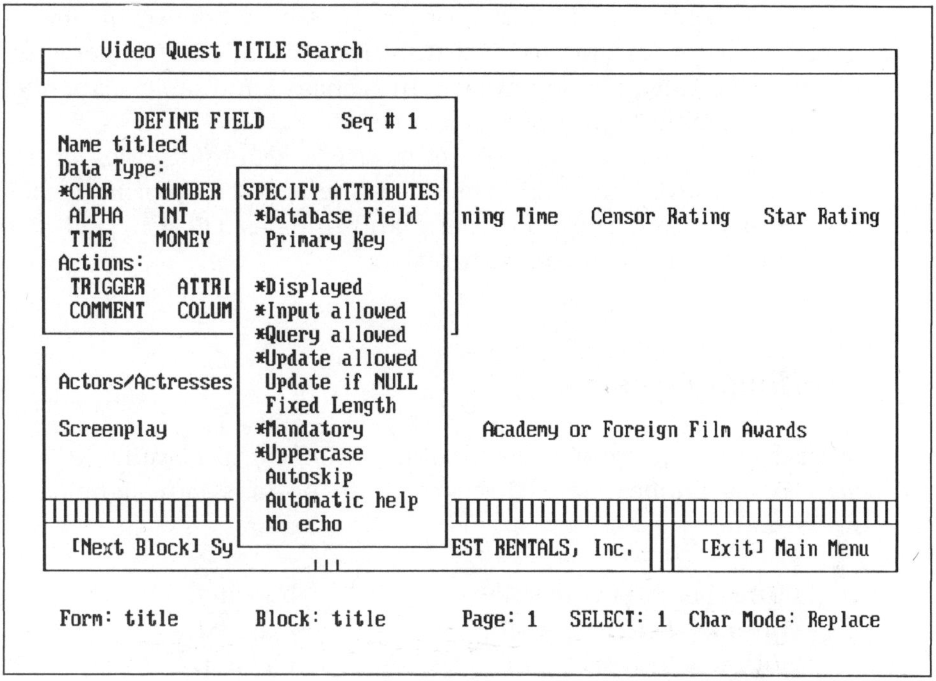

Figure 10.7   Primary Key Attribute on the TITLECD Field

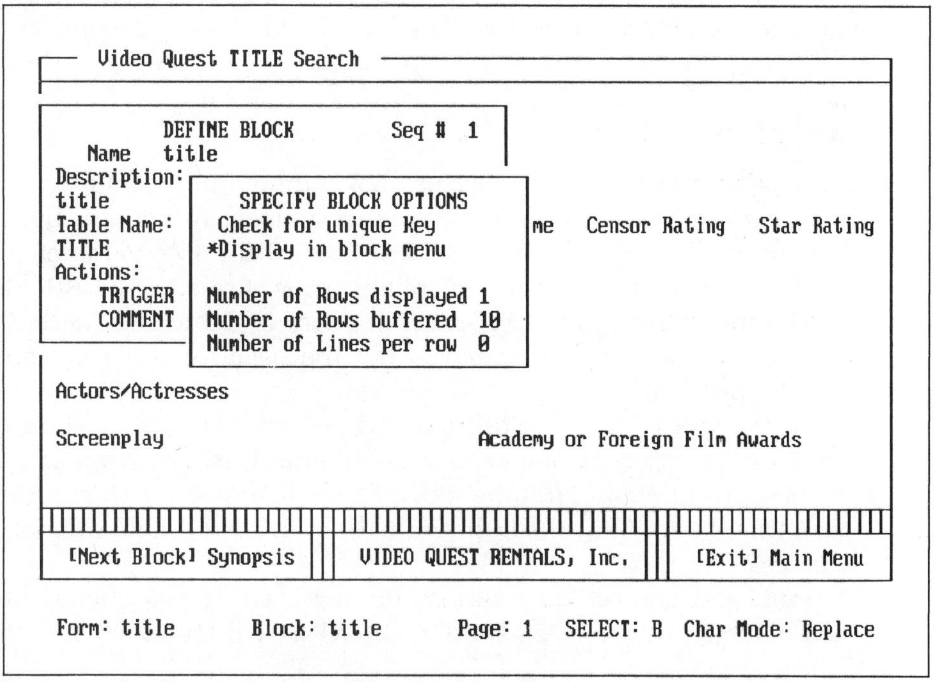

Figure 10.8   CHECK FOR UNIQUE KEY Option

The problem with this approach is that whenever a new record is added or a row is updated, ORACLE issues a SELECT statement to verify whether the value already exists. This causes a full table scan, often resulting in prohibitively poor performance.

A more efficient approach is to create a unique index on the *titlecd* column in the TITLE table. When creating the TITLE form, do not declare any primary keys. Then on inserts and updates, ORACLE will use the index and will not scan the entire table.

Runform Options

Several runtime options (also called *switches*) are available for running SQL*Forms applications. Three of these options can significantly affect performance:

Buffer Records with File	-b switch
Optimize SQL Processing	-o switch
Optimize Transaction Processing	-t switch

When running a form from the command line, you can set these options by adding the appropriate switches. From SQL*Forms (Design), you may use the SPECIFY RUN OPTION window to choose the options.

BUFFER RECORDS

On smaller machines, SQL*Forms may bump into memory constraints when running an application. If you are unable to increase the memory on your machine (or lower the CONTEXT_AREA size parameter in your INIT.ORA configuration file), you might resort to using the BUFFER RECORDS option. This option conserves memory by buffering queried records to a file instead of active memory—but the negative affect is significantly reduced performance.

If you reject this option, queried records are buffered to memory. SQL*Forms reserves enough space to buffer at least 300 rows for *all* blocks on the current form. Multiple block forms compete for this buffer space. Rows that do not fit in the buffer remain on disk and naturally take longer to access.

You can control the number of rows SQL*Forms should buffer for each block on the SPECIFY BLOCK OPTIONS window, as Figure 10.9 illustrates.

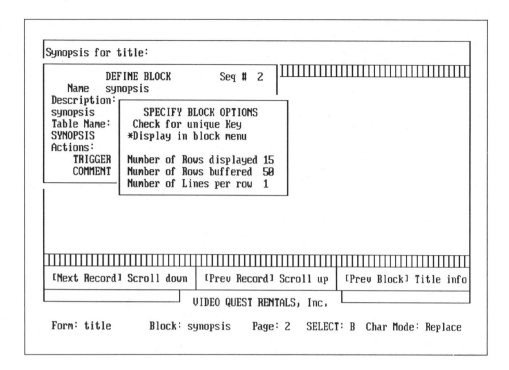

Figure 10.9   Number of Rows Buffered Item

SQL*Forms guarantees space for at least the number of rows defined here. Analyze the blocks of your form to determine those that will retrieve the most records and adjust the number of rows buffered accordingly, keeping in mind the 300-row buffer limit. Whenever possible, buffer at least *twice* as many rows as can be displayed at one time.

OPTIMIZE SQL PROCESSING

SQL*Forms defaults to this option. Deselect this option only if you run into serious memory constraints. This may happen on smaller machines running larger SQL*Forms applications loaded with triggers.

By default, SQL*Forms assigns a separate cursor (memory space) to each trigger (and further, to each trigger step), to optimize trigger execution. Deselecting this option causes trigger steps to share cursor data area, thus conserving memory.

SQL*Forms does let you have your cake and eat it too, however. If you are bumping up against memory limitations, you can deselect the OPTIMIZE SQL PROCESSING option for the entire form, but you can then *override* it for any individual SQL statement trigger steps. This speeds up processing by allowing frequently executed SQL triggers to run in their own cursor areas, while other triggers can share cursors to conserve memory. You can control this by selecting the *Separate Cursor Data Area attribute on the TRIGGER STEP ATTRIBUTES window (see Figure 10.10).

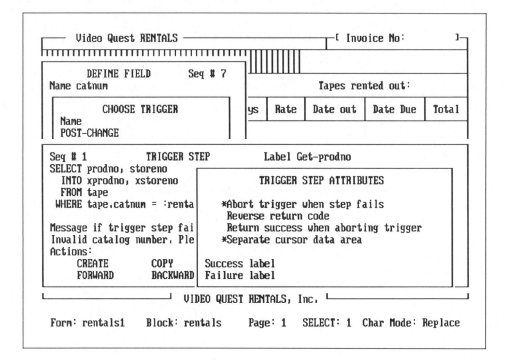

Figure 10.10   Separate Cursor Data Area Attribute

OPTIMIZE TRANSACTION PROCESSING

The OPTIMIZE TRANSACTION PROCESSING option is a slight variation of the OPTIMIZE SQL PROCESSING option. By deselecting this option, you also conserve memory, but not nearly as much; the option will assign a separate cursor area only to SQL SELECT statement triggers. All other SQL triggers (INSERTS, UPDATES, DELETES, LOCK TABLES, and SELECT-FOR-UPDATES) are forced to share cursor data area. This option is useful in query-intensive environments where you are experiencing memory problems. You can guarantee reasonable query performance while still conserving memory.

Managing Disk Space

In large database environments, an ORACLE database administrator (DBA) traditionally oversees disk space allocation and controls space requirements for many users accessing multiple databases. An ORACLE developer designing turnkey applications for smaller environments normally wears several hats, one of which is that of the DBA. To fulfill this role, the designer must be well versed in the tools available for managing the storage environment.

The Physical Storage Environment

An ORACLE database consists of a *database file* divided into logical *partitions*. A partition can hold one or more physical files. When first installed, ORACLE creates a SYSTEM partition corresponding to the DBS.ORA file and containing the data dictionary tables, temporary tables, and, optionally, help tables. Additional files may be added to the SYSTEM partition, or you may create other partitions and add files to them. A partition file is made up of *extents*, which are represented by a number of *blocks* or *pages*, as Figure 10.11 shows. The default block size is 1024 bytes on Professional ORACLE, Version 5. (It is 2048 on VMS and 4096 on VM/CMS.)

When you create a table, ORACLE automatically allocates more than enough data and index blocks in the SYSTEM partition to get you started. By default, ORACLE defines a 5-block extent for data and another 5-block extent for indexes. At 1024 bytes per block, each extent will hold roughly 5K bytes of data. When you completely fill these five data blocks, ORACLE allocates an additional extent of 25 blocks. ORACLE continues to allocate extents in 25-block increments as needed until you reach the file limit of 16 data extents. This translates to 760 blocks or 380K bytes of data storage per file. The same formula applies to index blocks; index data is limited to 16 extents per file. Once you exhaust the 380K bytes of space for either data or indexes, you must add another file to the partition.

As new rows are inserted into a block, ORACLE keeps at least 20% of the space free (this is an adjustable parameter) to allow for row expansion during subsequent updates. If an updated row can no longer fit in the physical block, the row is written to another physical block, or *chained*, in the same extent or a different one. Chained data is retrieved more slowly than data stored sequentially. If you know in advance that certain tables will be updated frequently, you can increase the amount of free space with the PCTFREE parameter in the CREATE SPACE command to lessen the impact of chaining on retrieval speed.

To see how much disk space is eaten up by tables in the database, you can query the ORACLE data dictionary view TABALLOC:

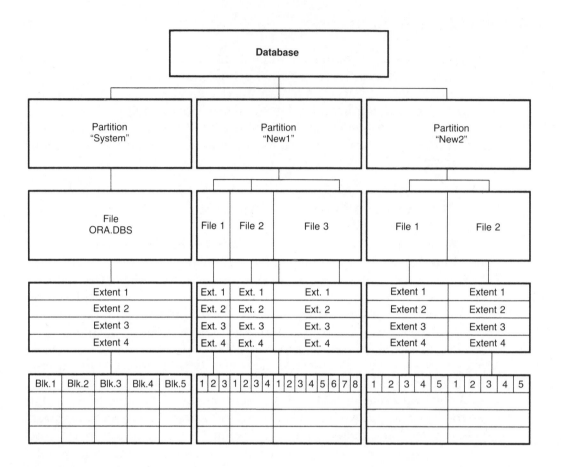

Figure 10.11   Database Partitions, Files, Extents, and Blocks

```
SELECT *
  FROM taballoc
```

The query might generate this display:

```
TNAME       D_BLKS   D_EXTS   I_BLKS   I_EXTS
----------  ------   ------   ------   ------

. . .
CNTL             5        1        5        1
. . .
CUSTOMER        30        2        5        1
. . .
TITLE          155        8      205       10
. . .
. . .
```

The TABALLOC view reports on the data and index blocks allocated for all tables created by all users of the database. If you want to review only the space allocation of the tables you own, you can query the STORAGE data dictionary view in the same manner.

The smallest table in the Video Quest database, CNTL, consists of a single row and no indexes, but ORACLE Version 5 is obliged to reserve a 5-block extent for data and another 5-block extent for indexes anyway. (ORACLE Version 6 corrects this problem.) Notice that the data space requirement for the CUSTOMER table has swollen to 30 blocks as new customers were added, but the index space hasn't exceeded the initial allocation. Since the CUSTOMER table is clustered, ORACLE automatically maintains an index on the cluster key and this space is not used.

The TITLE table presents an interesting picture of allocation. Remember that you optimized query performance by creating several indexes on the TITLE table. The index blocks reflect the cost in overhead, requiring 25 percent more space than data.

When either the data or the indexes exceed the threshold of 16 extents, ORACLE informs you with the error message

```
ORA-0116: cannot create extent, no more space in the par-
tition
```

It is possible that by freeing deleted space, you can reclaim enough space to continue working with this partition file. As data rows or index entries are deleted, the space is available to handle the overflow of updated rows, but new rows cannot be inserted into this space. Performing a full EXPort and IMPort of the partition tables ensures that ORACLE will restore the data to contiguous blocks, a procedure which reclaims the gaps of space caused by deleted rows.

An alternative is to enlarge the partition by adding another physical file to it. Be sure you have granted yourself DBA privilege, then perform the following steps:

1. Execute the Create Contiguous File (CCF) utility from the operating system to generate a new partition file and specify the number of contiguous blocks you wish to add.

   ```
   CCF new_file.ora 5000
   ```

   This adds 2.5 megabytes of space.

2. Now add the new file to the SYSTEM partition.

   ```
   ALTER PARTITION SYSTEM ADD FILE 'new_file.ora'
   ```

If desired, you could create a new partition with the CREATE PARTI-TION command, then add this new file to it instead of to the SYSTEM partition. By doing so, you can organize tables into groups and monitor space allocations separately from the ORACLE system and temporary tables.

Adding a new partition obviously alters the physical storage environment of your database. A relatively harmless error such as failing to specify the file by its correct name when altering the partition can produce tragic results; recovering from this error requires reinitialization of the entire database! As a precaution, *always* perform a full database file backup or EXPort before adding a new partition.

Planning for Growth of the Database

When you know that your table or indexes eventually will exceed the allotted 16 extents of space, you can preallocate space at the time you create the table. You use the CREATE SPACE command to do this.

For example, suppose your TITLE table starts out with a modest number of 1000 titles, requiring roughly 200 to 250 characters each. Within a couple of years, however, knowing that your tape inventory—actual copies of these titles—will expand to over 25,000 tapes, you expect the number of titles to grow to at least 5000. Since you've created several indexes to boost query performance, a few of them concatenated and noncompressed, you want to define at least 25% more index blocks than data blocks. To plan for such growth, you might reserve disk space by a statement like the following:

```
CREATE SPACE DEFINITION TITLE_SPACE
  DATAPAGES (INITIAL 500, INCREMENT 500, MAXEXTENTS 32,
  PCTFREE 20)
  INDEXPAGES (INITIAL 750, INCREMENT 750, MAXEXTENTS 32)
```

This allows for an initial allocation of 500 blocks, or 512 kilobytes of data, being increased in increments of 500 blocks as needed for 31 additional extents. The net allocation: 16 megabytes of space for TITLE data, and 25 percent more than that, or 20 megabytes, for indexes (assuming there is enough disk space available!).

You would then create the TITLE table as you would normally, except that you would add the new space definition name at the end of the CREATE TABLE statement like this:

```
CREATE TABLE title
 (column1, column2, column3)
 SPACE TITLE_SPACE
```

Data Integrity Facilities

Sophisticated database management systems offer automated facilities to preserve the integrity of data in the database. Typically, two kinds of problems threaten data integrity—a system failure leaving the database in an inconsistent state, and a situation in which several users attempt to update the same records concurrently. ORACLE provides the necessary facilities to maintain a consistent database in the event of either problem.

A system failure, such as a power outage or a computer program error, can easily disrupt the successful completion of an insert or update transaction. A transaction, by definition, is a single logical unit of work containing one or a series of actions—any one of which can modify the database. For example, suppose you are entering a RENTALS transaction. When you press the [Commit] key, three separate tables in the database might be affected: 1) a new record is first inserted into the RENTALS transaction table, and 2) the *qtyoh* position in the PRODUCT table must be decremented, and, if the customer had previously reserved the tape, 3) the RESERVATION transaction table would be updated.

If a program failure occurs in the middle of a transaction, such as *after* the application inserts a TRANSACTION record, but *before* the PRODUCT table had been updated, your database would be rendered inconsistent. ORACLE prevents this from happening with its ROLLBACK/RECOVERY mechanism. ORACLE maintains a "before-image" journal file which stores copies of database blocks as they appeared *before* they changed. If anything goes wrong during processing of a transaction, ORACLE automatically rolls back the database to the state it was in before the transaction began. Should the entire system shut down, affecting multiple users and transactions, ORACLE Version 5 relies on the "before-image" journal file to automatically return the database to a consistent state when started up again ("warm-started"). An "after-image" journal can optionally be maintained, allowing you to roll transaction changes *forward* to a specified point in the event of a system failure. In ORACLE Version 6, the logging facilities are significantly enhanced to improve performance, to improve space management, and to provide on-line archive, backup, and partial recovery.

Another data integrity problem can occur when multiple database users attempt to update the same records in the database concurrently. A user may overwrite another user's changes inadvertently, changing the data right out from under his nose. ORACLE Version 5 provides an automated locking facility to prevent users from interfering with each other's update or insert transactions. (A designer can explicitly control locking within the application, but this is seldom required except for tuning purposes.)

ORACLE Version 6 improves the locking scheme with true row-level locking. Row-level locking reduces the contention for data and indexes dramatically; a lock forces users to wait until the transaction is completed and the lock released. The higher the granularity of the lock (and it gets high at the page or table level), the greater the number of data and index rows being held; this increases the chance other users will be waiting to access rows being held by others. The more users waiting around, the less work being pushed through the system. The problem only gets worse as more concurrent users are added to the system, thus lowering *concurrency*. ORACLE's row-level locking model avoids this problem—it not only ensures data integrity through successful updates, but maximizes performance and system throughput.

Backup and Recovery

When a media failure occurs, such as a head crash that destroys data on the physical disk, your only recourse is to recover the data from a backup copy. How often should you back up your data? Obviously the answer to this question depends on how critical the data is to you. If your database changes frequently, back it up frequently. No business has ever been damaged by an overzealous backup policy. Routine, disciplined backup practices have bailed out more computerized businesses than one would hope to count.

ORACLE provides full backup and recovery in the EXPORT and IMPORT utilities. The EXPORT utility is used to back up data and database definitions for archiving or for restoration with the IMPORT utility. The EXPORT procedure is interrogative; it asks you a few simple questions, such as whether you wish to

choose Users, Tables, or Full Database Mode.
export GRANTS (resource privileges you've granted to other users)
export both rows and table definitions
compress data into a single extent on import to reduce fragmentation

The amount of information you can export depends on the export mode you choose to run—Users, Tables, or Full Database Mode. Most users can export only objects which they own. A DBA, however, can export or import tables or data belonging to any user. Table 10.2 summarizes what each export mode can and cannot do.

Table 10.2   Summary of Export Modes

Mode	User	Tables	Full DB
Will Export:	table definitions table data clusters indices first-level grants space definitions	table definitions table data space definitions	table definitions table data clusters indices grants views synonyms space definitions
Will *not* Export:	views synonyms	views synonyms grants indices clusters	SYS objects

Bulk Loading

The ORACLE RDBMS is a work-horse capable of managing very large databases with no more effort than managing a scattering of tables. But whether the database serves a single user with a small amount of data or multiple users with gigabytes of data, users need a tool that can load data—particularly large amounts of data—conveniently and economically into the database.

ORACLE's SQL*Loader facility moves data from a variety of external file formats into ORACLE tables. SQL*Loader is more versatile than the earlier loader product, the ORACLE Data Loader (ODL), and is intended to supersede it. SQL*Loader performs filtering, allowing you to selectively load records based on data values, and it can load multiple tables simultaneously. You have control over several loading options. You can

- handle fixed format, delimited format, and variable length records
- support a range of datatypes, including DATE, BINARY, and PACKED DECIMAL
- combine multiple physical records into a single logical record
- treat a single physical record as multiple logical records
- generate unique, sequential key values in specified columns
- load data from disk or tap

> ▸ provide thorough error handling so you can adjust and load all records

> ▸ use control files acceptable to IBM's DB2 Load Utility™, including those produced by IBM's Data Extract Utility (DXT™), which extracts from a variety of sources.

Security Administration

An ORACLE developer wearing the hat of the DBA must perform another important function for clients—setting up a secure database environment. In larger database environments, controlling database access is the dominion of the DBA, who often works in concert with the corporation's security administrator. Whether the ORACLE database is on a single-user PC, a mid-range VAX, or a large mainframe, chances are that several ORACLE users have access to the system. Access rights, the sharing of data, and data privacy must be closely guarded to protect the firm's critical asset—the corporate database.

Securing Database Objects

Via SQL*Menu, the security of your application forms and reports (called application *objects*) is controlled by user work class. Access to the SQL*Menu program itself is protected by usernames and password, which make up the underlying system that controls access to all other ORACLE tools. The same username/password scheme allows the ORACLE developer to control who can see data and who can change data at the database object level.

ORACLE organizes database users into a hierarchy based on user privileges:

1. The SYSTEM user who lords over the entire database environment. The SYSTEM user is the supreme DBA, hosting new users onto the system, granting one or more users DBA authority, and changing user passwords. The SYSTEM user can also alter the ORACLE database dictionary tables and views but would rarely need to do so.

2. Users with DBA authority who can set up new users and database privileges, terminate users, and access the ORACLE data dictionary.

3. Users with CONNECT and RESOURCE privileges who can log on to the database and are allowed to create new tables or indexes.

4. Users with CONNECT privilege only, who can access tables but cannot create any of their own tables.

Creating Users and Granting Privileges

When you first install ORACLE, the SYSTEM/MANAGER account (with full DBA authority) is automatically created. You should immediately change the default MANAGER password to ensure that no unauthorized user can impersonate the SYSTEM user and undermine the security controls you set up for the database environment.

As system designer and consultant to Video Quest, you are responsible for initially securing the database environment, but you will not be around forever. Video Quest is managed by the store owners, whose passwords are REXREED and GSISKEL, and who are directly responsible for the administration of the system. The Video Quest owners intend to use the SYSTEM account (and any others desired), but have authorized you to set up a DBA account for each of them for their private use. You will then grant the following privileges to the Video Quest personnel:

Store Owner	DBA privileges
Assistant Managers	RESOURCE and CONNECT privileges
Store Clerks	CONNECT only privileges

After logging on to ORACLE with the SYSTEM account, you might enter these GRANT commands to define the appropriate database privileges:

```
GRANT DBA to REXREED identified by opinionated
GRANT DBA to GSISKEL identified by argumentative
GRANT RESOURCE, CONNECT to SHUSTON identified by prolific
GRANT RESOURCE, CONNECT to GLUCAS identified by fantasy
GRANT CONNECT to BDIDDLY identified by fifties
GRANT CONNECT to BKEATON identified by glassyeye
GRANT CONNECT to CCHAPLIN identified by ibm
```

Only the store owners, REXREED or GSISKEL, have the authority to create user accounts or remove an account from the system. Suppose BKEATON leaves the company. The DBA would enter

```
REVOKE CONNECT FROM BKEATON
```

Whoever creates a table is the *owner* of the table; no one else can access this table unless authorized to do so by the owner. The owner controls who can see or change the data or table by issuing the GRANT command, selectively defining privileges with commands like this:

```
GRANT SELECT, INSERT, UPDATE, DELETE, ALTER, INDEX, CLUSTER
       or
       ALL (of the above privileges)
       ON table-or-view1 [,table-or-view2, table-or-view3 . . .]
       TO username1 ,username2
         or
       TO PUBLIC (all users on the system)
```

For example:

1. To allow all users, including store clerks, to query and modify the MASTER and TRANSACTION tables, enter

```
GRANT SELECT, INSERT, UPDATE, DELETE
    ON TITLE, PRODUCT, CUSTOMER, RENTALS, RETURNS
    TO PUBLIC
```

2. To allow Store Owners and Assistant Managers to have special resource privileges on the major Video Quest tables, enter

```
GRANT ALTER, INDEX, CLUSTER
    ON TITLE, PRODUCT, CUSTOMER, RENTALS, RETURNS
    TO REXREED, GSISKEL, SHUSTON, GLUCAS
```

3. To allow Store Owners and Assistant Managers to have ALL privileges on the restricted Code Maintenance tables, enter

```
GRANT ALL
    ON TAPE, CATEGORY, RENTCLASS, PAYMETHOD
    TO REXREED, GSISKEL, SHUSTON, GLUCAS
```

Having granted privileges on your tables to other users, you can also use REVOKE at any time.

When another user accesses a table you own, that user must reference the table explicitly by your ORACLE username. For example, if you had granted a store clerk privilege to query the TITLE you created, the clerk would have to construct the query like this:

```
SELECT *
  FROM ops$video.title
```

If the clerk does not reference the table by your username, ORACLE returns the confusing error message

```
#ORA-942: table or view does not exist
```

even though the clerk has been granted access privilege to it.

Typing in the full table name every time you want to query the table can be tedious. To save typing, you can create a synonym of the table name like this:

```
CREATE SYNONYM title1 FOR ops$video.title
```

and then query it by the synonym:

```
SELECT *
  FROM title1
```

You, as the application designer, will create a number of tables with the intention of allowing multiple users to access them via forms and reports. It would be silly to have users create their own synonyms for these commonly accessed tables. The appropriate solution is to create a unique public synonym for each table, allowing everyone to use that name. For example, to let all Video Quest personnel access the TITLE table via the TITLE form or a report, you would define

```
CREATE PUBLIC SYNONYM title for ops$video.title
```

Security through Views

While the GRANT command controls user access privileges on entire tables, a view can be used to control access to certain rows or columns of data in a table. You can build a view to extract only the parts of a table certain users may use, and then you can selectively grant privileges on that view. By creating views, you can thus ensure the privacy of sensitive information on a need-to-know basis.

Consider the classic example of access to employee salaries. A personnel application of our system contains an EMPLOYEE table with the columns *emp_id, name, deptno, job,* and *salary.* The firm's personnel department is responsible for maintaining employee records; however, selected information is available for the employees to browse. A feature of the application is to control access to salary information strictly on a need-to-know basis.

Security Problem 1
Allow everyone to see who's who in every department, but not their salaries.

Solution

Create a view that selects out every column except SALARY, then grant SELECT privileges to every employee (called PUBLIC). Enter

```
CREATE VIEW everyone
AS
SELECT emp_id, name, deptno, job
FROM employee

GRANT SELECT ON everyone TO PUBLIC
```

Security Problem 2

Allow department managers to see salary information on employees in their own departments, but not outside the department. Also, permit the department managers to update job and salary information.

Solution

Create a separate view for each department and restrict the department manager's update privilege to only the Job and Salary columns, not the entire view. Presumably, only the personnel manager has the proper authority to change other personnel information. Enter

```
CREATE VIEW sales_dept
AS
SELECT emp_id, name, deptno, job, salary
  FROM employee
 WHERE deptno = 'sales'

GRANT SELECT, UPDATE(job, salary)
   ON sales_dept
   TO sales_dept_manager
```

Security Problem 3

Permit an employee to view his or her own salary information, but no one else's.

Solution

Create a view that returns only the row of the EMPLOYEE table for the user currently logged on. You can create a single view to do this—not one for each user!—by enlisting the USER system variable, a SQL*Plus pseudo-column which returns the name of the current ORACLE log-on ID. To do this, enter

```
CREATE VIEW personal
AS
SELECT *
  FROM EMPLOYEE
 WHERE emp_id = USER

GRANT SELECT ON personal TO PUBLIC
```

For this technique to work, the company must follow a strict convention for creating log-on IDs. Each employee must use his or her unique employee ID as the ORACLE log-on ID as well. In highly secure environments this may not be advisable, because log-on IDs would be visible to anyone viewing the EMPLOYEE table.

The Security Audit Trail

ORACLE's sophisticated security audit facility is like a silent burglar alarm wired strategically throughout the database environment. ORACLE users who own tables can enable the audit facility to audit access attempts to their tables (and views and synonyms) and to monitor various SQL operations performed on the same objects. An ORACLE DBA can also use the audit trail facility to monitor DBA operations system-wide and examine log-on attempts to the database itself.

For example, suppose the DBA (or owner) wanted to audit access activities on the PRODUCT table. The DBA is interested in seeing both successful and unsuccessful attempts to modify the data or the table itself. The DBA would enter

```
AUDIT INSERT, UPDATE, DELETE, ALTER
   ON product
   BY ACCESS
```

The AUDIT parameter of the INIT.ORA file must also be switched on to enable auditing for the system.

To turn off the audit trail options on the PRODUCT table, you would use the NOAUDIT statement which mirrors the syntax of the AUDIT statement:

```
NOAUDIT INSERT, UPDATE, DELETE, ALTER
    ON product
    BY ACCESS
```

Different levels of auditing may be set for each database object, while the AUDIT statement specifies the operations to be audited. The syntax of the AUDIT statement is

```
AUDIT {<option> [,<option>] . . . ¦ ALL}
   ON { <table> ¦ DEFAULT }
  [BY {ACCESS ¦ SESSION }]
      [WHENEVER [NOT] SUCCESSFUL ]
```

The AUDIT table options include ALTER, AUDIT, COMMENT, DELETE, GRANT, INDEX, INSERT, LOCK, RENAME, SELECT, and UPDATE.

You can further qualify which records should be written out to the AUDIT_TRAIL table by including either the WHENEVER SUCCESSFUL or the WHENEVER NOT SUCCESSFUL clause. The former logs the audited operation only when it successfully completes, and the latter only when the operation does not successfully complete.

System Auditing

ORACLE DBAs have several other options at their disposal to enlarge the scope of their audit activities. The DBA-only options monitor activities across the entire database system and include such options as these:

CONNECT	monitors ORACLE log-on attempts
DBA	monitors system-wide GRANT, REVOKE, AUDIT, and NOAUDIT statements; CREATE/ALTER PARTITION, CREATE/DROP PUBLIC SYNONYM statements.
NOT EXISTS	references objects which result in ". . . does not exist" errors (except security violation errors such as ORA-942 table or view does not exist).
RESOURCE	provides CREATE/DROP TABLE, VIEW, SPACE, SYNONYM statements; CREATE/ALTER/DROP CLUSTER statements.

Documenting Your System

Though you are intimately familiar with the Video Quest application by now, the profusion of tables, views, columns, and indexes may be getting confusing to you. You have now defined 13 base tables and 4 views which collectively maintain data in 124 different columns and over 20 indexes.

Tracking this many database objects manually would be difficult, if not impossible.

The Video Quest application is small by most standards. Business applications supporting over 50 tables and views with hundreds of columns are common in production environments. If the Video Quest system were to get much bigger, you would be in a real pickle without an automated tool like the ORACLE data dictionary to organize and catalog the database objects for you.

The ORACLE Data Dictionary

The ORACLE data dictionary consists of roughly 50 system tables and views (this number varies between ORACLE versions and environments) that record detailed information about the database—the names of database objects, storage allocation parameters, and user profile information. The dictionary is an active data dictionary, available whenever the database is up and running. When a table is created, an index dropped, a column modified, a new space allocated, a table cluster created, or a new user added, the ORACLE dictionary knows about it, and records all changes automatically in realtime.

One keen advantage of ORACLE's dictionary is that objects are stored in tabular form which can be easily queried with SQL. You can manipulate dictionary data as you would any other data stored in ORACLE tables to produce detailed tabular reports, providing useful system documentation on your database application. The dictionary tables you will use most frequently for this purpose include

TAB	lists the tables, views, and clusters which you (the current ORACLE user) have created.
CATALOG	lists the tables, views, and clusters accessible to you (including objects you own and those to which you've been granted access.)
COLUMNS	lists the column definitions of the tables and views accessible to you.
INDEXES	lists the index definitions on the tables you have created.

The TAB and COLUMNS Tables

If you were to issue a simple query against the TAB (for Table) dictionary table, such as

```
SELECT *
  FROM tab
```

you would see all the tables, views, and clusters you have created for the
Video Quest database:

```
TNAME        TABTYPE   CLUSTERID
---------    -------   ---------
CATEGORY     TABLE
CNTL         TABLE
CUSTNAME     TABLE              1
CUSTOMER     TABLE              2
INVOICE      TABLE
PAYMETHOD    TABLE
```

The CATALOG table is similar to the TAB table but more robust. A look
inside this table reveals the following column definitions:

```
DESCRIBE CATALOG

Name       Null?      Type
--------   --------   ---------
TNAME      NOT NULL   CHAR(30)
CREATOR               CHAR(30)
TABLETYPE  NOT NULL   CHAR(7)
CLUSTERID             NUMBER
LOGBLK                NUMBER
REQBLK                NUMBER
IXCOMP                CHAR(10)
REMARKS               CHAR(240)
```

While interesting, some of the information in the CATALOG table is
not critical for generating system documentation. One feature that is particularly useful, however, is the ability to store comments about your tables
in the CATALOG dictionary table. If you have inserted comments about
your tables beforehand, you can generate a simple report organized by
TABLE or VIEW, that describes the objects as shown in Figure 10.12.

Comments about tables and columns can be stored with the SQL*Plus
COMMENT command. Table comments are stored in the CATALOG table,
whereas column comments are stored in the COLUMNS data dictionary
table, which we will examine momentarily. With a little advance preparation, you can thus create a more complete report of the internal workings
of your application.

```
Tue Jun  7                                                                page   1
                              Video Quest System Documentation
                                      List of Tables

Object  Table/View Name  Comments
------  ---------------  ------------------------------------------------------------------
TABLE   CATEGORY         Code Info        Tracks codes to identify film categories.

        CNTL             Control Info     Tracks Video Quest control information, including distributed store number,
                                          sales tax percentages, etc.

        CUSTNAME         Master Info      Tracks authorized members and viewing restrictions for this membership.

        CUSTOMER         Master Info      Tracks primary members by Id.  Stores vital statistics, mailing address and
                                          credit card info.

        INVOICE          Transaction Info Tracks payment received from rentals, sales and returns transactions.

        PAYMETHOD        Codes Info       Tracks validation codes for various payment methods accepted by the store.

        PRODUCT          Master Info      Product information, including product types, descriptions, prices and inventory
                                          positions.

        RENTALS          Transaction Info Tracks rental transaction information.

        RENTCLASS        Code Info        Tracks validation codes for rental classes.  Includes daily rental rates.

        RETURNS          Transaction Info Tracks returns transactions.  Used to update RENTALS.

        SYNOPSIS         Master Info      Tracks synopsis of the title.

        TAPE             Code Info        Catalog number associated with each product.

        TITLE            Master Info      Tracks title information.

VIEW    INVENTORY

        PRODUCTS_RENTED

        QTY_RENTED

        YR_RENTALS


                                          Have A Good Day!
                                          VDODOC.SQL
17 records selected.
```

Figure 10.12   The Video Quest Tables Report

To store the comment about the CATEGORY table shown above, you would enter

```
COMMENT ON TABLE category IS
'Code Table. Tracks Codes to identify film categories.'
```

To store a comment about any column in the CATEGORY table, you would enter

```
COMMENT ON COLUMN category.description IS
'Description of the category code, e.g., 100 = Adventure,
110 = Children'
```

The COLUMNS Table

The COLUMNS table breaks your tables and views down into more detail, listing column definitions and comments, if created. The COLUMNS table stores the following information:

```
DESCRIBE COLUMNS

Name            Null?        Type
----------      ---------    ----------
CNAME           NOT NULL     CHAR(30)
TNAME           NOT NULL     CHAR(30)
CREATOR                      CHAR(30)
COLNO           NOT NULL     NUMBER
COLTYPE         NOT NULL     CHAR(6)
WIDTH           NOT NULL     NUMBER
SCALE                        NUMBER
NULLS           NOT NULL     CHAR(8)
REMARKS                      CHAR(240)
DEFAULTVAL                   CHAR(240)
```

A simple join of the CATALOG and COLUMNS tables (joined on the *tname* column) might generate documentation describing the 124+ columns in the Video Quest database. A snapshot of this report is shown in Figure 10.13.

The COL # column records the column position, or the order in which the columns were defined. Also, don't be alarmed to see the width of certain number columns as 0—the default width of these columns is 22 bytes, which stores a number that can occupy 44 character positions when formatted. If you create number columns without specifying a width, SQL*Plus simply assigns a 0 value to them for convenience. The SCALE function refers to the decimal positions you defined for some numeric columns.

The INDEXES Table

The INDEXES dictionary table stores information about all indexes created on the tables you own. This includes entries for the indexes created by other users to whom you have granted access and RESOURCE privileges. An index listing is invaluable, especially while you are in the heat of battle performance tuning your application, creating and recreating index paths right and left. An example of this report is shown in Figure 10.14.

```
Tue Jun  7                                                                      page    1
                                   Video Quest System Documentation
                                   Table and View Column Definitions

Object   Table/View Name   Col #  Column          Datatype     Nulls?     Comments
------   ---------------   -----  ------          --------     ------     --------
TABLE    CATEGORY            1    Category        NUMBER(0)    NOT NULL   Category Code to identify categories. e.g.,
                                                                         100 = Adventure, 110 = Children, ...
                            2    Description      CHAR(20)     NULL       Description of the category. e.g.
              .                   .                             .
         CUSTNAME            1    Memberid        NUMBER(0)    NOT NULL   Member id to identify customer. Established
                                                                         when customer was created.
                            2    Name            CHAR(30)     NULL       Name of other authorized users allowed to use
                                                                         this membership.

                            3    Restrict_Cat    NUMBER(0)    NULL       Category of tapes which are restricted for
                                                                         each authorized user. Validated during rental

         CUSTOMER            1    Memberid        NUMBER(0)    NULL       Memberid to identify customer.  A sequential
                                                                         number generated by the system on insert.

                            2    Name            CHAR(30)     NULL       Name of primary member.
                            3    Ad1             CHAR(30)     NULL       Street address of customer.
                            4    Ad2             CHAR(30)     NULL       Additional line for address for customer.
                            5    City            CHAR(30)     NULL       City of address for customer.
                            6    State           CHAR(2)      NULL       State of address for customer.
                            7    Zip             CHAR(10)     NULL       Zip code of address for customer.
                            8    Day_Area        CHAR(3)      NULL       Area code of phone number to contact customer
                                                                         during the day.
                            9    Day_Prefix      CHAR(3)      NULL       Prefix of customer's daytime phone number.
                           10    Day_Suffix      CHAR(4)      NULL       Last four digits of daytime phone number.
                           11    Eve_Area        CHAR(3)      NULL       Area code of customer's evening phone number.
                           12    Eve_Prefix      CHAR(3)      NULL       Prefixe of customer's evening phone number.
                           13    Eve_Suffix      CHAR(4)      NULL       Last four digits of evening phone number.
                           14    Creditcard      CHAR(2)      NULL       Type of credit card, e.g., AX, MC, VI...
                           15    Credcdno        CHAR(20)     NULL       Credit card number.
                           16    Cardexp         DATE(7)      NULL       Date credit card expires. e.g. DD-MON)YY
                           17    Cdlno           CHAR(10)     NULL       Drivers license number for customer.
                           18    Cdlexp          DATE(7)      NULL       Expiration date on customers drivers licence.
                           19    Date_Created    DATE(7)      NULL       Date when member was created. Defaults to
                                                                         current date. DD-MON-YY
                           20    Last_Act        DATE(7)      NULL       Date of last activity.  Updated by rentals,
                                                                         sales,reservations transactions. DD-MON-YY
                           21    Format          CHAR(2)      NULL       Default format of customer's VCR.
              .                   .                             .          .
              .                   .                             .          .
              .                   .                             .          .

                                           Have A Good Day!
                                           VDODOC.SQL

124 records selected.
```

Figure 10.13   The Video Quest CATALOG/COLUMNS Join Report

Video Quest Documentation Procedure

The report examples on the preceding pages were generated with the 3-part procedure, VDODOC.SQL, derived from the CATALOG, COLUMNS, and INDEXES data dictionary tables (see Listing 10.1). The complete report output generated by this procedure appears in Appendix A, *Video Quest System Documentation*.

```
Tue Jun  7                                                                                    page    1
                                    Video Quest System Documentation
                                          Index Definitions

Table                                        Concat
Name              Index        Columns         Id    Unique?     Compress?
------------      ------------ -------------  ------  ----------  ------------
.                 .            .
CUSTOMER          CUSTOMER1    Ad1             1      Non Unique  Compress
                               City            1      Non Unique  Compress
                               Name            1      Non Unique  Compress
                               State           1      Non Unique  Compress

                  CUSTOMER2    Day_Area        2      Unique      Compress
                               Day_Prefix      2      Unique      Compress
                               Day_Suffix      2      Unique      Compress
.                 .            .
PRODUCT           PRODUCT0     Prodno          5      Unique      Nocompress
                               Storeno         5      Unique      Nocompress

                  PRODUCT1     Prodno          6      Non Unique  Nocompress
                               Storeno         6      Non Unique  Nocompress
                               Titlecd         6      Non Unique  Nocompress
.                 .            .
RENTALS           RENTALS0     Catnum          1      Unique      Compress
                               Dateout         1      Unique      Compress
                               Memberid        1      Unique      Compress
.                 .            .
TITLE             TITLE0       Titlecd                Unique      Compress

                  TITLE1       Category               Non Unique  Compress

                  TITLE2       Category        1      Non Unique  Nocompress
                               Titlecd         1      Non Unique  Nocompress

                  TITLE3       Actors          2      Non Unique  Nocompress
                               Directors       2      Non Unique  Nocompress

                  TITLE4       Actors          3      Non Unique  Compress
                               Awards          3      Non Unique  Compress
                               Starrtg         3      Non Unique  Compress
.                 .            .               .      .           .
.                 .            .               .      .           .

                                          Have A Good Day!
                                            VDODOC.SQL
49 records selected.
```

Figure 10.14   The Video Quest INDEXES Report

Listing 10.1   Video Quest System Documentation Procedure

```
rem * VDODOC.SQL
rem *
rem * Procedure to document the tables, columns and index
rem * definitions for the Video Quest Application
CLEAR BUFFER
CLEAR BREAKS
rem * Start Tables & View Listing'
SET NEWPAGE 0
SET LINESIZE 132
SET PAGESIZE 54
SET SPACE 2
SET TERM OFF
SET ECHO OFF
```

```
TTITLE 'Video Quest System Documentation¦List of Tables &
Views'
BTITLE 'Have A Good Day!¦VDODOC.SQL'
COLUMN tabletype HEADING 'Object' FORMAT a6
COLUMN tname HEADING 'Table/View Name'FORMAT a15
COLUMN remarks HEADING 'Comments' FORMAT a100 wrap
SPOOL vdodoc.lis
BREAK ON tabletype nodup skip 2 ON tname SKIP 1 ON cname
SKIP1
SELECT tabletype, tname, remarks
  FROM catalog
 ORDER BY tabletype, tname
/
rem * Start Table & View Columns Report
CLEAR BUFFER
TTITLE 'Video Quest System Documentation¦Table and View
Column Definitions'
SET SPACE 2
COLUMN tabletype        HEADING 'Object'        FORMAT a6
COLUMN tname            HEADING 'Table/View Name'  FORMAT
a15
COLUMN colno            HEADING 'Col #'FORMAT 99
COLUMN initcap(cname)   HEADING 'Column'        FORMAT a20
COLUMN ctype            HEADING 'Datatype'      FORMAT a10
COLUMN nulls            HEADING 'Nulls?'        FORMAT a8
COLUMN scale            HEADING 'Scale'         FORMAT 99
COLUMN remarks          HEADING 'Comments'      FORMAT a45
wrap
SELECT catalog.tabletype, catalog.tname, colno, init-
cap(cname),
        coltype¦¦'('¦¦WIDTH¦¦')' ctype, nulls, scale,
columns.remarks
  FROM catalog, columns
 WHERE catalog.tname                      columns.tname
 ORDER BY catalog.tabletype, catalog.tname, colno
/
rem * Start Index Definitions Report
CLEAR BUFFER
CLEAR BREAKS
TTITLE 'Video Quest System Documentation¦Index Defini-
tions'
COLUMN tname                    HEADING 'Table¦Name'    FORMAT
a12
```

continued

411

```
COLUMN iname                 HEADING 'Index' FORMAT a12
COLUMN initcap(colnames)     HEADING 'Columns'    FORMAT a15
COLUMN concatid HEADING 'Concat!Id'   FORMAT 99
COLUMN initcap(indextype)    HEADING 'Unique?'    FORMAT a10
COLUMN initcap(compression) HEADING 'Compress?'   FORMAT a12
SET SPACE 4
BREAK ON tname SKIP 2 NODUP ON iname SKIP 1 nodup
SELECT tname, iname, initcap(colnames), concatid,
    initcap(indextype), initcap(compression)
    FROM indexes
    ORDER BY tname, iname, initcap(colnames)
/
SPOOL OFF
TTITLE OFF
BTITLE OFF
CLEAR BUFFER
CLEAR BREAKS
rem * End Video Quest System Documentation Procedure
```

Summary

A separate treatise would be required to adequately cover the more advanced features and concepts of ORACLE's RDBMS and application development tools. This chapter merely scratched the surface, highlighting strategies for

- ▶ Application performance tuning via

    Indexes

    Query optimization

    Table clustering

    Denormalization

- ▶ SQL*Forms optimization
- ▶ Controlling disk space allocation
- ▶ Securing the database environment
- ▶ Documenting your application with the ORACLE Data Dictionary.

Afterword

Indeed you have traveled far and accomplished a lot in this book. You have toured inside ORACLE and its fourth-generation environment tools. You have scrutinized ORACLE's SQL database language and have learned how to build both simple and complex queries to solve specific problems. You now have the satisfaction of having completed a real-world business application from the ground up with database technology.

The application development process has been both creative and practical. Your application ultimately accommodated the information management needs of a typical business, while allowing room for business expansion and evolving information needs. You've had to weigh several design choices in order to fulfill the functionality and user interface requirements of myriad computer users. It's time for you to relax now and synthesize what you have learned. Take a moment or two or three. You've earned it.

Appendixes

Video Quest System Documentation

This appendix lists the database tables, views, columns, and indexes created for the sample Video Quest database. The listing was generated by the documentation procedure, VDODOC.SQL, defined in Chapter 10 in the section *Documenting Your System*.

Mastering ORACLE

```
Tue Jun  7                                                                                    page    1
                                      Video Quest System Documentation
                                             List of Tables

Object   Table/View Name  Comments
+-----    -------------    -------------------------------------------------------------------------------
TABLE    CATEGORY         Code Info          Tracks codes to identify film categories.

         CNTL             Control Info       Tracks Video Quest control information, including distributed store number,
                                             sales tax percentages, etc.
         CUSTNAME         Master Info        Tracks authorized members and viewing restrictions for this membership.

         CUSTOMER         Master Info        Tracks primary members by Id.  Stores vital statistics, mailing address  and
                                             credit card info.
         INVOICE          Transaction Info   Tracks payment received from rentals, sales and returns transactions.

         PAYMETHOD        Codes Info         Tracks validation codes for various payment methods accepted by the store.

         PRODUCT          Master Info        Product information, including product types, descriptions, prices and inventory
                                             positions.

         RENTALS          Transaction Info   Tracks rental transaction information.

         RENTCLASS        Code Info          Tracks validation codes for rental classes.  Includes daily rental rates.

         RETURNS          Transaction Info   Tracks returns transactions.  Used to update RENTALS.

         SYNOPSIS         Master Info        Tracks synopsis of the title.

         TAPE             Code Info          Catalog number associated with each product.

         TITLE            Master Info        Tracks title information.

VIEW     INVENTORY

         PRODUCTS_RENTED

         QTY_RENTED

         YR_RENTALS




                                             Have A Good Day!
                                             VDODOC.SQL
17 records selected.
```

List of Tables

418

```
Tue Jun  7                                                              page    1

                       Table and View Column Definitions

Object  Table/View Name  Col #  Column               Datatype    Nulls?    Comments
------  ---------------  -----  --------------------  ----------  --------  ---------------------------------------------
TABLE   CATEGORY           1    Category              NUMBER(0)   NOT NULL  Category Code to identify categories. e.g. 10
                                                                           0 = Adventure, 110 = Children, ...

                           2    Description           CHAR(20)    NULL      Description of the category. e.g. 100 = Adventure,
                                                                           110 = Children, ...


        CNTL               1    Storeno               NUMBER(0)   NULL      Store number to identify store at a specific
                                                                           location. Used for validation.

                           2    Last_Invoice          NUMBER(0)   NULL      Last assigned sequential number for invoice.
                                                                           System controlled.

                           3    Last_Memberid         NUMBER(0)   NULL      Last assigned sequential number for member id.
                                                                           System controlled.

                           4    Slstaxpct             NUMBER(0)   NULL      Sales tax percentage. e.g. 6.5

                           5    Latechgpct            NUMBER(0)   NULL      Late charge percentage. e.g. 1.5

                           6    Maxrent               NUMBER(0)   NULL      Maximum rental limit at store. e.g. 5


        CUSTNAME           1    Memberid              NUMBER(0)   NOT NULL  Member id to identify customer. Established
                                                                           when customer was created.

                           2    Name                  CHAR(30)    NULL      Name of other authorized users allowed to use
                                                                           this membership.

                           3    Restrict_Cat          NUMBER(0)   NULL      Category of tapes which are restricted for each
                                                                           authorized user. Validated during rental transaction.

        CUSTOMER           1    Memberid              NUMBER(0)   NULL      Member id to identify customer. A sequential
                                                                           number generated by the system on insert. Used
                           2    Name                  CHAR(30)    NULL      Name of authorized user who owns this members
                                                                           hip.
                           3    Ad1                   CHAR(30)    NULL      Street address of customer.

                           4    Ad2                   CHAR(30)    NULL      Additional line for address for customer.
                           5    City                  CHAR(30)    NULL      City of address for customer.
                           6    State                 CHAR(2)     NULL      State of address for customer.
                           7    Zip                   CHAR(10)    NULL      Zip code of address for customer.
                           8    Day_Area              CHAR(3)     NULL      Area code of phone number to contact customer
                                                                           during the day.




                                    Have A Good Day!
                                      VDODOC.SQL
```

Table and View Column Definitions, page 1

Mastering ORACLE

Video Quest System Documentation
Table and View Column Definitions

Object	Table/View Name	Col #	Column	Datatype	Nulls?	Comments
TABLE	CUSTOMER	9	Day_Prefix	CHAR(3)	NULL	The three digits after area code of phone number to contact customer during the day.
		10	Day_Suffix	CHAR(4)	NULL	Last four digits of phone number to contact customer during the day.
		11	Eve_Area	CHAR(3)	NULL	Area code of phone number to contact customer in the evening.
		12	Eve_Prefix	CHAR(3)	NULL	The three digits after area code of phone number to contact customer in the evening.
		13	Eve_Suffix	CHAR(4)	NULL	Last four digits of phone number to contact customer in the evening.
		14	Creditcard	CHAR(2)	NULL	Credit card type of customer. e.g. AX, MC, VI ...
		15	Credcdno	CHAR(20)	NULL	Credit card number.
		16	Cardexp	DATE(7)	NULL	Date on which credit card expires. e.g. DD-MON-YY
		17	Cdlno	CHAR(10)	NULL	Drivers license number for customer.
		18	Cdlexp	DATE(7)	NULL	Expiration date on customers drivers licence.
		19	Date_Created	DATE(7)	NULL	Date when member was created. Default to current date. DD-MON-YY
		20	Last_Act	DATE(7)	NULL	Date of last activity. Updated by transactions. DD-MON-YY
		21	Format	CHAR(2)	NULL	Default tape format for tape rental. e.g. V = VHS, B= BETA.
	INVOICE	1	Invno	NUMBER(0)	NOT NULL	Invoice number to identify transaction. Sequential number generated by the system.
		2	Memberid	NUMBER(0)	NOT NULL	Member id to identify customer. Validated with CUSTOMER table. Optional for sales transaction.
		3	Paymethod	CHAR(2)	NULL	Method of payment. Validated with PAYMETHOD table. e.g. CAsh, AX, MC, VI.
		4	Trantype	CHAR(1)	NOT NULL	Transaction type. S = Sales. R = Rentals. L = Latecharge.

Have A Good Day!
VDODOC.SQL

Table and View Column Definitions, page 2

```
Tue Jun  7                                                                         page     3
                               Video Quest System Documentation
                               Table and View Column Definitions

Object   Table/View Name   Col #   Column                Datatype     Nulls?     Comments
------   ---------------   -----   --------------------  ----------   --------   ------------------------------------------

TABLE    INVOICE             5     Trandate              DATE(7)      NOT NULL   Date when rental or sales transaction happene
                                                                                 d. DD-MON-YY. Default to current date.

                             6     Trantime              CHAR(8)      NOT NULL   Time when rental or sales transaction happene
                                                                                 d. e.g. 09:35 am. Set by system.

                             7     Total                 NUMBER(0)    NULL       Actual amount received from customer. Amount
                                                                                 includes gross sales plus tax.

                             8     Tax                   NUMBER(0)    NULL       Total amount of tax for this transaction.


         PAYMETHOD           1     Paymethod             CHAR(2)      NULL       Code to identify credit card or cash payment.
                                                                                 e.g. VI, MC, CA.

                             2     Description           CHAR(20)     NULL       Description of payment method. e.g. VISA, Mas
                                                                                 terCard, Cash.


         PRODUCT             1     Prodno                CHAR(25)     NOT NULL   Product number to identify a particular title
                                                                                 Used for validation.

                             2     Storeno               NUMBER(0)    NOT NULL   Store number to identify store at a specific
                                                                                 location.

                             3     Description           CHAR(30)     NULL       Description of product.
                             4     Titlecd               CHAR(15)     NULL       Title code to identify title of tape. Validat
                                                                                 ed with TITLE table.

                             5     Format                CHAR(1)      NULL       Format type of the tape. B = BETA. V = VHS. N
                                                                                 = None.

                             6     Prodtype              CHAR(2)      NULL       Product code. R = Rental. S = For sale. RS =
                                                                                 Both Rent/Sale.

                             7     Rentclass             NUMBER(0)    NULL       Rental class code to identify rental rate per
                                                                                 day. Validated with RCLASS table.

                             8     Cost                  NUMBER(10)   NULL       Cost price of product.
                             9     Suggrtl               NUMBER(10)   NULL       Suggested retail price of product.
                            10     Sellrtl               NUMBER(10)   NULL       Selling price of product.
                            11     Qtyrecvd              NUMBER(0)    NULL
                            12     Qtyoh                 NUMBER(0)    NULL       Quantity on hand.
                            13     Qtysold               NUMBER(0)    NULL
                            14     Qtyord                NUMBER(0)    NULL       Product quantity on order to date.
                            15     Qtyrsv                NUMBER(0)    NULL       Quantity reserved to be shipped.

                                   Have A Good Day!
                                      VDODOC.SQL
```

Table and View Column Definitions, page 3

```
Tue Jun  7                                                                    page    4
                                Video Quest System Documentation
                                Table and View Column Definitions


Object   Table/View Name   Col #   Column                Datatype     Nulls?    Comments
------   ---------------   -----   --------------------  ----------   --------  --------------------------------------------

TABLE    RENTALS           1       Memberid              NUMBER(0)    NOT NULL  Member id to identify customer. Validated wit
                                                                                h CUSTOMER table.

                           2       Catnum                NUMBER(0)    NOT NULL
                           3       Dateout               DATE(7)      NULL      Date when tape was rented out. DD-MON-YY
                           4       Rentdays              NUMBER(0)    NULL      The number of days of the rental period.
                           5       Schdrtn               DATE(7)      NULL      Date when tape is scheduled to return. DD-MON
                                                                                -YY

                           6       Actrtn                DATE(7)      NULL      Date when tape was actually returned. DD-MON-
                                                                                YY.

                           7       Ratepdy               NUMBER(10)   NULL      Rental rate per day.
                           8       Invno                 NUMBER(0)    NULL      Invoice number associated with the receipt of
                                                                                this rental transaction. System generated.


         RENTCLASS         1       Rentclass             NUMBER(0)    NOT NULL  Rental class code to identify various rental
                                                                                rates. Used for validation.

                           2       Ratepdy               NUMBER(0)    NULL      Rental rate per day for a specific rental cla
                                                                                ss.

                           3       Description           CHAR(20)     NULL      Rental class description.

         RETURNS           1       Memberid              NUMBER(0)    NOT NULL  Member id to identify member who rented the t
                                                                                ape.

                           2       Catnum                NUMBER(0)    NOT NULL
                           3       Actrtn                DATE(7)      NULL      Actual return date. Default to current date.
                           4       Latecharge            NUMBER(0)    NULL      Latecharge computed, based on due date and ac
                                                                                tual return date.


         SYNOPSIS          1       Titlecd               CHAR(15)     NOT NULL  Title code to identify title. Validated with
                                                                                TITLE table.

                           2       Lineno                NUMBER(0)    NOT NULL  System generated number to track line number
                                                                                as text is input.

                           3       Title                 CHAR(78)     NULL


         TAPE              1       Catnum                NUMBER(0)    NOT NULL
                           2       Prodno                CHAR(25)     NOT NULL  Product number to identify product. Validated
                                                                                with PRODUCT table.


                                        Have A Good Day!
                                          VDODOC.SQL
```

Table and View Column Definitions, page 4

```
Tue Jun  7                                                                    page    5
                              Video Quest System Documentation
                              Table and View Column Definitions


Object  Table/View Name  Col #  Column               Datatype    Nulls?    Comments
------  ---------------  -----  --------------------  ----------  --------  ----------------------------------------------

TABLE   TAPE               3    Storeno              NUMBER(0)   NOT NULL  Store number to identify store at a specific
                                                                           location. Validated with CNTL table.


        TITLE              1    Titlecd              CHAR(15)    NOT NULL  Title code to identify title. Used for valida
                                                                           tion.
                           2    Title                CHAR(78)    NULL
                           3    Category             CHAR(3)     NULL      Category of this title. e.g. 100 = adventure,
                                                                           110 = children ...
                           4    Directors            CHAR(78)    NULL      Names of directors for this title.
                           5    Producers            CHAR(78)    NULL      Names of names of producers for this title.
                           6    Screenplay           CHAR(78)    NULL      Names of screenplay writers for this title.
                           7    Actors               CHAR(78)    NULL      Names of actors and actresses for this title.
                           8    Awards               CHAR(78)    NULL      List of awards for this title, if any.
                           9    Release              CHAR(4)     NULL      Year when title was released. YYYY
                          10    Runtime              CHAR(10)    NULL      Total run time of this tape. e.g. 120 mins.
                          11    Censorrtg            CHAR(7)     NULL      Censor rating of this title. e.g. G, PG, PG-1
                                                                           3, R, ...
                          12    Starrtg              CHAR(5)     NULL      Star rating of this title. e.g *, **, ...
                          13    Studio               CHAR(15)    NULL      The studio which released this title. e.g. Pa
                                                                           ramount
                          14    Color_Bw             CHAR(15)    NULL      Described if film is in color or black and white.

VIEW    INVENTORY          1    Prodno               CHAR(25)    NULL
                           2    Description          CHAR(30)    NULL
                           3    Title                CHAR(78)    NULL
                           4    Cost                 NUMBER(10)  NULL
                           5    Qtyrecvd             NUMBER(0)   NULL
                           6    Qtyoh                NUMBER(0)   NULL
                           7    Qtysold              NUMBER(0)   NULL
                           8    Qty_Rented           NUMBER(0)   NULL
                           9    Total                NUMBER(0)   NULL
                          10    Variance             NUMBER(0)   NULL

        PRODUCTS_RENTED    1    Memberid             NUMBER(0)   NULL
                           2    Catnum               NUMBER(0)   NULL
                           3    Prodno               CHAR(25)    NULL




                                        Have A Good Day!
                                          VDODOC.SQL
```

Table and View Column Definitions, page 5

```
Tue Jun  7                                                                    page    6

                               Video Quest System Documentation
                               Table and View Column Definitions


Object  Table/View Name  Col #  Column                Datatype    Nulls?    Comments
------  ---------------  -----  --------------------  ----------  --------  -------------------------------------------
VIEW    PRODUCTS_RENTED    4    Dateout               DATE(7)     NULL
                           5    Schdrtn               DATE(7)     NULL


        QTY_RENTED         1    Prodno                CHAR(25)    NULL
                           2    Qty_Rented            NUMBER(0)   NULL


        YR_RENTALS         1    Titlecd               CHAR(15)    NULL
                           2    Format                CHAR(1)     NULL
                           3    Jan                   NUMBER(0)   NULL
                           4    Feb                   NUMBER(0)   NULL
                           5    Mar                   NUMBER(0)   NULL
                           6    Apr                   NUMBER(0)   NULL
                           7    May                   NUMBER(0)   NULL
                           8    Jun                   NUMBER(0)   NULL
                           9    Jul                   NUMBER(0)   NULL
                          10    Aug                   NUMBER(0)   NULL
                          11    Sep                   NUMBER(0)   NULL
                          12    Oct                   NUMBER(0)   NULL
                          13    Nov                   NUMBER(0)   NULL
                          14    Dec                   NUMBER(0)   NULL
                          15    Ttlqty                NUMBER(0)   NULL

























                                        Have A Good Day!
                                         VDODOC.SQL

124 records selected.
```

Table and View Column Definitions, page 6

```
Tue Jun  7                                                                page   1
                              Video Quest System Documentation
                                    Index Definitions

Table                              Concat
Name          Index      Columns       Id    Unique?       Compress?
------------  ---------- --------------- ------  ----------  -----------
CATEGORY      CATEGORY0  Category             Unique       Compress



CUSTOMER      CUSTOMER1  Ad1            1     Non Unique   Compress
                         City           1     Non Unique   Compress
                         Name           1     Non Unique   Compress
                         State          1     Non Unique   Compress

              CUSTOMER2  Day_Area       2     Unique       Compress
                         Day_Prefix     2     Unique       Compress
                         Day_Suffix     2     Unique       Compress




INVOICE       INVOICE0   Invno          1     Unique       Compress
                         Memberid       1     Unique       Compress



PRODUCT       PRODUCT0   Prodno         5     Unique       Nocompress
                         Storeno        5     Unique       Nocompress

              PRODUCT1   Prodno         6     Non Unique   Nocompress
                         Storeno        6     Non Unique   Nocompress
                         Titlecd        6     Non Unique   Nocompress

              PRODUCT2   Rentclass      3     Non Unique   Compress
                         Titlecd        3     Non Unique   Compress

              PRODUCT3   Format         4     Non Unique   Compress
                         Rentclass      4     Non Unique   Compress

RENTALS       RENTALS0   Catnum         1     Unique       Compress
                         Dateout        1     Unique       Compress
                         Memberid       1     Unique       Compress

RENTCLASS     RENTCLASS0 Rentclass            Unique       Compress




                              Have A Good Day!
                                 VDODOC.SQL
```

Index Definitions, page 1

```
Tue Jun  7                                                                   page    2
                               Video Quest System Documentation
                                      Index Definitions

Table                            Concat
Name            Index    Columns      Id   Unique?       Compress?
------------    ------------ ---------------- ------   ----------    ------------
RETURNS         RETURNS0     Actrtn        1   Unique        Compress
                             Catnum        1   Unique        Compress
                             Memberid      1   Unique        Compress


SYNOPSIS        SYNOPSIS0    Lineno        1   Unique        Compress
                             Titlecd       1   Unique        Compress


TAPE            TAPE0        Catnum        1   Unique        Nocompress
                             Storeno       1   Unique        Nocompress

                TAPE1        Catnum        2   Non Unique    Compress
                             Prodno        2   Non Unique    Compress
                             Storeno       2   Non Unique    Compress


TITLE           TITLE0       Titlecd           Unique        Compress

                TITLE1       Category          Non Unique    Compress

                TITLE2       Category      1   Non Unique    Nocompress
                             Titlecd       1   Non Unique    Nocompress

                TITLE3       Actors        2   Non Unique    Nocompress
                             Directors     2   Non Unique    Nocompress

                TITLE4       Actors        3   Non Unique    Compress
                             Awards        3   Non Unique    Compress
                             Starrtg       3   Non Unique    Compress

                TITLE5       Awards        4   Non Unique    Compress
                             Directors     4   Non Unique    Compress
                             Starrtg       4   Non Unique    Compress

                TITLE6       Runtime       5   Non Unique    Nocompress
                             Starrtg       5   Non Unique    Nocompress

                TITLE7       Release       6   Non Unique    Nocompress
                             Studio        6   Non Unique    Nocompress

                                     Have A Good Day!
                                        VDODOC.SQL
49 records selected.
```

Index Definitions, page 2

B

Program Listings for Video Quest Forms

This appendix presents the program listings for the SQL*Forms sample application used throughout this book. These program files list the .INP files for the following Video Quest forms, complete with field definitions, default validations, and triggers:

- ▶ TITLE form
- ▶ PRODUCT form
- ▶ CUSTOMER form
- ▶ RENTALS form
- ▶ RETURNS form
- ▶ OUTRENT form

OUTRENT is a query-only form called from either the RENTALS or RETURNS transaction forms. Details on defining the macros to call OUT-RENT are found in Chapter 7 in the section *Building the RENTALS Form*.

Program listings for the CODE Maintenance forms—CATEGORY, RENTAL_CLASS, PAYMETHOD, and CATALOG—are not included. These forms are simply generated with the SQL*Forms DEFAULT form facility.

Listing B.1   The TITLE Form

```
; Generated by SQL*Forms Version 2.0.18 on Sat Jun 11 11:57:48 1988
; Application owner is OPS$DCRONIN. Application name is title
; (Application ID is 0)
; --------------------------------------------------
;Application Title :
TITLE
;ORACLE workspace size :
```

continued

Listing B.1   *(continued)*

```
;Block name / Description :
**key-startup
;SQL>
$display-msg
SELECT 'x'
  FROM dual
 WHERE 1 = 1

;Message if value not found :
*Add title or update one. To query: [Enter], type query, [Execute Query].
;Must value exist Y/N :
Y
;Block name / Description :
*title/title
;Enter default WHERE and ORDER BY clause :
where titlecd > ' '

;Table name :
TITLE
;Check for uniqueness before inserting Y/N :
N
;Display/Buffer how many records :
1 / 10
;Field name :
*PRE-DELETE
;SQL>
$Chk-synopsis
SELECT 'x'
  FROM synopsis
 WHERE synopsis.titlecd = :title.titlecd

;Message if value not found :
*You cannot delete title as synopsis exists.! Delete synopsis first . . .
;Must value exist Y/N :
N
;Field name :
*key-nxtblk
;SQL>
$get_nxtblk
#EXEMACRO nxtblk;exeqry;

;Message if value not found :
Program error occurred while querying synopsis. Call your supervisor.
;Must value exist Y/N :
Y
;Field name :
titlecd
;Type of field :
CHAR
;Length of field / Display length / Query length :
15 / 15 / 15
;Is this field in the base table Y/N :
Y
;Is this field part of the primary key Y/N :
N
;Default value :

;Page :
1
;Line :
4
;Column :
3
;Prompt :
```

```
;Allow field to be entered Y/N :
**Y
;Allow field to be updated Y/N :
Y
;Allow entry of query condition Y/N :
Y
;Hide value of field Y/N :
N
;SQL>

;Is field mandatory Y/N :
Y
;Is field fixed length Y/N :
N
;Auto jump to next field Y/N :
N
;Convert field to upper case Y/N :
Y
;Help message :
Enter a unique title code for this film title.
;Lowest value :

;Highest value :

;Field name :
title
;Type of field :
CHAR
;Length of field / Display length / Query length :
61 / 61 / 61
;Is this field in the base table Y/N :
Y
;Is this field part of the primary key Y/N :
N
;Default value :

;Page :
1
;Line :
4
;Column :
19
;Prompt :

;Allow field to be entered Y/N :
**Y
;Allow field to be updated Y/N :
Y
;Allow entry of query condition Y/N :
Y
;Hide value of field Y/N :
N
;SQL>
**POST-CHANGE
/
;SQL>
$set-xtdesc
SELECT :title.title
  INTO title.xtdesc
  FROM dual

;Message if value not found :

;Must value exist Y/N :
Y
```

continued

Listing B.1   *(continued)*

```
;Is field mandatory Y/N :
Y
;Is field fixed length Y/N :
N
;Auto jump to next field Y/N :
N
;Convert field to upper case Y/N :
N
;Help message :
Title of the film.
;Lowest value :

;Highest value :

;Field name :
category
;Type of field :
CHAR
;Length of field / Display length / Query length :
3 / 3 / 3
;Is this field in the base table Y/N :
Y
;Is this field part of the primary key Y/N :
N
;Default value :
999
;Page :
1
;Line :
6
;Column :
3
;Prompt :

;Allow field to be entered Y/N :
**Y
;Allow field to be updated Y/N :
Y
;Allow entry of query condition Y/N :
Y
;Hide value of field Y/N :
N
;SQL>
**POST-CHANGE
/
;SQL>
$Get_cat
SELECT description
  INTO cdesc
  FROM category
 WHERE category.category = :title.category

;Message if value not found :
Invalid category. Use [List Values] to see valid choices.
;Must value exist Y/N :
Y
;Is field mandatory Y/N :
Y
;Is field fixed length Y/N :
N
;Auto jump to next field Y/N :
N
;Convert field to upper case Y/N :
Y
```

```
;Help message :
Category code to identify film category, e.g., 100 = Adventure.
;Lowest value :
@category.category
;Field name :
cdesc
;Type of field :
CHAR
;Length of field / Display length / Query length :
20 / 20 / 20
;Is this field in the base table Y/N :
N
;Default value :

;Page :
1
;Line :
6
;Column :
8
;Prompt :

;Allow field to be entered Y/N :
**N
;Allow entry of query condition Y/N :
N
;Hide value of field Y/N :
N
;SQL>

;Field name :
release
;Type of field :
CHAR
;Length of field / Display length / Query length :
4 / 4 / 4
;Is this field in the base table Y/N :
Y
;Is this field part of the primary key Y/N :
N
;Default value :

;Page :
1
;Line :
9
;Column :
5
;Prompt :

;Allow field to be entered Y/N :
**Y
;Allow field to be updated Y/N :
Y
;Allow entry of query condition Y/N :
Y
;Hide value of field Y/N :
N
;SQL>
**POST-CHANGE
/
;SQL>
$Chk-release
SELECT 'x'
  FROM dual
 WHERE to_date(:release, 'YYYY') <= sysdate
```

continued

Listing B.1   *(continued)*

```
;Message if value not found :
You cannot enter a release date that is later than today!
;Must value exist Y/N :
Y
;Is field mandatory Y/N :
N
;Is field fixed length Y/N :
N
;Auto jump to next field Y/N :
N
;Convert field to upper case Y/N :
Y
;Help message :
*Year film was released.  Enter the year only, e.g., 1987.
;Lowest value :

;Highest value :

;Field name :
studio
;Type of field :
CHAR
;Length of field / Display length / Query length :
14 / 14 / 14
;Is this field in the base table Y/N :
Y
;Is this field part of the primary key Y/N :
N
;Default value :

;Page :
1
;Line :
9
;Column :
12
;Prompt :

;Allow field to be entered Y/N :
**Y
;Allow field to be updated Y/N :
Y
;Allow entry of query condition Y/N :
Y
;Hide value of field Y/N :
N
;SQL>

;Is field mandatory Y/N :
N
;Is field fixed length Y/N :
N
;Auto jump to next field Y/N :
N
;Convert field to upper case Y/N :
N
;Help message :
Studio that distributes the film.
;Lowest value :

;Highest value :

;Field name :
color_bw
```

```
;Type of field :
CHAR
;Length of field / Display length / Query length :
6 / 6 / 6
;Is this field in the base table Y/N :
Y
;Is this field part of the primary key Y/N :
N
;Default value :

;Page :
1
;Line :
9
;Column :
27
;Prompt :

;Allow field to be entered Y/N :
**Y
;Allow field to be updated Y/N :
Y
;Allow entry of query condition Y/N :
Y
;Hide value of field Y/N :
N
;SQL>
**POST-CHANGE
/
;SQL>
$Chk-entry
SELECT color_bw
  FROM title
 WHERE title.color_bw = :title.color_bw

;Message if value not found :
Valid choices are 'Color' or 'BW'. Please re-enter . . .
;Must value exist Y/N :
Y
;Is field mandatory Y/N :
N
;Is field fixed length Y/N :
N
;Auto jump to next field Y/N :
N
;Convert field to upper case Y/N :
N
;Help message :
Enter 'Color' or  'BW'.
;Lowest value :

;Highest value :

;Field name :
runtime
;Type of field :
CHAR
;Length of field / Display length / Query length :
10 / 10 / 10
;Is this field in the base table Y/N :
Y
;Is this field part of the primary key Y/N :
N
;Default value :
```

continued

Listing B.1   *(continued)*

```
;Page :
1
;Line :
9
;Column :
38
;Prompt :

;Allow field to be entered Y/N :
**Y
;Allow field to be updated Y/N :
Y
;Allow entry of query condition Y/N :
Y
;Hide value of field Y/N :
N
;SQL>

;Is field mandatory Y/N :
N
;Is field fixed length Y/N :
N
;Auto jump to next field Y/N :
N
;Convert field to upper case Y/N :
N
;Help message :
*Running time of the film, e.g., '120 mins.'.
;Lowest value :

;Highest value :

;Field name :
censorrtg
;Type of field :
CHAR
;Length of field / Display length / Query length :
7 / 7 / 7
;Is this field in the base table Y/N :
Y
;Is this field part of the primary key Y/N :
N
;Default value :

;Page :
1
;Line :
9
;Column :
55
;Prompt :

;Allow field to be entered Y/N :
**Y
;Allow field to be updated Y/N :
Y
;Allow entry of query condition Y/N :
Y
;Hide value of field Y/N :
N
;SQL>

;Is field mandatory Y/N :
N
```

```
;Is field fixed length Y/N :
N
;Auto jump to next field Y/N :
N
;Convert field to upper case Y/N :
Y
;Help message :
Censorship rating of the film, e.g., G =General, PG-13 = Parental Guidance.
;Lowest value :

;Highest value :

;Field name :
starrtg
;Type of field :
CHAR
;Length of field / Display length / Query length :
6 / 5 / 6
;Is this field in the base table Y/N :
Y
;Is this field part of the primary key Y/N :
N
;Default value :
;Page :
1
;Line :
9
;Column :
71
;Prompt :

;Allow field to be entered Y/N :
**Y
;Allow field to be updated Y/N :
Y
;Allow entry of query condition Y/N :
Y
;Hide value of field Y/N :
N
;SQL>

;Is field mandatory Y/N :
N
;Is field fixed length Y/N :
N
;Auto jump to next field Y/N :
N
;Convert field to upper case Y/N :
Y
;Help message :
Star rating for this title. e.g. *, **, ***. ****, *****  (5 Stars is Tops!)

;Lowest value :

;Highest value :

;Field name :
directors
;Type of field :
CHAR
;Length of field / Display length / Query length :
78 / 77 / 78
;Is this field in the base table Y/N :
Y
;Is this field part of the primary key Y/N :
N
```

continued

Listing B.1   *(continued)*

```
;Default value :

;Page :
1
;Line :
12
;Column :
3
;Prompt :

;Allow field to be entered Y/N :
**Y
;Allow field to be updated Y/N :
Y
;Allow entry of query condition Y/N :
Y
;Hide value of field Y/N :
N
;SQL>

;Is field mandatory Y/N :
N
;Is field fixed length Y/N :
N
;Auto jump to next field Y/N :
N
;Convert field to upper case Y/N :
N
;Help message :
Names of the directors for this title.
;Lowest value :

;Highest value :

;Field name :
producers
;Type of field :
CHAR
;Length of field / Display length / Query length :
78 / 77 / 78
;Is this field in the base table Y/N :
Y
;Is this field part of the primary key Y/N :
N
;Default value :

;Page :
1
;Line :
14
;Column :
3
;Prompt :

;Allow field to be entered Y/N :
**Y
;Allow field to be updated Y/N :
Y
;Allow entry of query condition Y/N :
Y
;Hide value of field Y/N :
N
;SQL>
```

```
;Is field mandatory Y/N :
N
;Is field fixed length Y/N :
N
;Auto jump to next field Y/N :
N
;Convert field to upper case Y/N :
N
;Help message :
Names of the producers and co-producers of this film.
;Lowest value :

;Highest value :

;Field name :
actors
;Type of field :
CHAR
;Length of field / Display length / Query length :
78 / 77 / 78
;Is this field in the base table Y/N :
Y
;Is this field part of the primary key Y/N :
N
;Default value :

;Page :
1
;Line :
16
;Column :
3
;Prompt :

;Allow field to be entered Y/N :
**Y
;Allow field to be updated Y/N :
Y
;Allow entry of query condition Y/N :
Y
;Hide value of field Y/N :
N
;SQL>

;Is field mandatory Y/N :
N
;Is field fixed length Y/N :
N
;Auto jump to next field Y/N :
N
;Convert field to upper case Y/N :
N
;Help message :
Names of actors and actresses for this film.
;Lowest value :

;Highest value :

;Field name :
screenplay
;Type of field :
CHAR
;Length of field / Display length / Query length :
38 / 38 / 38
;Is this field in the base table Y/N :
Y
```

continued

Listing B.1   *(continued)*

```
;Is this field part of the primary key Y/N :
N
;Default value :

;Page :
1
;Line :
18
;Column :
3
;Prompt :

;Allow field to be entered Y/N :
**Y
;Allow field to be updated Y/N :
Y
;Allow entry of query condition Y/N :
Y
;Hide value of field Y/N :
N
;SQL>

;Is field mandatory Y/N :
N
;Is field fixed length Y/N :
N
;Auto jump to next field Y/N :
N
;Convert field to upper case Y/N :
N
;Help message :
Names of screen writers for this film.
;Lowest value :

;Highest value :

;Field name :
awards
;Type of field :
CHAR
;Length of field / Display length / Query length :
38 / 38 / 38
;Is this field in the base table Y/N :
Y
;Is this field part of the primary key Y/N :
N
;Default value :

;Page :
1
;Line :
18
;Column :
42
;Prompt :

;Allow field to be entered Y/N :
**Y
;Allow field to be updated Y/N :
Y
;Allow entry of query condition Y/N :
Y
```

```
;Hide value of field Y/N :
N
;SQL>

;Is field mandatory Y/N :
N
;Is field fixed length Y/N :
N
;Auto jump to next field Y/N :
N
;Convert field to upper case Y/N :
N
;Help message :
List of awards for this title, if any.
;Lowest value :

;Highest value :

;Field name :
xtdesc
;Type of field :
CHAR
;Length of field / Display length / Query length :
78 / 58 / 78
;Is this field in the base table Y/N :
N
;Default value :

;Page :
2
;Line :
2
;Column :
22
;Prompt :

;Allow field to be entered Y/N :
**N
;Allow entry of query condition Y/N :
N
;Hide value of field Y/N :
N
;SQL>

;Field name :
;Block name / Description :
*synopsis/synopsis
;Enter default WHERE and ORDER BY clause :
WHERE lineno > ''

;Table name :
SYNOPSIS
;Check for uniqueness before inserting Y/N :
N
;Display/Buffer how many records :
15 / 50
;Base crt line ?
5
;How many physical lines per record ?
1
;Field name :
*PRE-INSERT
;SQL>
;Must value exist Y/:
$Add-lineno
SELECT nvl(max(lineno),0) + 1
```

continued

Listing B.1   *(continued)*

```
  INTO lineno
  FROM synopsis
 WHERE synopsis.titlecd = :synopsis.titlecd
/
;Message if value not found :
$Okay-lineno $Line1
;Must value exist Y/N :
N
$Line1
SELECT 1, :title.titlecd
  INTO lineno, synopsis.titlecd
  FROM dual
/
;Message if value not found :
Pre-insert error. Problem inserting 1st line number.  Call your supervisor.
;Must value exist Y/N :
Y
$okay-lineno
SELECT 'x'
  FROM dual
 WHERE 1 = 1

;Message if value not found :

;Must value exist Y/N :
Y
;Field name :
*PRE-UPDATE
;SQL>
$no-update
#EXEMACRO null;

;Message if value not found :
*You cannot change the synopsis text.  Ask your supervisor.
;Must value exist Y/N :
Y
;Field name :
*key-nxtblk
;SQL>
$no-nxtblk
#exemacro null;

;Message if value not found :
*Press [PgUp] to return to TITLE page.
;Must value exist Y/N :
Y
;Field name :
titlecd
;Type of field :
CHAR
;Length of field / Display length / Query length :
15 / 15 / 15
;Is this field in the base table Y/N :
*Y
;Is this field part of the primary key Y/N :
Y
;Field to copy primary key from :
TITLE.TITLECD
;Page :

;SQL>
;Field name :
title
;Type of field :
```

```
CHAR
;Length of field / Display length / Query length :
78 / 78 / 78
;Is this field in the base table Y/N :
Y
;Is this field part of the primary key Y/N :
N
;Default value :

;Page :
2
;Line :
1
;Column :
2
;Prompt :

;Allow field to be entered Y/N :
**Y
;Allow field to be updated Y/N :
N
;Allow entry of query condition Y/N :
Y
;Hide value of field Y/N :
N
;SQL>

;Is field mandatory Y/N :
N
;Is field fixed length Y/N :
N
;Auto jump to next field Y/N :
Y
;Convert field to upper case Y/N :
N
;Help message :
Text for film synopsis.
;Lowest value :

;Highest value :

;Field name :
lineno
;Type of field :
INT
;Length of field / Display length / Query length :
6 / 6 / 6
;Is this field in the base table Y/N :
*Y
;Is this field part of the primary key Y/N :
Y
;Field to copy primary key from :

;Default value :

;Page :

;SQL>

;Field name :
;Block name / Description :

      Video Quest TITLE Search
%LINE
3
```

continued

Listing B.1   *(continued)*

```
  Title Code      Title
%LINE
5
  Film Category
%LINE
8
  Released    Studio     Color/BW    Running Time   Censor Rating
Star Rating
%LINE
11
  Directors
%LINE
13
  Producers/Co-Producers
%LINE
15
  Actors/Actresses
%LINE
17
  Screenplay                        Awards
%LINE
22
  [PgDn] Title Synopsis   VIDEO QUEST RENTALS, Inc.
[Exit] Main Menu
%LINE
1
%GRAPHICS
```

Listing B.2   The PRODUCT Form

```
; Generated by SQL*Forms Version 2.0.18 on Fri Jun 10 09:49:32 1988
; Application owner is OPS$DCRONIN. Application name is product
; (Application ID is 0)
; -------------------------------------------------
;Application Title :
PRODUCT
;ORACLE workspace size :

;Block name / Description :
**key-startup
;SQL>
$display-msg
SELECT 'x'
  FROM dual
 WHERE 1 = 1

;Message if value not found :
*Add new product or update existing one. To query: [F1], enter query, [F2].
;Must value exist Y/N :
Y
;Block name / Description :
*product/product
;Enter default WHERE and ORDER BY clause :
*order by storeno, prodno

;Table name :
PRODUCT
;Check for uniqueness before inserting Y/N :
N
```

```
;Display/Buffer how many records :
1 / 30
;Field name :
*POST-QUERY
;SQL>
;Tricky trigger!  Attribute for both steps to this trigger must be:
;    * Return success when abort!
;Why?  Because, if the title hasn't ever been rented, the post-query trigger
;step fails (can't select days_rented if there isn't any!) and the entire
; trigger aborts. Result: The entire query is disrupted & returns a LIE!
; What kept happening, when attribute was set to * Abort on failure, is
; the query halted, couldn't continue the query and returned "Query found
;  no records" message - EVEN IF IT WAS A LIE!
$get-days_rented
SELECT qty_rented
  INTO product.qty_rented
  FROM qty_rented
 WHERE prodno = :product.prodno
/
;Message if value not found :

;Must value exist Y/N :
*N
$calc-revenue
SELECT nvl(:product.qty_rented,0) * nvl(:product.ratepdy, 0)
  INTO product.revenue
  FROM dual

;Message if value not found :
Couldn't calculate rental revenue for this product.
;Must value exist Y/N :
*N
;Field name :
*PRE-INSERT
;SQL>
$init-product
SELECT 0, 0, 0
  INTO qtyoh, qtyord, qtyrsv
  FROM dual

;Message if value not found :
Error in initializing fields for product. Call supervisor.
;Must value exist Y/N :
Y
;Field name :
*key-delrec
;SQL>
$no-delete
#exemacro null;

;Message if value not found :
*Delete not allowed on product screen!
;Must value exist Y/N :
N
;Field name :
prodno
;Type of field :
CHAR
;Length of field / Display length / Query length :
25 / 10 / 25
;Is this field in the base table Y/N :
*Y
;Is this field part of the primary key Y/N :
Y
;Field to copy primary key from :

;Default value :
```

continued

Listing B.2   *(continued)*

```
;Page :
1
;Line :
3
;Column :
18
;Prompt :

;Allow field to be entered Y/N :
**Y
;Allow field to be updated Y/N :
N
;Allow entry of query condition Y/N :
Y
;Hide value of field Y/N :
N
;SQL>

;Is field mandatory Y/N :
N
;Is field fixed length Y/N :
N
;Auto jump to next field Y/N :
N
;Convert field to upper case Y/N :
Y
;Help message :
Product number to identify product.
;Lowest value :

;Highest value :

;Field name :
description
;Type of field :
CHAR
;Length of field / Display length / Query length :
30 / 30 / 30
;Is this field in the base table Y/N :
Y
;Is this field part of the primary key Y/N :
N
;Default value :

;Page :
1
;Line :
5
;Column :
18
;Prompt :

;Allow field to be entered Y/N :
**Y
;Allow field to be updated Y/N :
Y
;Allow entry of query condition Y/N :
Y
;Hide value of field Y/N :
N
;SQL>

;Is field mandatory Y/N :
N
```

```
;Is field fixed length Y/N :
N
;Auto jump to next field Y/N :
N
;Convert field to upper case Y/N :
N
;Help message :
Description of the product.
;Lowest value :

;Highest value :

;Field name :
prodtype
;Type of field :
CHAR
;Length of field / Display length / Query length :
2 / 2 / 2
;Is this field in the base table Y/N :
Y
;Is this field part of the primary key Y/N :
N
;Default value :

;Page :
1
;Line :
6
;Column :
18
;Prompt :

;Allow field to be entered Y/N :
**Y
;Allow field to be updated Y/N :
Y
;Allow entry of query condition Y/N :
Y
;Hide value of field Y/N :
N
;SQL>
**POST-CHANGE
/
;SQL>
$chk-prodtype
SELECT DECODE(:prodtype,'R','Rental','S','Sale','RS','Both Rent/Sale')
  INTO xdesc
  FROM dual
 WHERE :prodtype in ('R','S','RS')

;Message if value not found :
Invalid product type. R = Rental. S = Sale.  RS = Both Rent/Sale.
;Must value exist Y/N :
Y
;Is field mandatory Y/N :
Y
;Is field fixed length Y/N :
N
;Auto jump to next field Y/N :
N
;Convert field to upper case Y/N :
Y
;Help message :
Product type. R = Rental. S = Sale. RS = Both Rent/Sale.
;Lowest value :

;Highest value :
```

continued

445

Listing B.2   *(continued)*

```
;Field name :
xdesc
;Type of field :
CHAR
;Length of field / Display length / Query length :
22 / 20 / 22
;Is this field in the base table Y/N :
N
;Default value :

;Page :
1
;Line :
6
;Column :
21
;Prompt :

;Allow field to be entered Y/N :
**N
;Allow entry of query condition Y/N :
N
;Hide value of field Y/N :
N
;SQL>

;Field name :
titlecd
;Type of field :
CHAR
;Length of field / Display length / Query length :
15 / 15 / 15
;Is this field in the base table Y/N :
Y
;Is this field part of the primary key Y/N :
N
;Default value :
N/A
;Page :
1
;Line :
8
;Column :
18
;Prompt :

;Allow field to be entered Y/N :
**Y
;Allow field to be updated Y/N :
Y
;Allow entry of query condition Y/N :
Y
;Hide value of field Y/N :
N
;SQL>
**POST-CHANGE
/
;SQL>
$get-title
SELECT title.title
  INTO tdesc
  FROM title
 WHERE title.titlecd = :titlecd
```

```
;Message if value not found :
Invalid title code. Please re-enter.
;Must value exist Y/N :
Y
;Is field mandatory Y/N :
Y
;Is field fixed length Y/N :
N
;Auto jump to next field Y/N :
N
;Convert field to upper case Y/N :
Y
;Help message :
Enter title code.
;Lowest value :

;Highest value :

;Field name :
tdesc
;Type of field :
CHAR
;Length of field / Display length / Query length :
48 / 46 / 48
;Is this field in the base table Y/N :
N
;Default value :

;Page :
1
;Line :
8
;Column :
34
;Prompt :

;Allow field to be entered Y/N :
**N
;Allow entry of query condition Y/N :
N
;Hide value of field Y/N :
N
;SQL>

;Field name :
format
;Type of field :
CHAR
;Length of field / Display length / Query length :
1 / 1 / 1
;Is this field in the base table Y/N :
Y
;Is this field part of the primary key Y/N :
N
;Default value :
N
;Page :
1
;Line :
q
;Column :
18
;Prompt :

;Allow field to be entered Y/N :
**Y
```

continued

Listing B.2   *(continued)*

```
;Allow field to be updated Y/N :
Y
;Allow entry of query condition Y/N :
Y
;Hide value of field Y/N :
N
;SQL>
**POST-CHANGE
/
;SQL>
$get-format
SELECT DECODE(:format,'B','Beta','V','Vhs','N','N/A')
  INTO fdesc
  FROM dual
 WHERE :format in ('B','V','N')

;Message if value not found :
Invalid format. B = Beta. V = Vhs. N = Not applicable. Please re-enter.
;Must value exist Y/N :
Y
;Is field mandatory Y/N :
Y
;Is field fixed length Y/N :
N
;Auto jump to next field Y/N :
N
;Convert field to upper case Y/N :
Y
;Help message :
Tape format.  B = Beta, V = Vhs, N = Not applicable.
;Lowest value :

;Highest value :

;Field name :
fdesc
;Type of field :
CHAR
;Length of field / Display length / Query length :
20 / 20 / 20
;Is this field in the base table Y/N :
N
;Default value :

;Page :
1
;Line :
9
;Column :
20
;Prompt :
;Allow field to be entered Y/N :
**N
;Allow entry of query condition Y/N :
N
;Hide value of field Y/N :
N
;SQL>

;Field name :
rentclass
;Type of field :
INT
```

```
;Length of field / Display length / Query length :
2 / 2 / 2
;Is this field in the base table Y/N :
Y
;Is this field part of the primary key Y/N :
N
;Default value :
99
;Page :
1
;Line :
11
;Column :
18
;Prompt :

;Allow field to be entered Y/N :
**Y
;Allow field to be updated Y/N :
Y
;Allow entry of query condition Y/N :
Y
;Hide value of field Y/N :
N
;SQL>
**POST-CHANGE
/
;SQL>
$get-rentclass
SELECT RATEPDY, description
  INTO ratepdy, rdesc
  FROM rentclass
 WHERE rentclass.rentclass = :rentclass

;Message if value not found :
Invalid rental class. Use [List Values]. Please re-enter.
;Must value exist Y/N :
Y
;Is field mandatory Y/N :
Y
;Is field fixed length Y/N :
N
;Auto jump to next field Y/N :
N
;Convert field to upper case Y/N :
N
;Help message :
Rental class to establish rental rate. Use [List Values].
;Lowest value :
@rentclass.rentclass
;Field name :
rdesc
;Type of field :
CHAR
;Length of field / Display length / Query length :
20 / 20 / 20
;Is this field in the base table Y/N :
N
;Default value :

;Page :
1
;Line :
11
;Column :
21
```

continued

Listing B.2   *(continued)*

```
;Prompt :

;Allow field to be entered Y/N :
**N
;Allow entry of query condition Y/N :
N
;Hide value of field Y/N :
N
;SQL>

;Field name :
ratepdy
;Type of field :
RMONEY
;Length of field / Display length / Query length :
7 / 7 / 7
;Is this field in the base table Y/N :
N
;Default value :

;Page :
1
;Line :
12
;Column :
18
;Prompt :

;Allow field to be entered Y/N :
**N
;Allow entry of query condition Y/N :
N
;Hide value of field Y/N :
N
;SQL>

;Field name :
qty_rented
;Type of field :
RINT
;Length of field / Display length / Query length :
5 / 5 / 5
;Is this field in the base table Y/N :
N
;Default value :

;Page :
1
;Line :
11
;Column :
62
;Prompt :

;Allow field to be entered Y/N :
**N
;Allow entry of query condition Y/N :
N
;Hide value of field Y/N :
N
;SQL>

;Field name :
Revenue
```

```
;Type of field :
RMONEY
;Length of field / Display length / Query length :
9 / 9 / 9
;Is this field in the base table Y/N :
N
;Default value :

;Page :
1
;Line :
12
;Column :
62
;Prompt :

;Allow field to be entered Y/N :
**N
;Allow entry of query condition Y/N :
N
;Hide value of field Y/N :
N
;SQL>

;Field name :
cost
;Type of field :
RMONEY
;Length of field / Display length / Query length :
8 / 8 / 10
;Is this field in the base table Y/N :
Y
;Is this field part of the primary key Y/N :
N
;Default value :
0
;Page :
1
;Line :
21
;Column :
4
;Prompt :

;Allow field to be entered Y/N :
**Y
;Allow field to be updated Y/N :
Y
;Allow entry of query condition Y/N :
Y
;Hide value of field Y/N :
N
;SQL>

;Is field mandatory Y/N :
Y
;Is field fixed length Y/N :
N
;Auto jump to next field Y/N :
N
;Convert field to upper case Y/N :
N
;Help message :
Enter cost of product.
;Lowest value :

;Highest value :
```

continued

Listing B.2   *(continued)*

```
;Field name :
sellrtl
;Type of field :
RMONEY
;Length of field / Display length / Query length :
8 / 8 / 10
;Is this field in the base table Y/N :
Y
;Is this field part of the primary key Y/N :
N
;Default value :
0
;Page :
1
;Line :
21
;Column :
17
;Prompt :

;Allow field to be entered Y/N :
**Y
;Allow field to be updated Y/N :
Y
;Allow entry of query condition Y/N :
Y
;Hide value of field Y/N :
N
;SQL>

;Is field mandatory Y/N :
N
;Is field fixed length Y/N :
N
;Auto jump to next field Y/N :
N
;Convert field to upper case Y/N :
N
;Help message :
*No need to enter selling price if product is 'R' (Rental Only).
;Lowest value :

;Highest value :

;Field name :
suggrtl
;Type of field :
RMONEY
;Length of field / Display length / Query length :
8 / 8 / 10
;Is this field in the base table Y/N :
Y
;Is this field part of the primary key Y/N :
N
;Default value :
0
;Page :
1
;Line :
21
;Column :
31
;Prompt :
```

```
;Allow field to be entered Y/N :
**Y
;Allow field to be updated Y/N :
Y
;Allow entry of query condition Y/N :
Y
;Hide value of field Y/N :
N
;SQL>

;Is field mandatory Y/N :
N
;Is field fixed length Y/N :
N
;Auto jump to next field Y/N :
N
;Convert field to upper case Y/N :
N
;Help message :
Enter suggested retail price of product.
;Lowest value :

;Highest value :

;Field name :
qtyrecvd
;Type of field :
RINT
;Length of field / Display length / Query length :
6 / 6 / 8
;Is this field in the base table Y/N :
Y
;Is this field part of the primary key Y/N :
N
;Default value :
0
;Page :
1
;Line :
21
;Column :
44
;Prompt :

;Allow field to be entered Y/N :
**N
;Allow entry of query condition Y/N :
Y
;Hide value of field Y/N :
N
;SQL>

;Field name :
qtyoh
;Type of field :
RINT
;Length of field / Display length / Query length :
6 / 6 / 8
;Is this field in the base table Y/N :
Y
;Is this field part of the primary key Y/N :
N
;Default value :
0
;Page :
1
```

continued

Listing B.2   *(continued)*

```
;Line :
21
;Column :
52
;Prompt :

;Allow field to be entered Y/N :
**N
;Allow entry of query condition Y/N :
Y
;Hide value of field Y/N :
N
;SQL>

;Field name :
qtysold
;Type of field :
RINT
;Length of field / Display length / Query length :
6 / 6 / 8
;Is this field in the base table Y/N :
Y
;Is this field part of the primary key Y/N :
N
;Default value :
0
;Page :
1
;Line :
21
;Column :
59
;Prompt :

;Allow field to be entered Y/N :
**N
;Allow entry of query condition Y/N :
Y
;Hide value of field Y/N :
N
;SQL>

;Field name :
qtyrsv
;Type of field :
RINT
;Length of field / Display length / Query length :
6 / 6 / 8
;Is this field in the base table Y/N :
Y
;Is this field part of the primary key Y/N :
N
;Default value :
0
;Page :
1
;Line :
21
;Column :
67
;Prompt :

;Allow field to be entered Y/N :
**N
```

```
;Allow entry of query condition Y/N :
Y
;Hide value of field Y/N :
N
;SQL>

;Field name :
qtyord
;Type of field :
RINT
;Length of field / Display length / Query length :
6 / 6 / 8
;Is this field in the base table Y/N :
Y
;Is this field part of the primary key Y/N :
N
;Default value :
0
;Page :
1
;Line :
21
;Column :
74
;Prompt :

;Allow field to be entered Y/N :
**N
;Allow entry of query condition Y/N :
Y
;Hide value of field Y/N :
N
;SQL>

;Field name :
storeno
;Type of field :
INT
;Length of field / Display length / Query length :
3 / 3 / 3
;Is this field in the base table Y/N :
*Y
;Is this field part of the primary key Y/N :
Y
;Field to copy primary key from :

;Default value :
1
;Page :
1
;Line :
3
;Column :
73
;Prompt :

;Allow field to be entered Y/N :
**Y
;Allow field to be updated Y/N :
N
;Allow entry of query condition Y/N :
Y
;Hide value of field Y/N :
N
;SQL>
```

continued

Listing B.2   *(continued)*

```
;Is field mandatory Y/N :
N
;Is field fixed length Y/N :
N
;Auto jump to next field Y/N :
N
;Convert field to upper case Y/N :
N
;Help message :
Store number to identify location within distributed network of stores.
;Lowest value :

;Highest value :

;Field name :

;Block name / Description :

        Video Quest PRODUCT Database
%LINE
3
        Product No:                                              Store No.:
%LINE
5
     Description:
    Product Type:
%LINE
8
      Title Code:
          Format:
%LINE
11
    Rental Class:                        Times rented:
    Rate Per Day:                        Revenue to date:
%LINE
15
              Pricing and Inventory Positions
%LINE
18
Product    Selling     Suggested    Qty        On      Qty      On        On
Cost       Retail      Retail       Received    Hand    Sold    Reserve    Order
%LINE
23
                    VIDEO QUEST RENTALS, Inc.
%LINE
1
%GRAPHICS
```

Listing B.3   The CUSTOMER Form

```
; Generated by SQL*Forms Version 2.0.18 on Fri Jun 10 14:23:10 1988
; Application owner is OPS$DCRONIN. Application name is customer
; (Application ID is 0)
; ------------------------------------------------
;Application Title :
CUSTOMER
;ORACLE workspace size :
;Block name / Description :
**key-startup
```

```
;SQL>
$display-msg
SELECT 'x'
  FROM dual
 WHERE 1 = 1

;Message if value not found :
*Add new customer or update existing one. To query: [F1], enter query, [F2].
;Must value exist Y/N :
Y
;Block name / Description :
*customer/customer
;Enter default WHERE and ORDER BY clause :
where customer.memberid > 0
order by customer.memberid


;Table name :
CUSTOMER
;Check for uniqueness before inserting Y/N :
N
;Display/Buffer how many records :
1 / 30
;Field name :
*PRE-INSERT
;SQL>
$Lock-cntl
LOCK TABLE cntl IN SHARE UPDATE MODE
/
;Message if value not found :
Program error:  Problem locking CNTL table to generate new memberid.
;Must value exist Y/N :
Y
$New-memberid
UPDATE cntl
   SET last_memberid = nvl(last_memberid,0) + 1
/
;Message if value not found :
Program error: Problem updating CNTL table to generate new memberid.
;Must value exist Y/N :
Y
$Get_newid
SELECT last_memberid
  INTO customer.memberid
  FROM cntl

;Message if value not found :
Pre-Insert Error: Problem inserting new memberid. See your supervisor.
;Must value exist Y/N :
Y
;Field name :
*PRE-DELETE
;SQL>
$Lock-custname
LOCK TABLE custname IN SHARE UPDATE MODE
/
;Message if value not found :

;Must value exist Y/N :
Y
$Del-details
DELETE FROM custname
 WHERE custname.memberd = :customer.memberid

;Message if value not found :
Pre-Delete error: Problem deleting detail members when deleting master . . .
```

continued

Listing B.3   *(continued)*

```
;Must value exist Y/N :
Y
;Field name :
*Key-crerec
;SQL>
$Coord-crerec
#EXEMACRO exetrg clear_details; crerec;

;Message if value not found :
Program error: Problem executing [Create Record] in coordinated blocks.
;Must value exist Y/N :
Y
;Field name :
*key-delrec
;SQL>
$Coord-delete
#EXEMACRO exetrg clear_details; delrec; exetrg query_details;
;Message if value not found :
Program error: Problem executing [Delete Record] in coordinated blocks.
;Must value exist Y/N :
Y
;Field name :
*key-entqry
;SQL>
$Coord-entqry
#EXEMACRO entqry; exetrg query_details;

;Message if value not found :
Program error:  Problem executing [Enter Query] in coordinated block.
;Must value exist Y/N :
Y
;Field name :
*key-exeqry
;SQL>
$No_exeqry
#EXEMACRO null;

;Message if value not found :
*You must enter specific customer information to query.  Press [Enter Query].
;Must value exist Y/N :
N
;Field name :
*key-nxtblk
;SQL>
$Chk-master
SELECT 'x'
  FROM dual
 WHERE :customer.name is null
/
;Message if value not found :
*You must enter customer information before going to the next block.
;Must value exist Y/N :
Y
$Ok-nxtblk
#EXEMACRO nxtblk;

;Message if value not found :
Program error:  Problem executing [Next Block].  See your supervisor.
;Must value exist Y/N :
Y
;Field name :
*key-nxtrec
;SQL>
```

```
$Coord-nxtrec
#EXEMACRO nxtrec; exetrg query_details;

;Message if value not found :
Program error:  Problem executing [Next Record] in coordinated block.
;Must value exist Y/N :
Y
;Field name :
*KEY-PRVBLK
;SQL>
$No-prvblk
#EXEMACRO null;

;Message if value not found :
*Nowhere to go from here.  You're in the Master block . . .
;Must value exist Y/N :
Y
;Field name :
*key-prvrec
;SQL>
$Coord-prvrec
#EXEMACRO prvrec;exetrg query_details;

;Message if value not found :
Program error: Problem executing [Previous Record] in coordinated blocks.
;Must value exist Y/N :
Y
;Field name :
*Clear_details
;SQL>
$Clr-details
#EXEMACRO CASE customer.memberid IS
     WHEN '' then null;
     WHEN others THEN globlk custname; clrblk;
         goblk customer;
END CASE;

;Message if value not found :

;Must value exist Y/N :
Y
;Field name :
*Query_details
;SQL>
$Qry-details
#EXEMACRO CASE customer.memberid IS
     WHEN '' then null;
     WHEN others THEN goblk custname; exeqry;
         goblk customer;
END CASE;
;Message if value not found :
User trigger error:  Problem querying coordinated blocks.
;Must value exist Y/N :
Y
;Field name :
memberid
;Type of field :
INT
;Length of field / Display length / Query length :
? / ? / ?
;Is this field in the base table Y/N :
Y
;Is this field part of the primary key Y/N :
N
;Default value :
;Page :
1
```

continued

Listing B.3 *(continued)*

```
;Line :
3
;Column :
14
;Prompt :
;Allow field to be entered Y/N :
**N
;Allow entry of query condition Y/N :
Y
;Hide value of field Y/N :
N
;SQL>

;Field name :
name
;Type of field :
CHAR
;Length of field / Display length / Query length :
30 / 30 / 30
;Is this field in the base table Y/N :
*Y
;Is this field part of the primary key Y/N :
Y
;Field to copy primary key from :

;Default value :

;Page :
1
;Line :
5
;Column :
14
;Prompt :

;Allow field to be entered Y/N :
**Y
;Allow field to be updated Y/N :
Y
;Allow entry of query condition Y/N :
Y
;Hide value of field Y/N :
N
;SQL>

;Is field mandatory Y/N :
Y
;Is field fixed length Y/N :
N
;Auto jump to next field Y/N :
N
;Convert field to upper case Y/N :
N
;Help message :
*Primary member must be entered to establish membership.
;Lowest value :

;Highest value :

;Field name :
ad1
;Type of field :
CHAR
```

```
;Length of field / Display length / Query length :
30 / 30 / 30
;Is this field in the base table Y/N :
Y
;Is this field part of the primary key Y/N :
N
;Default value :

;Page :
1
;Line :
6
;Column :
14
;Prompt :

;Allow field to be entered Y/N :
**Y
;Allow field to be updated Y/N :
Y
;Allow entry of query condition Y/N :
Y
;Hide value of field Y/N :
N
;SQL>

;Is field mandatory Y/N :
Y
;Is field fixed length Y/N :
N
;Auto jump to next field Y/N :
N
;Convert field to upper case Y/N :
N
;Help message :
Street address of customer.
;Lowest value :

;Highest value :

;Field name :
ad2
;Type of field :
CHAR
;Length of field / Display length / Query length :
30 / 30 / 30
;Is this field in the base table Y/N :
Y
;Is this field part of the primary key Y/N :
N
;Default value :

;Page :
1
;Line :
7
;Column :
14
;Prompt :

;Allow field to be entered Y/N :
**Y
;Allow field to be updated Y/N :
Y
;Allow entry of query condition Y/N :
Y
```

continued

Listing B.3   *(continued)*

```
;Hide value of field Y/N :
N
;SQL>

;Is field mandatory Y/N :
N
;Is field fixed length Y/N :
N
;Auto jump to next field Y/N :
N
;Convert field to upper case Y/N :
N
;Help message :
Additional line for address, if necessary.
;Lowest value :

;Highest value :

;Field name :
city
;Type of field :
CHAR
;Length of field / Display length / Query length :
30 / 30 / 30
;Is this field in the base table Y/N :
Y
;Is this field part of the primary key Y/N :
N
;Default value :

;Page :
1
;Line :
8
;Column :
14
;Prompt :

;Allow field to be entered Y/N :
**Y
;Allow field to be updated Y/N :
Y
;Allow entry of query condition Y/N :
Y
;Hide value of field Y/N :
N
;SQL>

;Is field mandatory Y/N :
Y
;Is field fixed length Y/N :
N
;Auto jump to next field Y/N :
N
;Convert field to upper case Y/N :
N
;Help message :
City of customer's address.
;Lowest value :

;Highest value :

;Field name :
state
```

```
;Type of field :
CHAR
;Length of field / Display length / Query length :
2 / 2 / 2
;Is this field in the base table Y/N :
Y
;Is this field part of the primary key Y/N :
N
;Default value :
CA
;Page :
1
;Line :
9
;Column :
14
;Prompt :

;Allow field to be entered Y/N :
**Y
;Allow field to be updated Y/N :
Y
;Allow entry of query condition Y/N :
Y
;Hide value of field Y/N :
N
;SQL>

;Is field mandatory Y/N :
N
;Is field fixed length Y/N :
N
;Auto jump to next field Y/N :
N
;Convert field to upper case Y/N :
Y
;Help message :
State of customer's address.
;Lowest value :

;Highest value :

;Field name :
zip
;Type of field :
CHAR
;Length of field / Display length / Query length :
10 / 10 / 10
;Is this field in the base table Y/N :
Y
;Is this field part of the primary key Y/N :
N
;Default value :

;Page :
1
;Line :
9
;Column :
23
;Prompt :

;Allow field to be entered Y/N :
**Y
;Allow field to be updated Y/N :
Y
```

continued

Listing B.3   *(continued)*

```
;Allow entry of query condition Y/N :
Y
;Hide value of field Y/N :
N
;SQL>

;Is field mandatory Y/N :
N
;Is field fixed length Y/N :
N
;Auto jump to next field Y/N :
N
;Convert field to upper case Y/N :
Y
;Help message :
Zip code of customer's address.
;Lowest value :

;Highest value :

;Field name :
day_area
;Type of field :
CHAR
;Length of field / Display length / Query length :
3 / 3 / 3
;Is this field in the base table Y/N :
Y
;Is this field part of the primary key Y/N :
N
;Default value :

;Page :
1
;Line :
11
;Column :
15
;Prompt :

;Allow field to be entered Y/N :
**Y
;Allow field to be updated Y/N :
Y
;Allow entry of query condition Y/N :
Y
;Hide value of field Y/N :
N
;SQL>

;Is field mandatory Y/N :
N
;Is field fixed length Y/N :
N
;Auto jump to next field Y/N :
Y
;Convert field to upper case Y/N :
N
;Help message :
Area code for daytime phone number.
;Lowest value :

;Highest value :
```

```
;Field name :
day_prefix
;Type of field :
CHAR
;Length of field / Display length / Query length :
3 / 3 / 3
;Is this field in the base table Y/N :
Y
;Is this field part of the primary key Y/N :
N
;Default value :

;Page :
1
;Line :
11
;Column :
20
;Prompt :

;Allow field to be entered Y/N :
**Y
;Allow field to be updated Y/N :
Y
;Allow entry of query condition Y/N :
Y
;Hide value of field Y/N :
N
;SQL>

;Is field mandatory Y/N :
N
;Is field fixed length Y/N :
Y
;Auto jump to next field Y/N :
Y
;Convert field to upper case Y/N :
N
;Help message :
Prefix for daytime phone number.
;Lowest value :

;Highest value :

;Field name :
day_suffix
;Type of field :
CHAR
;Length of field / Display length / Query length :
4 / 4 / 4
;Is this field in the base table Y/N :
Y
;Is this field part of the primary key Y/N :
N
;Default value :

;Page :
1
;Line :
11
;Column :
24
;Prompt :
;Allow field to be entered Y/N :
**Y
;Allow field to be updated Y/N :
Y
```

continued

Listing B.3   *(continued)*

```
;Allow entry of query condition Y/N :
Y
;Hide value of field Y/N :
N
;SQL>

;Is field mandatory Y/N :
N
;Is field fixed length Y/N :
Y
;Auto jump to next field Y/N :
Y
;Convert field to upper case Y/N :
Y
;Help message :
Suffix for daytime phone number.
;Lowest value :

;Highest value :

;Field name :
eve_area
;Type of field :
CHAR
;Length of field / Display length / Query length :
3 / 3 / 3
;Is this field in the base table Y/N :
Y
;Is this field part of the primary key Y/N :
N
;Default value :

;Page :
1
;Line :
11
;Column :
37
;Prompt :

;Allow field to be entered Y/N :
**Y
;Allow field to be updated Y/N :
Y
;Allow entry of query condition Y/N :
Y
;Hide value of field Y/N :
N
;SQL>

;Is field mandatory Y/N :
N
;Is field fixed length Y/N :
Y
;Auto jump to next field Y/N :
Y
;Convert field to upper case Y/N :
Y
;Help message :
Area code for evening phone number.
;Lowest value :

;Highest value :
```

```
;Field name :
eve_prefix
;Type of field :
CHAR
;Length of field / Display length / Query length :
3 / 3 / 3
;Is this field in the base table Y/N :
Y
;Is this field part of the primary key Y/N :
N
;Default value :

;Page :
1
;Line :
11
;Column :
42
;Prompt :

;Allow field to be entered Y/N :
**Y
;Allow field to be updated Y/N :
Y
;Allow entry of query condition Y/N :
Y
;Hide value of field Y/N :
N
;SQL>

;Is field mandatory Y/N :
N
;Is field fixed length Y/N :
Y
;Auto jump to next field Y/N :
Y
;Convert field to upper case Y/N :
Y
;Help message :
Prefix for evening phone number.
;Lowest value :

;Highest value :

;Field name :
eve_suffix
;Type of field :
CHAR
;Length of field / Display length / Query length :
4 / 4 / 4
;Is this field in the base table Y/N :
Y
;Is this field part of the primary key Y/N :
N
;Default value :

;Page :
1
;Line :
11
;Column :
46
;Prompt :

;Allow field to be entered Y/N :
**Y
```

continued

467

Listing B.3   *(continued)*

```
;Allow field to be updated Y/N :
Y
;Allow entry of query condition Y/N :
Y
;Hide value of field Y/N :
N
;SQL>

;Is field mandatory Y/N :
N
;Is field fixed length Y/N :
Y
;Auto jump to next field Y/N :
Y
;Convert field to upper case Y/N :
Y
;Help message :
Suffix for evening phone number.
;Lowest value :

;Highest value :

;Field name :
creditcard
;Type of field :
CHAR
;Length of field / Display length / Query length :
2 / 2 / 2
;Is this field in the base table Y/N :
Y
;Is this field part of the primary key Y/N :
N
;Default value :

;Page :
1
;Line :
5
;Column :
55
;Prompt :

;Allow field to be entered Y/N :
**Y
;Allow field to be updated Y/N :
Y
;Allow entry of query condition Y/N :
Y
;Hide value of field Y/N :
N
;SQL>
**POST-CHANGE
/
;SQL>
$get-cdesc
SELECT paymethod.description
  INTO creditdesc
  FROM paymethod
 WHERE paymethod.paymethod = :customer.creditcard

;Message if value not found :
Invalid credit card code, e.g., VI, MC, AX.  Use [List Values] . . .
;Must value exist Y/N :
Y
```

```
;Is field mandatory Y/N :
Y
;Is field fixed length Y/N :
N
;Auto jump to next field Y/N :
N
;Convert field to upper case Y/N :
Y
;Help message :
Credit card code. e.g. VI, MC. Use [List Values].
;Lowest value :
@creditcard.creditcard
;Field name :
creditdesc
;Type of field :
CHAR
;Length of field / Display length / Query length :
20 / 20 / 20
;Is this field in the base table Y/N :
N
;Default value :

;Page :
1
;Line :
5
;Column :
58
;Prompt :

;Allow field to be entered Y/N :
**N
;Allow entry of query condition Y/N :
N
;Hide value of field Y/N :
N
;SQL>

;Field name :
credcdno
;Type of field :
CHAR
;Length of field / Display length / Query length :
20 / 20 / 20
;Is this field in the base table Y/N :
Y
;Is this field part of the primary key Y/N :
N
;Default value :

;Page :
1
;Line :
6
;Column :
55
;Prompt :

;Allow field to be entered Y/N :
**Y
;Allow field to be updated Y/N :
Y
;Allow entry of query condition Y/N :
Y
;Hide value of field Y/N :
N
;SQL>
```

continued

Listing B.3   *(continued)*

```
;Is field mandatory Y/N :
Y
;Is field fixed length Y/N :
N
;Auto jump to next field Y/N :
N
;Convert field to upper case Y/N :
Y
;Help message :
Credit card number.
;Lowest value :

;Highest value :

;Field name :
cardexp
;Type of field :
DATE
;Length of field / Display length / Query length :
9 / 9 / 9
;Is this field in the base table Y/N :
Y
;Is this field part of the primary key Y/N :
N
;Default value :

;Page :
1
;Line :
7
;Column :
55
;Prompt :

;Allow field to be entered Y/N :
**Y
;Allow field to be updated Y/N :
Y
;Allow entry of query condition Y/N :
Y
;Hide value of field Y/N :
N
;SQL>
**POST-CHANGE
/
;SQL>
$Chk-cardexp
SELECT 'x'
  FROM dual
 WHERE to_date(:cardexp) >= sysdate

;Message if value not found :
Credit card has expired! If entered incorrectly, try again . . .
;Must value exist Y/N :
Y
;Is field mandatory Y/N :
Y
;Is field fixed length Y/N :
N
;Auto jump to next field Y/N :
N
;Convert field to upper case Y/N :
Y
```

```
;Help message :
Credit card expiration date. e.g. 31-DEC-87
;Lowest value :

;Highest value :

;Field name :
cdlno
;Type of field :
CHAR
;Length of field / Display length / Query length :
10 / 10 / 10
;Is this field in the base table Y/N :
Y
;Is this field part of the primary key Y/N :
N
;Default value :

;Page :
1
;Line :
8
;Column :
55
;Prompt :

;Allow field to be entered Y/N :
**Y
;Allow field to be updated Y/N :
Y
;Allow entry of query condition Y/N :
Y
;Hide value of field Y/N :
N
;SQL>

;Is field mandatory Y/N :
Y
;Is field fixed length Y/N :
N
;Auto jump to next field Y/N :
N
;Convert field to upper case Y/N :
Y
;Help message :
Driver's license number or id number.
;Lowest value :

;Highest value :

;Field name :
cdlexp
;Type of field :
DATE
;Length of field / Display length / Query length :
9 / 9 / 9
;Is this field in the base table Y/N :
Y
;Is this field part of the primary key Y/N :
N
;Default value :

;Page :
1
;Line :
8
```

continued

Listing B.3   (*continued*)

```
;Column :
71
;Prompt :

;Allow field to be entered Y/N :
**Y
;Allow field to be updated Y/N :
Y
;Allow entry of query condition Y/N :
Y
;Hide value of field Y/N :
N
;SQL>
**POST-CHANGE
/
;SQL>
$chk-cdlexp
SELECT 1 from dual
 WHERE to_date(:cdlexp) >= sysdate

;Message if value not found :
License expiration date must be later than today's date. Please re-enter.
;Must value exist Y/N :
Y
;Is field mandatory Y/N :
Y
;Is field fixed length Y/N :
N
;Auto jump to next field Y/N :
Y
;Convert field to upper case Y/N :
Y
;Help message :
Date on which driver's license expires. e.g. 31-DEC-87
;Lowest value :

;Highest value :

;Field name :
format
;Type of field :
CHAR
;Length of field / Display length / Query length :
2 / 2 / 2
;Is this field in the base table Y/N :
Y
;Is this field part of the primary key Y/N :
N
;Default value :
V
;Page :
1
;Line :
9
;Column :
55
;Prompt :

;Allow field to be entered Y/N :
**Y
;Allow field to be updated Y/N :
Y
;Allow entry of query condition Y/N :
Y
```

```
;Hide value of field Y/N :
N
;SQL>
**POST-CHANGE
/
;SQL>
$get-format
SELECT DECODE(:format, 'V', 'Vhs', 'B', 'Beta', 'VB', 'Both
Vhs/Beta')
  INTO fdesc
  FROM dual
 WHERE :format in ('V', 'B', 'VB')

;Message if value not found :
Invalid tape format.  V = Vhs,  B = Beta, VB = Both Vhs/Beta.
;Must value exist Y/N :
Y
;Is field mandatory Y/N :
N
;Is field fixed length Y/N :
N
;Auto jump to next field Y/N :
N
;Convert field to upper case Y/N :
Y
;Help message :
Tape format.  Choices:  V = Vhs, B = Beta, or VB = Both Vhs/Beta.
;Lowest value :

;Highest value :

;Field name :
fdesc
;Type of field :
CHAR
;Length of field / Display length / Query length :
15 / 15 / 15
;Is this field in the base table Y/N :
N
;Default value :

;Page :
1
;Line :
9
;Column :
58
;Prompt :

;Allow field to be entered Y/N :
**N
;Allow entry of query condition Y/N :
N
;Hide value of field Y/N :
N
;SQL>

;Field name :
date_created
;Type of field :
DATE
;Length of field / Display length / Query length :
9 / 9 / 9
;Is this field in the base table Y/N :
Y
;Is this field part of the primary key Y/N :
N
```

continued

Listing B.3   *(continued)*

```
;Default value :
$$date$$
;Page :
1
;Line :
3
;Column :
34
;Prompt :

;Allow field to be entered Y/N :
**Y
;Allow field to be updated Y/N :
Y
;Allow entry of query condition Y/N :
Y
;Hide value of field Y/N :
N
;SQL>

;Is field mandatory Y/N :
N
;Is field fixed length Y/N :
N
;Auto jump to next field Y/N :
N
;Convert field to upper case Y/N :
N
;Help message :
Date membership first created.  Default is today's date.
;Lowest value :

;Highest value :

;Field name :
last_act
;Type of field :
DATE
;Length of field / Display length / Query length :
9 / 9 / 9
;Is this field in the base table Y/N :
Y
;Is this field part of the primary key Y/N :
N
;Default value :

;Page :
1
;Line :
3
;Column :
70
;Prompt :

;Allow field to be entered Y/N :
**N
;Allow entry of query condition Y/N :
Y
;Hide value of field Y/N :
N
;SQL>

;Field name :
```

```
;Block name / Description :
*custname/custname
;Enter default WHERE and ORDER BY clause :
where memberid > 0

;Table name :
CUSTNAME
;Check for uniqueness before inserting Y/N :
N
;Display/Buffer how many records :
3 / 12
;Base crt line ?
19
;How many physical lines per record ?
1
;Field name :
*Key-crerec
;SQL>
$Coord-crerec
#EXEMACRO clrblk; prvblk; crerec;

;Message if value not found :
Program error: Problem executing [Create Record] in coordinated blocks.
;Must value exist Y/N :
Y
;Field name :
memberid
;Type of field :
INT
;Length of field / Display length / Query length :
7 / 7 / 7
;Is this field in the base table Y/N :
*Y
;Is this field part of the primary key Y/N :
Y
;Field to copy primary key from :
CUSTOMER.MEMBERID
;Page :

;SQL>

;Field name :
name
;Type of field :
CHAR
;Length of field / Display length / Query length :
30 / 30 / 30
;Is this field in the base table Y/N :
Y
;Is this field part of the primary key Y/N :
N
;Default value :

;Page :
1
;Line :
1
;Column :
13
;Prompt :

;Allow field to be entered Y/N :
**Y
;Allow field to be updated Y/N :
Y
;Allow entry of query condition Y/N :
Y
```

continued

Listing B.3   *(continued)*

```
;Hide value of field Y/N :
N
;SQL>

;Is field mandatory Y/N :
N
;Is field fixed length Y/N :
N
;Auto jump to next field Y/N :
N
;Convert field to upper case Y/N :
N
;Help message :
Name of authorized user for this membership.
;Lowest value :

;Highest value :

;Field name :
restrict_cat
;Type of field :
INT
;Length of field / Display length / Query length :
3 / 3 / 3
;Is this field in the base table Y/N :
Y
;Is this field part of the primary key Y/N :
N
;Default value :

;Page :
1
;Line :
1
;Column :
44
;Prompt :

;Allow field to be entered Y/N :
**Y
;Allow field to be updated Y/N :
Y
;Allow entry of query condition Y/N :
Y
;Hide value of field Y/N :
N
;SQL>
**POST-CHANGE
/
;SQL>
$Get-catdesc
SELECT category.description
  INTO catdesc
  FROM category
 WHERE category.category = :custname.restrict_cat

;Message if value not found :
Invalid film category code.  Use [List Values].
;Must value exist Y/N :
Y
;Is field mandatory Y/N :
N
```

```
;Is field fixed length Y/N :
N
;Auto jump to next field Y/N :
N
;Convert field to upper case Y/N :
N
;Help message :
Restricted category code for authorized member. Use [List Values].
;Lowest value :
@category.category
;Field name :
catdesc
;Type of field :
CHAR
;Length of field / Display length / Query length :
20 / 20 / 20
;Is this field in the base table Y/N :
N
;Default value :

;Page :
1
;Line :
1
;Column :
48
;Prompt :

;Allow field to be entered Y/N :
**N
;Allow entry of query condition Y/N :
N
;Hide value of field Y/N :
N
;SQL>

;Field name :

;Block name / Description :

         Video Quest CUSTOMER Database
%LINE
3
   Member Id:          Created:             Account Last Active:
%LINE
5
      Member:                                  Credit:
     Address:                               Card No.:
                                             Expires:
         City:                               License:
Exp:
       State:      Zip:               Tape format:
%LINE
11
   Telephone: (   )    -        Eve: (   )    -
%LINE
14
          Add authorized users & rental restrictions for this membership
%LINE
18
              Authorized User           Category "Off Limits"
%LINE
23
```

continued

Listing B.3   *(continued)*

```
                              VIDEO QUEST RENTALS, Inc.
%LINE
1
%GRAPHICS
```

Listing B.4   The RENTALS Form

```
; Generated by SQL*Forms Version 2.0.18 on Fri Jun 10 15:42:44 1988
; Application owner is OPS$DCRONIN. Application name is rentals1
; (Application ID is 0)
; ------------------------------------------------
;Application Title :
RENTALS
;ORACLE workspace size :

;Block name / Description :
**key-duprec
;SQL>
$Chk-rental
SELECT 'x'
  FROM dual
 WHERE :customer.memberid is not null
   AND :rentals.catnum is not null
   AND :invoice.paymethod is not null
/
;Message if value not found :
Why print a blank invoice? Enter ALL rental information and try again . . .
;Must value exist Y/N :
Y
$Ok-print
#EXEMACRO print; redisp;

;Message if value not found :

;Must value exist Y/N :
Y
;Block name / Description :
**key-entqry / Query member(id)
;SQL>
$call-customer
#EXEMACRO call customer;

;Message if value not found :
Program error: Problem calling CUSTOMER form. See your supervisor.
;Must value exist Y/N :
Y
;Block name / Description :
**key-exeqry
;SQL>
$Chk-null
SELECT 'x'
  FROM dual
 WHERE :customer.name is not null
/
;Message if value not found :
You must enter a member(id) to query outstanding rentals.
;Must value exist Y/N :
Y
```

```
$copy-memberid
#COPY :customer.memberid global.memberid
/
;Message if value not found :

;Must value exist Y/N :
Y
$copy-name
#COPY :customer.name global.name
/
;Message if value not found :

;Must value exist Y/N :
Y
$Auto-query
#EXEMACRO callqry outrent;

;Message if value not found :
Program error: Problem moving to next block and executing query.
;Must value exist Y/N :
Y
;Block name / Description :
customer/customer
;Table name :
*
;Check for uniqueness before inserting Y/N :
N
;Display/Buffer how many records :
1 / 1
;Field name :
*key-nxtblk
;SQL>
$chk-null
select 'x'
  from dual
 where :customer.memberid is not null
/
;Message if value not found :
You must enter a member(id) to process rentals.
;Must value exist Y/N :
Y
#exemacro nxtblk;

;Message if value not found :

;Must value exist Y/N :
Y
;Field name :
*key-prvblk
;SQL>
#exemacro null;

;Message if value not found :
Nowhere to go from here, boyo!
;Must value exist Y/N :
Y
;Field name :
xslstaxpct
;Type of field :
CHAR
;Length of field / Display length / Query length :
10 / 10 / 10
;Is this field in the base table Y/N :
N
;Default value :
```

continued

Listing B.4   *(continued)*

```
;Page :

;SQL>

;Field name :
invno
;Type of field :
RINT
;Length of field / Display length / Query length :
7 / 7 / 7
;Is this field in the base table Y/N :
N
;Default value :

;Page :
1
;Line :
1
;Column :
70
;Prompt :

;Allow field to be entered Y/N :
**N
;Allow entry of query condition Y/N :
N
;Hide value of field Y/N :
N
;SQL>

;Field name :
day
;Type of field :
CHAR
;Length of field / Display length / Query length :
9 / 9 / 9
;Is this field in the base table Y/N :
N
;Default value :

;Page :
1
;Line :
3
;Column :
51
;Prompt :

;Allow field to be entered Y/N :
**N
;Allow entry of query condition Y/N :
N
;Hide value of field Y/N :
N
;SQL>

;Field name :
xdateout
;Type of field :
DATE
;Length of field / Display length / Query length :
9 / 9 / 9
;Is this field in the base table Y/N :
Y
```

```
;Is this field part of the primary key Y/N :
N
;Default value :
$$date$$
;Page :
1
;Line :
3
;Column :
61
;Prompt :

;Allow field to be entered Y/N :
**N
;Allow entry of query condition Y/N :
N
;Hide value of field Y/N :
N
;SQL>
**POST-CHANGE
/
;SQL>
$Convert-get-info
SELECT to_char(to_date(:xdateout),'Day'),
       to_char(sysdate,'hh:mi am'), slstaxpct
  INTO day, time, xslstaxpct
  FROM cntl

;Message if value not found :
Program error:  Problem converting date formats.  See your supervisor.
;Must value exist Y/N :
Y
;Field name :
time
;Type of field :
CHAR
;Length of field / Display length / Query length :
9 / 9 / 9
;Is this field in the base table Y/N :
N
;Default value :

;Page :
1
;Line :
3
;Column :
71
;Prompt :

;Allow field to be entered Y/N :
**N
;Allow entry of query condition Y/N :
N
;Hide value of field Y/N :
N
;SQL>

;Field name :
outrent
;Type of field :
RINT
;Length of field / Display length / Query length :
3 / 3 / 3
;Is this field in the base table Y/N :
N
;Default value :
```

continued

Listing B.4   *(continued)*

```
;Page :
1
;Line :
5
;Column :
71
;Prompt :

;Allow field to be entered Y/N :
**N
;Allow entry of query condition Y/N :
N
;Hide value of field Y/N :
N
;SQL>

;Field name :
memberid
;Type of field :
INT
;Length of field / Display length / Query length :
7 / 7 / 7
;Is this field in the base table Y/N :
Y
;Is this field part of the primary key Y/N :
N
;Default value :

;Page :
1
;Line :
5
;Column :
14
;Prompt :

;Allow field to be entered Y/N :
**Y
;Allow field to be updated Y/N :
N
;Allow entry of query condition Y/N :
N
;Hide value of field Y/N :
N
;SQL>
**POST-CHANGE
/
;SQL>
$Get-name
SELECT name
  INTO name
  FROM customer
 WHERE customer.memberid = :customer.memberid
/
;Message if value not found :
Invalid Id.  Verify card, or clear block  press [Exeqry] to query customer.
;Must value exist Y/N :
Y
;Must value exist Y/N:
$Get-outrent
SELECT count(*)
  INTO outrent
  FROM rentals
```

```
 WHERE rentals.memberid = :customer.memberid
   AND rentals.actrtn is null
/
;Message if value not found :
Program error: Problem computing outstanding rentals for this customer.
;Must value exist Y/N :
Y
$chk-outrent
select 1 from cntl
 where :outrent > maxrent
/
;Message if value not found :
*Customer has exceeded rental limit! No rentals until tapes returned . . .
;Must value exist Y/N :
Y
;SQL>
**key-nxtfld
/
;SQL>
$Go-nxtblk
#EXEMACRO nxtblk;

;Message if value not found :
Program error:  Problem executing NXTBLK on memberid.  See your supervisor.
;Must value exist Y/N :
Y
;Is field mandatory Y/N :
N
;Is field fixed length Y/N :
N
;Auto jump to next field Y/N :
N
;Convert field to upper case Y/N :
N
;Help message :
Enter membership Id.
;Lowest value :

;Highest value :

;Field name :
name
;Type of field :
CHAR
;Length of field / Display length / Query length :
28 / 28 / 28
;Is this field in the base table Y/N :
N
;Default value :

;Page :
1
;Line :
5
;Column :
22
;Prompt :

;Allow field to be entered Y/N :
**N
;Allow entry of query condition Y/N :
N
;Hide value of field Y/N :
N
;SQL>

;Field name :
```

continued

Listing B.4 *(continued)*

```
;Block name / Description :
*rentals/rentals
;Enter default WHERE and ORDER BY clause :
where rentals.memberid > 0 and rentals.memberid is not null

;Table name :
RENTALS
;Check for uniqueness before inserting Y/N :
N
;Display/Buffer how many records :
3 / 12
;Base crt line ?
9
;How many physical lines per record ?
2
;Field name :
*PRE-INSERT
;SQL>
$Chk-maxrent
SELECT count(*)
  FROM rentals
 WHERE rentals.memberid = :rentals.memberid
   AND actrtn is null
 GROUP by rentals.memberid
having count(*) >=
(select maxrent
       from cntl)
/
;Message if value not found :
*Customer exceeded rental limit!  Please have customer return tapes.
;Must value exist Y/N :
Y
$Chk-custinvno
SELECT 'x'
  FROM dual
 WHERE :customer.invno is null
/
;Message if value not found :
$lock-cntl $init-rental
;Must value exist Y/N :
Y
$lock-cntl
LOCK TABLE cntl IN SHARE UPDATE MODE
/
;Message if value not found :
Program error:  Problem locking CNTL table to generate new invoice number.
;Must value exist Y/N :
Y
$Get-newinvno
UPDATE cntl
   SET last_invoice = last_invoice + 1
/
;Message if value not found :
Program error: Problem updating CNTL table to generate new invoice number.
;Must value exist Y/N :
Y
$Display-invno
SELECT last_invoice
  INTO customer.invno
  FROM cntl
/
;Message if value not found :
Problem inserting new invoice number. See your supervisor.
```

```
;Must value exist Y/N :
Y
$Init-rental
SELECT null, :customer.xdateout, :customer.invno
  INTO actrtn, dateout, rentals.invno
  FROM dual

;Message if value not found :
Program error:  Problem initializing rental fields.  See your supervisor.
;Must value exist Y/N :
Y
;Field name :
*POST-INSERT
;SQL>
$Lock-product
LOCK TABLE product IN SHARE UPDATE MODE
/
;Message if value not found :
Program error:  Problem locking PRODUCT table to decrement QTYOH.
;Must value exist Y/N :
Y
$Update-product
UPDATE product
   SET qtyoh = qtyoh - 1
 WHERE product.prodno = :xprodno
   AND product.storeno = :xstoreno
/
;Message if value not found :
Program error:  Problem decrementing QTYOH in PRODUCT table to reflect rent.
;Must value exist Y/N :
Y
$Lock-customer
LOCK TABLE customer IN SHARE UPDATE MODE
/
;Message if value not found :
Program error:  Problem locking CUSTOMER table to update LAST_ACT.
;Must value exist Y/N :
Y
$Update-customer
UPDATE customer
   SET last_act = sysdate
 WHERE customer.memberid = :rentals.memberid

;Message if value not found :
Program error: Problem updating LAST_ACT in CUSTOMER table. See supervisor.
;Must value exist Y/N :
Y
;Field name :
*key-commit
;SQL>
$no-commit
#exemacro null;

;Message if value not found :
*Commit is allowed only on receipt of payment.
;Must value exist Y/N :
N
;Field name :
*key-delrec
;SQL>
$no-delete
#exemacro null;

;Message if value not found :
*Rentals may not be deleted.
;Must value exist Y/N :
N
```

continued

Listing B.4   *(continued)*

```
;Field name :
memberid
;Type of field :
INT
;Length of field / Display length / Query length :
7 / 7 / 7
;Is this field in the base table Y/N :
*Y
;Is this field part of the primary key Y/N :
N
;Copy field value from :
CUSTOMER.MEMBERID
;Page :

;SQL>

;Field name :
invno
;Type of field :
INT
;Length of field / Display length / Query length :
7 / 7 / 7
;Is this field in the base table Y/N :
*Y
;Is this field part of the primary key Y/N :
N
;Copy field value from :
CUSTOMER.INVNO

;Page :

;SQL>

;Field name :
xprodno
;Type of field :
CHAR
;Length of field / Display length / Query length :
25 / 25 / 25
;Is this field in the base table Y/N :
N
;Default value :

;Page :

;SQL>

;Field name :
xstoreno
;Type of field :
INT
;Length of field / Display length / Query length :
3 / 3 / 3
;Is this field in the base table Y/N :
N
;Default value :

;Page :

;SQL>

;Field name :
actrtn
;Type of field :
DATE
```

```
;Length of field / Display length / Query length :
9 / 9 / 9
;Is this field in the base table Y/N :
Y
;Is this field part of the primary key Y/N :
N
;Default value :

;Page :

;SQL>

;Field name :
xcategory
;Type of field :
INT
;Length of field / Display length / Query length :
3 / 3 / 3
;Is this field in the base table Y/N :
N
;Default value :

;Page :

;SQL>

;Field name :
catnum
;Type of field :
INT
;Length of field / Display length / Query length :
10 / 7 / 10
;Is this field in the base table Y/N :
*Y
;Is this field part of the primary key Y/N :
Y
;Field to copy primary key from :
;Default value :
;Page :
1
;Line :
1
;Column :
3
;Prompt :

;Allow field to be entered Y/N :
**Y
;Allow field to be updated Y/N :
N
;Allow entry of query condition Y/N :
Y
;Hide value of field Y/N :
N
;SQL>
**POST-CHANGE
/
;SQL>
$Get-prodno
SELECT prodno, storeno
  INTO xprodno, xstoreno
  FROM tape
 WHERE tape.catnum = :rentals.catnum
/
;Message if value not found :
Invalid catalog number. Please re-enter.
```

continued

Listing B.4   *(continued)*

```
;Must value exist Y/N :
Y
$Chk-if-rented
SELECT 'x'
  FROM rentals
 WHERE rentals.catnum = :rentals.catnum
   AND rentals.actrtn is null
/
;Message if value not found :
*Rental with this catalog number is already checked out!  Please re-enter
;Must value exist Y/N :
Y
$Get-titlecd
SELECT titlecd, ratepdy,
       DECODE(product.format, 'V', 'Vhs', 'B', 'Beta', null)
  INTO titlecd, ratepdy, fdesc
  FROM product, rentclass
 WHERE product.prodno = :xprodno
   AND product.storeno = :xstoreno
   AND product.rentclass = rentclass.rentclass
   AND product.prodtype in ('R', 'RS')
/
;Message if value not found :
Invalid product number OR  product is not a rental item. Please re-enter.
;Must value exist Y/N :
Y
$Get-title
SELECT title, category
  INTO tdesc, xcategory
  FROM title
 WHERE title.titlecd = :titlecd
/
;Message if value not found :
Invalid title or category not fetched for this title.  See your supervisor.
;Must value exist Y/N :
*N
;Trigger will FAIL, if you reverse the order of the where clauses; trigger
;must test memberid 1st to identify only those rows in custname table
;that belong to the member you're working with on screen. If you let the
;trigger test the restricted category first, SQL stops at the first row in
;the table that contains that restricted category - and will stop! The query
;has succeeded (returned a row!) at that point without even giving a hoot
;whether the film category found belongs to the memberid you need!
$Chk-restrict
SELECT 'x'
  FROM custname
 WHERE custname.memberid = :customer.memberid
   AND custname.restrict_cat = :xcategory
/
;Message if value not found :
*Authorized user(s) restricted from viewing this tape!  Consult key member
;Must value exist Y/N :
Y
$Chk-custformat
SELECT 'x'
  FROM customer
 WHERE customer.memberid = :customer.memberid
   AND (customer.format = decode(:fdesc, 'Vhs', 'V', 'Beta', 'B')
    OR customer.format = 'VB')
;Message if value not found :
Format of this tape doesn't match customer's default tape format.  Check it.
;Must value exist Y/N :
Y
```

```
;Is field mandatory Y/N :
N
;Is field fixed length Y/N :
N
;Auto jump to next field Y/N :
N
;Convert field to upper case Y/N :
N
;Help message :
Enter catalog number of rental tape.
;Lowest value :

;Highest value :

;Field name :
titlecd
;Type of field :
CHAR
;Length of field / Display length / Query length :
15 / 15 / 15
;Is this field in the base table Y/N :
N
;Default value :

;Page :
1
;Line :
1
;Column :
12
;Prompt :

;Allow field to be entered Y/N :
**N
;Allow entry of query condition Y/N :
N
;Hide value of field Y/N :
N
;SQL>

;Field name :
rentdays
;Type of field :
RINT
;Length of field / Display length / Query length :
3 / 3 / 3
;Is this field in the base table Y/N :
Y
;Is this field part of the primary key Y/N :
N
;Default value :

;Page :
1
;Line :
1
;Column :
39
;Prompt :

;Allow field to be entered Y/N :
**Y
;Allow field to be updated Y/N :
N
;Allow entry of query condition Y/N :
N
```

continued

Listing B.4   *(continued)*

```
;Hide value of field Y/N :
N
;SQL>
**POST-CHANGE
/
;SQL>
$Calc-schdrtn
SELECT sysdate + to_number(:rentdays)
  INTO schdrtn
  FROM dual
;Message if value not found :
Program error:  Problem calculating scheduled return date.  See supervisor.
;Must value exist Y/N :
Y
;Is field mandatory Y/N :
Y
;Is field fixed length Y/N :
N
;Auto jump to next field Y/N :
N
;Convert field to upper case Y/N :
N
;Help message :
Number of days customer will rent this tape.
;Lowest value :

;Highest value :

;Field name :
ratepdy
;Type of field :
RMONEY
;Length of field / Display length / Query length :
5 / 5 / 5
;Is this field in the base table Y/N :
Y
;Is this field part of the primary key Y/N :
N
;Default value :

;Page :
1
;Line :
1
;Column :
44
;Prompt :

;Allow field to be entered Y/N :
**Y
;Allow field to be updated Y/N :
N
;Allow entry of query condition Y/N :
Y
;Hide value of field Y/N :
N
;SQL>
**POST-CHANGE
/
;SQL>
$Calc-total
SELECT (nvl(:rentals.rentdays, 0) * nvl(:rentals.ratepdy, 0))
  INTO rentals.linettl
  FROM dual
/
```

```
;Message if value not found :
Program error: Can't calculate line total on RATEPDY.  See your supervisor.
;Must value exist Y/N :
Y
$Calc-subtotals
SELECT nvl(:invoice.total, 0) + nvl(:rentals.linettl, 0),
       round(nvl(:invoice.tax, 0) +
       nvl(:rentals.linettl, 0) * (nvl(:customer.xslstaxpct,
       0)/100),2)
  INTO invoice.total, invoice.tax
  FROM dual
/
;Message if value not found :
Program error:  Can't calculate subtotals on RATEPDY.  See your supervisor.
;Must value exist Y/N :
Y
$calc-grandtotals
SELECT nvl(:invoice.total, 0) + nvl(:invoice.tax, 0)
  INTO invoice.grand_total
  FROM dual

;Message if value not found :
Program error:  Can't calculate grand total on RATEPDY. See your supervisor.
;Must value exist Y/N :
Y
;Is field mandatory Y/N :
N
;Is field fixed length Y/N :
N
;Auto jump to next field Y/N :
N
;Convert field to upper case Y/N :
N
;Help message :
Rate per day for this rental.  You may overwrite the displayed (default) value.
;Lowest value :

;Highest value :

;Field name :
dateout
;Type of field :
DATE
;Length of field / Display length / Query length :
9 / 9 / 9
;Is this field in the base table Y/N :
Y
;Is this field part of the primary key Y/N :
N
;Default value :
$$date$$
;Page :
1
;Line :
1
;Column :
51
;Prompt :

;Allow field to be entered Y/N :
**N
;Allow entry of query condition Y/N :
N
;Hide value of field Y/N :
N
;SQL>
```

continued

Listing B.4   *(continued)*

```
;Field name :
schdrtn
;Type of field :
DATE
;Length of field / Display length / Query length :
9 / 9 / 9
;Is this field in the base table Y/N :
Y
;Is this field part of the primary key Y/N :
N
;Default value :

;Page :
1
;Line :
1
;Column :
62
;Prompt :

;Allow field to be entered Y/N :
**N
;Allow entry of query condition Y/N :
N
;Hide value of field Y/N :
N
;SQL>

;Field name :
linettl
;Type of field :
RMONEY
;Length of field / Display length / Query length :
7 / 7 / 7
;Is this field in the base table Y/N :
N
;Default value :

;Page :
1
;Line :
1
;Column :
73
;Prompt :

;Allow field to be entered Y/N :
**N
;Allow entry of query condition Y/N :
N
;Hide value of field Y/N :
N
;SQL>

;Field name :
fdesc
;Type of field :
CHAR
;Length of field / Display length / Query length :
4 / 4 / 4
;Is this field in the base table Y/N :
N
;Default value :
```

```
;Page :
1
;Line :
1
;Column :
30
;Prompt :

;Allow field to be entered Y/N :
**N
;Allow entry of query condition Y/N :
N
;Hide value of field Y/N :
N
;SQL>

;Field name :
tdesc
;Type of field :
CHAR
;Length of field / Display length / Query length :
?? / ?? / ??
;Is this field in the base table Y/N :
N
;Default value :

;Page :
1
;Line :
2
;Column :
3
;Prompt :

;Allow field to be entered Y/N :
**N
;Allow entry of query condition Y/N :
N
;Hide value of field Y/N :
N
;SQL>

;Field name :
;Block name / Description :
INVOICE/Invoice
;Table name :
INVOICE
;Check for uniqueness before inserting Y/N :
N
;Display/Buffer how many records :
1 / 1
;Field name :
*PRE-INSERT
;SQL>
$Init-invoice
SELECT to_number(:customer.invno), 'R', to_date(:customer.xdateout),
       to_char(sysdate, 'hh:mi am'), :customer.memberid
  INTO invoice.invno, trantype, invoice.trandate,
invoice.trantime,
       invoice.memberid
  FROM dual

;Message if value not found :
Program error: Problem initializing the INVOICE fields. See your supervisor.
;Must value exist Y/N :
Y
```

continued

Listing B.4   *(continued)*

```
;Field name :
*key-duprec
;SQL>
$ok-print
#exemacro print; redisp;

;Message if value not found :

;Must value exist Y/N :
Y
;Field name :
*key-entqry
;SQL>
$no-entqry
#exemacro null;

;Message if value not found :
*Add/update customer disabled here.  Go to previous block and try again.
;Must value exist Y/N :
N
;Field name :
*key-exeqry
;SQL>
$no-exeqry
#exemacro null;

;Message if value not found :
Query of rentals disabled here.  Go to previous block and try again.
;Must value exist Y/N :
Y
;Field name :
*key-listval
;SQL>
$no-titlesout
#exemacro null;

;Message if value not found :
Query of titles out disabled here.  Go to previous block and try again.
;Must value exist Y/N :
Y
;Field name :
memberid
;Type of field :
INT
;Length of field / Display length / Query length :
7 / 7 / 7
;Is this field in the base table Y/N :
*Y
;Is this field part of the primary key Y/N :
N
;Copy field value from :
CUSTOMER.MEMBERID
;Page :

;SQL>

;Field name :
invno
;Type of field :
INT
;Length of field / Display length / Query length :
7 / 7 / 7
;Is this field in the base table Y/N :
*Y
```

```
;Is this field part of the primary key Y/N :
N
;Copy field value from :
RENTALS.INVNO
;Page :

;SQL>

;Field name :
trantype
;Type of field :
CHAR
;Length of field / Display length / Query length :
1 / 1 / 1
;Is this field in the base table Y/N :
Y
;Is this field part of the primary key Y/N :
N
;Default value :
R
;Page :

;SQL>

;Field name :
trandate
;Type of field :
DATE
;Length of field / Display length / Query length :
9 / 9 / 9
;Is this field in the base table Y/N :
*Y
;Is this field part of the primary key Y/N :
N
;Copy field value from :
RENTALS.DATEOUT
;Page :

;SQL>

;Field name :
trantime
;Type of field :
CHAR
;Length of field / Display length / Query length :
8 / 8 / 8
;Is this field in the base table Y/N :
Y
;Is this field part of the primary key Y/N :
N
;Default value :

;Page :

;SQL>

;Field name :
paymethod
;Type of field :
CHAR
;Length of field / Display length / Query length :
2 / 2 / 2
;Is this field in the base table Y/N :
Y
;Is this field part of the primary key Y/N :
N
;Default value :
```

continued

Listing B.4   *(continued)*

```
;Page :
1
;Line :
16
;Column :
35
;Prompt :

;Allow field to be entered Y/N :
**Y
;Allow field to be updated Y/N :
N
;Allow entry of query condition Y/N :
N
;Hide value of field Y/N :
N
;SQL>
**POST-CHANGE
/
;SQL>
$Get-paydesc
SELECT description
  INTO paydesc
  FROM paymethod
 WHERE paymethod.paymethod = :invoice.paymethod
;Message if value not found :
Invalid payment method. CAsh, AX, MC, VI  Use [List Values].
;Must value exist Y/N :
Y
;Is field mandatory Y/N :
Y
;Is field fixed length Y/N :
N
;Auto jump to next field Y/N :
N
;Convert field to upper case Y/N :
Y
;Help message :
*Enter pay method.  CAsh,VI,AX,MC, etc.  Use [List Values]
;Lowest value :
@paymethod.paymethod
;Field name :
paydesc
;Type of field :
CHAR
;Length of field / Display length / Query length :
20 / 20 / 20
;Is this field in the base table Y/N :
N
;Default value :

;Page :
1
;Line :
16
;Column :
38
;Prompt :

;Allow field to be entered Y/N :
**N
;Allow entry of query condition Y/N :
N
```

```
;Hide value of field Y/N :
N
;SQL>

;Field name :
cashtend
;Type of field :
RMONEY
;Length of field / Display length / Query length :
10 / 10 / 10
;Is this field in the base table Y/N :
N
;Default value :
0
;Page :
1
;Line :
17
;Column :
38
;Prompt :

;Allow field to be entered Y/N :
**Y
;Allow field to be updated Y/N :
N
;Allow entry of query condition Y/N :
N
;Hide value of field Y/N :
N
;SQL>
**POST-CHANGE
/
;SQL>
$chk-cashamt
SELECT DECODE(:paymethod, 'CA',
                 nvl(:cashtend, 0) - nvl(:grand_total, 0), 0)
  INTO change
  FROM dual
/
;Message if value not found :
Program error:  Problem calculating change.  See your supervisor.
;Must value exist Y/N :
Y
$Chk-cash-or-charge
SELECT 'x'
  FROM dual
 WHERE :paymethod = 'CA'

;Message if value not found :
Change given only with CASH transactions.  Clear field and commit, please
;Must value exist Y/N :
Y
;Is field mandatory Y/N :
N
;Is field fixed length Y/N :
N
;Auto jump to next field Y/N :
N
;Convert field to upper case Y/N :
N
;Help message :
If cash, enter amount received from customer.
;Lowest value :

;Highest value :
```

continued

Listing B.4   *(continued)*

```
;Field name :
change
;Type of field :
RMONEY
;Length of field / Display length / Query length :
10 / 10 / 10
;Is this field in the base table Y/N :
N
;Default value :
0
;Page :
1
;Line :
18
;Column :
38
;Prompt :

;Allow field to be entered Y/N :
**N
;Allow entry of query condition Y/N :
N
;Hide value of field Y/N :
N
;SQL>

;Field name :
total
;Type of field :
RMONEY
;Length of field / Display length / Query length :
9 / 9 / 9
;Is this field in the base table Y/N :
Y
;Is this field part of the primary key Y/N :
N
;Default value :

;Page :
1
;Line :
16
;Column :
71
;Prompt :

;Allow field to be entered Y/N :
**N
;Allow entry of query condition Y/N :
N
;Hide value of field Y/N :
N
;SQL>

;Field name :
tax
;Type of field :
RMONEY
;Length of field / Display length / Query length :
9 / 9 / 9
;Is this field in the base table Y/N :
Y
```

```
;Is this field part of the primary key Y/N :
N
;Default value :
;Page :
1
;Line :
17
;Column :
71
;Prompt :

;Allow field to be entered Y/N :
**N
;Allow entry of query condition Y/N :
N
;Hide value of field Y/N :
N
;SQL>

;Field name :
grand_total
;Type of field :
RMONEY
;Length of field / Display length / Query length :
9 / 9 / 9
;Is this field in the base table Y/N :
N
;Default value :

;Page :
1
;Line :
18
;Column :
71
;Prompt :

;Allow field to be entered Y/N :
**N
;Allow entry of query condition Y/N :
N
;Hide value of field Y/N :
N
;SQL>

;Field name :
;Block name / Description :
      Video Quest RENTALS                          [ Invoice No:]
%LINE
5
  Member Id:                                   Tapes rented out:
%LINE
7
   Catalog    Title    Format    Days    Rate   Date out   Date Due   Total
%LINE
16
                     Paid:                            Subtotal:
             Cash tendered:                                Tax:
                   Change:                   Pay this amount:
%LINE
21
    [EntQry] Add/Update Member    [ExeQry] Tapes Out    [DupRec] Print Invoice Amt
%LINE
23
```

continued

Listing B.4   *(continued)*

```
                    VIDEO QUEST RENTALS, Inc.
%LINE
1
%GRAPHICS
```

Listing B.5   The RETURNS Form

```
; Generated by SQL*Forms Version 2.0.18 on Fri Jun 10 19:49:27 1988
; Application owner is OPS$DCRONIN.  Application name is returns1
; (Application ID is 0)
; -------------------------------------------------
;Application Title :
RETURNS
;ORACLE workspace size :

;Block name / Description :
**key-commit
;SQL>
$no-commit
#exemacro null;

;Message if value not found :
Commit allowed only on payment block (or after receipt of latecharges)
;Must value exist Y/N :
Y
;Block name / Description :
**key-duprec
;SQL>
$chk-return
SELECT 'x'
  FROM dual
 WHERE :customer.memberid is not null
   AND :returns.catnum is not null
   AND :invoice.total is not null
/
;Message if value not found :
Why print a blank invoice?  Enter returns information and try again . . .
;Must value exist Y/N :
Y
$ok-print
#exemacro print; redisp;

;Message if value not found :

;Must value exist Y/N :
Y
;Block name / Description :
**key-entqry
;SQL>
$no-entqry
#exemacro null;

;Message if value not found :
*Enter memberid and press [F2] to query rentals checked out by this member.
;Must value exist Y/N :
N
;Block name / Description :
**key-exeqry
```

```
;SQL>
$chk-null
select 1
  from dual
 where :customer.name is not null
/
;Message if value not found :
You must identify a member to query rentals outstanding.
;Must value exist Y/N :
Y
$copy-memberid
#copy customer.memberid global.memberid
/
;Message if value not found :

;Must value exist Y/N :
Y
$copy-name
#copy customer.name global.name
/
;Message if value not found :
;Must value exist Y/N :
Y
$out-rental
#exemacro callqry outrent;

;Message if value not found :

;Must value exist Y/N :
Y
;Block name / Description :
customer/customer
;Table name :
*
;Check for uniqueness before inserting Y/N :
N
;Display/Buffer how many records :
1 / 1
;Field name :
*key-nxtfld
;SQL>
#exemacro goblk returns;

;Message if value not found :

;Must value exist Y/N :
Y
;Field name :
latechgpct
;Type of field :
RNUMBER
;Length of field / Display length / Query length :
7 / 7 / 7
;Is this field in the base table Y/N :
N
;Default value :

;Page :

;SQL>

;Field name :
xslstaxpct
;Type of field :
RNUMBER
```

continued

Listing B.5 *(continued)*

```
;Length of field / Display length / Query length :
6 / 6 / 6
;Is this field in the base table Y/N :
N
;Default value :

;Page :

;SQL>

;Field name :
invno
;Type of field :
RINT
;Length of field / Display length / Query length :
7 / 7 / 7
;Is this field in the base table Y/N :
N
;Default value :

;Page :
1
;Line :
1
;Column :
70
;Prompt :

;Allow field to be entered Y/N :
**N
;Allow entry of query condition Y/N :
N
;Hide value of field Y/N :
N
;SQL>

;Field name :
memberid
;Type of field :
INT
;Length of field / Display length / Query length :
7 / 7 / 7
;Is this field in the base table Y/N :
Y
;Is this field part of the primary key Y/N :
N
;Default value :

;Page :
1
;Line :
5
;Column :
14
;Prompt :

;Allow field to be entered Y/N :
**Y
;Allow field to be updated Y/N :
N
;Allow entry of query condition Y/N :
N
;Hide value of field Y/N :
N
```

```
;SQL>
**POST-CHANGE
/
;SQL>
$get-name
SELECT name
  INTO name
  FROM customer
 WHERE customer.memberid = :customer.memberid
/
;Message if value not found :
Invalid member id. Please verify member info.
;Must value exist Y/N :
Y
;Must value exist Y/N:
$get-outrent
SELECT count(*)
  INTO outrent
  FROM rentals
 WHERE rentals.memberid = :customer.memberid
   AND actrtn is null
/
;Message if value not found :

;Must value exist Y/N :
N
$chk-outrent
select 1 from cntl
 where :outrent > maxrent

;Message if value not found :
*Customer has exceeded rental limit!  No rentals until tapes are returned . . .
;Must value exist Y/N :
Y
;Is field mandatory Y/N :
N
;Is field fixed length Y/N :
N
;Auto jump to next field Y/N :
N
;Convert field to upper case Y/N :
N
;Help message :
;Lowest value :

;Highest value :

;Field name :
name
;Type of field :
CHAR
;Length of field / Display length / Query length :
30 / 27 / 30
;Is this field in the base table Y/N :
N
;Default value :
;Page :
1
;Line :
5
;Column :
22
;Prompt :

;Allow field to be entered Y/N :
**N
```

continued

Listing B.5   *(continued)*

```
;Allow entry of query condition Y/N :
N
;Hide value of field Y/N :
N
;SQL>

;Field name :
outrent
;Type of field :
RINT
;Length of field / Display length / Query length :
3 / 3 / 3
;Is this field in the base table Y/N :
N
;Default value :
0
;Page :
1
;Line :
5
;Column :
71
;Prompt :

;Allow field to be entered Y/N :
**N
;Allow entry of query condition Y/N :
N
;Hide value of field Y/N :
N
;SQL>

;Field name :
day
;Type of field :
CHAR
;Length of field / Display length / Query length :
9 / 9 / 9
;Is this field in the base table Y/N :
N
;Default value :
;Page :
1
;Line :
3
;Column :
51
;Prompt :

;Allow field to be entered Y/N :
**N
;Allow entry of query condition Y/N :
N
;Hide value of field Y/N :
N
;SQL>

;Field name :
xactrtn
;Type of field :
DATE
;Length of field / Display length / Query length :
9 / 9 / 9
;Is this field in the base table Y/N :
Y
```

```
;Is this field part of the primary key Y/N :
N
;Default value :
$$date$$
;Page :
1
;Line :
3
;Column :
61
;Prompt :

;Allow field to be entered Y/N :
**N
;Allow entry of query condition Y/N :
N
;Hide value of field Y/N :
N
;SQL>
**POST-CHANGE
/
;SQL>
SELECT to_char(to_date(:xactrtn),'Day'),
       to_char(sysdate,'hh:mi am'), slstaxpct, latechgpct
  INTO day, time, xslstaxpct, latechgpct
  FROM cntl
;Message if value not found :

;Must value exist Y/N :
N
;Field name :
time
;Type of field :
CHAR
;Length of field / Display length / Query length :
9 / 9 / 9
;Is this field in the base table Y/N :
N
;Default value :

;Page :
1
;Line :
3
;Column :
71
;Prompt :

;Allow field to be entered Y/N :
**N
;Allow entry of query condition Y/N :
N
;Hide value of field Y/N :
N
;SQL>

;Field name :
;Block name / Description :
*returns/returns
;Enter default WHERE and ORDER BY clause :
where customer.memberid > 0

;Table name :
RETURNS
;Check for uniqueness before inserting Y/N :
N
```

continued

Listing B.5   *(continued)*

```
;Display/Buffer how many records :
3 / 50
;Base crt line ?
q
;How many physical lines per record ?
2
;Field name :
*PRE-INSERT
;SQL>
$init-returns
SELECT :customer.memberid, sysdate, nvl(:latecharge,0)
  INTO returns.memberid, actrtn, latecharge
  FROM dual

;Message if value not found :
Error in initializing fields in returns block.
;Must value exist Y/N :
Y
;Field name :
*POST-INSERT
;SQL>
$lock-rentals
lock table rentals in share update mode
/
;Message if value not found :
Post-insert. Error in locking RENTALS for update. Call for help.
;Must value exist Y/N :
Y
$update-rentals
update rentals
   set actrtn = sysdate
 where rentals.memberid = :customer.memberid
   and rentals.catnum = :catnum
/
;Message if value not found :
Post-insert. Error in relocating rentals record. Call
for help.
;Must value exist Y/N :
Y
$lock-product
lock table product in share update mode
/
;Message if value not found :
Post-insert. Error in locking PRODUCT for update. Call for help.
;Must value exist Y/N :
Y
$update-product
update product
   set qtyoh = qtyoh + 1
 where product.prodno = :xprodno
   and product.storeno = :xstoreno
/
;Message if value not found :
Post-insert. Error in relocating rentals record. Call for help.
;Must value exist Y/N :
Y
$lock-customer
lock table customer in share update mode
/
;Message if value not found :
Post-insert.  Error in locking CUSTOMER table for update.
;Must value exist Y/N :
Y
```

```
$update-customer
update customer
   set last_act = sysdate
 where customer.memberid = :customer.memberid

;Message if value not found :
Post-insert.  Error in updating last activity date in CUSTOMER table.
;Must value exist Y/N :
Y
;Field name :
*key-delrec
;SQL>
$no_delete
#exemacro null;

;Message if value not found :
*Delete is not allowed on returns screen.
;Must value exist Y/N :
N
;Field name :
memberid
;Type of field :
INT
;Length of field / Display length / Query length :
7 / 7 / 7
;Is this field in the base table Y/N :
*Y
;Is this field part of the primary key Y/N :
Y
;Field to copy primary key from :
CUSTOMER.MEMBERID
;Page :

;SQL>

;Field name :
xprodno
;Type of field :
CHAR
;Length of field / Display length / Query length :
25 / 25 / 25
;Is this field in the base table Y/N :
N
;Default value :

;Page :

;SQL>

;Field name :
xstoreno
;Type of field :
INT
;Length of field / Display length / Query length :
2 / 2 / 2
;Is this field in the base table Y/N :
N
;Default value :

;Page :

;SQL>

;Field name :
dateout
;Type of field :
DATE
```

continued

Listing B.5   *(continued)*

```
;Length of field / Display length / Query length :
9 / 9 / 9
;Is this field in the base table Y/N :
N
;Default value :

;Page :

;SQL>

;Field name :
ratepdy
;Type of field :
RMONEY
;Length of field / Display length / Query length :
7 / 7 / 7
;Is this field in the base table Y/N :
N
;Default value :

;Page :

;SQL>

;Field name :
catnum
;Type of field :
INT
;Length of field / Display length / Query length :
7 / 7 / 10
;Is this field in the base table Y/N :
*Y
;Is this field part of the primary key Y/N :
Y
;Field to copy primary key from :
;Default value :
;Page :
1
;Line :
1
;Column :
3
;Prompt :

;Allow field to be entered Y/N :
**Y
;Allow field to be updated Y/N :
N
;Allow entry of query condition Y/N :
Y
;Hide value of field Y/N :
N
;SQL>
**POST-CHANGE
/
;SQL>
$get-prodno
select prodno, storeno
  into xprodno, xstoreno
  from tape
 where tape.catnum = :catnum
/
;Message if value not found :
Serial number does not exist. Please re-enter.
```

```
;Must value exist Y/N :
Y
$get-titlecd
select title.titlecd, title.title,
       decode(product.format, 'V', 'Vhs', 'B', 'Beta', null)
  into titlecd, tdesc, format
  from title, product
 where title.titlecd = product.titlecd
   and product.prodno = :xprodno
   and product.storeno = :xstoreno
/
;Message if value not found :
Cannot locate title for serial no.
;Must value exist Y/N :
Y
$xref-rental
select max(dateout)
  into dateout
  from rentals
 where rentals.catnum = :catnum
/
;Message if value not found :
Can't locate (max) dateout for this tape.  Are you sure it's been rented?
;Must value exist Y/N :
Y
$chk-dateout
select 1 from dual
 where :dateout is null
/
;Message if value not found :
*Cannot locate rental with this serial number. Please re-enter.
;Must value exist Y/N :
Y
$get-other-fields
select rentals.memberid, schdrtn, ratepdy
  into returns.memberid, schdrtn, ratepdy
  from rentals
 where rentals.catnum = :catnum
   and rentals.dateout = to_date(:dateout)
   and actrtn is null
/
;Message if value not found :
Rental has already been returned. Please cancel transaction.
;Must value exist Y/N :
Y
$calc-latecharge
select (trunc(sysdate _ to_date(:schdrtn))) *
       (:customer.latechgpct) * to_number(:ratepdy),
       trunc(sysdate _ to_date(:schdrtn)), sysdate
  into latecharge, latedays, actrtn
  from dual
 where trunc(sysdate _ to_date(:schdrtn)) > 0
/
;Message if value not found :
 ;Must value exist Y/N :
N
$calc-total
select nvl(:invoice.total, 0) + nvl(:returns.latecharge, 0),
       round(nvl(:invoice.tax,0) +
             (nvl(:returns.latecharge,0) *(nvl(:customer.xslstaxpct,0)/100)))
  into invoice.total, invoice.tax
  from dual
/
;Message if value not found :
Error in calculating total late charges on commit of
transaction.
```

continued

Listing B.5   *(continued)*

```
;Must value exist Y/N :
Y
$calc-grandtotal
select (nvl(:invoice.total,0) + nvl(:invoice.tax,0))
  into invoice.grand_total
  from dual
;Message if value not found :

;Must value exist Y/N :
Y
;Is field mandatory Y/N :
N
;Is field fixed length Y/N :
N
;Auto jump to next field Y/N :
N
;Convert field to upper case Y/N :
N
;Help message :
Serial number of the returned tape.
;Lowest value :

;Highest value :

;Field name :
titlecd
;Type of field :
CHAR
;Length of field / Display length / Query length :
15 / 15 / 15
;Is this field in the base table Y/N :
N
;Default value :

;Page :
1
;Line :
1
;Column :
13
;Prompt :

;Allow field to be entered Y/N :
**N
;Allow entry of query condition Y/N :
N
;Hide value of field Y/N :
N
;SQL>

;Field name :
format
;Type of field :
CHAR
;Length of field / Display length / Query length :
4 / 4 / 4
;Is this field in the base table Y/N :
N
;Default value :

;Page :
1
;Line :
1
```

```
;Column :
31
;Prompt :

;Allow field to be entered Y/N :
**N
;Allow entry of query condition Y/N :
N
;Hide value of field Y/N :
N
;SQL>

;Field name :
schdrtn
;Type of field :
DATE
;Length of field / Display length / Query length :
9 / 9 / 9
;Is this field in the base table Y/N :
N
;Default value :

;Page :
1
;Line :
1
;Column :
38
;Prompt :

;Allow field to be entered Y/N :
**N
;Allow entry of query condition Y/N :
N
;Hide value of field Y/N :
N
;SQL>

;Field name :
actrtn
;Type of field :
DATE
;Length of field / Display length / Query length :
9 / 9 / 9
;Is this field in the base table Y/N :
*Y
;Is this field part of the primary key Y/N :
N
;Copy field value from :
CUSTOMER.XACTRTN
;Page :
1
;Line :
1
;Column :
48
;Prompt :

;Allow field to be entered Y/N :
**N
;Allow entry of query condition Y/N :
N
;Hide value of field Y/N :
N
;SQL>
```

continued

Listing B.5   *(continued)*

```
;Field name :
latedays
;Type of field :
RINT
;Length of field / Display length / Query length :
3 / 3 / 3
;Is this field in the base table Y/N :
N
;Default value :
0
;Page :
1
;Line :
1
;Column :
63
;Prompt :

;Allow field to be entered Y/N :
**N
;Allow entry of query condition Y/N :
N
;Hide value of field Y/N :
N
;SQL>

;Field name :
latecharge
;Type of field :
RMONEY
;Length of field / Display length / Query length :
7 / 7 / 7
;Is this field in the base table Y/N :
Y
;Is this field part of the primary key Y/N :
N
;Default value :
0
;Page :
1
;Line :
1
;Column :
72
;Prompt :

;Allow field to be entered Y/N :
**N
;Allow entry of query condition Y/N :
N
;Hide value of field Y/N :
N
;SQL>

;Field name :
tdesc
;Type of field :
CHAR
;Length of field / Display length / Query length :
77 / 67 / 78
;Is this field in the base table Y/N :
N
;Default value :
```

```
;Page :
1
;Line :
2
;Column :
13
;Prompt :

;Allow field to be entered Y/N :
**N
;Allow entry of query condition Y/N :
N
;Hide value of field Y/N :
N
;SQL>

;Field name :

;Block name / Description :
INVOICE/Invoice
;Table name :
INVOICE
;Check for uniqueness before inserting Y/N :
N
;Display/Buffer how many records :
1 / 1
;Field name :
*PRE-INSERT
;SQL>
$lock-cntl
lock table cntl in share update mode
/
;Message if value not found :
Pre-insert.  Error in locking CNTL table to update last
invoice number.
;Must value exist Y/N :
Y
$get-newinvno
update cntl
   set last_invoice = last_invoice + 1
/
;Message if value not found :

;Must value exist Y/N :
Y
$init-invoice
select last_invoice, 'L', sysdate, to_char(sysdate, 'hh:mi am'),
       :customer.memberid, to_char(sysdate, 'hh:mi
  into invoice.invno, trantype, invoice.trandate,
invoice.trantime,
       invoice.memberid, customer.time
  from cntl
/
;Message if value not found :
Error in initializing fields in INVOICE record.
;Must value exist Y/N :
Y
$init-customer
select to_char(sysdate, 'hh:mi am'), :invoice.invno
  into customer.time, customer.invno
  from dual

;Message if value not found :
Error initializing customer control block
;Must value exist Y/N :
Y
```

continued

Listing B.5   *(continued)*

```
;Field name :
*key-commit
;SQL>
$ok-commit
#exemacro commit; goblk customer;

;Message if value not found :

;Must value exist Y/N :
Y
;Field name :
*key-delrec
;SQL>
$no-delete
#exemacro null;

;Message if value not found :
*Delete record not allowed on this screen.
;Must value exist Y/N :
N
;Field name :
*key-exeqry
;SQL>
$no-exeqry
#exemacro null;

;Message if value not found :
*Query disabled in invoice block.  Go to previous block and try again.
;Must value exist Y/N :
N
;Field name :
invno
;Type of field :
INT
;Length of field / Display length / Query length :
7 / 7 / 7
;Is this field in the base table Y/N :
*Y
;Is this field part of the primary key Y/N :
Y
;Field to copy primary key from :

;Default value :

;Page :

;SQL>

;Field name :
memberid
;Type of field :
INT
;Length of field / Display length / Query length :
7 / 7 / 7
;Is this field in the base table Y/N :
*Y
;Is this field part of the primary key Y/N :
N
;Copy field value from :
CUSTOMER.MEMBERID
;Page :

;SQL>
```

```
;Field name :
trantype
;Type of field :
CHAR
;Length of field / Display length / Query length :
1 / 1 / 1
;Is this field in the base table Y/N :
Y
;Is this field part of the primary key Y/N :
N
;Default value :
L
;Page :

;SQL>

;Field name :
trandate
;Type of field :
DATE
;Length of field / Display length / Query length :
9 / 9 / 9
;Is this field in the base table Y/N :
*Y
;Is this field part of the primary key Y/N :
N
;Copy field value from :
RETURNS.ACTRTN
;Page :

;SQL>

;Field name :
trantime
;Type of field :
CHAR
;Length of field / Display length / Query length :
8 / 8 / 8
;Is this field in the base table Y/N :
Y
;Is this field part of the primary key Y/N :
N
;Default value :

;Page :

;SQL>

;Field name :
paymethod
;Type of field :
CHAR
;Length of field / Display length / Query length :
2 / 2 / 2
;Is this field in the base table Y/N :
Y
;Is this field part of the primary key Y/N :
N
;Default value :

;Page :
1
;Line :
16
;Column :
37
;Prompt :
```

continued

Listing B.5   *(continued)*

```
;Allow field to be entered Y/N :
**Y
;Allow field to be updated Y/N :
Y
;Allow entry of query condition Y/N :
Y
;Hide value of field Y/N :
N
;SQL>
**POST-CHANGE
/
;SQL>
$get-paydesc
select description
  into paydesc
  from paymethod
 where paymethod.paymethod = :invoice.paymethod

;Message if value not found :
Invalid payment method.  Choices are: CAsh, AX, MC, etc.  Use [List Values].
;Must value exist Y/N :
Y
;Is field mandatory Y/N :
N
;Is field fixed length Y/N :
N
;Auto jump to next field Y/N :
N
;Convert field to upper case Y/N :
Y
;Help message :
*Payment method choices are:  CAsh, AX, MC, VI, DI, WF, etc.  Use [List Values].
;Lowest value :
paymethod.paymethod
;Field name :
paydesc
;Type of field :
CHAR
;Length of field / Display length / Query length :
18 / 18 / 18
;Is this field in the base table Y/N :
N
;Default value :

;Page :
1
;Line :
16
;Column :
40
;Prompt :

;Allow field to be entered Y/N :
**N
;Allow entry of query condition Y/N :
N
;Hide value of field Y/N :
N
;SQL>

;Field name :
total
;Type of field :
RMONEY
```

```
;Length of field / Display length / Query length :
9 / 9 / 9
;Is this field in the base table Y/N :
Y
;Is this field part of the primary key Y/N :
N
;Default value :

;Page :
1
;Line :
16
;Column :
70
;Prompt :

;Allow field to be entered Y/N :
**N
;Allow entry of query condition Y/N :
N
;Hide value of field Y/N :
N
;SQL>

;Field name :
cashtend
;Type of field :
RMONEY
;Length of field / Display length / Query length :
9 / 9 / 9
;Is this field in the base table Y/N :
N
;Default value :

;Page :
1
;Line :
17
;Column :
37
;Prompt :

;Allow field to be entered Y/N :
**Y
;Allow field to be updated Y/N :
N
;Allow entry of query condition Y/N :
N
;Hide value of field Y/N :
N
;SQL>
**POST-CHANGE
/
;SQL>
$chk-cash-or-credit
select 1
  from dual
 where :paymethod = 'CA'
/
;Message if value not found :
Change given only for CASH transactions.  Commit transaction now.
;Must value exist Y/N :
Y
$chk-cashtend
select 'x'
  from dual
```

continued

Listing B.5   *(continued)*

```
 where to_number(:cashtend) > to_number(:grand_total)
/
;Message if value not found :
Cash received must be greater than or equal to total sale amount.
;Must value exist Y/N :
Y
$calc-change
select decode(:paymethod, 'CA', nvl(:cashtend, 0) _ nvl(:grand_total,0), 0)
  into change
  from dual

;Message if value not found :
Error in calculating change.
;Must value exist Y/N :
Y
;Is field mandatory Y/N :
N
;Is field fixed length Y/N :
N
;Auto jump to next field Y/N :
N
;Convert field to upper case Y/N :
N
;Help message :
If cash, enter cash amount received fromcustomer.
;Lowest value :

;Highest value :

;Field name :
tax
;Type of field :
RMONEY
;Length of field / Display length / Query length :
9 / 9 / 9
;Is this field in the base table Y/N :
Y
;Is this field part of the primary key Y/N :
N
;Default value :

;Page :
1
;Line :
17
;Column :
70
;Prompt :

;Allow field to be entered Y/N :
**N
;Allow entry of query condition Y/N :
N
;Hide value of field Y/N :
N
;SQL>

;Field name :
change
;Type of field :
RMONEY
;Length of field / Display length / Query length :
9 / 9 / 9
```

```
;Is this field in the base table Y/N :
N
;Default value :

;Page :
1
;Line :
18
;Column :
37
;Prompt :

;Allow field to be entered Y/N :
**N
;Allow entry of query condition Y/N :
N
;Hide value of field Y/N :
N
;SQL>

;Field name :
Grand_total
;Type of field :
RMONEY
;Length of field / Display length / Query length :
9 / 9 / 9
;Is this field in the base table Y/N :
N
;Default value :

;Page :
1
;Line :
18
;Column :
70
;Prompt :

;Allow field to be entered Y/N :
**N
;Allow entry of query condition Y/N :
N
;Hide value of field Y/N :
N
;SQL>

;Field name :

;Block name / Description :
      Video Quest RETURNED Tapes                        [ Invoice No.
%LINE
5
   Member Id:                                 Tapes rented out:
%LINE
7
   Catalog    Title    Format    Due In    Returned    Days Late    Latechg
%LINE
9
                                                                      $
%LINE
16
                   Payment method:                    Subtotal:
                       Cash given:                         Tax:
                          Change:          Total latecharges:
%LINE
21
```

continued

Listing B.5 *(continued)*

```
  [ExeQry] Tapes Checked Out      [Exit] Main Menu      [DupRec]  Print Invoice
%LINE
23
                      VIDEO QUEST RENTALS, Inc.
%LINE
1
%GRAPHICS
```

Listing B.6   The OUTRENT Form

```
; Generated by SQL*Forms Version 2.0.18 on Sun Jan 17 19:10:01 1988
; Application owner is BOOK.  Application name is outrent
; (Application ID is 0)
; ----------------------------------------------------
;Application Title :
OUTRENT
;ORACLE workspace size :

;Block name / Description :
**key-clrblk
;SQL>
$no-clearblk
#exemacro null;

;Message if value not found :
*Form is query only!
;Must value exist Y/N :
N
;Block name / Description :
**key-clrfrm
;SQL>
$no-clearform
#exemacro null;

;Message if value not found :
*Form is query only!
;Must value exist Y/N :
N
;Block name / Description :
**key-clrrec
;SQL>
$no-clearcrd
#exemacro null;

;Message if value not found :
*Form is auto-query only!
;Must value exist Y/N :
N
;Block name / Description :
**key-startup
;SQL>
$copy-memberid
#copy global.memberid customer.memberid
/
;Message if value not found :
;Must value exist Y/N :
Y
$copy-name
```

```
#copy global.name customer.name
/
;Message if value not found :

;Must value exist Y/N :
Y
$auto-query
#exemacro goblk outrent;exeqry;

;Message if value not found :

;Must value exist Y/N :
Y
;Block name / Description :
customer/customer
;Table name :
*
;Check for uniqueness before inserting Y/N :
N
;Display/Buffer how many records :
1 / 1
;Field name :
memberid
;Type of field :
INT
;Length of field / Display length / Query length :
7 / 7 / 7
;Is this field in the base table Y/N :
N
;Default value :

;Page :
1
;Line :
4
;Column :
14
;Prompt :

;Allow field to be entered Y/N :
**Y
;Allow field to be updated Y/N :
N
;Allow entry of query condition Y/N :
N
;Hide value of field Y/N :
N
;SQL>

;Is field mandatory Y/N :
N
;Is field fixed length Y/N :
N
;Auto jump to next field Y/N :
N
;Convert field to upper case Y/N :
N
;Help message :

;Lowest value :

;Highest value :

;Field name :
name
```

continued

Listing B.6   *(continued)*

```
;Type of field :
CHAR
;Length of field / Display length / Query length :
30 / 30 / 30
;Is this field in the base table Y/N :
N
;Default value :

;Page :
1
;Line :
4
;Column :
22
;Prompt :

;Allow field to be entered Y/N :
**N
;Allow entry of query condition Y/N :
N
;Hide value of field Y/N :
N
;SQL>

;Field name :

;Block name / Description :
*outrent/outrent
;Enter default WHERE and ORDER BY clause :
where rentals.memberid > 0 and actrtn is null

;Table name :
RENTALS
;Check for uniqueness before inserting Y/N :
N
;Display/Buffer how many records :
6 / 20
;Base crt line ?
8
;How many physical lines per record ?
2
;Field name :
xprodno
;Type of field :
CHAR
;Length of field / Display length / Query length :
25 / 25 / 25
;Is this field in the base table Y/N :
N
;Default value :

;Page :

;SQL>

;Field name :
xstoreno
;Type of field :
INT
;Length of field / Display length / Query length :
3 / 3 / 3
;Is this field in the base table Y/N :
N
;Default value :
```

```
;Page :

;SQL>

;Field name :
actrtn
;Type of field :
DATE
;Length of field / Display length / Query length :
9 / 9 / 9
;Is this field in the base table Y/N :
Y
;Is this field part of the primary key Y/N :
N
;Default value :

;Page :

;SQL>

;Field name :
memberid
;Type of field :
INT
;Length of field / Display length / Query length :
7 / 7 / 7
;Is this field in the base table Y/N :
*Y
;Is this field part of the primary key Y/N :
Y
;Field to copy primary key from :
CUSTOMER.MEMBERID
;Page :

;SQL>

;Field name :
xcategory
;Type of field :
INT
;Length of field / Display length / Query length :
3 / 3 / 3
;Is this field in the base table Y/N :
N
;Default value :

;Page :

;SQL>

;Field name :
CATNUM
;Type of field :
INT
;Length of field / Display length / Query length :
10 / 7 / 10
;Is this field in the base table Y/N :
*Y
;Is this field part of the primary key Y/N :
Y
;Field to copy primary key from :

;Default value :

;Page :
1
```

continued

Listing B.6 *(continued)*

```
;Line :
1
;Column :
3
;Prompt :

;Allow field to be entered Y/N :
**Y
;Allow field to be updated Y/N :
N
;Allow entry of query condition Y/N :
Y
;Hide value of field Y/N :
N
;SQL>
**POST-CHANGE
/
;SQL>
$get-prodno
select prodno, storeno
  into xprodno, xstoreno
  from tape
 where tape.catnum = :outrent.catnum
/
;Message if value not found :
Invalid Serial number. Please re-enter.
;Must value exist Y/N :
Y
$get-titlecd
select titlecd, ratepdy
  into titlecd, ratepdy
  from product, rentclass
 where product.prodno = :xprodno
   and product.storeno = :xstoreno
   and product.rentclass = rentclass.rentclass
   and product.prodtype in ('R','RS')
/
;Message if value not found :
Invalid Product number. OR  Product is not a rental item. Please re-enter.
;Must value exist Y/N :
Y
$get-title
select title, category
  into title, xcategory
  from title
 where title.titlecd = :titlecd
/
;Message if value not found :
;Must value exist Y/N :
*N
$calc-latecharge
select (trunc(sysdate _ to_date(:schdrtn))) * (latechgpct * :ratepdy)
  into latecharge_todate
  from cntl
 where trunc(sysdate _ to_date(:schdrtn)) > 0

;Message if value not found :
;Must value exist Y/N :
Y
;Is field mandatory Y/N :
N
;Is field fixed length Y/N :
N
```

```
;Auto jump to next field Y/N :
N
;Convert field to upper case Y/N :
N
;Help message :

;Lowest value :

;Highest value :

;Field name :
titlecd
;Type of field :
CHAR
;Length of field / Display length / Query length :
15 / 15 / 15
;Is this field in the base table Y/N :
N
;Default value :

;Page :
1
;Line :
1
;Column :
13
;Prompt :

;Allow field to be entered Y/N :
**N
;Allow entry of query condition Y/N :
N
;Hide value of field Y/N :
N
;SQL>

;Field name :
rentdays
;Type of field :
RINT
;Length of field / Display length / Query length :
3 / 3 / 3
;Is this field in the base table Y/N :
Y
;Is this field part of the primary key Y/N :
N
;Default value :

;Page :
1
;Line :
1
;Column :
30
;Prompt :

;Allow field to be entered Y/N :
**N
;Allow entry of query condition Y/N :
N
;Hide value of field Y/N :
N
;SQL>
**POST-CHANGE
/
;SQL>
$calc-linetotal
```

continued

Listing B.6   *(continued)*

```
select (:rentdays * :ratepdy)
  into line_total
  from dual

;Message if value not found :
;Must value exist Y/N :
Y
;Field name :
ratepdy
;Type of field :
RMONEY
;Length of field / Display length / Query length :
5 / 5 / 5
;Is this field in the base table Y/N :
Y
;Is this field part of the primary key Y/N :
N
;Default value :

;Page :
1
;Line :
1
;Column :
34
;Prompt :

;Allow field to be entered Y/N :
**N
;Allow entry of query condition Y/N :
N
;Hide value of field Y/N :
N
;SQL>

;Field name :
line_total
;Type of field :
RMONEY
;Length of field / Display length / Query length :
6 / 6 / 6
;Is this field in the base table Y/N :
N
;Default value :

;Page :
1
;Line :
1
;Column :
40
;Prompt :

;Allow field to be entered Y/N :
**N
;Allow entry of query condition Y/N :
N
;Hide value of field Y/N :
N
;SQL>

;Field name :
dateout
;Type of field :
DATE
```

```
;Length of field / Display length / Query length :
9 / 9 / 9
;Is this field in the base table Y/N :
Y
;Is this field part of the primary key Y/N :
N
;Default value :
$$date$$
;Page :
1
;Line :
1
;Column :
48
;Prompt :

;Allow field to be entered Y/N :
**N
;Allow entry of query condition Y/N :
Y
;Hide value of field Y/N :
N
;SQL>

;Field name :
schdrtn
;Type of field :
DATE
;Length of field / Display length / Query length :
9 / 9 / 9
;Is this field in the base table Y/N :
Y
;Is this field part of the primary key Y/N :
N
;Default value :

;Page :
1
;Line :
1
;Column :
59
;Prompt :

;Allow field to be entered Y/N :
**N
;Allow entry of query condition Y/N :
Y
;Hide value of field Y/N :
N
;SQL>

;Field name :
latecharge_todate
;Type of field :
RMONEY
;Length of field / Display length / Query length :
8 / 8 / 8
;Is this field in the base table Y/N :
N
;Default value :
    0
;Page :
1
;Line :
1
```

continued

Listing B.6   *(continued)*

```
;Column :
71
;Prompt :

;Allow field to be entered Y/N :
**N
;Allow entry of query condition Y/N :
N
;Hide value of field Y/N :
N
;SQL>

;Field name :
title
;Type of field :
CHAR
;Length of field / Display length / Query length :
77 / 67 / 78
;Is this field in the base table Y/N :
N
;Default value :

;Page :
1
;Line :
2
;Column :
13
;Prompt :

;Allow field to be entered Y/N :
**N
;Allow entry of query condition Y/N :
N
;Hide value of field Y/N :
N
;SQL>

;Field name :
;Block name / Description :

     RENTALS OUT by Member
%LINE
4
  Member Id:
%LINE
6
  Catalog    Title    Days Rate    Total    Date Out    Date Due    Latechrg
%LINE
8
                                                                  $
%LINE
21
     Press [Exit] to return to Rental Screen
%LINE
23
                            VIDEO QUEST RENTALS, Inc.
%LINE
1
%GRAPHICS
```

C

ORACLE-Supported Hardware Platforms

Mainframes, Minicomputers, and Workstations

Company	Operating System(s)
AT&T	UNIX System V
Altos	UNIX System V
Amdahl	MVS/SP, MVS/XA, VM/CMS, UTS
Apollo	Aegis-Domain/IX
Comparex	MVS/SP, MVS/XA, VM/CMS, UTS
Control Data	NOS/VE
Convergent Technologies	CTIX
Dansk Data	UNIX System V
DDE	UNIX
DEC	VMS, ULTRIX
Edge	UNIX
Encore	UNIX
Gould	UNIX
Harris	VOS, UNIX System V
Hewlett-Packard	HP-UX
Honeywell-Bull	GCOS, UNIX System V
IBM	MVS/SP, MVS/XA, VM/CMS, UTS, AIX
ICL	UNIX System V, VME
Motorola	UNIX
NAS	MVS/SP, MVS/XA, VM/CMS, UTS
NCR	UNIX System V
Nixdorf	OSx
Norsk	SINTRAN
PCS	UNIX System V
Plexus	UNIX System V
Prime	PRIME, UNIX
Pyramid	OSx
Sequent	DYNIX
Siemens	BS2000, SINIX
Stratus	VOS
Sun	SunOS 3.X
Unisys	UNIX System V
Wang	VS

continued

Microcomputers

Hardware	Software
IBM PC/AT and compatibles	PC-DOS, MS-DOS, XENIX, OS/2
COMPAQ DESKPRO 386 and compatibles	MS-DOS, XENIX, OS/2
IBM PS/2	PC-DOS, XENIX, OS/2

D

For Further Reference

Codd, E. F. *Extending the Database Model to Capture More Meaning*. Communications of the ACM. No 4. December, 1979.

Codd, E. F. *Keynote Speech of Oracle User Conference*. August 19, 1985.

Date, C. J. *A Guide to DB2*. Addison-Wesley, 1984.

Date, C. J. *A Guide to the SQL Standard*. Addison-Wesley, 1987.

Gane, Chris. *Developing Business Systems in SQL*. Rapid Systems Development, Inc., 1986.

Quick Reference Guide
to Video Quest Schema

Table Column	Displayed As (in Queries and Reports)	Entity	Key
TAPE Table			
catnum	Catalog Number	TAPE	\<Pr\>
prodno	Product Number	PRODUCT	\<F\>
storeno	Store Number	STORE	\<F\>
PRODUCT Table			
prodno	Product Number	PRODUCT	\<Pr\>
description	Product Description	PRODUCT	
storeno	Store Number	STORE	\<F\>
titlecd	Title Code	TITLE	\<F\>
format	Format Type	FORMAT TYPE	\<F\>
prodtype	Product Type	PRODUCT TYPE	\<F\>
rentclass	Rental Class	RENTAL CLASS	\<F\>
cost	Cost	PRODUCT	
suggrtl	Suggested Retail	PRODUCT	
sellrtl	Selling Retail	PRODUCT	
qtyrecvd	Quantity Received	PRODUCT	
qtyoh	Quantity On Hand	PRODUCT	
qtysold	Quantity Sold	PRODUCT	
qtyord	Quantity On Order	PRODUCT	
qtyrsv	Quantity Reserved	PRODUCT	
TITLE Table			
titlecd	Title Code	TITLE	\<Pr\>
category	Film Category	FILM CATEGORY	\<F\>
title	Title Description	TITLE	
directors	Directors	TITLE	
producers	Producers	TITLE	
screenplay	Screenplay Writer	TITLE	
actors	Actors/Actresses	TITLE	
awards	Film Awards	TITLE	*continued*

Table Column	Displayed As (in Queries and Reports)	Entity	Key
TITLE Table, cont.			
release	Year Film Released	TITLE	
runtime	Running Time (Length)	TITLE	
censorrtg	Censorship Rating	TITLE	
starrtg	Star Rating	TITLE	
studio	Studio Producer	TITLE	
color_bw	Color or B/W Format	TITLE	
SYNOPSIS Table			
titlecd	Title Code	TITLE	\<F\>
description	Synopsis (1 line of)	TITLE	
lineno	Line Number	TITLE	
CATEGORY Table			
category	Category Code	FILM CATEGORY	\<Pr\>
description	Category Description	FILM CATEGORY	
RENTAL CLASS Table			
rentclass	Rental Class Code	RENTAL CLASS	\<Pr\>
description	Class Description	RENTAL CLASS	
ratepdy	Rate Per Day	RENTAL CLASS	
CUSTOMER Table			
memberid	Member ID	PRIMARY MEMBER	\<Pr\>
name	Name	PRIMARY MEMBER	
ad1	Address	PRIMARY MEMBER	
ad2	Address	PRIMARY MEMBER	
city	City	PRIMARY MEMBER	
state	State	PRIMARY MEMBER	
zip	Zip	PRIMARY MEMBER	
day_area	Day Phone	PRIMARY MEMBER	
day_prefix	Day Phone	PRIMARY MEMBER	
day_suffix	Day Phone	PRIMARY MEMBER	
eve_area	Eve Phone	PRIMARY MEMBER	
eve_prefix	Eve Phone	PRIMARY MEMBER	
eve_suffix	Eve Phone	PRIMARY MEMBER	
creditcard	Credit Card	PRIMARY MEMBER	
cardexp	Expiration Date	PRIMARY MEMBER	
cdlno	Driver's License	PRIMARY MEMBER	
cdlexp	Expiration Date	PRIMARY MEMBER	
date_created	Date Membership Created	PRIMARY MEMBER	
last_act	Last Activity Date	PRIMARY MEMBER	
format	Default Tape Format	PRIMARY MEMBER	
CUSTNAME Table			
memberid	Member ID	PRIMARY MEMBER	\<F\>
name	Authorized Member Name	AUTHORIZED MEMBER	
restrict_cat	Restricted Tape	AUTHORIZED MEMBER	

Table Column	Displayed As (in Queries and Reports)	Entity	Key
RENTALS Table			
memberid	Member ID	CUSTOMER	\<F\>
catnum	Catalog Number	TAPE	\<F\>
actrtn	Date Tape Returned	RETURN	\<F\>
dateout	Date Tape Rented	RENTAL	
rentdays	Number of Days Rented	RENTAL	
schdrtn	Date Tape Due Back	RENTAL	
RETURNS Table			
memberid	Member ID	CUSTOMER	\<F\>
catnum	Catalog Number	TAPE	\<F\>
actrtn	Date Tape Returned	RETURN	
latecharge	Late Charges Accrued	RETURN	
INVOICE Table			
invno	Invoice Number	INVOICE	\<Pr\>
memberid	Member ID	CUSTOMER	\<F\>
paymethod	Paymethod	PAYMETHOD	\<F\>
trantype	Transaction Type	INVOICE	
trandate	Transaction Date	INVOICE	
trantime	Transaction Time	INVOICE	
total	Total Invoice Amount	INVOICE	
tax	Total Tax Amount	INVOICE	
PAYMETHOD Table			
paymethod	Paymethod	PAYMETHOD	\<Pr\>
description	Payment Description	PAYMETHOD	

Index